WRITING INSTRUCTION TO SUPPORT LITERACY SUCCESS

LITERACY RESEARCH, PRACTICE AND EVALUATION

Series Editors: Evan Ortlieb and Earl H. Cheek, Jr.

Recent Volumes:

Volume 1: Using Informative Assessments towards Effective Literacy Instruction

Volume 2: Advanced Literary Practices: From the Clinic to the Classroom

Volume 3: School-based Interventions for Struggling Readers, K-8

Volume 4: Theoretical Models of Learning and Literacy Development

Volume 5: Video Reflection in Literacy Teacher Education and Development: Lessons from Research and Practice

Volume 6: Video Research in Disciplinary Literacies

Emerald Group Publishing Limited
Howard House, Wagon Lane, Bingley BD16 1WA, UK

First edition 2017

Copyright © 2017 Emerald Group Publishing Limited

Reprints and permissions service
Contact: permissions@emeraldinsight.com

No part of this book may be reproduced, stored in a retrieval system, transmitted in any form or by any means electronic, mechanical, photocopying, recording or otherwise without either the prior written permission of the publisher or a licence permitting restricted copying issued in the UK by The Copyright Licensing Agency and in the USA by The Copyright Clearance Center. Any opinions expressed in the chapters are those of the authors. Whilst Emerald makes every effort to ensure the quality and accuracy of its content, Emerald makes no representation implied or otherwise, as to the chapters' suitability and application and disclaims any warranties, express or implied, to their use.

British Library Cataloguing in Publication Data
A catalogue record for this book is available from the British Library

ISBN: 978-1-78635-526-3
ISSN: 2048-0458 (Series)

Printed and bound by CPI Group (UK) Ltd, Croydon, CR0 4YY

ISOQAR certified
Management System,
awarded to Emerald
for adherence to
Environmental
standard
ISO 14001:2004.

Certificate Number 1985
ISO 14001

INVESTOR IN PEOPLE

LITERACY RESEARCH, PRACTICE AND EVALUATION
VOLUME 7

WRITING INSTRUCTION TO SUPPORT LITERACY SUCCESS

EDITED BY

EVAN ORTLIEB
St. John's University, New York, NY, USA

EARL H. CHEEK, JR.
Louisiana State University, Baton Rouge, LA, USA

WOLFRAM VERLAAN
University of Alabama in Huntsville, Huntsville, AL, U

United Kingdom – North America – Japan
India – Malaysia – China

CONTENTS

LIST OF CONTRIBUTORS   *ix*

ABOUT THE EDITORS   *xi*

INTRODUCTION   *xiii*

RETHINKING WRITING PRODUCTS AND
PROCESSES IN A DIGITAL AGE
   Evan Ortlieb, Wolfram Verlaan, Earl H. Cheek Jr. and   *1*
   Danielle DiMarco

TURNING AROUND THE PROGRESS OF
STRUGGLING WRITERS: KEY FINDINGS FROM
RECENT RESEARCH
   Sinéad Harmey and Emily Rodgers   *19*

ACCELERATING STUDENT PROGRESS IN WRITING:
EXAMINING PRACTICES EFFECTIVE IN NEW
ZEALAND PRIMARY SCHOOL CLASSROOMS
   Judy M. Parr   *41*

IDEAS AS A SPRINGBOARD FOR WRITING IN
K-8 CLASSROOMS
   Kathleen M. Alley and Barbara J. Peterson   *65*

PROCESS WITH A PURPOSE: LOW-STAKES WRITING
IN THE SECONDARY ENGLISH CLASSROOM
   Sue Verlaan and Wolfram Verlaan   *95*

LEARNING LANGUAGE AND VOCABULARY IN
DIALOGUE WITH THE REAL AUDIENCE:
EXPLORING YOUNG WRITERS' AUTHENTIC
WRITING AND LANGUAGE LEARNING
EXPERIENCES
    Ewa McGrail, J. Patrick McGrail and Alicja Rieger   117

UNDERSTANDING A DIGITAL WRITING CYCLE:
BARRIERS, BRIDGES, AND OUTCOMES IN TWO
SECOND-GRADE CLASSROOMS
    Jessica S. Mitchell, Rachael F. Thompson and   137
    Rebecca S. Anderson

CLASSROOM WRITING COMMUNITY AS
AUTHENTIC AUDIENCE: THE DEVELOPMENT OF
NINTH-GRADERS' ANALYTICAL WRITING AND
ACADEMIC WRITING IDENTITIES
    Susan S. Fields   157

ENGAGING STUDENTS IN MULTIMODAL
ARGUMENTS: INFOGRAPHICS AND PUBLIC
SERVICE ANNOUNCEMENTS
    Emily Howell   183

THE USE OF GOOGLE DOCS TECHNOLOGY TO
SUPPORT PEER REVISION
    Jessica Semeraro and Noreen S. Moore   203

A FRAMEWORK FOR LITERACY: A
TEACHER–RESEARCHER PARTNERSHIP
CONSIDERS THE "C-S-C PARAGRAPH" AND
LITERACY OUTCOMES
    Christopher W. Johnson   221

POWERFUL WRITING INSTRUCTION: SEEING,
UNDERSTANDING, AND INFLUENCING PATTERNS
    Marla Robertson, Leslie Patterson and Carol Wickstrom   241

FOURTH GRADERS AS RESEARCHERS: AUTHORS
AND SELF-ILLUSTRATORS OF
INFORMATIONAL BOOKS
    Anita Nigam and Carole Janisch   *263*

SENIORS, SCHOLARS, RESEARCHERS: USING AN
INQUIRY APPROACH TO WRITING THE
RESEARCH PAPER
    Sarah M. Fleming   *281*

AUGMENTING ACADEMIC WRITING
ACHIEVEMENT FOR ALL STUDENTS
    Wally Thompson, Debra Coffey and Traci Pettet   *303*

LIST OF CONTRIBUTORS

Kathleen M. Alley	Mississippi State University, Mississippi State, MS, USA
Rebecca S. Anderson	The University of Memphis, Memphis, TN, USA
Earl H. Cheek, Jr.	Louisiana State University, Baton Rouge, LA, USA
Debra Coffey	Kennesaw State University, Kennesaw, GA, USA
Danielle DiMarco	St. John's University, Jamaica, NY, USA
Susan S. Fields	Boston University, Boston, MA, USA
Sarah M. Fleming	Syracuse University, New York, NY, USA
Sinéad Harmey	Queens College, CUNY, Flushing, NY, USA
Emily Howell	Iowa State University, Ames, IA, USA
Carole Janisch	Texas Tech University, Lubbock, TX, USA
Christopher W. Johnson	University of Minnesota Duluth, Duluth, MN, USA
Ewa McGrail	Georgia State University, Atlanta, GA, USA
J. Patrick McGrail	Jacksonville State University, Jacksonville, FL, USA
Jessica S. Mitchell	University of North Alabama, Florence, AL, USA
Noreen S. Moore	William Paterson University, Wayne, NJ, USA
Anita Nigam	Texas Tech University, Lubbock, TX, USA

Evan Ortlieb	St. John's University, Jamaica, NY, USA
Judy M. Parr	The University of Auckland, Auckland, New Zealand
Leslie Patterson	Human Systems Dynamics Institute, Circle Pines, MN, USA
Barbara J. Peterson	University of South Florida, Tampa, FL, USA
Traci Pettet	University of North Texas, Denton, TX, USA
Alicja Rieger	Valdosta State University, Valdosta, GA, USA
Marla Robertson	Utah State University, Logan, UT, USA
Emily Rodgers	The Ohio State University, Columbus, OH, USA
Jessica Semeraro	William Paterson University, Wayne, NJ, USA
Rachael F. Thompson	The University of Memphis, Memphis, TN, USA
Wally Thompson	Eastern New Mexico University, Portales, NM, USA
Sue Verlaan	University of Alabama in Huntsville, Huntsville, AL, USA
Wolfram Verlaan	University of Alabama in Huntsville, Huntsville, AL, USA
Carol Wickstrom	University of North Texas, Denton, TX, USA

ABOUT THE EDITORS

Evan Ortlieb (Ph.D.) is Professor and the Coordinator of Literacy Programs at St. John's University. His academic accomplishments and innovative history include his co-edited book series, *Literacy Research, Practice, and Evaluation*, along with his publication of more than 100 manuscripts, which substantiate some of his contributions to the field. His research remains on school literacy improvement in diverse and disadvantaged communities worldwide. He is also the founder and active President of the Ortlieb Foundation − a non-profit organization that aims to financially assist those who have been diagnosed with cancer in pursuing their collegiate education through scholarships.

Earl H. Cheek, Jr. (Ph.D.) is Patrick and Edwidge Olinde Endowed Professor Emeritus at Louisiana State University. His primary area of expertise is Literacy Education, specifically; assessment, diagnostic-prescriptive, grades 1−12, content reading, struggling readers, and dyslexia. His academic accomplishments include the co-edited book series, *Literacy Research, Practice, and Evaluation*, and the publication of more than 100 manuscripts including articles, chapters in books, and textbooks. In addition to his publications, he has presented over 100 papers at state, regional, national, and international conferences, and has served as the major professor/dissertation director for 70 Ph.D. students.

Wolfram Verlaan (Ph.D., N.B.C.T.) is Assistant Professor of Literacy and Reading and the Coordinator of the M.Ed. Reading Specialist Program at the University of Alabama in Huntsville. As a former middle- and high-school teacher for nine years with a National Board teaching certification (NBCT) in Early Adolescence English/Language Arts, he brings a wealth of knowledge to bear regarding ELA instruction in secondary classrooms. In addition to a research interest in the relationship between listening comprehension and reading comprehension, he is also interested in methods of improving pre-service teacher preparation, effective literacy instruction, and ways to address the literacy achievement gap in the United States between less-advantaged and more-advantaged students.

INTRODUCTION

Although writing has always been considered an important component of literacy instruction, writing instruction in many classrooms has frequently been shunted aside to allow instructional time to be devoted to curriculum deemed more immediately important, such as reading, math, and science. Recent initiatives such as the Common Core State Standards, however, have reemphasized the importance of writing by acknowledging that subject matter knowledge is more completely demonstrated and solidified when one is able to cogently communicate one's thoughts about a given topic via writing. And unlike speaking, writing is not a natural act — students require significant amounts of instruction and practice to develop their writing ability. To that end, this volume, in the book series Literacy Research, Practice, and Evaluation, provides a collection of researched-based instructional practices drawn from the authors' experiences with writing instruction in primary and secondary school classrooms. The volume's 15 chapters address a wide scope of writing instructional methods that range from an analysis of successful writing practices employed in primary schools in New Zealand, to engaging ninth-grade students with multimodal writing assignments in US classrooms, to using low-stakes writing assignments to allow teachers to build relationships with and insights into their students as a basis for successful writing instruction. The instructional methodologies employed in these varying contexts are described in detail, and most can be modified for younger or older students to address writing instruction apropos to a given grade range.

Successful writing instruction is never formulaic; it is an iterative process that relies, among other things, on modeling, guidance, feedback, and practice, and it is always contextualized by the social, cultural, and academic milieux in which the instruction occurs. The writing instruction described in this volume affords the reader the opportunity to view both the process and the context of writing instruction through varying lenses and perspectives. Consequently, this volume should be of significant interest to educators, researchers, literacy specialists, and others who are engaged in writing instruction.

Wolfram Verlaan
Co-editor

RETHINKING WRITING PRODUCTS AND PROCESSES IN A DIGITAL AGE

Evan Ortlieb, Wolfram Verlaan, Earl H. Cheek, Jr. and Danielle DiMarco

ABSTRACT

Purpose — *Writing as a hot topic in literacy has recently gained a foothold in terms of importance to academic and career success, finally receiving the attention it warrants and thus, this chapter provides timely information about how to teach writing products and processes in the 21st century.*

Design/methodology/approach — *Through a historical examination of writing instruction, this chapter provides a contextual lens for how writing has not always been a priority in the field of literacy; how writing and reading are interconnected; and how differing theories aim to explain writing development.*

Findings — *Writing has taken on a balanced approach between writing for product and writing as a practice. Teacher pedagogy has been heavily influenced by the advent of high-stakes assessments. Other factors such as maintaining motivation and engagement for writing affect student performance. Writing and reading benefit from an integrated instructional approach.*

Practical implications — *Elements of writing instruction are deconstructed to provide information for teachers to support students' confidence in their writing abilities, build their identity as writers, and promote individualization and creativity to flourish through independence.*

Keywords: Writing product; writing process; theory; digital writing; writing-reading connection

Literacy is said to be the thread that connects all content areas and academic disciplines. But if you were to observe in most classrooms today, you could very well see a fragmented approach to teaching reading and writing throughout all grade levels that has prevailed for ages. The manner in which literacy is viewed is departmentalized just like the content areas (e.g., now is time for our 90-minute literacy block inclusive of a 20-minute writing block of time). As countries like Finland do away with teaching separate subject areas all together to teach topics (Garner, 2015), perhaps reconsideration needs to be given to how we approach reading and writing instruction in the classroom. After all, the very nature of reading and writing is connected in the ways in which we think, plan, envision, problem solve, proceed through a process, and apply skills to create products.

Writing as a topic for research has historically taken a back seat to reading including topics like phonological awareness, phonics, fluency, vocabulary, and comprehension (Allington, 2005). Over the past 20 years, writing has very rarely been listed as a hot topic by experts in the field of literacy as evidenced by the ongoing What's Hot, What's Not Survey in Literacy (Cassidy, Ortlieb, & Grote-Garcia, 2016). Moreover, some may consider writing to be a rudimentary skill is that is learned in the early childhood years and that no further instruction or development is needed; after all, this is also a commonly held belief outside of education circles for the ability to read.

THE RE-MEMBERED LITERACY COMPONENT

Although writing was not deemed one of the five pillars of literacy instruction by the National Reading Panel (2001) as part of the No Child Left Behind Act, recommendations for writing instruction have taken on a balanced approach inclusive of both process writing and skills instruction (Cutler & Graham, 2008) in recent years. The Institute of Education Sciences (2012) report, *Teaching Elementary School Students to be Effective Writers*, offered the following recommendations for teaching the writing process:

- Teachers should explain and model how the fluid nature of the writing process works together, so that students can learn to apply strategies flexibly — separately or in combination — when they write.
- Teachers should engage students in writing activities in which the writing process does not move in a lockstep fashion from planning to drafting to revising several iterations to editing to publishing.

While these tenets are foundational to every writing program, they do not provide explicit direction regarding models of what this would look like in the classroom environment. Thus, there has been considerable variability in pedagogical planning, delivery, and in the frequency of strategy selection to yield desired standards-based outcomes (Cassidy et al., 2016). However, there have also been other external forces that have influenced the state of writing instruction today — none more so than the introduction, continuation, and increase in high-stakes testing associated with writing proficiency (Dutro, Selland, & Bien, 2013; Ketter & Pool, 2001).

The High Stakes of Writing Development

High-stakes testing has altered the structure of many writing programs, eroding significant gains in achievement (Au, 2013; Cassidy & Ortlieb, 2013; Kell & Kell, 2013). How does a test do this? Well, when prescribed ways of writing determine whether a student passes a grade level, teaching to the test becomes commonplace to ensure no child is left behind (that grade level), leading to a narrowing of the curriculum. These approaches come at the cost of implementing best practices in writing pedagogy toward students' development as competent writers capable of doing what real writers do — engage in story creation, plot development, content knowledge extension, and image creation often times more detailed than if we saw them with our own eyes (Sampson, Ortlieb, & Leung, 2016).

These standardized assessments often place a premium on the writing product (e.g., argumentative essay, summary statement, descriptive representation) rather than the process itself and, moreover, do not adequately assess all that students need to know and be able to do as successful writers in K-12 and higher education settings, as well as in the work place (Applebee & Langer, 2009). A dearth of data on what writing instruction looks like in schools persists despite national reports like that of the National Commission on Writing (2003), which indicated that writing should be a cornerstone of all school curricula (Graham & Perin, 2007a, 2007b).

Write Now

Writing as a hot topic in literacy has recently gained a foothold in terms of importance to academic and career success (Cassidy, Ortlieb, & Grote-Garcia, 2015), finally receiving the attention it warrants and thus, the time is ripe for continued research and inquiry into how writing instruction can support literacy success. This movement was spurred by the increase in standards associated with the Common Core State Standards that were adopted by 46 states starting in the year 2011. Universal expectations for diverse and sophisticated writing now exist for the first time beginning in the early childhood years; and as a result, high-stakes tests are associated with these standards; if these writing benchmarks are not met, students cannot advance to subsequent grade levels (Ortlieb, 2012).

Moreover, writing was added to standardized tests for college entry (SAT, ACT) beginning in 2005, as it was thought to serve as another predictor of potential collegiate success. But why is writing now linked to collegiate success if it has often been viewed as simply a minor component of one's literacy — a tenet that is learned in the early childhood years, and a tenet that seems relatively straightforward in its process and product? We believe that writing today, its products, and the process for mastery contrast with what writing has been in years past. What follows is a re-examination of writing through both theoretical and practical lenses to understand the purposes, products, and processes of writing today in the digital age.

THEORETICAL UNDERPINNINGS OF WRITING

Huey (1908/1968) famously noted over 100 years ago that "... to completely analyze what we do when we read would ... be to describe very many of the most intricate workings of the human mind ... ." (p. 6); this same statement would be equally if not more applicable to what we do when we write. Research investigating the act of writing has been heavily influenced by models seeking to describe the interaction of the cognitive processes involved in writing. Hayes and Flower (1980) posited one of the most influential of these models, identifying three overarching cognitive functions controlling the writing process of accomplished writers: planning, translating, and reviewing. This model has generated a significant body of research and parts of it have since been revised and augmented (Chenoweth & Hayes, 2001; Hayes, 1996, 2004; Kellogg, 1999).

Because the cognitive processes involved in writing can differ depending on whether one is a beginning or an accomplished writer, models such as the one proposed by Bereiter and Scardamalia (1987) have sought to examine which processes are involved as writing develops in novice writers. Until recently, much of the research investigating the cognitive processes involved in writing has used indirect measures of cognitive functioning to arrive at conclusions regarding these processes. Now, however, technological advances in medicine and brain research make it possible to examine what specifically happens in the brain during the writing process from both a neurological and physiological perspective (Berninger & Richards, 2002).

And yet, despite what might be termed "inside the head" factors that influence the writing process, the act of writing does not take place in a vacuum. Not only is the manner in which we craft a written composition influenced by factors such as our intended audience, our purpose for writing, and our choice of rhetorical style, these factors themselves are influenced by the society and culture within which we were brought up and/or find ourselves (Leki, 1991). Sociocultural theories of writing have sought to examine how cultural and societal factors, including, school itself exert an influence on how we communicate through the writing act (Bazerman & Prior, 2005; Bruner, 1996; Gee, 2000; Rogoff, 2003). For example, as Heath (1983) showed in her famous study, the home language environment in which we learn to communicate prior to the time we start school can either support or hinder our ability to adapt to the language requirements of our school environment.

In addition, what it means to be considered "literate" is largely situated in and contextualized by the environment in which we want to communicate. Hence, the language choices we make to communicate within a particular community, what Gee has termed a "discourse community," are typically dictated by what that community has considered acceptable, regardless of what our "literate" status might be outside of that community (Gee, 2011). As the Internet has given us the potential to communicate via writing with an extraordinary number of different communities across the globe, awareness of how sociocultural influences shape the manner of that communication is exceedingly important.

Research investigating the cognitive and sociocultural aspects that influence writing has contributed to the determining of "best practices" for the manner in which writing instruction proceeds in our schools. For example, research investigating the overarching processes of planning, translating, and reviewing posited in the original Hayes and Flower model (1980) has led to instructional approaches in which students are provided strategy-based methods for planning, writing, and revising, with research demonstrating the effectiveness of strategy-based instruction for a wide range of students (Graham, McKeown, Kiuhara, & Harris, 2012; Graham & Perin, 2007c). In addition, sociocultural theory has shed light on the importance of collaboration and mentorship in the writing process, indicating that the quality of a student's writing can be significantly improved when students collaborate and provide support to one another as they proceed through the writing process (Graham et al., 2012; Graham & Perin, 2007c). Moreover, affective components that influence student achievement such as motivation and self-efficacy can be strengthened through collaborative writing (De Bernardi & Antolini, 2007; Paquette, 2009; Schultz, 1997).With the advent of the digital age, the cognitive and sociocultural factors that influence writing development have been significantly affected by the proliferation of computer technologies over the last two decades. Although research investigating the effects of technology on the various aspects of writing instruction is still limited, the use of word processors has been shown to have a positive effect on both the quality and quantity of writing (Bangert-Drowns, 1993; Goldberg, Russel, & Cook, 2003). In addition, computer and networking technologies allow students to collaborate online not only with other students in their classroom, but also potentially with other students across the globe. Furthermore, web pages consisting almost entirely of "hypertextual" writing, through which audio, pictures, video, and/or other text are interwoven with a given piece of writing, have had a dramatic impact on changing the traditional conception of writing as something that proceeds in a linear fashion (Mehrubeoglu, Ortlieb, McLauchlan, & Pham, 2012).

Writing instruction in today's classrooms, then, will include the application of research-based best practices in the context of a world that is increasingly connected online. What this looks like will certainly differ from classroom to classroom depending on the instructional goals for the students, but important parts of the writing process (e.g., planning, writing, and revising) will be retained. However, their execution can now be informed by the knowledge of a global community. Having students collaborate while giving them a voice to express what is important to them can also support those affective factors that help improve student writing. In addition, providing students with authentic writing assignments for authentic audiences (Duke, Caughlan, Juzwik, & Martin, 2011) can help students view writing as a meaningful part of their education. For example, students in an elementary school classroom might conduct online research to produce a pamphlet informing visitors to a local zoo about the feeding habits of some of the animals (Duke et al., 2011). Or, a group of middle school students might build a website to draw attention to a cause, such as recycling on their school campus or water quality in natural bodies of water in or near their community. Regardless of the particular structure or subject of the assignments used to facilitate writing instruction in today's classrooms, writing activities will be more effective when they are informed by research and allow students to engage with each other and the world around them in a meaningful context.

WRITING AS A PRACTICE

A Shift toward Student-Centered Pedagogies

During the writing process movement of the 1970s through the early 1990s, the focus of research on writing shifted from the products of writing to the process of writing (Durst, 2015; Shelton & Altwerger, 2014). Some literacy researchers began to describe the writing process as they saw it practiced by professional authors (Emig, 1973; Murray, 1972) while others like Peter Elbow encouraged risk-taking toward writing excellence (e.g., generating, critiquing, and extending ideas in multiple directions [Campbell, 1996]). Meanwhile, composition theorists (Hayes & Flowers, 1986) urged educators to teach writing as a recursive and iterative cognitive process rather than the linear, five-step model that prevails in many schools today.

Hillocks (1995) urged teachers to prudently analyze the particular writing task students would perform to: (a) determine the specific production strategies required to compose a given form of writing; (b) provide directed, explicit instruction through carefully sequenced "gateway activities," and (c) engage students in developing the procedural knowledge and in performing the production strategies for a given type of writing. Some researchers argue that a true writer's process is recursive and that using a fixed linear process to writing instruction may inhibit learners' writing development. Yet, classroom instruction continues to be centered on production via a linear process. Calkins (1986) furthers "when our students resist writing, it's usually because writing has be treated as a little more than a place to display their command of spellmanship, penmanship, and grammar" (p. 33). And thus the challenge is set – how can teachers balance the demands of high-stakes writing assessments while promoting students to take a positive stance in writing process activities? The alternative focus of "length, correctness, and evaluation" is no longer an option (not that it ever was), as it reduces writing motivation to extrinsic scare tactics (Lindsey, 1996, p. 104).

Maintaining the Motivation to Write

Reflexive writers want to engage in writing to satisfy their own needs; they are task-oriented and independent writers. Calkins (1986) argues that children want to write when it is personal. Writing habits are formed in environments where writing is modeled, valued, and praised. These habits are solidified through the maintenance of student interest beyond the activity. Here are some examples of how the first author has incubated students' writing development:

(1) Sharing my own identity as a writer, genre preferences, and text structures. For instance, discussing how I enjoy reading the works of fiction writers (e.g., John Grisham, Stephen King) as they have an uncanny ability to keep the readers' attention through provocative vocabulary usage and unpredictable story structures; and how this serves as a backbone for the writing style that I use in my own fictional craft. Moreover, I enjoy informational writing to inform others teachers about the latest in my research findings on the writing process (just as they might want to inform their peers about fashion styles, fascinating books to read, or helpful websites to learn more about travel destinations).

(2) Promoting situational interest in writing topics by using *jolts,* or presenting something counter or new to students' existing understanding of a topic (Ortlieb, 2014) (e.g., some schools in the United States have no summer break; some schools prefer to have students in multiple grade levels in the same class; and even best-selling authors struggle

most with plot development (Sampson, Ortlieb, & Leung, in press)). The jolt causes the learner to react; in turn, the students will be curious. Instances of perturbation involve questioning, contradicting, and challenging (Duit & Treagust, 1998) previously held beliefs, understandings, and assumptions. Thus, meaning making, or making sense of the world, is a process and product of "puzzlement, perturbation, expectation violations, curiosity, or cognitive dissonance" (Jonassen, 2002, p. 45).

(3) Maintain interest through diverse pedagogies through a re-engagement activity or event (e.g., responding to a critique; introducing an article that features an opposing perspective; in-class debate; peer review). Hidi, Berndorff, and Ainley (2002) highlight that both children and adults interested in a topic tend to engage, maintain focus on, and enjoy an activity more than people without the interest (p. 431).

A longitudinal study conducted by Nolen (2007) revealed several factors that "appeared to contribute to the development and maintenance of situational interest over time" (p. 27). Overall, these factors include providing students with a positive emotional environment and encouraging autonomy. In addition, teachers capable of providing social supports and instruction designed to foster cognitive and emotional learning were also identified as contributors to the development of individual interests (Nolen, 2007). Utilizing varied instructional methods addressing the purposes and skills students identify as being important or request to learn are ways in which teachers can demonstrate and communicate to students the importance of autonomy and self-direction. Allowing students to pursue writing activities that interest them and promote self-direction may contribute to the production of texts students care about as well as boosting their overall self-efficacy and positive associations with successful writing experiences (Nolen & Ward, 2008). Success in writing should be viewed at least in part on the production of self-selected pieces and not merely on an evaluation of an assigned writing topic or task.

Opportunity and Challenge

Today's teachers face a bevy of challenges: (a) ensuring their students score highly on high-stakes writing assessments; (b) enhancing students' identities as writers, and (c) guaranteeing all their students meet grade level expectations for writing proficiency. What can get lost in the fray is the attention paid to the audience for whom we write and its importance in a writer's motivation and meaningfulness of the writing task (Fields, 2016).

The concept of combining school-based writing tasks with reflexive, self-based writing begs further discussion. What if teachers openly discuss the criteria for writing outlined in the standards but highlighted the areas where creative control was still in the hands of the writer? For example, the standards may state that an opinion piece of writing including several supporting reasons and a sense of closure is required. As teachers, we can point out that nowhere in the standards does it say dictate writing topics. Students will share a teachers' excitement of realizing "Hey! I still get to make the most important decisions here!"

Mixing the Process and Product Approaches

Badger and White (2000) propose that maximizing the effectiveness of writing instruction is possible if elements from both the product and process approaches are combined. For example, they suggest that writers "start with one approach and adapt it" (p. 157). In addition, the authors suggest utilizing a combination of approaches they refer to as the *genre approach to writing*, embedding instruction in a social context where the writing is constructed for a specific purpose (Badger & White, 2000). The role of the teacher within this amalgamated approach is to model the process of constructing a written piece by exposing students to exemplar writing samples (products) and providing them with an instructional sequence (processes) they can replicate to independently create writing. In short, this approach is based on immersion and imitation. Greene (1992) refers to this approach as *mining*.

Once teachers have modeled the process of mining texts, Greene (1992) explains that the instructional goal for students is to independently "attend to specific features of the texts they read, selecting, organizing, and connecting ideas for the purpose of writing" (p. 156), and more readily see writing as a cyclical process of constant improvement. This wide-angle lens, or metacognitive approach to deconstructing elements of writing, supports students' confidence in their writing abilities, builds their identity as writers, and promotes individualization and creativity to flourish through independence. Instruction that accompanies this combination of approaches should be direct and include mentoring, as previously discussed, as well as modeling and thinking aloud to explain the mental processes necessary to construct a piece of writing.

Digital Writing

Researchers agree that when writing is authentic, social, and interactive students tend to be more motivated and actively engaged in writing activities (Candlin & Hyland, 2014; Pigg et al., 2013). The results of recent studies have revealed that when students are permitted to choose the topics they write about they are more likely to be motivated to construct writing (Johnson & Scarbrough, 2015; Wolsey & Grisham, 2007). Although computers have primarily been utilized in classrooms as tools for researching or as word processors, more recent research had been building the argument that blogging can be a socially engaging form of writing that supports students and classroom instruction (Ortlieb, McVee, & Shanahan, 2015; Ortlieb, Shanahan, & McVee, 2015).

According to Boas (2011), a blog is defined as "a web page with regular diary or journal entries that incorporated different postings by authors and responses to these posts by an audience" (p. 28). It provides a social, interactive, and motivational platform for the creation of writing. Blogs are an ideal choice within writing classes of all ages because they can be created and developed by students utilizing a process approach. Drexler, Dawson, and Ferdig (2007) further "educational blogs employ technology to offer practice, thoughtful feedback and revisions based on feedback-fundamental steps in the writing process to improve student writing" (p. 140). For example, a writer can brainstorm and post lists of topic ideas on their blog, and then elicit and receive feedback from the audience about which topics are best to pursue. As a draft is being constructed, it is posted for audience review repeatedly. Teacher and peer feedback offered during reviews guide the drafting, revision, or editing of any piece that is posted. Lessons presented either whole class, small group, or individually can be centered on the learning and application of strategies to improve the quality of writing or these lessons can be focused on how to review and offer feedback in a co-constructed and iterative process.

Blogs are not limited to a narrative form of writing such as journaling or constructing diary entries though. Drexler et al. (2007) examined the use of collaborative blogging on third graders' school-based expository writing. The results of the study revealed that blogging supported classroom instruction in several ways as students were engaged and motivated to write, collaborated, improved their writing skills, and demonstrated a transfer of knowledge from the blogging project to other subject areas through a differentiated pedagogical approach. The use of technology can benefit students in their writing skills and production; the only pedagogical limits are those we set upon ourselves. Advancing our understanding of how writing instruction supports literacy success is paramount, and certainly digital technologies and literacies play a significant role toward preparing learners for the known and unknown demands of writers in the 21st century.

CONNECTING WRITING TO READING TODAY

The advent of the digital age has intensified the need for teaching students to become more effective writers, and to integrate the basic tenants of writing into the literacy curriculum. As explicated earlier in this chapter, that has not always been the case. Reading instruction has typically been viewed as the more critical component of the instructional process with writing being treated as not much more than an afterthought. As stated earlier, over the past 20 years, writing has rarely been listed as a hot topic by experts on the What's Hot, What's Not Survey in Literacy. This has become much more of a concern as the demands of the digital age have increased the need for more literate writers as well as readers. Effective written communication is critical with the increased use of electronic discourse in emails, blogs, social media, and other digital forums. The inability to communicate effectively leads to misunderstandings, and missed opportunities.

We have discussed the issues surrounding the debate among advocates of writing as a product, and those that support process writing. Others, as we have indicated, strongly believe that combining elements of the process and product approaches is necessary to maximize the effectiveness of writing instruction. The process writing movement beginning in the 1970s emphasized the importance of allowing students to become more involved in how they express themselves, and to explore their inner self throughout this process. Some encouraged more risk-taking (Campbell, 1996) while others urged educators to move away from the linear, five-step model to a more recursive and iterative cognitive process (Hays & Flowers, 1986). During this period, renewed efforts to emphasize writing as an integral component of the instructional process gained support, as advocates drew attention to the writing-reading connection suggesting that they should be taught together (Tierney & Shanahan, 1991).

Clearly, it is essential to today's digital world to emphasize writing as a crucial component of the instructional writing and reading process. The writing-reading connection is vital to success in the digital age (Ortlieb,

2014; Sampson et al., 2016). A recently published study in *Reading Research Quarterly* found clear evidence that there is a close connection between reading and writing. Lee and Schallert (2016) explored the reading-writing connection in a yearlong study of 300 middle school students developing literacy in a new language. In this case, South Korean students were learning English. The study examined whether the development of reading improved writing and vice versa. They found that reading and writing did share cognitive processes, and that improving reading positively impacted writing, and that the same was true for writing. Their results showed that in the experimental group where there was an intensive effort to connect reading to writing, there was a significant improvement in writing performance, and reading comprehension. In the control group where students received regular instruction, the growth was not as pronounced. They concluded that extensive reading enhances writing skills, and that extensive writing facilitated the development of reading skills, suggesting that reading and writing are connected and facilitate the development of both activities.

Although the National Reading Panel did not identify writing as one of the five pillars of literacy instruction, we believe that a more balanced approach to writing instruction is appropriate and crucial to increasing the writing abilities of students in this digital age of instantaneous communication between individuals and among groups. Students are expected to perform at a higher level of proficiency in writing at an earlier age, and to be able to transfer this skill to other areas outside of a school setting. The demands on students to write well can be somewhat attributed to the demands of society for better performance in the work place. The movement advocating better writing skills has always been a factor in educational settings, but has more recently manifested itself through the demand for higher standards such as the Common Core Standards movement that led to the adoption of these standards in 46 states beginning in 2011. This demand has precipitated the higher expectations for more diverse and sophisticated writing. Although the advocacy for the Common Core Standards has abated to some extent with some states reevaluating their stand on this particular movement, there continues to be a desire to improve the writing skills of students at an early age.

After analyzing the research related to the writing-reading connection, we conclude that there is a symbiotic relationship between the two activities that strongly suggests both writing and reading benefit from an integrated instructional approach. In the digital age, we believe that it is more crucial than ever to teach students to be effective writers.

REFERENCES

Allington, R. L. (2005). The other five "pillars" of effective reading instruction. *Reading Today, 22*(6), 3.
Applebee, A. N., & Langer, J. A. (2009). What is happening in the teaching of writing? *English Journal, 98*(5), 15–28.
Au, K. (2013). *Multicultural issues and literacy achievement.* New York, NY: Routledge.
Badger, R., & White, G. (2000). A process genre approach to teaching writing. *ELT Journal, 54*(2), 153–160.
Bangert-Drowns, R. (1993). The word processor as an instructional tool: A meta-analysis of word processing in writing instruction. *Review of Educational Research, 63*(1), 69–93.
Bazerman, C., & Prior, P. (2005). Participating in emergent socio-literate worlds: Genre, disciplinarity, interdisciplinarity. In R. Beach, J. Green, M. Kamil, & T. Shanahan (Eds.), *Multidisciplinary perspectives on literacy research* (2nd ed., pp. 133–178). Creskil, NJ: Hampton Press.
Bereiter, C., & Scardamalia, M. (1987). *The psychology of written composition.* Hillsdale, NJ: Lawrence Erlbaum.
Berninger, V. W., & Richards, T. L. (2002). *Brain literacy for educators and psychologists.* Amsterdam: Academic Press.
Boas, I. V. (2011). Process writing and the internet: Blogs and Ning Networks in the classroom. *English Teaching Forum, 49*(2), 26–33.
Bruner, J. (1996). *The culture of education.* Cambridge, MA: Harvard University Press.
Calkins, L. M. (1986). *The art of teaching writing.* Portsmouth, NH: Heinemann.
Campbell, C. H. (1996). Taking stock and a fresh look at writing. *Harvard Educational Review, 66*(1), 137–142.
Candlin, C. N., & Hyland, K. (2014). *Writing: Texts, processes and practices.* New York, NY: Routledge.
Cassidy, J., & Ortlieb, E. (2013). What was hot (and not) in literacy: What we can learn. *Journal of Adolescent & Adult Literacy, 57*(1), 21–29. doi:10.1002/JAAL.215
Cassidy, J., Ortlieb, E., & Grote-Garcia, S. (2016). Beyond the common core: Examining 20 years of literacy practices and their impact on struggling readers. *Literacy Research and Instruction, 55*(2), 91–104.
Chenoweth, A., & Hayes, J. R. (2001). Fluency in writing: Generating text in L1 and L2. *Written Communication, 18*, 80–98.
Cutler, L., & Graham, S. (2008). Primary grade writing instruction: A national survey. *Journal of Educational Psychology, 100*(4), 907–919.
De Bernardi, B., & Antolini, E. (2007). Fostering students' willingness and interest in argumentative writing: An intervention study. In G. Rijlaarsdam (Ed.), *Studies in writing and motivation* (pp. 183–202). Oxford: Elsevier.
Drexler, W., Dawson, K., & Ferdig, R. E. (2007). Collaborative blogging as a means to develop elementary expository writing skills. *Electronic Journal for the Integration of Technology in Education, 6*, 140–160.
Duit, R., & Treagust, D. F. (1998). Learning in science-from behaviourism towards social constructivism and beyond. In B. J. Fraser & K. G. Tobin (Eds.), *International handbook of science education* (pp. 3–25). Lancaster: Kluwer Academic Publishers.
Duke, N. K., Caughlan, S., Juzwik, M. M., & Martin, N. M. (2011). *Reading and writing genre with purpose in K-8 classrooms.* Portsmouth, NH: Heinemann.

Durst, R. K. (2015). The stormy times of James Moffett. *English Education, 47*(2), 111–130.
Dutro, E., Selland, M. K., & Bien, A. C. (2013). Revealing writing, concealing writers: High-stakes assessment in an urban elementary classroom. *Journal of Literacy Research, 45*, 99–141.
Emig, J. (1977). Writing as a mode of learning. *College Composition and Communication, 28*(2), 122–128.
Fields, S. (2016). Classroom writing community as authentic audience: The development of ninth-graders' analytical writing and academic writing identities. In E. T. Ortlieb, E. H. Cheek Jr., & W. Verlaan (Eds.), *Writing instruction to support literacy success* (Vol. 7, pp. 157–181). Literacy Research, Practice and Evaluation. Bingley, UK: Emerald Group Publishing Limited.
Garner, R. (2015, March 25). Finland schools: Subjects scrapped and replaced with 'topics' as country reforms its education system. *The Independent*. Retrieved from http://www.independent.co.uk/news/world/europe/finland-schools-subjects-are-out-and-topics-are-in-as-country-reforms-its-education-system-10123911.html
Gee, J. P. (2000). The new literacy studies: From "socially situated" to the work of the social. In D. Barton, M. Hamilton, & R. Ivanic (Eds.), *Situated literacies: Reading and writing in context* (pp. 180–196). London: Routledge.
Gee, J. P. (2011). *Social linguistics and literacies: Ideology in discourses* (4th ed.). London: Taylor and Francis.
Goldberg, A., Russel, M., & Cook, A. (2003). The effect of computers on student writing: A meta-analysis of studies from 1992 to 2002. *The Journal of Technology, Learning, and Assessment, 2*(1), 3–51.
Graham, S., McKeown, D., Kiuhara, S., & Harris, K. (2012). A meta-analysis of writing instruction for students in the elementary grades. *Journal of Educational Psychology, 104*(3), 879–896. doi:10.1037/A0029185
Graham, S., & Perin, D. (2007a). *Writing next: Effective strategies to improve the writing of adolescents in middle and high schools*. New York, NY: Carnegie Corporation.
Graham, S., & Perin, D. (2007b). A meta-analysis of writing instruction for adolescent students. *Journal of Educational Psychology, 99*(3), 445–476.
Graham, S., & Perin, D. (2007c). A meta-analysis of writing instruction for adolescent students. *Journal of Educational Psychology, 99*(3), 445–476. doi:10.1037/0022-0663.99.3.445
Greene, S. (1992). Mining texts in reading to write. *Journal of Advanced Composition, 12*(1), 151–170.
Hayes, J. R. (1996). A new framework for understanding cognition and affect in writing. In C. M. Levy & S. Ransdell (Eds.). *The science of writing: Theories, methods, individual differences, and applications* (pp. 1–27). Mahwah, NJ: Lawrence Erlbaum.
Hayes, J. R. (2004). What triggers revision? In L. Allal, L. Chanquoy, & P. Largy (Eds.), *Studies in writing* (Vol. 13, pp. 9–20). Revision: Cognitive and Instructional Processes. Norwell, MA: Kluwer Academic Press.
Hayes, J. R., & Flowers, L. (1986). Identifying the organization of writing processes. In L. W. Gregg & E. R. Steinberg (Eds.), *Cognitive processes in writing* (pp. 3–30). Mahwah, NJ: Erlbaum.
Heath, S. B. (1983). *Ways with words: Language, life, and work in communities and classrooms*. Cambridge: Cambridge University Press.

Hidi, S., Berndorff, D., & Ainley, M. (2002). Children's argument writing, interest and self-efficacy: An intervention study. *Learning and instruction, 12*(4), 429–446.
Hillocks, G. (1995). *Teaching writing as reflective practice*. New York, NY: Teachers College Press.
Huey, E. B. (1908/1968). *The psychology and pedagogy of reading*. Cambridge, MA: MIT Press.
Institute of Education Sciences. (2012). *Teaching elementary school students to be effective writers*. Washington, DC: U.S. Department of Education, What Works Clearinghouse. Retrieved from http://ies.ed.gov/ncee/wwc/pdf/practice_guides/writing_pg_062612.pdf
International Reading Association. (1999). *High-stakes assessments in reading: A position statement of the International Reading Association*. Retrieved from http://www.reading.org/Libraries/position-statements-and-resultions/ps1035_high_stakes.pdf
Johnson, C. W., & Scarbrough, B. (2015). The role of video in a literacy collaboration to re-engage struggling students. In E. Ortlieb, L. Shanahan, & M. McVee (Eds.), *Video research in disciplinary literacies* (pp. 79–94). Bingley, UK: Emerald Group Publishing Limited.
Jonassen, D. H. (2002). Learning as activity. *Educational Technology, 42*(2), 45–51.
Kell, M., & Kell, P. (2013). High stakes testing, literacy wars, globalization and Asia. In M. Kell & P. Kell (Eds.), *Education in the Asia Pacific region: Issues, concerns, and prospects* (Vol. 24, pp. 15–24). Literacy and language in East Asia: Shifting meanings, values and approaches. Singapore: Springer.
Kellogg, R. T. (1999). Components of working memory in writing. In M. Torrance & G. Jeffery (Eds.), *The cognitive demands of writing: Processing capacity and working memory effects in text production* (pp. 43–61). Amsterdam: Amsterdam University Press.
Ketter, J., & Pool, J. (2001). Exploring the impact of a high-stakes direct writing assessment in two high school classrooms. *Research in the Teaching of English, 35*(3), 344–393.
Lee, J., & Schallert, D. L. (2016). Exploring the reading-writing connection: A yearlong classroom-based experimental study of middle school students developing literacy in a new language. *Reading Research Quarterly, 51*(2), 143–164.
Leki, I. (1991). Twenty-five years of contrastive rhetoric: Text analysis and writing pedagogies. *TESOL Quarterly, 25*(1), 123–143.
Lindsey, M. (1996). Connections between reading and writing: What the experts say. *The Clearing House, 70*(2), 103–105.
Mehrubeoglu, M., Ortlieb, E., McLauchlan, L., & Pham, L. M. (2012). Capturing reading patterns through a real-time smart camera iris tracking system. *Proceedings of the SPIE* 8437, Real-Time Image and Video Processing, 843705. doi:10.1117/12.922875.
Murray, D. (1972). Teach writing as a process not product. *The Leaflet, 71*(3), 11–14.
National Commission on Writing. (2003, April). *The neglected R: The need for a writing revolution*. Retrieved from http://www.writingcommission.org/report.html. Accessed on April 28, 2016.
National Reading Panel (U.S.), National Institute of Child Health, & Human Development (US). (2000). *Report of the national reading panel: Teaching children to read: An evidence-based assessment of the scientific research literature on reading and its implications for reading instruction: Reports of the subgroups*. National Institute of Child Health and Human Development, National Institutes of Health.
Nolen, S. B. (2007). Young children's motivation to read and write: Development in social contexts. *Cognition and Instruction, 25*(2–3), 219–270.

Nolen, S. B., & Ward, C. J. (2008). Sociocultural and situative approaches to studying motivation. *Advances in motivation and achievement, 15*, 425–460.

Ortlieb, E. (2012). Examining the utility of high stakes assessment. In J. Cassidy & S. Grote-Garcia (Eds.), *What's hot in literacy: Trends and issues* (pp. 29–33). Dubuque, IA: Kendall Hunt.

Ortlieb, E. (2014). *Theoretical models of learning and literacy development.* Bingley, UK: Emerald Group Publishing Limited.

Ortlieb, E., McVee, M., & Shanahan, L. (Eds.). (2015). *Video reflection in literacy teacher education and development.* Bingley, UK: Emerald Group Publishing Limited.

Ortlieb, E., Shanahan, L., & McVee, M. (2015). *Literacy research, practice and evaluation* (Vol. 6). Video research in disciplinary literacies. Bingley, UK: Emerald Publishing Group.

Paquette, K. (2009). Integrating the 6 + 1 writing traits model with cross-age tutoring: An investigation of elementary students' writing development. *Literacy Research and Instruction, 48*(1), 28–38. doi:10.1080/19388070802226261

Pigg, S., Grabill, J. T., Brunk-Chavez, B., Moore, J. L., Rosinski, P., & Curran, P. G. (2013). Ubiquitous writing, technologies, and the social practice of literacies of coordination. *Written Communication, 31*(1), 91–117.

Rogoff, B. (2003). *The cultural nature of human development.* New York, NY: Oxford University Press.

Sampson, M. R., Ortlieb, E., & Leung, C. B. (2016). Rethinking the writing process: What best-selling and award-winning authors have to say. *Journal of Adolescent & Adult Literacy, 59*(7). Retrieved from http://onlinelibrary.wiley.com/wol1/doi/10.1002/jaal.557/abstract

Schultz, K. (1997). 'Do you want to be in my story?': Collaborative writing in an urban elementary classroom. *Journal of Literacy Research, 29*(2), 253–287.

Shelton, N. R., & Altwerger, B. (2014). *Literacy policies and practices in conflict: Reclaiming classrooms in networked times.* New York, NY: Routledge.

Tierney, R. J., & Shanahan, T. (1991). Research on the reading-writing relationship: Interactions, transactions, and outcomes. In R. Barr, M. L. Kamil, P. Mosenthal, & P. D. Pearson (Eds.), *Handbook of reading research* (Vol. 2, pp. 246–280). New York, NY: Longman.

Wolsey, T. D., & Grisham, D. L. (2007). Adolescents and the new literacies: Writing engagement. *Action in Teacher Education, 29*(2), 29–38.

TURNING AROUND THE PROGRESS OF STRUGGLING WRITERS: KEY FINDINGS FROM RECENT RESEARCH

Sinéad Harmey and Emily Rodgers

ABSTRACT

Purpose — *To identify features of teacher support associated with children who made accelerated progress in writing in an early literacy intervention.*

Design/methodology/approach — *Mixed methods were used to describe the paths, rates, variability, and potential sources of change in the writing development of 24 first grade students who participated in an early literacy intervention for 20 weeks. To describe the breadth and variability of change in children's writing within a co-constructed setting, two groups who made high and low progress were identified.*

Findings — *We focus on one child, Paul, who made high progress (became more independent in the writing of linguistically complex messages) and the features of teacher support that this child received compared to those who made lower progress. We compare him to another child, Emma, who made low progress. Teacher support associated with high progress included a conversational style and flexibility to adapt to the child's message intent as the student composed, supporting students to write linguistically more complex and legible messages, and supporting students to orchestrate a broad range of problem-solving behaviors while writing.*

Practical implications — *We describe how teachers can support children to gradually take control of the composition process, how they can recognize complexity in early written messages and we provide suggestions as to how teachers can systematically assess, observe, and support children's self-regulation of the writing process.*

Keywords: Writing development; writing instruction; writing difficulties; early intervention

According to the Common Core State Standards [CCSS] (National Governors Association Center for Best Practices & Council of Chief State School Officers, 2010) for English Language Arts, by first grade children should be able to write narratives that recount two or more appropriately sequenced events that include details regarding what happened, using temporal words to signal event order, and provide a sense of closure. For many teachers, supporting young children, particularly those with literacy difficulties, to achieve such levels of complexity in their written messages is a challenging task because writing involves not only the generation of an idea that is then purposefully constructed and communicated from letters, words, and sentences, but also involves the orchestration and control of directional and strategic behaviors, phonological and orthographic encoding, and fine motor skills (Alamargot & Fayol, 2009; Clay, 2001; Graham & Harris, 2009).

A large body of research exists that provides guidance on best practices for general writing instruction (cf. Calkins, 2013; Graham et al., 2012) but there remains less information for teachers of children in kindergarten and first grade who struggle early in their school career with writing. Knowing how to best support this population of children, however, is crucial for at least two reasons: we know that children who struggle early in their school career with writing are more likely to struggle with other literacy tasks and that this will continue throughout the child's school career (Ritchey & Coker, 2014), and we know that writing plays a critical supporting role in early reading development in that what one learns about in writing can help with reading and vice versa (Clay, 2004; Rodgers, 2008).

In this chapter, we present findings about effective teaching from a study that we conducted with first grade struggling writers. We begin by describing our study and the key features of early writing progress that emerged from it; features that can be used to guide instruction and inform assessment. We bring these features to life with examples from two cases, Paul, a child who made high progress in writing, and Emma who made low progress that was not sufficient to catch up to her peers. For each feature of high progress, we describe what the teachers did to promote it. Finally, we conclude the chapter with practical implications for teachers to turn around the progress of young struggling writers.

DESIGN OF OUR STUDY

We conducted a study of change over time in the co-constructed writing of 24 children as they engaged in a short-term early literacy intervention, Reading Recovery [RR] (Clay, 2005). Daily RR lessons include a writing component where the teacher and child compose and co-construct a written message.

Our study was theoretically informed by literacy processing theory (Clay, 2001). This theory describes change over time in the sources of information children use and the actions they take (what they do) as they problem-solve the task of reading and writing meaningful texts. As children develop expertise in both reading and writing, these problem-solving actions move from simple and faltering to complex and efficient, with regressions and progressions as the task, context, or activity changes or becomes more challenging (Granott, 2002). This theory fits with our theoretical orientation to writing because we view writing as a complex problem-solving process that involves generation of an idea that is then purposefully constructed and communicated from sources of information like letters, words, and sentences and involves orchestration of a range of problem-solving behaviors (e.g., editing) (Harmey, 2015, p. 32).

A consequence of such a perspective is that, in studying writing development, we were particularly interesting in describing change over time in what children used and did as they composed and constructed messages during the RR lesson. We, therefore, chose to use a microgenetic design. Such a design is used to answer questions about *how* learning occurs (Siegler, 2006) and involve an elevated density of observations which are intensively analyzed during a period of rapid developmental change (e.g., learning to walk) (Lavelli, Pantoja, Hsu, Messinger, & Fogel, 2005). This design was particularly suited to the purpose of our study, which was to describe changes that occurred in what children wrote over time, how they wrote it, and how the teachers interacted with them during a period of rapid change (a short-term early literacy intervention).

Participants

This study was conducted with an extant data set comprising videos and instructional records for 24 first grade students selected for RR (14 boys and 10 girls). Six children spoke English as an additional language and all were entitled to free school meals. They attended 22 schools in a mid-western city of the United States and were taught by 22 teachers (two teachers had two students each) who between them had an average of 17.45 (SD = 6.2) years of experience teaching.

The students' average pre-intervention total score on the *Observation Survey of Early Literacy Achievement* [OSELA] (Clay, 2013) was 361.8 (SD = 40.6) placing them in the 9th percentile nationally, meaning that only 9% of a national random sample of children scored lower than they did (see D'Agostino, 2012 for an explanation of total scores and the OSELA).

Sources of Data

Sources of data included the daily written messages of all students totaling 1,150 ($M = 47$), and two or three videos of each child's lessons ($n = 52$ videos). Each written message was rated for linguistic complexity and legibility and each video was rated to ascertain where the locus of control lay, or the degree to which the child or teacher controlled the production of the message. To do this we used the Early Writing Observational Rubric (Harmey, D'Agostino, & Rodgers, 2015) (see appendix for a description of the items on the rubric).

Analysis

Our analysis had three main phases; (1) we analyzed the rate and path of children's change over time, (2) we identified different patterns of progress, and (3) we examined the breadth, variability, and potential sources of change (including teacher support) by identifying and conducting a rich descriptive analysis of children who characterized differential patterns of progress. We plotted empirical growth plots (Singer & Willett, 2003) and used hierarchical linear modeling (HLM) (Raudenbush & Bryk, 2002) to ascertain individual and group paths and rates of change. To ascertain the breadth, variability, and potential sources of change we examined the path and rate of change and overall gains for individuals to ascertain if there were particular patterns of progress. The data were organized and reorganized to permit analyses of similarities, differences, and patterns of progress (for a detailed description of this analysis see Harmey, 2015).

In this chapter, we focus our attention on groups who made high or low progress. Our identification of the groups was made solely on their progress in writing but was supported by evidence of their overall literacy gains. Indeed, the high progress group increased from the 6th percentile (total score $M = 352.8$, $SD = 31.85$) to the 33rd percentile (total score $M = 497.2$, $SD = 17.85$) in 20 weeks, while the low progress group increased from the 8th percentile (total score $M = 357.83$, $SD = 28.18$) to just the 19th percentile ($M = 479.83$, $SD = 31.19$).

We present two cases, Paul and Emma, who typified the type of progress each group made. Over the course of the RR intervention, high progress students like Paul exhibited growing independence in multiple writing behaviors, including problem-solving, and wrote increasingly more complex messages. Low progress students like Emma, in contrast, exhibited growth in certain aspects of observed writing behaviors but demonstrated no change in the complexity of the messages she wrote. We consider what it was that students like Paul did as he wrote in a co-constructed setting, how it differed from what students like Emma did, and how the features of teacher support that they received differed.

FINDINGS

Key Feature of High Progress Students: Increasing Message Complexity

From our larger study, we found that the children who made high progress were supported to write longer, more syntactically complex and legible sentences. Their messages were logically organized and often spanned more than one sentence. Even when they only wrote one-sentence messages they tended to be more linguistically complex and textured (Halliday & Hassan, 1976). In other words, they used cohesive ties like temporal connectives ("then," "next," and "before"), logical connectives (words like "because") and demonstrative referents (words that refer to something referred to previously like "Dan is my friend. *He* is funny").

Compare, for example, the written texts of Paul and Emma who characterized high and low patterns of progress respectively (see Fig. 1). At week five, Paul wrote just a simple short message that was logically organized into one sentence and contained three cohesive ties, all personal pronouns ("I," "my," and "my"). By week 20, the last week of his intervention, Paul wrote two sentences that were both expanded: he wrote about a Christmas tree and added extra detail about lights, then wrote about stickers in his bathroom and added extra details about them being for Christmas. So over two sentences, he logically organized his thoughts. He also used three personal referents and a demonstrative referent to "point back" toward the Christmas tree he had described earlier.

The linguistic complexity of Emma's messages, however, rarely changed. She seldom wrote more than one sentence, and although the one-sentence messages were logically organized they were generally short and quite simple, with little extension. There was some variation over time in terms of the linguistic texture of her messages but the cohesive ties that she did use were simple. At week five, she used personal referents (like "I" and "my") and demonstrative referents (like the word "the"). At week 20, she again used a personal referent ("she").

Paul: Week 5	Paul: Week 20
I clean my car with my dad.	I have a christmas tree with lights on it. I have stickers in my bathroom for christmas.
Emma: Week 5	Emma: Week 20
Here I am on the swing.	She went fishing with Grandpa.

Fig. 1. Paul and Emma: Writing Samples at Week 5 and Week 20.

Teacher Support to Increase Message Complexity

We hypothesize that the quality of the conversation between teacher and student as they compose a message to write is largely responsible for the complexity of the message that is written. Clay (1998) describes these quality conversations as personalized and grounded in experience and notes that the skillful teacher simultaneously extends the language and learning of the child (p. 31). Extension of the message may take different forms. For example, expansion of a short message to a longer message may occur by the teacher reiterating the sentence but adding descriptive adjectives or adverbs. The teacher might also ask the child to elaborate to clarify the meaning of the message.

Consider, for example, this vignette and note how Paul's teacher expands his message:

Ms. Kelly: I heard that you have some very good news at your house. What happened at your house?

Paul: My baby cried.

Ms. Kelly: Your baby cried? Did you just have a baby at your house?

Paul: (smiles) My mom.

Ms. Kelly: Your mom just had a baby at your house. What should we write about your baby?

Paul: I love my baby too much.

Ms. Kelly: I love my baby too much. I bet you do. You waited a long time to have a sister.

Paul: And my dad

Ms. Kelly: I love my baby and my dad too much? Or I love my baby too much and my dad does too.

Paul: I love too much and my no. I love my baby sister and my dad.

Ms. Kelly: I love my baby sister and my dad.

Paul: Yeah.

Ms. Kelly: That's what we're changing it to?

Paul: Yeah.

Ms. Kelly: I love my baby sister and my dad. Okay

(Week 10, Lesson 40)

In this instance Ms. Kelly started the conversation similar to any typical conversation would start, bringing what she knows about the child to the conversation to invite Paul to share about something important that is happening in his life (cf. Clay, 2005). As the conversation continued, she took what Paul brought to the conversation and helped him to expand his message by both asking clarifying questions and by reiterating with elaboration. For example, when she asked Paul whether they had a baby at his house and he responded "My Mom" she reiterated what he said and repeated the expansion: "Your Mum just had a baby at your house?" In the same conversation, however, she demonstrated flexibility, or stayed open to unexpected turns in the conversation (cf. Clay, 1998). When Paul decided he wanted to add his Dad to the message she helped him by re-voicing his message to write about how he loved his baby sister and his Dad. Indeed, by the final observation, 15 weeks later, Paul was observed to compose and alter his message with little teacher support. For example, Ms. Kelly and Paul started by talking about a book he had read (*The Three Billy Goats Gruff*) but by the end of the conversation Paul turned the conversation around to something he wanted to write about, his new pencils.

For many children, one of the hardest aspects of writing is composing and many factors may obstruct composition. Closely linked to composing are the child's motivations to write, message intent, and control of oral language structures (Dyson, 1983) and Ms. Kelly's conversational style, flexibility, and reframing of Paul's message appeared to attend to these three factors. In contrast, the conversations between Emma and her teacher did not possess a conversational quality. Instead, the interactions before writing seemed more focused on the end product then a genuine personalized conversation. Take, for example, this exchange that occurred prior to writing in week 15:

> Ms. Byrne: Okay we need to write your story real quick. I want you to tell me about Ben and his cake. What happened?
>
> Emma: Uh, he Mom and Ben was, uh, making a cake.
>
> Ms. Byrne: Okay, you know how to start, right?
>
> Week 15, Lesson 50.

In this short 19-second conversation, the teacher was solely focused on the end product. In fact, in all three observations the teacher's opening remark as they set to co-construct the message was about what they would write rather than inviting the child into a genuine conversation. Despite the fact that Emma's response was fragmented grammatically, there was little attention on the part of the teacher to expand or aid Emma to structure the sentence in a more grammatically acceptable manner or to reiterate the sentence in a more acceptable manner.

Key Feature of High Progress Students: Improved Legibility

Legibility sounds like an old-fashioned concept, after all, it is no longer emphasized in the early grades; many researchers argue however, that kindergartners and first grade students should learn how to form letters fluently and well. Findings from the microgenetic analysis that was undertaken for this study support that assertion: children who made progress in the intervention also made progress on legibility on the rubric.

A very legible writing sample would be described as being easily readable, with appropriate height, width and spacing of words, and with letters formed correctly and not overly large (Harmey, 2015). Why is this so important?

Recall that we wrote earlier in this chapter that reading and writing share a reciprocal relationship; writing helps with reading and vice versa. One reason that legibility is so important is that it is easier for the child who wrote the message, to read it. A written message (see Fig. 2) with poor legibility, would be very difficult for a child to read back after writing it; it is difficult to tell the letters from the words and some letters look nothing like the way they would appear in a book. If the child cannot read back the message after writing it then some opportunity for reciprocity is lost, and just like the young, emerging writers in Clay (1975)'s research, the child will be left wondering, "What did I write?"

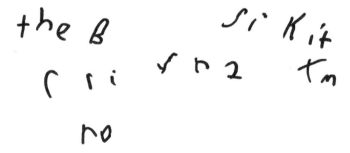

Fig. 2. Illegible Writing Sample.
*The child wrote: The bus is coming. It will stop here to let me get on.

Another reason legibility is so important has to do with its links to achievement (Dinehart & Manfra, 2013). As Dinehart (2014), noted in her review of the literature, children who struggle with writing down their ideas may opt to write shorter, simpler messages in order to finish the task more quickly, consequently having a negative impact on the complexity of the message. From a different perspective, when children can form letters quickly and well, cognitive resources are freed up, allowing the child to attend more to writing complex messages and worry less about forming letters or writing words.

Let's return to our anchor student, Paul. Over time, Paul gradually demonstrated a stable control of legibility. His letters, on the whole, were correctly formed, uniform in height, and oriented correctly. On the weeks that his legibility did waver, it often coincided with increases in average ratings of the linguistic complexity of his messages (see Fig. 3). From week nine, when weekly rating for the linguistic complexity of his messages rose there were corresponding dips in terms of the legibility of his messages and vice versa. These changes were characteristic of the regressions suggested by Thelen and Corbetta (2002) as features of developmental change. In other words, as children learn to master something new (writing linguistically more complex sentences) something that was previously stable (legibility) may make a seemingly backward transition.

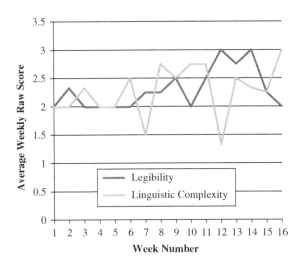

Fig. 3. Average Weekly Ratings* for Legibility and Linguistic Complexity, Paul.
*Ratings ranged from zero to three.

Children who made lower progress, however, appeared to consistently struggle or fail to improve the legibility of their messages over time. Emma's writing samples, for example, from both week 5 and week 20 differed little in the quality of legibility (see Fig. 1). She had difficulty forming letters, they were not uniform in height and had a "shaky" appearance that seemed to represent how she struggled to control fine motor control as she wrote.

Teacher Support of Legibility

In the previous section, we described how we noticed that, for the children who made high progress that there was a "give and take" in terms legibility and message complexity: when messages were more complex, legibility decreased temporarily. Paul's teacher, Ms. Kelly, demonstrated flexibility and understanding that as he pushed the length and complexity of their sentence that legibility "dipped." Consider the two writing samples in

Week	Written Message
36	I like to eat oranges and apples and pears. *(Good legibility but rather simple message.)* *I like to eat oranges and apples and pears.*
45	I play with my toys and I don't put them away. Then I go upstairs to sleep at night. *(Legibility dip with more complex message)* *I play with my toys and I don't put them away. Then I go upstairs to sleep at night.*

Fig. 4. Week 36 and Week 45 Writing Samples, Paul.

Fig. 4. In the first from lesson 36 of the intervention, Paul wrote a simple sentence that was legible with uniformity of height and spacing of correctly formed letters. In the second, from lesson 45 (just 9 lessons later), he wrote two longer sentences. On this occasion his letters were not at as uniform or "upright" and letter formation was not as exact. Had Ms. Kelly insisted on the level of penmanship demonstrated in lesson 36 it is questionable whether Paul would have been able to produce the more linguistically complex message that he did in lesson 45. It seemed that as Paul made steps forward to write more complex messages his teacher accepted, for a time, a lapse in legibility as evidenced by the drop in ratings for his legibility.

Unlike Paul, Emma's writing was large and she demonstrated tenuous control of letter formation over time. Indeed, even in the last week of her intervention, Emma's writing remained large (see Fig. 5), letters were rarely uniform in height, and many letters appeared to be awkwardly formed. There was little evidence, therefore, of the "give and take" that we noted for high progress students like Paul.

It should be noted that despite the fact that Paul's teacher was prepared to accept dips in legibility she was observed to provide very high levels of support in terms of letter formation at the beginning of the intervention. She did this by demonstrating formation on the practice page (a blank page that is used to practice spelling and letter formation). She also physically shared the pen, guiding his hand movements as he struggled to form letters.

In contrast, Emma's teacher was not observed to attend to letter formation in the three observations of the writing lesson, and did not take the opportunity to use the practice page for letter formation. It seems, therefore, that the key feature of teacher support of legibility for children that made high progress was flexibility. Flexibility, to pay particular attention to legibility early in the intervention (that appeared to pay dividends later) but a cognizance that legibility may "dip" as the child invested cognitive resources to write longer messages.

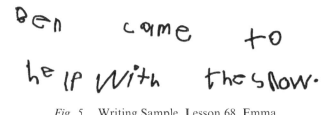

Fig. 5. Writing Sample, Lesson 68, Emma.

Key Feature of High Progress Students: Growing Independence

Another way that children who made high progress differed from those who made limited progress in writing was in what children did, or their observable behaviors, as they wrote in this co-constructed setting. The key feature that set these groups apart was their growth in independence. Growth in independence meant that children's actions were observed to move from teacher supported to teacher prompted to, finally, independent. In the larger study, we noted growth in independence in two key areas for the group that made high progress:

(a) Use of sources of knowledge (like spelling patterns or use of a bank of know words in writing).
(b) Monitoring the accuracy of the message.

In other words, for children who made high progress there was a gradual "handing over of the reins" of responsibility for writing the message within the co-constructed setting. We used event-listing matrices (Miles, Huberman, & Saldana, 2014) to display the foci of our observations of the writing event in a chronological order. The matrix (see Table 1) provided a clear visual representation of how our focal students Paul and Emma differed in terms of their growth in independence in multiple facets of the co-construction of their written messages.

It is evident from Table 1 that, over time, Paul accumulated a broader writing vocabulary, contributing, no doubt, to his ability to write longer messages. He transitioned from needed high teacher support to hear and record sounds in words to contributing all letter-sound information except for the word "pencils" in the last observation. While his teacher told him the next word to write and he did not notice any errors in the first observation, he did with prompting on the second occasion, and by the last observation he was monitoring the accuracy of his own message and even self-corrected an error.

Emma did show some growth over time in terms of moving from hearing initial, to final, to medial sounds in simple words. She was, however, rarely, observed to contribute spelling patterns. This was compounded by the simplicity of her messages, which provides a rationale for the need to write complex messages because of the learning opportunities the messages provide. In addition to this, and unlike Paul, Emma rarely monitored the accuracy of her message. At the last observation she did start to contribute the next word herself but she seldom noticed if she made mistakes. Rather, in this setting, her teacher assumed the role of editor.

Table 1. Event-Listing Matrix: Growing Independence of Observed Writing Behaviors.

	Observation 1 (Week 5)	Observation 2 (Week 10)	Observation 3 (Week 20)
Paul			
Message	I will play cars with my sister	I love my baby sister and my dad	I have lots of pencils in my pencil box. I work with my pencils at home and at school.
Spelling	Heard /si/ in sisters. Teacher used counters to help him hear and record "car." Teacher contributed spelling patterns.	Heard and recorded most sounds in sequence. Wrote the /e/ in love. Wrote the /y/ in "baby"	He contributed all letter-sound information including spelling patterns (except pencils)
Words written independently	My	I/ love/ my/ baby/ and/ my/ dad	I/ have/ a/ in/ my/ at/ lot/ work.
Monitoring of accuracy	Teacher told next word. Did not notice errors.	Wrote next words without prompt. Noticed errors if prompted (e.g., does that look right?).	Wrote next words without prompt. Noticed and self-corrected 2 errors. Asked questions (e.g., do I need an "s" in pencil?)
Emma			
Message	Baby bear goes fishing and he gets lots of fish	I will make pumpkin pie	Mom and Ben made the best cake
Spelling	Heard /b/ in baby and /f/ in fish. Teacher contributed spelling patterns	Heard initial and some final sounds. Teacher contributed spelling patterns	Heard initial and final sounds. Confused medial sounds a/e. Teacher contributed spelling patterns
Words written independently	A/ he/ of	I/ my/ mom	Mom/ and/ the/ cake
Monitoring of accuracy	Teacher reread for her on four occasions. Did not notice errors.	Teacher told next words. Did not notice errors and was not prompted to.	Searched for next words. Noticed one error but did not correct.

Teacher Support for Growing Independence

Increasing Responsibility to Use Sources of Knowledge

For children in our study who made high progress we noted that, at the beginning of the intervention, teachers contributed much of the necessary information, then moved toward accepting approximations and, by the end of the intervention, contributed very little. For example, for Paul during the first observation we noted that the teacher contributed spelling information freeing Paul to using his phonetic knowledge to write new words. Paul could hear and record the initial and final sounds in words, but needed high teacher support at times to hear the sounds in a sequence. This is exemplified in the following interaction, where Paul tries to spell the word "play":

Ms. Kelly: Let's try to do play. Can you push the sounds up? (teacher drew Elkonin boxes).

Paul: /p/ /a/ /l/

Ms. Kelly: Try it again. Plllaaay

Paul: /p/ /ay/

Ms. Kelly: plllay. Plllay

Paul: P.

Ms. Kelly: Okay can you write the P in the box?

Paul: (writes P in first box)

Ms. Kelly: /p/ /l/ /ay/ what sound-

Paul: L.

Ms. Kelly: Good. Yeah.

Paul: (writes L in second box)

Ms. Kelly: Say the sounds?

Paul: /p/ /p/ /uh/

Ms. Kelly: /p/ /l/ /ay/

Paul: A

Ms. Kelly: Write your A.

Paul: (writes A in third box)

Ms. Kelly: And this one has a /y/ that you really don't hear (writes y for Paul). Can you practice it right here? Play.

(Week 5, Lesson 25)

We noted in this interaction high levels of teacher support tempered by an expectation that Paul would write what he could. Ms. Kelly used Elkonin boxes (Clay, 2005) to support segmenting the word, but provided the orthographic information that was, perhaps at this point, too difficult for Paul. She concluded by telling him to practice writing the word, which may have helped him to commit the word to his writing vocabulary. Indeed, by the last week of the intervention Paul wrote most words in his messages independently and contributed orthographic information (like the /e/ in have).

In contrast, we noted that support was not withdrawn for children like Emma. By the end of the intervention teachers of children who made low progress continued to provide high support, similar to that observed in week 5 for Paul. For example, they still slowly articulated words and children did not have the opportunity to say and hear the sounds that they needed to record the word in written form.

Creating Spaces for Problem-Solving
In our observations we examined where the locus of control lay between child and teacher as they co-constructed the written message, in terms of deciding what letter or word to write next and monitoring the accuracy of what was written.

Children who made high progress were gradually supported to take more responsibility for problem-solving. For example, as Paul wrote his message during the first observation, Ms. Kelly told him all but one of the next words to write, leaving him no opportunity to think about what came next. In contrast, by the last observation she no longer told Paul what to do next, he thought about his message and made the decision quickly on his own. Ms. Kelly simply prompted Paul now and then to reread his message, creating a "space" for him to monitor and problem-solve on his own.

Teachers of students who made low progress, as we described previously, assumed the role of editor: monitoring for the child when a mistake was made, telling the next word or letter to write, and assumed a "dictation role" when it came to encoding the letters into words. Take, for example, Emma, who together with her teacher, co-constructed the sentence "*Baby bear goes fishing and he gets lots of fish*" on the fifth week of her intervention. On four occasions her teacher reread the message to her providing her with limited opportunities to search for the next word as she wrote. This pattern of telling continued when she attempted to spell words. In the vignette below, her teacher is helping her spell the word "fish":

> Ms. Byrne: Okay now we've got this fish. I'm gonna help you with it but I want you to put the first sound.
>
> Emma: (writes /f/ on practice page).
>
> Ms. Byrne: Okay, so you've got /f/. And then you hear this /i/ sound. And then we've got this /sh/ sound.
>
> (Week 6, Lesson 24)

This example illustrates that in this co-constructed setting, Ms. Cooper was telling Emma the next word, which did not provide her the opportunity to think about it for herself. Some element of responsibility was handed over to Emma by prompting her to write the first sound, which required thinking about letter-sound information, but then the teacher provided the rest of the information. This pattern was repeated across time, where the teacher provided most information and the chance or opportunity to problem-solve only occurred after a teacher prompt.

PRACTICAL IMPLICATIONS

In this study, teachers were faced with the challenging task of providing instructional support that would effectively guide struggling children toward being able to independently write the types of texts demanded by the CCSS (National Governors Association Center for Best Practices & Council of Chief State School Officers, 2010). We described in this chapter how high and low progressing students in our study changed in their writing and the nature of teacher support that seemed connected to these outcomes. In this final section we want to highlight two practical implications that arise from this study.

Become familiar with linguistic complexity

In order to help young students move from writing simple messages to more complex ones, it helps to have a good understanding of what makes a message more linguistically complex. Harmey (2015) developed a rubric that includes rating linguistic complexity on a scale of 0–3, from least to most linguistically complex.

0. The message could not be considered a complete or simple sentence. Example: The student writes a list of words.
1. The message is a simple short sentence (one independent clause that contains one thought) Example: *I want to do my Grinch.* This message contains one thought; if it was any shorter it would not be considered a full thought.
2. The message is one long sentence (one clause with an extension) or two or more simple sentence. Example: *I went to the grocery shop and ate a red apple.* This message contains one clause with an extension (.and ate a red apple). It could have been parsed into two sentences.
3. The message is two or more sentences. At least one is compound or is a long sentence (one clause with an extension) Example: *I have a lot of pencils in my pencil box. I work with my pencils at home and at school.*

In this case, the child wrote two sentences. One of the sentences is a compound sentence (I word with my pencils at home AND at school).

Teach for linguistic complexity

As we learned in this study, unless teachers prompted students to extend and expand on ideas, the written messages continued to be fairly simple. In order to teach for more linguistic complexity, prompt the student to add temporal connectives (words like "then," "next," and "before"), logical connectives (words like "at," "because," and "in order to"), and cohesive or co-referential ties (words that refer to something mentioned previously in a sentence, e.g., "Dan is my friend. He is funny."). Encourage the student to expand on ideas by adding more detail to the message, but at the same time, expect that legibility may lapse for a short while as the student places cognitive resources on writing a more complex message.

It is also helpful to consider the linguistic complexity of books that students are reading. The 0–3 rubric provided in the first bullet can be used to analyze text selection. Consider for example the range in linguistic complexity of these two stories about the same characters on the same topic, both from the first page of each little book, and both stories intended for children just learning to read.

Table 2.

Father Bear Goes Fishing (Randell, 1994a)	*Baby Bear Goes Fishing* (Randell, 1994b)
Father Bear went fishing. He went down to the river.	I'm going fishing, said Father Bear. "I like fishing, too," said Baby Bear. "I will go with you and help you."

As we mentioned in this chapter, reading and writing are reciprocal processes, meaning that what one learns in reading can help with writing, and vice versa. Usually when we select little books for beginning readers we consider its vocabulary: will it be too hard to read? We suggest also considering the text's linguistic complexity and choosing stories that will challenge and extend the student's present control. Reading stories with linguistic complexity just beyond what the student can produce in writing will support the production of more complex messages, and supporting the student to write more linguistically complex messages will make it easier to read stories with longer and more complex sentence structures.

REFERENCES

Alamargot, D., & Fayol, M. (2009). Modeling the development of written composition. In R. Beard, D. Myhill, J. Riley, & M. Nystrand (Eds.), *The Sage handbook of writing development* (pp. 23–47). London: Sage.

Calkins, L. (2013). *Writing pathways: Performance assessments and learning progressions, Grades K-8*. Portsmouth, NH: Heinemann.

Clay, M. M. (1975). *What did I write?* Portsmouth, NH: Heinemann.

Clay, M. M. (1998). *By different paths to common outcomes*. Portsmouth, NH: Heinemann.

Clay, M. M. (2001). *Change over time in children's literacy development*. Portsmouth, NH: Heinemann.

Clay, M. M. (2004). Talking, reading and writing. *Journal of Reading Recovery, 3*(2), 1–15.

Clay, M. M. (2005). *Literacy lessons designed for individuals: Part 2 – Teaching procedures*. Portsmouth, NH: Heinemann.

Clay, M. M. (2013). *An observation survey of early literacy achievement*. Portsmouth, NH: Heinemann.

D'Agostino, J. V. (2012). Technical review committee confirms highest NCRTI rating for observation survey of early literacy achievement. *Journal of Reading Recovery, 12*(1), 46–53.

Dinehart, L. H., & Manfra, I. (2013). Association between early fine motor movement and later math and reading achievement in early elementary school. *Early Childhood Education and Development, 24*(2), 138–161.

Dinehart, L. J. (2014). Handwriting in early childhood education: Current research and future implications. *Journal of Early Childhood Literacy, 15*(1), 97–118. doi:10.1177/1468798414522825

Dyson, A. H. (1983). Role of oral language in early writing processes. *Research in the Teaching of English, 17*, 1–30.

Graham, S., Bollinger, A., Booth Olson, C., D'Aoust, C., MacArthur, C., McCutchen, D., & Olinghouse, N. (2012). *Teaching elementary school students to be effective writers: A practice guide*. (NCEE 2012-4058). Washington, DC: National Center for Education Evaluation and Regional Assistance, Institute of Education Sciences, U.S. Department of Education. Retrieved from http://ies.ed.gov/ncee/wwc/publications_reviews.aspx#pubsearch

Graham, S., & Harris, K. R. (2009). Almost 30 years of writing research: Making sense of it all with 'The Wrath of Khan'. *Learning Disabilities Research & Practice, 24*(2), 58–68. doi:10.1037/0022-0663.92.4.620

Granott, N. (2002). How microdevelopment creates macrodevelopment: Reiterated sequences, backwards transitions, and the zone of proximal development. In N. Grannott & G. Parziale (Eds.), *Microdevelopment: Transition processes in development and learning* (pp. 213–242). Cambridge: Cambridge University Press.

Halliday, M., & Hassan, R. (1976). *Cohesion in English*. London: Longman.

Harmey, S. (2015). *Change over time in children's co-constructed writing*. Electronic Dissertation. Retrieved from https://etd.ohiolink.edu/

Harmey, S., D'Agostino, J. V., & Rodgers, E. (2015, December). Capturing change over time in early writing: The design of an early writing observational rubric. Paper presented at the 65th annual meeting of the Literacy Research Association, Carlsbad, California.

Lavelli, M., Pantoja, A. P. F., Hsu, H. C., Messinger, D., & Fogel, A. (2005). Using microgenetic designs to study change processes. In D. M. Teti (Ed.), *Handbook of research methods in developmental science* (pp. 40–65). Oxford: Blackwell Publishing Ltd. doi:10.1002/9780470756676.ch3

Miles, M. B., Huberman, A. M., & Saldaña, J. (2014). *Qualitative data analysis: A methods sourcebook*. Thousand Oaks, CA: Sage.

National Governors Association Center for Best Practices & Council of Chief State School Officers. (2010). *Common core state standards for English language arts and literacy in history/social studies, science, and technical subjects*. Washington, DC: Author.

Randall, B. (1994a). *Father Bear goes fishing*. Wellington, NZ: Nelson Price Milburn.

Randall, B. (1994b). *Baby Bear goes fishing*. Wellington, NZ: Nelson Price Milburn.

Raudenbush, S. W., & Bryk, A. S. (2002). *Hierarchical linear models: Applications and data analysis methods*. Thousand Oaks, CA: Sage.

Ritchey, K. D., & Coker, D. L. (2014). Identifying writing difficulties in first grade: An investigation of writing and reading measures. *Learning Disabilities Research and Practice, 29*(2), 54–65. doi:10.1111/ldrp.12030

Rodgers, E. (2008). Write now: Don't wait to teach struggling readers about writing. In G. S. Pinnell & P. Scharer (Eds.), *Guiding K-3 writers to independence: The new essentials* (pp. 193–208). New York, NY: Scholastic.

Siegler, R. S. (2006). Microgenetic analysis of learning. In D. Kuhn, R. S. Siegler, & W. Damon (Eds.), *Handbook of child psychology* (Vol. 2, pp. 464–509). Hoboken, NJ: Wiley.

Singer, J., & Willett, J. (2003). *Applied longitudinal data analysis: Modeling change and event occurrence*. Retrieved from http://www.oxfordscholarship.com. doi:10.1093/acprof:oso/9780195152968.003.0001.

Thelen, E., & Corbetta, D. (2002). Microdevelopment and dynamic systems: Applications to infant motor development. In N. Grannott & J. Parziale (Eds.), *Microdevelopment: Transition processes in development and learning* (pp. 59–79). New York, NY: Cambridge University Press.

APPENDIX

Table A1. Elements, Constructs, and Items of the Early Writing Observational Rubric.

Element of Rubric	Construct	Item
Part A: Writing behaviors		
(i) Using	Composition Encoding	Use of language to compose a message
		Use of visual information
		Use of letter-sound relationships
	Conceptual awareness about print	Concept of word
		Directionality
	Production	Writing vocabulary
(ii) Doing	Strategic activity on text	Searching
		Monitoring/crosschecking
		Self-correcting
		Fluency
Part B: Written message	Transcription	Legibility
	Micro-levels of language	Linguistic complexity
		Linguistic texture
		Punctuation and capital letters
	Macro-levels of language	Organization of message

ACCELERATING STUDENT PROGRESS IN WRITING: EXAMINING PRACTICES EFFECTIVE IN NEW ZEALAND PRIMARY SCHOOL CLASSROOMS

Judy M. Parr

ABSTRACT

Purpose — *Writing performance is an international issue and, while the quality of instruction is key, features of the context shape classroom practice. The issues and solutions in terms of teacher practice to address underachievement need to be considered within such a context and the purpose of the chapter is to undertake such an analysis.*

Design/methodology/approach — *Data from five different research projects (national and regional) of the author and colleagues, and two studies of the author's doctoral students, are synthesized to identify both common and specific elements of primary/elementary (years 1–8, ages 5–13) teacher practice in writing. These data provide an indication of the practices which appear to be the most powerful levers for developing writing and for accelerating student progress in the context in which the teachers work. These practices are discussed.*

Findings − The identified practices are: (1) acquiring and applying deep knowledge of your writers; (2) making connections with, and validating, relevant cultural and linguistic funds of knowledge; (3) aligning learning goals in writing with appropriately designed writing tasks and ensuring that students understand what they are learning and why; (4) providing quality feedback; (5) scaffolding self-regulation in writers; (6) differentiating instruction (while maintaining high expectations) and (7) providing targeted and direct instruction at the point of need. A discussion and a description of writing-specific instantiations of these help to illustrate their nature and the overlaps and interconnections.

Practical implications − As much of the data are drawn from the practices of teachers deemed to be highly effective, classroom practices associated with these teachers can be targeted as a means to improve the quality of instruction more widely in the particular context.

Keywords: Primary/elementary school; accelerating progress; effective classroom practices; context

INTRODUCTION

The ability of students to write is both an ongoing concern and a concern shared internationally. Consistent with international trends, the writing performance of students in New Zealand is problematic. Fewer primary students (years 1−8 of schooling, ages 5−13) meet national standards in writing than in reading and mathematics. A recent report of student achievement (2014) concluded that 70.6% met or exceeded the year level expectations in writing, compared with 77% that met or exceeded national expectations for achievement in reading and 75% in mathematics. Moreover, the writing achievement of particular groups of students, namely indigenous Maori, and also Pasifika, is, on average, about 15% below that of the rest of the student population and primary school boys lag behind girls to a similar extent (http://www.educationcounts.govt.nz/statistics/schooling/national-standards/National_Standards).

Students' instructional experiences are acknowledged to be a major contributor to performance with teachers having the largest single system-level impact on student achievement (Alton-Lee, 2003; Nye, Konstantopoulos, & Hedges, 2004). The quality of teaching is key (Hattie, 2003). Ongoing professional learning and resourcing are required to ensure quality, given that knowledge about pedagogy as well as content does not remain constant; definitions of literacy change and the extent of diversity of the student body is increasing. Providing the opportunity for high quality professional learning is a key policy initiative of the New Zealand Literacy Strategy (1999) and of successive governments.

Arguably, there is evidence of pedagogies that are regarded as having instructional force generally (Grossman, Loeb, Cohen, & Wyckoff, 2013; Hattie, 2009). There is relatively little data on writing instruction in elementary or middle schools (Gilbert & Graham, 2010). There are a number of studies of exemplary literacy teachers, commonly teachers of reading (Block & Mangieri, 2003; Pressley, Gaskins, Solic, & Collins, 2006; Wray, Medwell, Fox, & Poulson, 2000). These have, in part, contributed to the identification, from systematic research, of effective practices in teaching writing (Graham & Perin, 2007). However, instructional experiences are shaped at various layers, recontextualized as it were (after Bernstein, 2000). Features of the context and the implications of them are significant in a consideration of classroom instruction. Contexts shape classroom activities and student learning (Lipson, Mosenthal, Daniels, & Woodside-Jiron, 2000); they both enable and channel practice. In considering how to address underperformance in writing, the issues and solutions need to be considered within a particular context.

The Context

The New Zealand schooling context is somewhat different to many countries. New Zealand is one educational jurisdiction approximately the size of Scotland, Norway or a small state like Vermont in the United States. The national curriculum (*New Zealand Curriculum (NZC)*, Ministry of Education, 2007) is intended as a broad, guiding document to 'set the direction for student learning' (p. 6) and schools, which are autonomous, self-governing entities, are urged to adapt it to their local context. Writing is nominally within all eight learning areas of the curriculum as students learn 'how to communicate knowledge and ideas in appropriate ways' (p. 16) within each but the skills for writing largely tend to be described within the English learning area. The *New Zealand Curriculum* (2007) was fully implemented by 2010 and then schools were required to set out in their individual charters, priorities and targets for accelerating student achievement.

There are no mandated national tests or qualifications until the last three years of schooling. Since 2012, changed requirements regarding reporting to Ministry of Education mean that primary schools (years 1–8) report to the Ministry, in literacy against *National Standards in Reading and Writing* (Ministry of Education, 2009). The writing standards are not empirically based on student performance in writing or based on a theory of writing. They are derived from a close analysis of the nature of writing (and reading) required to access and be successful in all areas of the *New Zealand Curriculum*, after six months at school, and at each of Years 1–10 of schooling. The emphasis is on reading and writing in the service of learning. The standards represent aspirational goals in two senses: they are the standards that students need to achieve to be on track to succeed in the National Certificate for Educational Achievement (Level 2) at years 11–13 and, in devising the standards, there was a clear sense that they were in advance of what available normative data would suggest.

Further, the national curriculum document says and implies little specifically about pedagogy but, significantly, it does describes teaching as 'inquiry' (Ministry of Education, 2007, p. 35). The intention is that teachers undertake evidence-informed professional inquiry into challenges in terms of their practice; that they be adaptive experts, able to alter practice to better meet student need. Teachers have to understand their students' learning needs in writing, their strengths and gaps; the likely effective (research-informed) ways to address the needs, and how to action such pedagogically within their particular context. Teachers have to have deep knowledge of every student in their class as teachers make, on the basis of an overall teacher judgement, using evidence from a range of sources, the decision about whether a student meets, or is above or below national expectations in relation to national standards.

With a curriculum that essentially provides broad guidelines, with no mandated common testing and with a philosophy of teaching as inquiry, there needs to be support and development opportunities for professionals at all levels. These include high quality professional learning and tools and resources. In the area of writing there are several tools and resources, for example: a tool to provide diagnostic assessment of writing that also allows national normative comparisons, namely, *e-asTTle: Writing (revised)* (Ministry of Education & New Zealand Council for Educational Research, 2012); The *Literacy Learning Progressions* or *LLP* (Ministry of Education, 2010); a *Progress and Consistency Tool (PACT)* (Ministry of Education, 2015), designed to support teachers to make dependable judgements about students' progress and achievement in writing in relation to the standards, and research-based literacy handbooks for teachers, limited numbers of which are provided to schools free of charge (*Effective Literacy Practice Years 1–4* (2006) and *Effective Literacy Practice Years 5–8* (2007)). Tools, resources and professional learning opportunities effectively provide a mediating layer between the classroom and national guidelines.

The nature of the student body is another significant feature of the context. This body, largely in urban areas, is increasingly diverse. Some schools in Auckland, where around a third of the New Zealand population lives, register more than 60 different cultural groups. While indigenous Maori form a sizeable proportion in certain rural areas, Maori and Pasifika combined will form a majority of the students in Auckland schools by 2020. Thus, many classrooms are multi-cultural and multi-lingual, an additional factor for teachers in a bi-cultural nation.

A Theoretical Lens

The context or environment in which writing instruction occurs is complex. Employing an activity systems framing helps us to think about individual activity in relation to its context and how the individual, his/her activities, and the context affect one another (Yamagata-Lynch, 2010). Activity systems framing commonly uses the triangular model developed by Engestrom (1987). In this model the subject is the individual or group that is involved in the activity; the object is the goal of the activity and, at the apex of the triangle, sit both social others and material and psychological artefacts that can act as resources for the subject in the activity. When we are considering, as we are here, the instructional practices for writing that are effective in a context, there are two activity systems operating. One concerns the teacher as subject; the effective writing instructional practice as object, while the resources are those, like curriculum, assessment practices and professional learning opportunities that both support and channel teacher learning and practice. The other triangle contains the student as subject with the goals of enhanced writing development and performance and the resources include the teacher, the teacher's instructional practices and materials and, possibly, peers.

Instructional capacity, the capacity to produce worthwhile and substantial learning, according to Ball and Cohen (1996), is shaped by interactions between teachers, materials or technology, and students. Teachers' are key as they mediate instruction. In interpreting existing resources, including, in the current case, curriculum and standards; in evaluating the constraints of the classroom setting; in balancing trade-offs and devising strategies in the pursuit of instructional goals, teaching is seen as a design activity (Brown & Edleson, 2003). This dovetails with the idea of teaching as professional inquiry; design activity particularly emphasizes the active role of the teacher in the complexity that is practice.

Aims and Scope of the Chapter

This chapter will present a synthesis of data drawn from five different research projects (national and regional) of the author and colleagues, and two studies of the author's doctoral students, to identify both common and specific elements of primary/elementary (years 1−8, ages 5−13) teacher practice in writing. There are indications from these data of the practices which appear to be the most powerful levers for developing writing and for accelerating student progress in the context in which the teachers work. It is these practices that are focused on here. However, it is acknowledged that the quality of practice is underpinned and influenced by teachers' content knowledge of writing − how language works to achieve its communicative purposes and knowledge of the processes that writers engage in as they write; by their knowledge of effective pedagogy; their beliefs about teaching and learning of writing, and their personal dispositions and aptitudes for writing and the teaching of writing.

In some instances the selected practices are those that characterize purposively selected expert teachers of writing, that is, those whose students consistently make accelerated (beyond the expected gains of a national, normative sample) progress in writing (Gadd, 2014; Parr & Limbrick, 2010; Si'ilata, 2014; Si'ilata, Dreaver, Parr, Timperley, & Meissel, 2012). While, as noted, the literature on writing instruction is not extensive, relative to that on reading, much of it draws from the practices of teachers deemed to be effective. This focus is premised on the idea that those classroom practices associated with more effective teachers can be targeted as a means to improve the quality of instruction more widely (Grossman et al., 2013). In other instances, the data drawn on here are from studies that relate student progress to teacher level of proficiency in terms of specific practices (Gadd, 2014; Parr & Timperley, 2010) or teacher practice to student understanding (Timperley & Parr, 2009). And, in yet other instances, the data are those reported by a range of classroom teachers to be a practice they consider to be important or to be one reported from observation of peers, although they may be variously confident or proficient in executing the practice (Hawe & Parr, 2014; Parr & Jesson, 2016).

While the dimensions of practice selected as key to effective teaching of writing are, essentially, those the author infers from the various research projects drawn on, the resulting list largely aligns with the more general research findings on effective literacy practice alluded to above and with reviews of such (Hall & Harding, 2003). However, the list may be more constrained or focussed and the way in which the practices or dimensions of practices are described may be different. And, there are, arguably, additional ones that could be placed on the list, but it is the potentially most powerful practices in the context in which they occur that have been singled out for discussion and description. While, in some cases, the research shows a particular practice to be related to student achievement gains in writing and, thus, likely to be a key practice, it needs to be stressed that, in the classroom of an effective teacher, such practices are likely to operate in concert with others.

POTENTIAL, POWERFUL PRACTICES FOR DEVELOPING WRITING AND FOR ACCELERATING PROGRESS

The selected dimensions of practice are: (1) acquiring and applying deep knowledge of your writers; (2) making connections with, and validating, relevant cultural and linguistic funds of knowledge; (3) aligning learning goals in writing with appropriately designed writing tasks and ensuring that students understand what they are learning and why; (4) providing quality feedback; (5) scaffolding self-regulation in writers; (6) differentiating instruction (while maintaining high expectations), and (7) providing targeted and direct instruction at the point of need. A discussion and a description of writing-specific instantiations of these will help to illustrate their nature and the overlaps and interconnections.

Knowing Your Writers

In positioning teaching as involving a process of inquiry and teachers as inquiring practitioners, the NZC regards teachers as responsible for their own learning, for inquiring into student learning and making appropriate adjustments to practice to better meet the needs of their students. Observing, gathering and interpreting information on students' writing behaviours and outcomes is the key. Knowing where students are in relation to where they should be is one of the interdependent strategies that comprise assessment for learning (AfL); The National Assessment Strategy of 1999 was set in the context of, 'current thinking about the impact of formative assessment on teaching, learning and student achievement' (Chamberlain, 2000, p. 23). Related professional learning programmes such as Assessment for Better Learning (ABeL) and Assessment to Learn (AtoL) have reached over two-thirds of all primary schools and have had a significant impact on teachers' practice with both focused on development of teachers' assessment understandings about formative assessment and the use of associated strategies (Gilmore, 2008).

The investigation of strategies to support more effective assessment for learning, as Parr and Jesson (2015) note in their article 'Mapping the landscape of writing instruction in New Zealand classrooms', is a strong theme in the intervention and other research literature in New Zealand. In the survey of writing practices reported in that article, primary teachers rated the practice of 'rove and assist', that is to move around the classroom as students were writing, monitoring writing behaviours and noticing incidences where a comment or question or prompt may move the writer forward, as a practice they emphasized to a considerable extent. It was also a practice they were reportedly very confident in carrying out.

The use of evidence of student learning to frame professional development underpins research and development projects in literacy in New Zealand. A major, highly successful example of evidence-informed learning was the national Literacy Professional Development Project (LPDP). In this project learning at all levels was needs-based but the starting point was the identified learning needs of students to inform what teachers needed to know and do to address those needs. The project employed a whole school facilitation model of professional development where a visiting expert worked within the school over a two-year period upskilling leaders and teachers. The project was highly successful. The average effect size gain (Cohen's *d*) was calculated to show gain over and above the expected average gain in the two-year period of each cohort. In writing these effect sizes for each of the three cohorts were 0.79, 0.62, and 0.88, respectively. The gain for the lowest 20% of students (identified at the first time point) in each of the three cohorts was five to six times the expected gain (effect size gains of 1.81, 1.93 and 2.07) (Parr, Timperley, Reddish, Adams, & Jesson, 2007; Timperley, Parr, & Meissel, 2010).

In this project, resources and tools available to all schools were employed to find out about students' learning and teachers were supported to learn to use them effectively. A key indicator of student writing performance and their learning needs was obtained using the diagnostic assessment of writing tool that also allows national normative comparisons, namely, *Assessment Tools for Teaching and Learning (asTTle): Writing* (Ministry of Education & University of Auckland, 2004). An important design feature of this original version of the tool was the positioning of writing and writing instruction. Writing was described as serving major communicative purposes (relevant to the curriculum and context of schooling). To illustrate the features associated with different purposes for writing, detailed scoring rubrics specified, for seven different dimensions of writing (audience, content, structure, language resources, grammar, spelling and punctuation), the criteria commonly associated with each purpose at various curriculum levels of primary schooling.

The tool locates strengths, what the writer knows so that the teacher is able to build on this; it also identifies gaps in the knowledge base, providing data at both an individual and aggregated (e.g. class, year group) level. Teachers moderate writing collegially. During the project this moderation process was initially led by the expert visiting facilitator. The diagnostic focus, together with the fact that teachers can select when to utilize the assessment tool, reinforces the idea of assessment as an integral, ongoing part of learning and teaching. Research data from LPDP showed that teachers became more proficient at interpreting student achievement data in writing although the application of these data to adjust practice was a more challenging endeavour, requiring further support (Parr & Timperley, 2008).

Another tool (initially in its draft form) helped teachers participating in LPDP with descriptions and examples to cue them regarding what to notice as students write, as well as what to attend to in the pieces produced. The *Literacy Learning Progressions* or *LLP* (Ministry of Education, 2010) describe and illustrate writing behaviours and features of writing characteristic of particular year levels. In a study shortly after the draft of *LLP* was introduced, LPDP teachers reported finding the tool useful in providing a broader picture of development in writing; they reported learning in relation to expectations for student writing at different levels. Actions resulting from such learning were reportedly taken with respect to setting goals or targets and in terms of using the *LLP* to build profiles of students (Parr, 2011).

Making Connections with and Validating Cultural and Linguistic Funds of Knowledge

The belief that existing knowledge and experience that students have of language can be harnessed and built on productively to enable new learning in writing is an important precursor to pedagogies that draw on and validate existing cultural and linguistic funds of knowledge. Some of our sources would suggest New Zealand primary teachers have not yet embraced this notion or are unsure about their expertise. In ratings of importance in their practice, incorporating cultural and linguistic diversity rated lowest while teachers were also least confident regarding knowing about the out-of-school literacies of their students (Parr & Jesson, 2016). The Pasifika Literacy Professional Development Project (Si'ilata, 2014; Si'ilata et al., 2012) informs the descriptions of effective practices in terms of this dimension. This project was an extension of LPDP and was designed to examine the practices of teachers in five schools, with sizeable numbers of Pasifika students, who were successful in raising achievement of these students (Pasifika are the lowest performing group in literacy in New Zealand). A group of schools struggling with Pasifika achievement subsequently joined for two years and the knowledge from the successful group was used to help design their professional development.

Six specific practices with indicators and examples of those practices were developed, drawing on the teachers in successful schools who had become more proficient in using and that those teachers in less successful schools had begun to employ, with effect (Si'ilata, 2014). Clearly, some of the practices are the same as those discussed here but are couched in terms that refer specifically to Pasifika (e.g. knowledge of the learner or building agency/self-regulation or direct instruction through ensuring a focus on form that includes explicit teaching of academic vocabulary and language features within a meaningful context). The specification of dimensions of practice and the giving of examples is, of necessity, given teachers' lack of knowledge, very detailed. Here I simply draw attention to a small section related to instructional strategies. One indicator specifies explicitly teaching English language and vocabulary by building on Pasifika home languages and oral practices while another, closely related indicator, includes teaching strategies for written language that include the use of Pasifika literacy practices. Examples of practices from these include facilitating learners to write (and read) in first languages to support bi-literacy development; promoting receptive and productive language development by linking listening, reading, and viewing, with speaking, writing, and presenting; using Pasifika literacy practices, for example text memorization, recitation, choral reading and the use of metaphor, silence, song, and humour to build on Pasifika learners' strengths and, more generally, designing communicative tasks that allow for tuakana/teina pairings (more expert helping less expert or older helping younger), providing familiar, comfortable contexts for Pasifika learners to retrieve, practise and generate academic vocabulary, develop fluency and build accuracy.

Learning Goals and Tasks: Alignment and Transparency

Relatively little attention has been given to the quality of the instructional goals teachers set, how teachers convey them through lesson tasks and activities and how they are understood by students. The nature of goals is a particular issue in writing. There is debate about the extent to which it is possible to delineate specific and consistent features of writing in terms of criteria and particular dimensions (Marshall, 2004; Sadler, 1989). Marshall (2004) has argued that progression in writing should be construed as moving towards a broad horizon where learning outcomes and expectations are less precisely defined at the outset and where multiple pathways to successful achievement are possible. Students develop understanding of these broad horizons and different ways to achieve success as they engage in writing and participate in authentic evaluative activities designed to bring them into the subject community or guild (Hogden & Marshall, 2005; Marshall, 2004; Sadler, 1989). So, teachers have to balance this notion of broader goals with the need to help students to gain a sense of what is aimed for. Being specific about what students are learning about writing requires knowledge about how language works to achieve its communicative purpose, and teachers varied in their reported knowledge of linguistic features of text, for example (Parr & Limbrick, 2010).

How to achieve this balance and also more specific understandings was illustrated by one of our expert teachers in the Parr and Limbrick (2010) study. She gave students time to explore the current aims for writing: 'We are going to be doing response writing. Now before I even tell you what the intentions of the unit are, I want you to talk to a partner and decide what a response is. What is a response?' This elicitation of students' prior knowledge was followed by clarification of students' comments through discussion. Students in this class, when asked what the lesson was about, noted that they were learning to write their 'opinions, feelings and judgements' about events or books for specific audiences. Throughout the interviews with these students, they made frequent reference to an awareness of writing for an audience. They had, together, detailed the horizon.

The way in which goals are framed influences student understanding of writing and directs their attention to certain aspects (Hawe, Dixon, & Watson, 2008; Timperley & Parr, 2009). These studies in New Zealand writing classrooms more generally suggest a prevalence of performance goals such as 'I will use more interesting words in my stories' and 'we are writing a narrative'. The first goal draws attention to counting and comparing the number of interesting words used while the second directs the focus to the task or activity. If performance goals are common, students may tend to avoid more challenging pursuits and seek the easiest way to meet requirements (Dweck, 1986). Goals need to be sufficiently challenging and focussed on learning rather than performance so students are likely to be more motivated to master new skills and endeavour to understand content (Zimmerman, 2008). Framing goals as broad, cognitive communication processes, such as 'we will understand how to craft a persuasive argument' or 'I will make a strong argument that convinces the reader to support my point of view', draws attention to the discursive nature of writing and the notion that writing is for a purpose and/or an audience (Hawe & Parr, 2014).

It is also important that both learning goals and related performance criteria are clearly articulated and that a purposeful writing task is arrived at that gives students opportunities to achieve the goals. In a study of 17 writing classrooms (Timperley & Parr, 2009), we illustrated the confusion for students when there is a lack of clarity or alignment. The observational and interview data showed that, in instances where goals and mastery criteria were implicit or not articulated clearly or when lesson goals were clearly articulated but the mastery criteria and/or lesson tasks or activities were misaligned with them, students, at interview, were unable to articulate what they were learning or what a quality performance would looked like. Instead, they defaulted to nominating surface features or similar low level concerns or broad performance goals like 'write a report'. Also, as we found in this study, when teachers clearly convey substantive learning goals and what it is that constitutes successful writing in a way that students understand, they are more likely to generate feedback related to these qualities, and as a consequence are more likely to have students who are successful writers.

The design of the writing task is key to engagement and to achieving goals, and purposefulness is paramount. The notion of task purposefulness involves teachers ensuring that their students are interested in the content, link expected outcomes to their prior knowledge, interests or experiences, and value the learning that is inherent within tasks (Lodewyk & Winne, 2005; Lodewyk, Winne, & Jamieson-Noel, 2009). In a different study, of purposively selected exemplary teachers of writing, those whose students consistently progress well beyond normative expectations, the teacher level of expertise in devising writing tasks that students saw as purposeful and that they were invested in was correlated to extent of student progress (Gadd, 2014; Gadd & Parr, 2016). As a teacher explained, <we> 'have to seize the moment ... because topic is so essential ... I find the best writing is the writing that's, you know, got real purpose'. She added that she did not plan writing topics for the longer term because they 'arise according to kids' experiences, and needs, and interests', concluding that, '...<students> having something to say ... something to write about ... is of paramount importance to me as a teacher of writing' (Gadd & Parr, 2016).

A key contributor to task purposefulness involves teachers encouraging their students to select or even construct their own writing tasks so as to enhance their ownership of them (Marshall & Weinstein, 1984). This is an area where even some expert teachers appear not to capitalize. While teachers provided some choice of topic selection within broad and open-ended learning tasks, only one of Gadd's (2014) highly expert teachers involved students fully in the construction of a learning task. She asked students at the beginning of a lesson, 'What things have we been doing lately that we can really write about? Have a think ... Now talk to your partner.' Having decided on a topic (a recent market day that the students had run), she went on to ask, 'So what do you want your readers to know about market day?'

In the design of a writing task a teacher has to arrive at a task that allows students to work towards valued goals, goals which likely encompass both personal interests and communicative goals, and wider curriculum goals. And, to promote engagement, student input has to be achieved in some way or in some measure. Research suggests that this is an area of practice that continues to develop, even amongst many exemplary teachers.

Providing Quality Feedback

Feedback refers to, 'information provided by an agent (e.g. teacher, peer, book, parent, self, experience) regarding aspects of one's performance or understanding' (Hattie & Timperley, 2007, p. 81). There are different types of feedback, some more powerful than others. According to Hattie and

Timperley (2007), powerful types include information aimed at cognitive processes (skills, concepts, knowledge) underlying a task. This draws attention to the substantive aspects of learning and leads to deeper thinking and understanding. In a writing context, such feedback would address understandings about the purpose in writing a particular kind of text, the articulation of ideas and the use of language as a resource to express those ideas. Feedback about aspects of student self-regulation (monitoring, directing and controlling of actions towards the goals of learning) has a similar impact and degree of effectiveness. This type of feedback would include information about students' meta-cognitive awareness of the writing process, for example, their ongoing crafting and reworking of text. A further type of feedback focuses on how well a student is accomplishing a learning task or goal. Such feedback is of greatest value when focused on improvement and provided in conjunction with information about cognitive processing and/or student self-regulation.

Feedback is vital if students are to have information that helps them to learn and to take responsibility for regulating their own learning. New Zealand teachers have received significant exposure to the results of meta-analyses conducted by Hattie (2009) that show feedback as one of the most significant influences on student achievement (formative evaluation is also listed). Feedback, as an aspect of practice within writing instruction was rated the most important in a survey of New Zealand primary teachers with 98% reporting that they emphasized feedback to a great or very great extent. They were also very confident that they could do this well (Parr & Jesson, 2016).

More specifically, two studies have examined the nature and quality of this feedback in writing. Feedback and its nature were examined in the Hawe and Parr (2014) study. While almost all teachers gave feedback that focussed on learning, feedback that was achievement and improvement related, it was of variable quality. Of the 18 teachers, 17 were rated as providing students with achievement-related feedback. But four referred only in a general manner to the current learning focus such as '[I can see a] great range of describing words as I walk around' and a further two gave feedback in relation to more generic aspects of literacy learning like 'Your grammar and punctuation in this piece is perfect'. The rest, however, were observed telling students about the ways in which their work had met expectations in relation to the criteria for successful performance that has been established: Fran (addressing the class) '[Student] noticed that she has used seven 'she's'. [Student] only noticed when she stopped and highlighted − great' [the current goal of learning was to reduce needless repetition in the narrative]. Regarding improvement-related feedback, again, almost all (16 of 18) provided such. However, only 11 teachers informed their students about specific aspects of their work that needed improvement, together with ideas about how to carry out this improvement, with reference to the success criteria and/or generic features of literacy learning. For instance, during a short individual conference, Helen said to the student, 'What is needed here is a brief, effective ending ...' With one exception, there was little evidence of teachers and students jointly evaluating, reconstructing or revising text; students appeared to be assigned a more passive and restricted role as recipients of, and respondents to, their teachers' ideas.

The second study, of feedback within LPDP, showed that the ability of teachers to give quality written feedback on student writing was significantly and highly correlated to the rate of progress in writing of students in their class (Parr & Timperley, 2010). Quality feedback in this instance was defined (and scored) in terms of providing specific information with regard to (i) letting the student know how well s/he was going with respect to expectations in terms of the learning goal(s), (ii) indicating clearly what the key elements expected in a quality performance were in terms of the learning goals(s), (iii) clarifying what the nature of the gap was between the current performance and the desired performance, and (iv) giving guidance on how best to bridge that gap – how to work on the gap in order to improve. This research also showed that, with professional learning, teachers, over time, moved from providing feedback on lower level, mechanical concerns like spelling and gave feedback at higher levels such as with respect to the structure of the piece (at text or paragraph level) or regarding rhetorical concerns of audience or employing specific language as a resource for effect.

As noted above and confirmed in other projects (Gadd, 2014), while teachers were comfortable with, and could build considerable expertise in giving quality feedback, feedback theoretically and empirically considered to enhance learning, they were less adept at involving students in generating their own feedback and evaluating their own learning.

Scaffolding Self-Regulation in Writers

The idea of self-regulation as important to enhancing learning is widespread and certainly not new. In literacy, Clay (1991) saw the endpoint of instruction as when children have a self-improving system. If students are to generate meaningful feedback, monitor progress towards intended learning and become self-regulating, they need to know and understand where they are going and what counts as successful achievement (discussed in section 'Learning Goals and Tasks: Alignment and Transparency') (Hattie & Timperley, 2007; Sadler, 1989). Feedback (discussed in section 'Providing Quality Feedback') plays an important role in developing self-regulation. The teacher, according to Sadler (1989), is key in bringing about the transition from receiving and using feedback to becoming self-monitoring. When the source of information about learning and achievement moves from feedback provided *to* the student, to information generated *by* the student, the act becomes part of the process of self-monitoring. Appraising your own writing, for example, and that of your peers is a way to develop evaluative and productive knowledge and expertise and strengthen the self-regulating system for learning and development.

Only five of the teachers in the Hawe and Parr (2014) study explicitly included activities during lessons where students provided feedback to peers about where and how to improve their work in relation to goals or success criteria. Fran's students, for example, were asked, during the lesson, to stop writing and 'discuss what they have in their writing, relate to the SC [success criteria] and use other ideas to help improve work'. A further five teachers reminded their students to talk with peers about their work. With respect to involving students in self-assessment, half of the teachers made some attempt to do this. One means was again through reminding students, in this case of the need to identify where their work had not met the success criteria and needed improvement. However, another way was by means of a specifically allocated time for this activity when, during the lesson, students were asked to stop writing and to read their work (with a particular focus) and carry out improvements.

We have conducted two larger-scale survey studies (one within LPDP and one within a subsequent project) to investigate the extent to which students perceive themselves to have the type of knowledge of their writing performance needed to participate in their own learning and develop self-regulation. These studies suggest that suggest that, in general, students have not been given, through ongoing goal clarification and feedback, or have not been involved in generating, the necessary knowledge about their performance to begin to develop self-regulatory skills (Parr, Timperley, & Meissel, 2009).

Notably, self-regulation was the dimension in Gadd's (2014) study of exemplary teachers of writing which indicated the greatest difference in operational proficiency between the practice of two teacher participants whose students made by far the greatest learning gains, and other exemplary teachers. An examination of the actions of the 'best' of these exemplary teachers identified four instructional strategies: time and opportunities for students to write on self-selected topics (reinforcing the importance of learner involvedness in topic selection); to write outside writing instructional time (self-directed writing); opportunities for students to work collaboratively (testing ideas and giving and receiving feedback), and encouragement for students to take responsibility for seeking support for their writing (encouraging self-monitoring). Within this study, a move towards independence was particularly well illustrated by teachers encouraging students to maintain a writer's notebook in which they recorded possible writing topics for independent writing, decided which process tasks they needed to undertake in order to craft and re-craft texts, noted what assistance they considered they needed to complete tasks effectively, and listed outlets (such as class blogs) in which they could present their independent writing.

Direct, Targeted Instruction

Acts associated with direct, targeted instruction are known, in New Zealand, as deliberate acts of teaching (DATs) (Ministry of Education, 2006, 2007). Employing strategies associated with direct, targeted instruction was significantly related to student progress in Gadd's (2014) study of exemplary teachers where the important acts or strategies were modelling, that is, demonstrating or indicating clearly what students are expected to do and questioning students effectively.

A range of researchers identify the importance of demonstrating in effective literacy teaching (Englert, Raphael, Anderson, Anthony, & Stevens, 1991; Purcell-Gates, Duke, & Martineau, 2007). Demonstrating through modelling is a pedagogical feature of direct instruction that New Zealand teachers reported they most emphasized (after feedback); 91% of survey respondents said they emphasized it to a great or very great extent in their teaching of writing and it was a practice which they felt confident about (Parr & Jesson, 2016). Active modelling (as opposed to passive which involves text as model) was a feature of the very best of Gadd's (2014) expert teachers. These teachers engaged in composing texts with their students, utilizing prompts such as: 'What happened next? What's our next idea going to be? ... Talk with your buddy and have a go at coming up with a sentence ... Does that adjective help us to imagine anything in our heads? Does it need something else? ... Shall we go back to the word list we made?'

The nature of questioning, as a deliberate, directed act of teaching, also relates to progress in writing. Teachers whose students made the greatest learning gains asked three times as many high-cognitive-demand questions (those requiring learners to analyse, evaluate and synthesize issues in text-related conversations and think more deeply and metacognitively about them) of their students as other teachers, whether interacting with the whole class, groups, or individual students (Gadd, 2014). Examples, during text-related discussion in writing, of such questions (which are largely how and why questions) include: 'Why do you want to use metaphor in your description? How will it help the reader get a clear picture in their mind?' These are in stark contrast to questions like, 'Who can remember what a recount is?' or 'What sort of sentences do we put in our instructions?'

Differentiating Instruction

Differentiation of teaching to meet students' specific learning need has been identified as a characteristic of effective teaching practice (Allington, Johnston, & Day, 2002). Differentiating instruction is ensured in a number of ways. Across the several research projects where teachers were asked about, or observed as to how, they catered for individual needs in the classroom, the responses included: grouping for needs; monitoring, checking and individual teaching and re-teaching, and having individualized goals and criteria for success for students to work on.

Regarding grouping, it should be emphasized that this does not necessarily involve ability grouping. In reading, New Zealand teachers employ grouping, largely ability grouping to a far greater extent than in any other country participating in PIRLS (Chamberlain & Ministry of Education, 2013). In reading, teacher expectations of student progress and achievement bear a strong relationship to reading achievement (they account for a sizeable 20% of the variance in reading performance) and there are suggestions that, in reading, practices like levelled books to take home and reading groups based on ability give messages of lower expectations (Peterson, Rubie-Davies, Osborne, & Sibley, 2016). However, in writing, New Zealand teachers report that they tend not to ability group (Parr & Jesson, 2016) but rather to have flexible groupings whereby students come together for mini lessons, targeted to a particular need; at times they engage in shared and interactive writing with small groups. Developing groupings for some was based on students' patterns of strengths and weaknesses obtained from detailed diagnostic information which allowed targeted instruction to a particular need. However, these groups were fluid and changed over time (Parr & Limbrick, 2010).

Responses as to how individual needs were catered for also included ongoing monitoring, checking and re-teaching. One teacher in our Northland study showed us a series of lessons on the basis of identified need of individuals or small groups of students. But, more tellingly, this teacher reported making further informal checks as to whether these lessons were having an impact and, when it appeared that a small group of students were still not making progress, made adjustments like teaching in a different way, using new examples. These adjustments often involved taking steps like making the reason for learning salient and clear to ensure more ownership of the learning on the part of the students. This was an unsolicited reporting of something akin to a cycle of teaching as inquiry, happening within a classroom.

There were instances observed when scaffolding was provided for the individual. One such time occurred during conferencing with students. With a focus on the learning aim, which was 'to put [a character's] thoughts into writing', the teacher prompted the student to record his thinking about specific events. 'I'm just going to put a little star here and I want you to put in … write some thoughts. This is a perfect place to put your thoughts in. What were you thinking inside your head as you were …? Put yourself back to your game of soccer …' (Parr & Limbrick, 2010).

In observations of effective teachers, many routes to expertise in writing were possible and there were multiple levels at which students could operate. Further instances of differentiation were observed including where the success criteria varied for students and students were reminded to use their individual success criteria and where individuals had written goals that related specifically to 'gaps' identified in that student's writing (Parr & Limbrick, 2010).

CONCLUSION

Although these dimensions of practice have been considered individually, this is somewhat arbitrary. Several, for example, cohere as strategies or practices that together support and further student learning. Helping students to understand the goal(s) of learning and what constitutes expected performance, together with providing quality feedback about the relationship between current and desired performance and fostering the development of self-regulation through writer engagement in peer feedback and self-monitoring are considered to constitute, collectively, assessment for learning (James & Pedder, 2006; Swaffield, 2011), an approach linked to improved learning outcomes. In relation to assessment for learning, James and Pedder (2006) and Willis (2011) stress that achieving enhanced outcomes through AfL, is more complex than teachers adding individual strategies onto existing class programmes. The same notion holds when thinking about the practices discussed in this chapter. They should be viewed as a plaited rope where successive strands strengthen the facilitative link between teaching and student performance in writing.

The focus on these aspects of practice as hallmarks of exemplary teachers or as areas where improvement in practice is related to gains in achievement, is, in part, a function of the New Zealand context. The policy context stimulates and, arguably, focuses research to investigate the efficacy of, for example, assessment policy or models of professional development provision in literacy. The practices align with views instantiated in policy that teachers remain the best judge of student performance against national standards. An assessment policy whereby teachers make an overall teacher judgement about whether a student meets the standard in writing for the year level encourages the use of a range of sources of information collected in a variety of contexts.

The notion of differentiation extends the long history in New Zealand of teaching the individual student rather than a curriculum. Differentiation is consistent with a policy context where the expectation is that curriculum and pedagogy will be adapted to meet the needs of students in the local context. Such is also consistent with beliefs that teachers are professionals and are expected to inquire into their practice and adapt it to better meet the learning needs of their students. And, given stated Ministry of Education and government aims of reducing inequalities in achievement, investigation of practices that may be specifically associated with the achievement of targeted groups is also a focus of research. The foregrounding of practices that connect to, and validate, cultural and linguistic funds of knowledge related to language is highly significant in a bi-cultural country with special responsibilities to Pacific neighbours. Maori and Pasifika students are disproportionally represented in the lower bands of achievement in writing and identifying practices that optimize their engagement and progress is paramount.

REFERENCES

Allington, R. L., Johnston, P. H., & Day, J. (2002). Exemplary fourth-grade teachers. *Language Arts, 79*(6), 462–466.

Alton-Lee, A. (2003). *Quality teaching for diverse students in schooling: Best evidence synthesis.* Wellington: Ministry of Education.

Ball, D. L., & Cohen, D. K. (1996). Reform by the book: What is − or might be − the role of curriculum materials in teacher learning and instructional reform? *Educational Researcher, 25*(6–8), 14.

Bernstein, B. (2000). *Pedagogy, symbolic control and identity: Theory, research and critique.* London: Taylor and Francis.

Block, C. C., & Mangieri, J. N. (2003). *Exemplary literacy teachers: Promoting success for all children in grades K-5.* New York, NY: The Guilford Press.

Brown, M., & Edleson, D. C. (2003). *Teaching as design: Can we better understand the ways in which teachers use materials so we can better design materials to support their changes in practice?* Evanston, IL: Northwestern University.

Chamberlain, M. (2000, October). *The national assessment strategy and the relationships between teaching, learning and student achievement.* Keynote address at the National Assessment Regional Seminar, Auckland.

Chamberlain, M., & Ministry of Education. (2013). *PIRLS 2010/11 in New Zealand: An overview of findings from the third cycle of the progress in international reading literacy study.* Wellington: Ministry of Education.

Clay. (1991). *Becoming literate: The construction of inner control.* Auckland: Heineman Education.

Dweck, C. S. (1986). Motivational processes affecting learning. *American Psychologist, 41*, 1040–1048.

Engestrom, Y. (1987). *Learning by expanding.* Helsinki: Orienta-Konsultit Oy Press.

Englert, C. S., Raphael, T. E., Anderson, L. M., Anthony, H. M., & Stevens, D. D. (1991). Making strategies and self-talk visible: Writing instruction in regular and special education classrooms. *American Educational Research Journal, 28*(2), 337–372. doi:10.3102/00028312028002337

Gadd, M. (2014). *What is critical in the effective teaching of writing?: A study of the classroom practice of some Year 5 to 8 teachers in the New Zealand context.* Unpublished PhD thesis. University of Auckland.

Gadd, M., & Parr, J. M. (2016). It's all about Baxter: Task orientation in the effective teaching of writing. *Literacy, 50*(2), 93–99. doi:10.1111/lit.12072

Gilbert, J., & Graham, S. (2010). Teaching writing to elementary students in grades 4–6: A national survey. *The Elementary School Journal, 110*, 1–15. doi:10.1086/651193

Gilmore, A. (2008). *Professional learning in assessment.* Report to the Ministry of Education for the National Assessment Strategy Review. Canterbury: University of Canterbury.

Graham, S., & Perin, D. (2007). A meta-analysis of writing instruction for adolescent students. *Journal of Educational Psychology, 99*(3), 445–476. doi:10.1037/0022-0663.99.3.445

Grossman, P. L., Loeb, S., Cohen, J., & Wyckoff, J. (2013). Measure for measure: The relationship between measures of instructional practice in middle school English language arts and teachers' valued-added scores. *American Journal of Education, 119*, 445–470. doi:10.1086/669901

Hall, K., & Harding, A. (2003). *A systematic review of effective literacy teaching in the 4 to 14 age range of mainstream schooling.* Research Evidence in Education Library. London: Social Science Research Unit, Institute of Education.

Hattie, J. (2003, October). Teachers make a difference: What is the research evidence? Paper presented at the Australian Council for Educational Research Annual Conference on Building Teacher Quality, Melbourne.

Hattie, J. (2009). *Visible learning: A synthesis of 800 meta-analyses on achievement.* Abingdon: Routledge.

Hattie, J., & Timperley, H. (2007). The power of feedback. *Review of Educational Research, 77*(1), 81–112. doi:10.3102/003465430298487

Hawe, E., Dixon, H., & Watson, E. (2008). Oral feedback in the context of written language. *Australian Journal of Language and Literacy, 31*(1), 43–58.

Hawe, E., & Parr, J. M. (2014). Assessment for Learning in the writing classroom: An incomplete realisation. *Curriculum Journal, 25*(2), 210–237.

Hogden, J., & Marshall, B. (2005). Assessment for learning in English and mathematics: A comparison. *The Curriculum Journal, 16*(2), 153–176. doi:10.1080/09585170500135954

James, M., & Pedder, D. (2006). Beyond method: Assessment and learning practices and values. *The Curriculum Journal, 17*(2), 109–138. doi:10.1080/09585170600792712

Lipson, M., Mosenthal, J., Daniels, R., & Woodside-Jiron, H. (2000). Process writing in the classrooms of eleven fifth grade teachers with different orientations to teaching and learning. *Elementary School Journal, 10,* 209–232.

Lodewyk, K. R., & Winne, P. H. (2005). Relations among the structure of learning tasks, achievement and changes in self-efficacy in secondary students. *Journal of Educational Psychology, 97*(1), 3–12. doi:10.1037/0022-0663.97.1.3

Lodewyk, K. R., Winne, P. H., & Jamieson-Noel, D. L. (2009). Implications of task structure on self-regulated learning and achievement. *Educational Psychology, 29*(1), 1–25. doi:10.1080/01443410802447023

Marshall, B. (2004). Goals or horizons: The conundrum of progressions in English: Or a possible way of understanding formative assessment in English. *The Curriculum Journal, 15*(2), 101–113. doi:10.1080/0958517042000226784

Marshall, H. M., & Weinstein, R. S. (1984). Classroom factors affecting students' self-evaluations: An interactional model. *Review of Educational Research, 54*(3), 301–325. doi:10.3102/00346543054003301

Ministry of Education. (1999). *The literacy and numeracy strategy.* Ministry of Education, Wellington, New Zealand.

Ministry of Education. (2006). *Effective literacy practice years 1–4.* Wellington: Learning Media.

Ministry of Education. (2007). *Effective literacy practice years 5–8.* Wellington: Learning Media.

Ministry of Education. (2007). The New Zealand curriculum. Learning Media, Wellington, New Zealand.

Ministry of Education. (2009). *National standards for reading and writing.* Wellington: Author.

Ministry of Education. (2010). *Literacy learning progressions.* Wellington: Author.

Ministry of Education. (2015). *Progress and Consistency Tool (PACT).* Wellington: Author.

Ministry of Education & New Zealand Council for Educational Research. (2012). *e-asTTle: Writing (revised).* Retrieved from http://e-asTTle.tki.org.nz/user-manuals

Ministry of Education & University of Auckland. (2004). *asTTle: Assessment tools for teaching and learning*. Wellington: Ministry of Education.
Nye, B., Konstantopoulos, S., & Hedges, L. (2004). How large are teacher effects? *Education Evaluation and Policy Analysis, 26*, 237–257.
Parr, J. M. (2011). Repertoires to scaffold teacher learning and practice in assessment of writing. *Assessing Writing, 16*, 32–48.
Parr, J. M., & Jesson, R. (2016). Mapping the landscape of writing instruction in New Zealand primary school classrooms. *Reading and Writing: An Interdisciplinary Journal, 29*(5), 981–1011. doi:10.107/s11145-015-9589-5
Parr, J. M., & Limbrick, E. (2010). Contextualising practice: Hallmarks of effective teachers of writing. *Teaching and Teacher Education, 26*, 583–590.
Parr, J. M., & Timperley, H. (2008). Teachers, schools and using evidence: Considerations of preparedness. *Assessment in Education: Principles, Policy and Practice, 15*, 57–71.
Parr, J. M., Timperley, H., & Meissel, K. (2009, August 25–29). Letting students in on the secret of what they are learning: Student reported knowledge related to self-assessment. *European Association for Research in Learning and Instruction*, Amsterdam.
Parr, J. M., Timperley, H., Reddish, P., Adams, R., & Jesson, R. (2007). *Literacy professional development project: Identifying effective teaching and professional development practices for enhanced student learning*. Report to Ministry of Education, New Zealand. Retrieved from http://www.educationcounts.govt.nz/publications/literacy/16813
Parr, J. M., & Timperley, H. S. (2010). Feedback to writing: Assessment for teaching and learning and student progress. *Assessing Writing, 15*, 68–85. doi:10.1016/j.asw.2010.05.004
Peterson, E., Rubie-Davies, C., Osborne, D., & Sibley, C. (2016). Teachers' explicit and implicit prejudiced attitudes to educational achievement: Relations with student achievement and the ethnic achievement gap. *Learning and Instruction, 42*, 123–140.
Pressley, M., Gaskins, T., Solic, K., & Collins, S. (2006). A portrait of benchmark high school: How a school produces high achievement in students who previously failed. *Journal of Educational Psychology, 98*, 282–306.
Purcell-Gates, V., Duke, N. K., & Martineau, J. A. (2007). Learning to read and write genre-specific text: Roles of authentic experience and explicit teaching. *Reading Research Quarterly, 42*(1), 8–45. doi:10.1598/RRQ.42.1.1
Sadler, R. (1989). Formative assessment and the design of instructional systems. *Instructional Science, 18*, 119–144.
Si'ilata, R. (2014). *Va'a Tele: Pasifika learners riding the success wave on linguistically and culturally responsive pedagogies*. Unpublished PhD thesis. University of Auckland. Retrieved from http://hdl.handle.net/2292/23402
Si'ilata, R., Dreaver, K., Parr, J., Timperley, H., & Meissel, K. (2012). *Tula'i Mai! Making a difference to Pasifika student achievement in literacy*. Final Research Report on the Pasifika Literacy Professional Development Project 2009–2010. Auckland: Auckland UniServices Ltd. Retrieved from http://www.educationcounts.govt.nz/publications/pasifika_education/literacy-professional-development-project-2009-2010
Swaffield, S. (2011). Getting to the heart of authentic assessment for learning. *Assessment in Education: Principles, Policy & Practice, 18*(4), 433–449. doi:10.1080/0969594X.2011.582838
Timperley, H., Parr, J. M., & Meissel, K. (2010). *Making a difference to student achievement in literacy: Final research report on the literacy professional development project*. Report to

Learning Media and the Ministry of Education. Auckland: UniServices, University of Auckland.

Timperley, H. S., & Parr, J. M. (2009). What is this lesson about? Instructional processes and student understandings in writing classrooms. *The Curriculum Journal, 20*(1), 43–60. doi:10.1080/09585170902763999

Willis, J. (2011). Affiliation, autonomy and assessment for learning. *Assessment in Education: Principles, Policy & Practice, 18*(4), 399–415. doi:10.1080/0969594X.2011.604305 Willis (2011).

Wray, D., Medwell, J., Fox, R., & Poulson, L. (2000). The teaching practices of effective teachers of literacy. *Educational Review, 52*(1), 75–85.

Yamagata-Lynch, L. C. (2010). *Activity systems analysis methods: Understanding complex learning environments.* Dordrecht: Springer Science & Business.

Zimmerman, B. J. (2008). Goal setting: A key proactive source of academic self-regulation. In D. H. Schunk & B. J. Zimmerman (Eds.), *Motivation and self-regulated learning: Theory, research and applications* (pp. 267–295). London: Lawrence Erlbaum.

IDEAS AS A SPRINGBOARD FOR WRITING IN K-8 CLASSROOMS

Kathleen M. Alley and Barbara J. Peterson

ABSTRACT

Purpose — *To review and synthesize findings from peer-reviewed research related to students' sources of ideas for writing, and instructional dimensions that affect students' development of ideas for composition in grades K-8.*

Design/methodology/approach — *The ideas or content expressed in written composition are considered critical to ratings of writing quality. We utilized a Systematic Mixed Studies Review (SMSR) methodological framework (Heyvaert, Maes, & Onghena, 2011) to explore K-8 students' ideas and writing from a range of theoretical and methodological perspectives.*

Findings — *Students' ideas for writing originate from a range of sources, including teachers, peers, literature, content area curriculum, autobiographical/life experiences, popular culture/media, drawing, and play. Intertextuality, copying, social dialogue, and playful peer interactions are productive strategies K-8 writers use to generate ideas for composing, in addition to strategies introduced through planned instruction. Relevant dimensions of instruction include motivation to write, idea planning and organization, as well as specific instructional strategies, techniques, and tools to facilitate idea generation and selection within the composition process.*

Practical implications — *A permeable curriculum and effective instructional practices are crucial to support students' access to a full range of ideas and knowledge-based resources, and help them translate these into written composition. Instructional practices for idea development and writing: (a) connect reading and writing for authentic purposes; (b) include explicit modeling of strategies for planning and "online" generation of ideas throughout the writing process across genre; (c) align instructional focus across reading, writing, and other curricular activities; (d) allow for extended time to write; and (e) incorporate varied, flexible participation structures through which students can share ideas and receive teacher/peer feedback on writing.*

Keywords: Writing; composition; writing instruction; idea generation

Students in Mr. M.'s fifth-grade writer's workshop work in pairs to compose poems as part of a poetry unit of study (Christianakis, 2011). Ron suggests to his partner, Rayjon, that they browse through a folder of clipart on the computer to jump-start their writing process.

Ron: She cool. [*refers to a clipart image of an elderly woman*]. We should write a poem about her.

Rayjon: We can't write no poem about her.

Ron: Yeah. Yeah we can. We can make her a kickboxing grandma.

Rayjon: You crazy. That ain't no poem.

Ron: We can make it one. "Kick Boxing Grandmas they're really cool."

Rayjon: "they can whoop on anybody up in the school."

Ron: Hey that's tight! Let's put it down.

Rayjon: (*types what they just said*) Is this a poem?

Ron: It rhymes don't it?

Mr. M.: Hey, let's see what you've got. *(reads their first two lines)* This is good. What could your next stanza start with?

Ron: "They make good food"

Rayjon: "Like fried chicken so don't mess around up in their kitchen."

Ron: "If you do you'll get a licken." Ha Ha! Write it down. (Christianakis, 2011, p. 43)[1]

For Ron and Rayjon, a clipart image serves as inspiration for their poem about "Kickboxing Grandmas." Through playful banter, these fifth-grade writers experiment with ideas and language, then appraise and negotiate the form of their text. Their boundary-pushing poem draws upon "textual terrains" (Christianakis, 2011, p. 44), interweaving themes from domestic life as well as popular culture discourses of rap music and martial arts. In their lively collaboration, humor and emotional energy fuel creative idea generation, and solidify Ron and Rayjon's close relationship as writing partners and friends.

This vignette offers a window on the centrality of ideas to writing and the complexity of how developing writers generate ideas for composing within the social context of the classroom. Young writers' sources and processes for idea generation, and instructional dimensions that support idea generation for writing in K-8 classrooms is the focus of this chapter.

THEORETICAL PERSPECTIVES ON IDEA GENERATION AND COMPOSING

Ideas figure prominently in theories and models of proficient writing. Influential in the field of writing instruction, Flower and Hayes' (1981) cognitive model describes composing as a complex and recursive problem-solving activity, composed of three major processes: *planning* (generating ideas, goal-setting, organizing), *translating* or *text production*, and *reviewing* (revising, evaluating). Within this model, planning is envisioned in a broad sense as the formulation of an internal representation of knowledge or ideas for composing. Idea generation is one of several subprocesses writers

---

[1]Christianakis (2011). Copyright © 2011 by the National Council of Teachers of English. www.ncte.org. Reprinted with permission.

use in conjunction with self-regulatory functions (goal-setting, monitoring). Bereiter and Scardamalia (1987) also proposed a cognitive developmental model that situates writing as a tool for thinking and knowledge construction. Within this model, novice writers link ideas together using knowledge telling strategies. As writers gain expertise, they shift toward synthesizing ideational sources through knowledge building or transformational processes.

Sociocultural or contextual perspectives on writing development frequently draw upon the work of Vygotsky (1978, 1986) and Bakhtin (1981, 1986). Vygotskian conceptualizations relevant to ideas and composition include: (a) oral and written language as culturally based tools for thinking and learning, acquired within socially situated contexts and used for meaningful purposes; (b) young learners' expression of ideas on an external plane through language, with a gradual internalization of language into mental thought processes; and (c) the importance of socially mediated scaffolding of young learners through interactions with more proficient adults or peers. Other sociocultural writing theories draw upon Bakhtinian notions that language (including writing) is dialogic; it mediates interactions between writers and their audiences, writers' own ideas and words, and the ideas and words of others in the discourse community. Within this view, written texts combine multiple voices and reflect intertextual connections to ideas of others over historical time and space, and according to "speech genre" or types of discourse patterns learned within different communities. For further discussion of theoretical models of writing, readers may look to Graham, Gillespie, and McKeown (2013) for an overview of writing development; Jones (2014) for a review of idea generation as a cognitive process; and Siegel and Rowe's (2011) discussion of social semiotic perspectives.

QUALITY OF IDEAS AND WRITING ACHIEVEMENT

Given the prominent role of idea development to the writing process, it is not surprising that the ideas or content expressed in written composition are central to ratings of writing proficiency (National Center for Education Statistics [NCES], 2012; Purves, 1992). For the 2011 National Assessment of Educational Progress (NAEP; NCES, 2012), two of the three indicators of writing quality pertained to proficiency in development and organization of ideas. However, 2011 NAEP data present a worrisome landscape with respect to student achievement in writing. Only 27 percent of eighth and twelfth graders achieved at a proficient level or better; an achievement level that has not changed substantially since 1998. These findings raise concerns about the quality of students' writing and the instruction that effectively develops their expression of ideas in written form. Moreover, writing and literacy curricular initiatives continue to focus on generation and development of ideas as a critical dimension of writing quality (e.g., 6 + 1 traits writing approach; Culham, 2003), and as a transformative tool for disciplinary knowledge construction across curriculum (Chuy, Scardamalia, & Bereiter, 2012).

Considering the importance of ideas to quality writing, we reviewed and synthesized findings from the research on K-8 written composition to answer the following questions:

1. What sources and processes do young writers use to generate and develop ideas for composing?
2. How do different dimensions of K-8 instruction influence young writers' development of ideas for writing?

METHODS

In order to explore K-8 writing from a range of research perspectives, we utilized a Systematic Mixed Studies Review (SMSR) methodological framework (Heyvaert, Maes, & Onghena, 2011; Pluye, Gagnon, Griffiths, & Johnson-Lafleur, 2009). SMSR is an emerging methodology in health and behavioral sciences that integrates primary research findings from diverse theoretical and methodological perspectives in a systematic manner. Our SMSR framework included the following steps: (a) question formulation and development of explicit inclusion criteria; (b) search and identification of potential research investigations pertaining to our inquiry focus on ideas and writing; (c) selection of relevant studies applying explicit inclusion criteria; (d) appraisal of the methodological quality of studies included in the SMSR; and (e) analysis and synthesis of study findings through a critical and transparent interpretive process. Studies included in this SMSR were: (a) quantitative, qualitative, or mixed methods research published from 1990 to 2015 in peer-reviewed journals; (b) focused on K-8 students and/or teachers from English-speaking, mainstream classrooms in public or private school settings; (c) written with clearly articulated research design elements and methodology. In addition, study findings had a strong focus on ideas/

writing (i.e., idea generation, sources of ideas, instructional strategies related to ideas and writing).

Literature Search Methods

We conducted our search of the literature in three phases; electronic, manual, and bibliographic. During each search phase, we previewed article titles and abstracts to determine whether they met our inclusion criteria. During selection and appraisal of SMSR steps, we read studies more closely to appraise methodological quality, and rated the salience of ideas/writing within the findings of each study on a 0–5 scale. We included articles with 4 or 5 ratings in the review, and excluded articles with 0 to 2 ratings. Both authors re-read and discussed articles with ratings of 3 to reach agreement on inclusion in the SMSR.

We conducted an electronic search through ERIC and Academic Search Premier using the following terms in combination: *writing, writing instruction, writing strategies, teaching writing, written discourse, composition, composing* AND *ideas, ideation, topic selection, topic choice, topic generation, theme, storyline, content, elaboration, details, insight, planning, prewriting* AND *elementary, middle school, child(*)*. In the manual search phase, we reviewed article titles and abstracts from 21 key literacy and education journals. In the bibliographic search phase, we identified additional studies from references of articles retrieved through previous phases. These search phases yielded 83 studies for final data analysis and synthesis.

Data Analysis and Synthesis

In an initial phase of data extraction and analysis, we read each study several times and highlighted key research design features and findings relevant to ideas/writing. We annotated this information through an inductive, open coding procedure (Miles & Huberman, 1994). Next, we created descriptive memos that summarized research design features and key findings, as well as critical reflections and theoretical questions that arose during reading. We analyzed and refined emerging codes together, discussed developing patterns of themes across the body of research, and organized themes/codes using semantic mapping software. In the second phase of data analysis, we tabulated key design features and codes for each study on a retrieval table. We then interpreted and synthesized findings through an iterative process of referencing the semantic map of the corpus, tabulated codes, descriptive memos, as well as coded data and annotations on the original articles.

FINDINGS

The reviewed studies incorporated a range of design features, and reflected a theoretical divide between cognitive/sociocognitive and sociocultural perspectives on children's writing. Table 1 provides a broad overview of selected design features of the 83 studies in this review. Codes for design features reported in Table 1, were primarily based on key descriptors of context and participants researchers typically included in their reports of research (e.g., Urban, Suburban, or Rural Setting; Mixed Settings). We coded a feature as "Not Reported" for studies for which we were unable to find specific information to definitively code that particular design feature (e.g., a researcher might have reported a study setting/location as "a school in the Northeastern United States" rather than as Urban, Suburban, Rural, or Mixed geographical location). However, studies with inadequate reporting on key contextual or participant dimensions for more than one of these categories were eliminated from our research base in the methodological appraisal step within our SMSR methodological framework. Researchers provided much more detailed information about the study context, participants, and methodologies of research, beyond what we coded and reported here. Our intention in Table 1 was to simply highlight the overall landscape of design features of the reviewed research, rather than to provide an exhaustive accounting of contexts, participants, or methodological approaches of these studies.

Across the research base, the construct of "ideas for writing" was ill-defined and conceptualized in different ways: (a) "content" of writing; (b) global topics, subtopics, or themes; (c) specific elements within linguistic texts or drawings, such as ideas about characters, setting, plot events, problem/solution, dialogue; (d) elaborative or descriptive details; (e) concepts and conceptual schema; (f) gendered stereotypes or thematic elements; (g) topic knowledge, facts, information, or insights; (h) theories, hypotheses, observations, problems, or predictions (especially for science-based writing); and (i) theses, evidence, or claims (particularly for argumentation). The dimension of ideas was often linked to writing organization, particularly on rubrics assessing quality of writing "content." Within writing

Table 1. Overview of Reviewed Research: Context, Participants, and Methods (n = Number of Studies Out of 83 Studies in Total Data Set).

Context – Setting/Location[a]	n	Context/Participants – Diversity Level[c]	n
Urban	36	High	31
Suburban	13	Medium	6
Rural	10	Low	18
Mixed locations (multi-site)	10	Varied diversity levels (multi-site)	8
Not reported	14	Not reported	20
Total	83	*Total*	83

Context/Participants – SES Level[b]	n	# Participants (Students/Teachers)	n
Upper	1	<10	29
Middle	13	11–50	28
Lower	20	51–100	8
Mixed levels	25	101–150	10
Not reported	24	>151	8
Total	83	*Total*	83

Participants' Grade Level	n	Methods	n
K-2	29	Quantitative	21
3–5	25	Qualitative	52
6–8	14	Mixed Methods	10
Multiple Levels	15	*Total*	83
Total	83		

Notes: [a]*Context – Setting/Location* – Code labels Urban, Suburban, and Rural were derived through *in vivo* coding of researchers' descriptions of geographical locations of contexts/settings. The code Mixed Locations was assigned to multi-site studies located across geographical locations.
[b]*Context/Participants – Socioeconomic [SES] Level* – Code labels Upper, Middle, and Lower SES levels were derived through *in vivo* coding of researchers' descriptions of SES levels of participants, schools, or districts. Where researchers did not use these terms, we assigned codes based on other reported SES indicators (e.g., percentage of students receiving free-or-reduced lunch). We assigned the code Mixed Levels to multi-site studies that crossed these SES levels.
[c]*Context/Participants – Diversity Level* – Code labels High, Medium, and Low diversity levels were primarily derived from the *in vivo* coding of researchers' descriptions of the participant sample or community served by a school/district. Researchers' use of the term "diversity" reflected the historic use of this term in the field of education to refer to "students who may be distinguished [from the mainstream culture] by ethnicity, social class, and/or language" (Pérez, 2004, p. 6). Thus, in Table 1, "Low" diversity level describes contexts with primarily White, English-speaking students. We also considered reported demographic information on contexts/participants in assigning studies to diversity level categories. We assigned the code Mixed Levels to multi-site studies that reflected different levels of diversity across sites.

strategy research, idea generation was frequently subsumed under the umbrella of planning. However, planning also involved selecting and organizing ideas for particular rhetorical purposes, along with self-regulation of the writing process. This necessitated close reading of studies during the review process and a purposeful, interpretive qualitative analysis of how the researcher and participants conceptualized ideas/writing in each study.

With few exceptions, ideas/writing was not the main focus of researchers' questions. We adopted a qualitative approach to analyzing findings of quantitative studies within the research base, because these studies did not specifically address idea development separately from other aspects of instructional intervention, or the outcome measures integrated assessment of ideas with other aspects of writing quality (e.g., combining ideas/organization or ideas/organization/vocabulary in ratings of content quality of writing).

Students' Sources and Processes for Idea Generation and Composing

Students generate ideas for writing through multiple and overlapping sources or "funds of knowledge" (Moll, Amanti, Neff, & Gonzalez, 1992) including: (a) autobiographical or life experiences; (b) content-curriculum such as fiction and non-fiction literature, and other curricular texts or materials; (c) popular culture and media; (d) the teacher; (e) peers; (f) play and dramatic performance; and (g) drawing and images (see Fig. 1, *Students' Sources of Ideas for Writing*). Researchers contrasted "official world" or schooled sources, such as the teacher, classroom peers, literature, content area curriculum and certain autobiographical experiences, with students' "unofficial world" sources for writing ideas, such as popular culture and media, play/drama, drawing, as well as certain types of peer and personal or autobiographic experiences (Christianakis, 2011; Dyson, 1992, 1999, 2001a; Hoewisch, 2001; Ranker, 2007).

Knowledge Sources and Preferences for Composing
When composing, students frequently drew from autobiographical/life experiences as writing; for example, family events, recreational interests, pets, self and personal issues, as well as social relationships and problems (Chapman, 1995; Dyson, 2010; McGinley & Kamberelis, 1996). Many students regularly wrote from their daily experiences, and teachers often encouraged "true" or real-life autobiographical topics for composition.

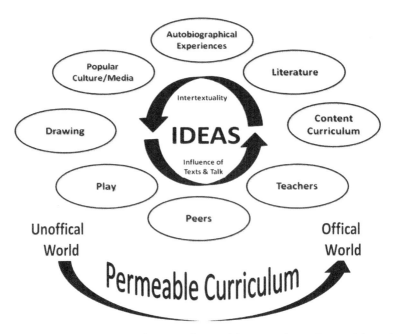

Fig. 1. Students' Sources of Ideas for Writing: Students Draw Ideas from Multiple, Generative Sources During Written Composition, Including the Official Worlds of School and Unofficial Worlds of Home, Community, and Society.

Writing from "true" autobiographical experiences was problematic for many young writers, however. Some students found autobiographical writing as "boring" or preferred not to share details of their personal lives with the teacher or peers. Alternatively, some students wrote about experiences that teachers interpreted as troublesome or inappropriate ("taboo") for classroom sharing (e.g., domestic or neighborhood violence, family problems with money or imprisonment, etc.). Other students chose to embellish on autobiographical themes to fit in with the social experiences of peers or to create possible social worlds through writing (Dutro, Selland, & Bien, 2013; Dyson, 2010; Schneider, 2003; Wohlwend, 2009). Fiction and non-fiction literature and content area materials comprised a major teacher/school sanctioned source of ideas that fostered close reading/ writing connections. Students composed regularly from these sources within literature-based and content curricular literacy activities (e.g., Corden, 2007; Klein, 2000; Many, Fyfe, Lewis, & Mitchell, 1996; Monte-Sano & Harris, 2012; see "Influences of Content Curriculum and

Literature" in the "Instructional Dimensions Mediating Students' Development of Ideas" section for discussion of these findings).

A prevalent finding across the research base was that many students eschewed autobiographical or other teacher-assigned fiction or non-fiction topics, and showed a strong preference for imaginary or fantasy writing (e.g., topics such as monsters, war craft, cops/robbers, superheroes, Disney princesses, or other popular culture/media themes). Young writers also enjoyed writing about imaginary play, and geared their writing toward play-based themes from the playground, home, or community. Writing about fantasy or popular culture themes provided a dialogic space for students to explore and deconstruct ideas and ideologies related to gender roles, power, cultural identity, and social justice (Dyson, 1999; Ghiso, 2011; Lewison & Heffernan, 2008; MacGillivray & Martinez, 1998; Peterson & Ladky, 2001; Wohlwend, 2009). In some classrooms, teachers accepted and encouraged fantasy, popular culture, or play-based topics, while other teachers discouraged or even censored this type of writing.

Researchers explored a continuum of choice and control over topics and genre of writing affecting not only idea generation, but also issues of authenticity and motivation for composing (Behizadeh, 2014, 2014/2015; Dutro et al., 2013; Dyson, 1999; Schneider, 2001). Some researchers expressed concerns that when instructional practices limit or censor students' access to certain knowledge sources or multimodal processes for composing (e.g., drawing, play, drama), this ostensibly limits their access to a full range of semiotic resources for literacy and learning success. Consequently, this may disadvantage or privilege certain students whose resources (funds of knowledge) align with or differ substantially from the types of knowledge most valued in school settings. A key recommendation was the importance of teachers fostering students' agency and choice for topic and genre selection, and enacting a "permeable curriculum" (Dyson, 2001a) that allows K-8 writers to draw upon their funds of knowledge for composing. Permeable curricular practices also build upon and extend this knowledge base through classroom experiences and exposure to varied textual resources (see "Motivation to Write" in section "Instructional Dimensions Mediating Students' Development of Ideas" for further discussion of these findings).

Intertextual Processes for Idea Generation and Composing
Several studies explored the complex dialogic and intertextual processes students use to interweave ideas and texts from "official world" and "unofficial world" sources of home, school, community, and society

(Christianakis, 2011; Dyson, 2001a, 2002; Pantaleo, 2009; Ranker, 2007; Read, 2005). These processes were multimodal in nature, as students typically drew upon oral language, gesture, dramatic and embodied action, visual/drawing, sound/music modes while composing. Analysis of classroom composing practices, texts, and student interviews also revealed how they reproduced, remixed, and recontextualized a range of ideational content (e.g., themes, facts, symbols, characters, plot lines, and drawings, etc.). The resultant heteroglossic texts (Bakhtin, 1981) were created through students' highly dynamic and iterative composing processes (Dyson, 2001b; Hoewisch, 2001; Lancia, 1997; Pantaleo, 2009; Wohlwend, 2009).

Classroom Dialogue
The importance of "texts and talk" within the dialogic space of the classroom was also a consistent thread with respect to sources and processes for generating ideas when composing. Researchers consistently found that dialogic interactions involving oral language, social interactions, and peer collaboration supported students' access to ideas for composition (Cairney, 1990; Chung & Walsh, 2006; Daiute, 1990; Daiute & Dalton, 1993; Dyson, 1999; McCarthey, 1994; Read, 2005). Informal forms of talk – including self-talk, peer-talk, and teacher talk, as well as more formal teacher/peer conferencing and feedback, had an impact on generation and shaping of ideas for composition (Daiute, 1990; DeGroff, 1992; Dyson, 2006; Matsamura, Patthey-Chavez, Valdes, & Garnier, 2002; McCarthey, 1992, 1994; Sipe, 1998). Findings related to self-talk and peer-talk are discussed in the sections that follow; see findings in section "Instructional Dimensions Mediating Students' Development of Ideas" for the influence of teacher talk/dialogue on students' idea generation and composing.

Self-Talk. Young writers used self-talk as a form of oral rehearsal as they generated and translated ideas for writing (Dyson, 2010; Myhill & Jones, 2009; Wiseman, 2003). Self-talk appeared to serve a meta-cognitive function that supported writers as they (a) planned or played with different ideas verbally prior to and during the composing process; (b) managed the cognitive demands of generating and holding onto ideas while transcribing; or (c) appraised, revised, and connected new ideas with those in the evolving text (Schneider, 2003; Schultz, 1997; Vass, 2007). Teachers commonly modeled this type of meta-cognitive self-talk for students within mini-lessons and instruction.

Self-talk also reflected an additional oral layer of the unfolding text, such as when students added character dialogue, sound effects, or narrated actions or events that may or may not have been included in the final written or drawn modes of the composition. The traces of this oral layer would not be evident to a teacher or researcher examining written artifacts, unless they observed the composing process as a whole or interviewed the student about the composition (Chapman, 1995; Dyson, 2001b, 2002; Watanabe & Hall-Kenyon, 2011; Wiseman, 2003). Self-talk also served a social function as writers might declare their topics or writing intentions to draw peer attention to their composition or to invite peers into collegial or collaborative talk while composing in pairs or small groups (Christianakis, 2011; Dyson, 2010; Schneider, 2003; Schultz, 1997).

Peer-Talk. Many researchers documented the importance of students' social relationships and types of collaborative interactions that supported and shaped students' idea generation and composing (Chung & Walsh, 2006; Daiute & Dalton, 1993; Dyson, 2010; McGinley & Kamberelis, 1996; Schneider, 2003; Schultz, 1997; Sutherland & Topping, 1999; Vass, 2007; Wiseman, 2003; Wohlwend, 2009). A continuum of peer-talk ranged from collegial talk that allowed pairs or small groups of students to informally share ideas, copy or coordinate the writing themes and plots for writing and drawing, to collaborative talk in which peers more closely negotiated ideas for topics, characters, dialogue, plot lines, as well as other semiotic resources for composing (Dyson, 2010; McGinley & Kamberelis, 1996; Schultz, 1997; Vass, 2007; Vass, Littleton, Miell, & Jones, 2008). Young composers invited, adopted, or rejected ideas of peers during these interactions, and through this process also negotiated friendships, affinities with peer groups, and social roles within the context of the classroom. In this way, peer-talk mediated idea generation and social goals for composing; in a reciprocal manner, composing mediated peer social interactions in complex ways within the classroom.

Play, Drama, and Drawing
Play, drama, and drawing were powerful, creative tools for generation and remixing ideas and texts, and appeared to contribute to creative flow for composition (Christianakis, 2011; Cremin, Goouch, Blakemore, Goff, & Macdonald, 2006; Crumpler & Schneider, 2002; Daiute, 1990; Dyson, 2001b, 2002; Lysacker, Wheat, & Benson, 2010; Ranker, 2007; Vass, 2007; Wohlwend, 2009). Researchers documented a continuum of students' playful interactions, including verbal play with words and ideas; play related talk in words, drawings and written texts; as well as play-acting through physical, embodied dramatic movements. Dramatic performance of texts

while composing and through author sharing in the classroom, as well as more formalized, process drama approaches also contributed to the creative generation of ideas and quality of composing (Cremin et al., 2006; Crumpler & Schneider, 2002; Schneider, 2003). In some research, teachers encouraged playfulness as a creative process, while others interpreted these behaviors as immature, off-task or disruptive to writing productivity.

Drawing was another common mode and source of idea generation that young writers frequently used along with other composing modalities, and was documented as a powerful tool for generating and communicating ideas (Christianakis, 2011; Dyson, 2001b; Mackenzie & Veresov, 2013; Ranker, 2007; Wohlwend, 2009). However, research revealed that beyond the early primary grades, drawing generally was not valued as an idea generation process, or as a legitimate multimodal text as compared to linguistic/written texts. A limited focus on visual/drawing and multimodal forms of idea generation and textual forms, both by teachers and researchers, was a key finding in this review.

Instructional Dimensions Mediating Students' Development of Ideas

Research supports the notion that instructional strategies can affect students' development as writers, including generation of ideas or content for assigned topics. Studies located for this review assessed students' use of a variety of planning techniques and tools to support ideation and development of quality writing, including: the influence of content curriculum and literature, strategy instruction, visual and symbolic tools, and approaches to writing instruction such as Writers Workshop. Teacher and peer dialogue were also entwined within each of these discussions.

Influences of Content Curriculum and Literature
Research examining writing in content curriculum focused on multiple ways teachers incorporated writing for a variety of purposes, frequently with an emphasis on writing to learn, that required taking an active role in making the writing process apparent, purposeful, and relevant. In science and social studies classrooms, the purpose of writing was often to develop understanding by "doing and writing about it" as well as to generate a record of experiences (Baxter, Bass, & Glasser, 2001; Monte-Sano & Harris, 2012). Instructional strategies included: brainstorming to elicit students' prior knowledge of topic and questions they wanted to answer (Baxter et al., 2001); Self-Regulated Strategy Development (SRSD; e.g.,

Danoff, Harris, & Graham, 1993; Tracy, Reid, & Graham, 2009); as well as group sharing, and inquiry discussions (Honig, 2010; Klein, 2000; Klein & Rose, 2010; Read, 2005). Such activities provided a context for upcoming discussions and investigations, acknowledged students' current understandings, and created a reference for future changes in ideation (Baxter et al., 2001).

Collaborative partnerships also supported work that was embedded in social interaction, and took advantage of the social nature of learning. In this respect, students' talk (e.g., feedback from partners) centered on content suggestions, generating ideas, syntax negotiations, spelling, concern for conventions, organization or categorization of information, rereading the writing, and revision (Dyson, 2006; McGinley & Kamberelis, 1996; Read, 2005; Vass, 2007). However, research findings also indicated teachers regularly established the quantity and accuracy of facts as traits of successful work which sometimes constrained students' independent development of ideas in writing-to-learn activities (Honig, 2010; Klein, 2000). Thus, students were sometimes positioned as recorders of sanctioned information instead of being supported to generate their own ideas in writing. Students used brief wordings they took from class discussion, and consistently represented facts gleaned from books and class charts. These elements allowed students to develop and shape ideas and provided a mechanism for the transformation of knowledge through writing (Many et al., 1996; Morrow, Pressley, Smith, & Smith, 1997).

Literature-based instruction, also referred to as a "study of models" approach (Graham, Kiuhara, McKeown, & Harris, 2012) and genre study, provided textual models for good writing and served as a springboard for idea development and creative expression (Brodney, Reeves, & Kazelskis, 1999; Muhammad, 2015; Tracy & Headley, 2013). Students drew upon specific genre elements (e.g., characters, settings, themes, interactive literary devices, etc.) to develop ideas for writing based on literature read and discussed in class (Cantrell, 1999; Lancia, 1997; Pantaleo, 2009; Watanabe & Hall-Kenyon, 2011), and through teachers' dialogic modeling of mentor texts and studying of author's craft through mini-lessons (Corden, 2007; Dressel, 1990). Using high-quality children's literature, engaging students in extensive reading and writing, teaching skills in the context of meaningful reading and writing experiences were key findings. In addition, research highlighted the importance of teachers' explicit modeling and metacognitive explanations of idea generation and other composing strategies, as well as the alignment of instructional focus across reading and writing activities (Alston, 2012; Corden, 2007; Silby & Watts, 2015).

Strategy Instruction
Teaching pre-writing strategies through highly explicit, teacher-directed instructional routines, including teacher dialogue when modeling, was related to the quality and length of stories produced (Brodney et al., 1999; Hacker et al., 2015; Silby & Watts, 2015). Students who were taught metacognitive dialogue ("self-talk") for goal-setting, brainstorming, and other organizational techniques as a part of a comprehensive writing program, spent more time planning ideas/content before they wrote and produced better quality writing (Behizadeh, 2014/2015; Bui, Schumaker, & Deshler, 2006; Hacker et al., 2015). In contrast, struggling writers minimized the role of planning, telling what they knew about a topic and planning as they wrote. They utilized a "retrieve-and-write" approach, summoning from memory anything they recalled that may have been pertinent and wrote it down, using each idea to stimulate the next idea in their writing (Bui et al., 2006). Vass et al. (2008) posited this "retrieve-and-write" approach, though often considered a negative means, supported students' online development of ideas, translating, appraising, and generation of more ideas.

Features of writing quality in writing plans were also associated with higher writing scores (Chai, 2006). Chai shared, "When examined for degree of detail (Elaboration), writing plans that had a substantial pool of ideas, including a brief summary of topic, were associated with essays that received the highest mean writing scores" (p. 213). Further, proficient writers developed goals to guide the writing process, generating and organizing ideas/content to meet their objectives. Conversely, students who minimized their planning or minimally engaged in metacognitive self-talk tended to generate ideas as they wrote, without recursively monitoring the composing process (Chai, 2006). Vass (2007) observed young writers frequently would repeat aloud what they had written while engaged in both non-explicit and explicit appraisal of texts within collaborative writing pairs. Use of dialogue in narrative, where characters talked to each other directly, supported students' ability to generate ideas and write longer narratives (Andrews, Beal, Corson, & Beal, 1990). Students who were taught this task and who wrote on a self-selected topic, authored longer stories and enjoyed the sessions more when using dialogue.

Research provides strong documentation for the positive influence cognitive strategy instruction has on students' writing (Benedek-Wood, Mason, Wood, Hoffman, & McGuire, 2014; Hacker et al., 2015; Zumbrunn & Bruning, 2013). Findings indicated self-regulatory dimensions of instruction (e.g., self-instructions, self-monitoring, and goal-setting) all had some level of positive impact on students' quality of writing, their ability to write longer selections, or their motivation regarding topic choice and the requirement to communicate in written form (Danoff et al., 1993). These findings were consistent with metanalyses of writing instruction outside our reviewed body of research, that showed self-regulation procedures increased the effectiveness of writing strategy training designed to improve students writing performance (Graham et al., 2012; Graham & Perin, 2007).

Visual and Symbolic Tools
Visual tools such as drawing, graphic organizers, cognitive/semantic mapping and story-boarding also supported students' idea generation and written expression. Drawing and story-boarding served as a viable and effective form of rehearsal, sustaining fluid movement between drawing and writing to express thought (Caldwell & Moore, 1991; Chapman, 1995; Dyson, 1999; Norris, Mokhtari, & Reichard, 1998; Wohlwend, 2009). In addition, cognitive/semantic mapping and graphic organizers provided a visual display of information; a structure that helped students generate ideas, and facilitated topic maintenance, idea organization, and sequence (Benedek-Wood et al., 2014; Dutro et al., 2013). Graphic organizers supported students as they connected new ideas to background knowledge, and helped them conceptualize information in ways that relationships amongst ideas/concepts were more apparent.

Approaches to Writing Instruction
As a framework for writing instruction and practice in the classroom, various approaches such as Writer's Workshop and process drama incorporated multiple elements that supported development of ideas and quality writing. Successful approaches allowed for idea generation through verbalizations, flexibility for students to initially plan and then generate creative content in multiple contexts, collaboration and playful interactions, as well as writing for authentic audiences. Research findings indicated students engaged in writers' workshop were active participants in social dialogue, constructing written genres in response to texts with which they engaged and in response to structured writing tasks (Chapman, 1995; Dyson, 1999; McGinley & Kamberelis, 1996). In the reviewed research, writers' workshop went beyond a simplistic view of the writing process (plan-draft-revise/edit-final draft) with its emphasis on both product and process. Teachers not only created opportunities for students to write, but also helped students connect ideas and feelings with language through play

(Ghiso, 2011; Wohlwend, 2009); peer interaction (Cantrell, 1999; Daiute & Dalton, 1993; Wiseman, 2003); interactive drawing and writing (Christianakis, 2011; Roth & Guinee, 2011); teaching writing skills in the context of their own writing via teacher conferencing and feedback (Alston, 2012; Matsamura et al., 2002; McCarthey, 1992, 1994; Zheng, Lawrence, Warschauer, & Lin, 2015); using literature to model effective writing (Cantrell, 1999; Lancia, 1997); process drama (Cremin et al., 2006; Crumpler & Schneider, 2002); and by encouraging students to formally and informally share their writing with each other (Behizadeh, 2014/2015; Chapman, 1995; Daiute & Dalton, 1993).

Motivation to Write
The act of writing is a complex, protracted, problem-solving task in which motivation is critical, but difficult to establish and maintain (Bruning & Horn, 2000). When students experience writing as a purposeful, authentic task, they see writing as a way to participate in a discourse community rather than as the creation of a product (Behizadah, 2014, 2014/2015; Nolen, 2001; Zumbrunn & Bruning, 2013). At times, teachers' imposition of topics and specific genre requirements served to constrain ideas, creativity, knowledge construction, motivation, and overall composition quality (Behizadeh, 2014, 2014/2015; Dutro et al., 2013; Engelhard, Gordon, & Gabrielson, 1992; Honig, 2010; Lewison & Heffernan, 2008). Writing to a topic or a prescribed prompt was a prevalent practice that dominated writing instruction in many classrooms across the reviewed research, and was often associated with concerns about high-stakes assessments of writing (Dutro et al., 2013; McCarthey, 2008). This prompt-oriented writing instruction was problematic in that it constrained students' access to ideas for writing, and negatively impacted their motivation to write. Moreover, researchers considered teacher censorship of specific topics (e.g., blood, violence, popular culture, or media themes), genre (e.g., non-realistic fiction or fantasy), marginalization of play and drawing as planning and writing options, as well as prioritization of conventions over content/ideas as having a potential negative impact on students' creativity and motivation for writing (Christianakis, 2011; DeGroff, 1992; Dyson, 2002, 2006; Ranker, 2007; Schneider, 2001). Additionally, when teacher's feedback was primarily on conventions of text, students' focus tended to shift from content toward conventions. This also impacted students' motivation for writing, as well as their revision and overall quality of ideas/content for composing (Dyson, 2006; Zheng et al, 2015). Overall, writing quality and motivation are fostered in classrooms where there is a culture of tolerance and respect

for a diversity of ideas, a continuum of choice in topics and practices, and a permeable curriculum that allows for interplay across boundaries of students' unofficial and official worlds.

DISCUSSION AND PRACTICAL IMPLICATIONS

The reviewed research offers rich information on students' idea generation sources and processes, and the dimensions of instruction that influence quality of idea generation for composing in K-8 classrooms. As we consider key findings and implications of this body of research, we invite readers to revisit Ron and Rayjon's collaborative composition of Kickboxing Grandmas (Christianakis, 2011). K-8 writers, such as Ron and Rayjon, draw upon varied semiotic or knowledge sources for composing, and generate ideas in complex ways. These knowledge sources are influenced by students' diverse experiences both inside and outside of school (i.e., "official and unofficial worlds"). In their composing, Ron and Rayjon interweave ideas from outside of school within their school-based text — knowledge of martial arts moves, as well as personal experiences with the formidable dispositions and culinary feats of certain grandmas. The boys capture the voice and linguistic elements of rhythm, rhyme, slang, boasts, and hyperbole characteristic of rap poetic genre (another unofficial world resource). From the research literature, we see that students' social and cultural backgrounds may encompass "funds of knowledge" (Moll et al., 1992) that are less or more valued within school curriculum and instruction. Ron and Rayjon's teacher, Mr. M., valued and encouraged rap as a legitimate poetic form. When teachers identify and build upon the full range of students' knowledge sources through classroom experiences, talk (self-talk, peer/teacher dialogue, conferencing), and texts (developing intertextual reading/writing connections), this facilitates students' access to ideas and knowledge base for composing, as well as their success in literacy and learning.

The degree of students' agency and control over topic choice for composing in the classroom influenced their access to these idea or knowledge sources, the quality of ideas in their compositions, as well as interest and motivation for writing. A recurrent finding was the prevalence of popular culture themes and media as an idea source for students' writing, and the impact that teachers' valuing or censorship of these themes had on students' idea generation and motivation for composing. The kickboxing theme for Ron and Rayjon's composition was accepted by their teacher, Mr. M. However the same choice might be censored within another classroom, as too violent or irreverent for school-based composing. Related to choice and control was the concept of authenticity of ideas/ topics, as well as authenticity of goals and purposes for writing. Increased authenticity was linked to better writing motivation and quality. However, students' perspectives on the authenticity in writing may differ from those of the teacher, and interpretation of what is relevant or authentic will vary from student to student. As well, young writers can direct their writing toward topics, objectives, and rhetorical purposes that may differ greatly from teacher or school-based goals. Student goals for writing might include negotiating social relationships, exploring social identity, or entertaining peers in the classroom. Through their composing, Ron and Rayjon coordinated the goal of meeting Mr. M.'s poetry assignment expectations, with their own rhetorical objectives of performing the poem for appreciative peers. Students exercise agency in setting their own social goals for writing; these goals may either subvert the teacher-established writing goals, or the teacher can acknowledge and build upon them through instruction.

Another recurrent finding across the research base was that the assessment paradigm of writing to an assigned topic/prompt within a limited time period fostered a similar approach within writing instruction, with resultant negative impact on the students' idea generation and motivation for writing. Implications of these findings are that educators need to thoughtfully plan writing instruction to include a continuum of social participation structures and practices that maximize students' agency, choice, and authenticity of topics and purposes for writing. Strategies for successful idea generation and composition within testing situations can be addressed as a specialized type of rhetorical writing task, but not as the primary paradigm for writing instruction. Classroom surveys and individual writing interviews with students are strategies that may help students generate and develop topics of high interest, and explore what they consider meaningful or authentic writing for their own lives.

Although the instructional research emphasizes effective strategies for idea generation through advanced planning (e.g., brainstorming, topic lists, graphic organizers, semantic mapping etc.), observational research on students' composing also reveals the importance of "online" idea generation that continues throughout the composing process. Research suggests students' idea generation and translation of ideas into textual forms are often distributed across various modalities, as well as across the writing of collaborative writing peers or partners. These multiple modes include oral, visual, dramatic gestural/embodied performance, as well as written linguistic modes. For young writers, the processes of talking, writing/drawing, playing, dramatic enactments, copying or imitating others are essential to generating ideas from pre-writing through all composing phases. We can see the online, dialogic nature of Ron and Rayjon's idea generation and how playing with ideas and linguistic forms drives their creative process forward. The reviewed research reinforces our own concerns as educators that these various modes of idea generation and translation through multimodalities are often considered immature processes or interpreted as off-task behaviors, rather than productive idea generation and composing strategies for writers. In Ron's classroom, Mr. M. allowed him to draw to get started with writing, but Ron's proficient cartooning and design of multimodal texts were not valued as legitimate forms of composition, or as evidence of writing achievement by district standards (Christianakis, 2011).

Despite the changing, contemporary landscape of technology and multimedia texts, the research base also reinforces our own observations that multimodal forms of writing are not valued in K-8 classroom instruction or assessments of writing achievement. At best, expression of ideas through multimodal composing practices and textual forms are viewed as acceptable for novice writers in the early primary grades before they have transitioned to more mature, conventional, and linguistic modes of writing. This finding is a concern in its marginalization of multimodal processes for idea generation and composition, but also because developing students' proficiency with reading and writing multimodal texts is foundational to 21st century literacy. Consequently, we recommend teachers explicitly focus on multimodal strategies writers use productively for composing, both for advanced planning and online idea generation. Explicit instruction should also include a range of multimodal texts drawn from in- and out-of-school sources. Moreover, assessment of student writing achievement will need to undergo radical reform in order to align with a 21st century framework of multimodal texts and literacy practices.

In our review of the literature, we found few researchers focused directly on questions of idea generation and composing processes. Moreover, the conceptualization of ideas for writing was ill-defined, and often considered broadly to include topic knowledge, as well as genre knowledge as sources of ideas for composing. However, the reviewed research provides strong evidence for the effectiveness of literature and content curriculum-based approaches for developing both students' topic and genre knowledge. Although there is an increased emphasis on informational reading and writing as a tool for knowledge construction and content area learning, we argue for a balance of informational and literary genre as the focus of writing instruction and as a means for students' efferent and aesthetic communication of ideas. As well, we recommend literature-based approaches incorporate both traditional and multimodal textual forms as models and resources for idea generation and composing.

Research on instructional practices that influence students' idea generation and composing overlaps with and supports the conclusions of other major meta-analyses of instructional approaches, and recommendations for best practices in K-8 writing instruction (Graham & Perin, 2007; Graham & Sandmel, 2011; Graham et al., 2012). Instructional practices that support idea development and writing: (a) connect reading and writing for authentic purposes; (b) include explicit modeling of strategies for planning and "online" generation of ideas throughout the writing process across genre; (c) align instructional focus across reading, writing, and other curricular activities; (d) allow for extended time to write; and (e) incorporate varied, flexible participation structures through which students can share ideas and receive teacher/peer feedback on writing. However, our review of research across methodologies also led us to conclude that the "best available evidence" on the complex process of idea generation and composing could not be reduced to quantifiable values and prescriptive practices applicable to all students. We argue that certain instructional approaches strategies for planning and idea generation (e.g., SRSD; genre-based instruction; writing from real-life, personal experiences) may be effective for some students, but might also stifle creative idea generation and motivation of other writers, such as Ron and Rayjon. Therefore, we believe instructional approaches to fostering students' idea generation for writing should not be prescriptive or implemented as a fixed set of practices across all students and educational contexts. Rather, teachers should enact a range of practices flexibly to support students' quality of idea generation for composing, creativity and motivation for writing, and development of writerly identity.

Overall, the reviewed research suggests that teachers may support students' idea generation for writing by designing a permeable curriculum that (a) highlights the socially situated and dialogic nature of composing; (b) includes a continuum of students' agency, choice and control over topics, participation structures, and composing goals; (c) considers both composing *processes* and *products*; (d) develops and expands the range of resources, tools, and multimodal processes students may draw upon for idea generation and writing; and (e) guides young writers' efforts to set and accomplish multiple goals throughout the composing process. A permeable curriculum and effective instructional practices are crucial to support students' access to a full range of ideas and knowledge-based resources, and help them translate these into written composition.

Research on writing and assessments of students' writing achievement present a concerning picture about the quality of writing instruction in schools and the inadequate preservice and in-service preparation in the area of writing (Cutler & Graham, 2008; Gilbert & Graham, 2010). There is an urgent need for comprehensive programs of professional development and preservice teacher preparation in the area of writing development and instruction. Beyond a focus on effective approaches to K-8 writing instruction, teachers need support in adopting a permeable curriculum and "funds of knowledge" approach to promoting young writers' idea generation and composing.

CONCLUSION

Through writing, we communicate our ideas to others, record and reflect upon them and our experiences, create a sense of personal identity and social belonging, advance knowledge, and preserve a common culture. Moreover, proficient writing is a critical tool for students' thinking, learning, and knowledge transformation across curricular areas, as well as for access to educational and career opportunities at the post-secondary level. Ideas or content expressed in written composition are central to ratings of writing quality and proficiency, and to student achievement in writing. In an increasingly diverse global society, educators must design a permeable curriculum that allows students' to draw upon a wide range of personal, social, and cultural sources and creative strategies for idea generation as a basis for proficient writing. The synthesized findings in this chapter illuminate the complexity of students' sources and processes for idea generation, as well as the salient dimensions of instructional design that support student's idea development for writing in K-8 classrooms. As researchers and teacher educators, we hope this review contributes to practical understandings of pedagogical dimensions that promote young writers' idea generation as a foundation for proficient writing and literacy success. We also hope the ideas we share serve as a springboard for further research and theoretical consideration of developing writers' idea generation and composing practices.

REFERENCES

Asterisks indicate SMSR studies cited (*) and SMSR studies not cited in chapter (**).

*Alston, C. L. (2012). Examining instructional practices, intellectual challenge, and supports for African American student writers. *Research in the Teaching of English, 47*(2), 112–144.

*Andrews, P., Beal, C. R., Corson, J., & Beal, C. (1990). Talking on paper: Dialogue as a writing task for sixth graders. *The Journal of Experimental Education, 58*(2), 87–94.

Bakhtin, M. M. (1981). The dialogic imagination: Four essays *(M. Holquist & C. Emerson, Trans.)*. Austin, TX: University of Texas Press.

Bakhtin, M. M. (1986). *Speech genres and other late essays.* (V. W. McGee, Trans.; C. Emerson & M. Holquist, Eds.). Austin, TX: University of Texas Press. (Original work published 1974).

*Baxter, G. P., Bass, K. M., & Glasser, R. (2001). Notebook writing in three fifth-grade science classrooms. *The Elementary School Journal, 102*(2), 123–140.

*Behizadeh, N. (2014). Adolescent perspectives on authentic writing. *Journal of Language and Literacy Education, 10*(1), 27–44.

*Behizadeh, N. (2014/2015). Xavier's take on authentic writing: Structuring choices for expression and impact. *Journal of Adolescent & Adult Literacy, 58*(4), 289–298.

*Benedek-Wood, E., Mason, L. H., Wood, P. H., Hoffman, K. E., & McGuire, A. (2014). An experimental examination of quick writing in the middle school science classroom. *Learning Disabilities: A Contemporary Journal, 12*(1), 69–92.

*Brodney, B., Reeves, C., & Kazelskis, R. (1999). Selected prewriting treatments: Effects on expository compositions written by fifth-grade students. *The Journal of Experimental Education, 68*(1), 5–20.

*Bui, Y., Schumaker, J., & Deshler, D. (2006). The effects of a strategic writing program for students with and without learning disabilities in inclusive fifth-grade classes. *Learning Disabilities Research & Practice, 21*(4), 244–260.

*Cairney, T. (1990). Intertextuality: Infectious echoes from the past. *The Reading Teacher, 43*(7), 478–484.

*Caldwell, H., & Moore, B. (1991). The art of writing: Drawing as preparation for narrative writing in the primary grades. *Studies in Art Education, 32*(4), 207–219.

*Cantrell, S. C. (1999). The effects of literacy instruction on primary students' reading and writing achievement. *Reading Research and Instruction, 39*(1), 3–26.

*Chai, C. (2006). Writing plan quality: Relevance to writing scores. *Assessing Writing, 11*(3), 198–223.

*Chapman, M. (1995). The sociocognitive construction of written genres in first grade. *Research in the Teaching of English, 29*(2), 164–192.

*Christianakis, M. (2011). Children's text development: Drawing, pictures, and writing. *Research in the Teaching of English, 46*(1), 22–54.

*Chung, Y., & Walsh, D. H. (2006). Constructing a joint story-writing space: The dynamics of young children's collaboration at computers. *Early Education & Development, 17*(3), 373–420.

Chuy, M., Scardamalia, M., & Bereiter, C. (2012). Development of ideational writing through knowledge building. In E. L. Grigorenko, E. Mambrino, & D. D. Preiss (Eds.), *Writing: A mosaic of new perspectives* (pp. 175–190). Hoboken, NJ: Psychology Press.

*Corden, R. (2007). Developing reading-writing connections: The impact of explicit instruction of literary devices on the quality of children's narrative writing. *Journal of Research in Childhood Education, 21*(3), 269–289.

*Cremin, T., Goouch, K., Blakemore, L., Goff, E., & Macdonald, R. (2006). Connecting drama and writing: Seizing the moment to write. *Research in Drama Education: The Journal of Applied Theatre and Performance, 11*(3), 273–291.

*Crumpler, T., & Schneider, J. J. (2002). Writing with their whole being: A cross study analysis of children's writing from five classrooms using process drama. *Research in Drama Education: The Journal of Applied Theatre and Performance, 7*(1), 61–79.

Culham, R. (2003). *6 + 1 traits of writing: The complete guide*. New York, NY: Scholastic Professional Books.

Cutler, L., & Graham, S. (2008). Primary grade writing instruction: A national survey. *Journal of Educational Psychology, 100*(4), 907–919.

*Daiute, C. (1990). The role of play in writing development. *Research in the Teaching of English, 24*(1), 4–47.

*Daiute, C., & Dalton, B. (1993). Collaboration between children learning to write: Can novices be masters? *Cognition and Instruction, 10*(4), 281–333.

*Danoff, B., Harris, K., & Graham, S. (1993). Incorporating strategy instruction within the writing process in the regular classroom: Effects on the writing of students with and without learning disabilities. *Journal of Reading Behavior, 25*(3), 295–322.

*DeGroff, L. (1992). Process-writing teachers' responses to fourth-grade writers' first drafts. *The Elementary School Journal, 93*(2), 131–144.

*Dressel, J. H. (1990). The effects of listening to and discussing different qualities of children's literature on the narrative writing of fifth graders. *Research in the Teaching of English, 24*(4), 397–414.

*Dutro, E., Selland, M. K., & Bien, A. C. (2013). Revealing writing, concealing writers: High-stakes assessment in an urban elementary classroom. *Journal of Literacy Research, 45*(2), 99–141.

*Dyson, A. H. (1992). Whistle for Willie, lost puppies, and cartoon dogs: The sociocultural dimensions of young children's composing. *Journal of Reading Behavior, 24*(4), 434–462.

*Dyson, A. H. (1999). Coach Bombay's kids learn to write: Children's appropriation of media material for school literacy. *Research in the Teaching of English, 33*(4), 367–402.

*Dyson, A. H. (2001a). Where are the childhoods in childhood literacy? An exploration in outer(school) space. *Journal of Early Childhood Literacy, 1*(1), 9–39.

*Dyson, A. H. (2001b). Donkey Kong in Little Bear country: A first grader's composing development in the media spotlight. *The Elementary School Journal, 101*(4), 417–433.

*Dyson, A. H. (2002). The drinking god factor: A writing development remix for "all" children. *Written Communication, 19*(4), 545–577.

*Dyson, A. H. (2006). On saying it right (write): "Fix-its" in the foundations of learning to write. *Research in the Teaching of English, 41*(1), 8–42.

*Dyson, A. H. (2010). Writing childhoods under construction: Re-visioning 'copying' in early childhood. *Journal of Early Childhood Literacy, 10*(1), 7–31.

**Eitelgeorge, J. S., & Barrett, R. (2003). Multiple continua of writing development in a first grade classroom. *Reading Research and Instruction, 43*(2), 17–64.

*Engelhard, G., Gordon, B., & Gabrielson, S. (1992). The influences of mode of discourse, experiential demand, and gender on the quality of writing. *Research in the Teaching of English, 26*(2), 315–336.

Flower, L., & Hayes, J. R. (1981). A cognitive process theory of writing. *College Composition and Communication, 32*(4), 364–387.

*Ghiso, M. P. (2011). Playing with/through non-fiction texts: Young children authoring their relationships with history. *Journal of Early Childhood Literacy, 13*(1), 26–51.

Gilbert, J., & Graham, S. (2010). Teaching writing to elementary students in grades 4–6: A national survey. *Elementary School Journal, 110*(4), 494–518.

Graham, S., Gillespie, A., & McKeown, D. (2013). Writing: Importance, development, and instruction. *Reading and Writing Quarterly, 26*(1), 1–15.

Graham, S., Kiuhara, S., McKeown, D., & Harris, K. R. (2012). A meta-analysis of writing instruction for students in the elementary grades. *Journal of Educational Psychology, 104*(4), 879–896.

Graham, S., & Perin, D. (2007). What we know, what we still need to know: Teaching adolescents to write. *Scientific Studies of Reading, 11*(4), 313–335.

Graham, S., & Sandmel, K. (2011). The process writing approach: A meta-analysis. *The Journal of Educational Research, 104*(6), 396–407.

*Hacker, D. J., Dole, J. A., Ferguson, M., Adamson, S., Roundy, L., & Scarpulla, L. (2015). The short-term and maintenance effects of self-regulated strategy development in writing for middle school students. *Reading & Writing Quarterly, 31*(4), 351–372.

Heyvaert, M., Maes, B., & Onghena, P. (2011). Mixed methods research synthesis: Definition, framework, and potential. *Quality & Quantity, 47*(2), 659–676.

*Hoewisch, A. (2001). "Do I have to have a princess in my story?": Supporting children's writing of fairytales. *Reading and Writing Quarterly, 17*, 249–277.

*Honig, S. (2010). What do children write in science? A study of the genre set in a primary science classroom. *Written Communication, 27*(1), 87–119.

Jones, S. (2014). From ideas in the head to words on the page: Young adolescents' reflections on their own writing processes. *Language and Education, 28*(1), 52–67.

*Klein, P. D. (2000). Elementary students' strategies for writing-to-learn in science. *Cognition and Instruction, 18*(3), 317–348.

*Klein, P. D., & Rose, M. R. (2010). Teaching argument and explanation to prepare junior students for writing to learn. *Reading Research Quarterly, 45*(4), 433–461.

**Knudson, R. E. (1993). Effects of different instructional tasks on students' narrative writing. *The Journal of Experimental Education, 61*(3), 205–214.

**Kos, R., & Maslowski, C. (2001). Second graders' perceptions of what is important in writing. *The Elementary School Journal, 101*(5), 567–584.

*Lancia, P. J. (1997). Literary borrowing: The effects of literature on children's writing. *The Reading Teacher, 50*(6), 470–475.

*Lewison, M., & Heffernan, L. (2008). Rewriting writers workshop: Creating safe spaces for disruptive stories. *Research in the Teaching of English, 42*(4), 435–465.

*Lysacker, J. T., Wheat, J., & Benson, E. (2010). Children's spontaneous play in writer's workshop. *Journal of Early Childhood Literacy, 10*(2), 209–229.

*MacGillivray, L., & Martinez, A. M. (1998). Princesses who commit suicide: Primary children writing within and against stereotypes. *Journal of Literacy Research, 30*(1), 53–84.

*Mackenzie, N., & Veresov, N. (2013). How drawing can support writing acquisition: Text construction in early writing from a Vygotskian perspective. *Australasian Journal of Early Childhood, 38*(4), 22–29.

*Many, J. E., Fyfe, R., Lewis, G., & Mitchell, E. (1996). Traversing the topical landscape: Exploring students' self-directed reading-writing-research processes. *Reading Research Quarterly, 36*(1), 12–35.

*Matsamura, L. C., Patthey-Chavez, G., Valdes, R., & Garnier, H. (2002). Teacher feedback, writing assignment quality, and third-grade students' revisions in lower and higher-achieving urban schools. *The Elementary School Journal, 103*(1), 3–25.

*McCarthey, S. J. (1992). The teacher, the author, and the text: Variations in form and content of writing conferences. *Journal of Literacy Research, 24*(1), 51–82.

*McCarthey, S. J. (1994). Authors, text, and talk: The internalization of dialogue from social interaction during writing. *Reading Research Quarterly, 29*(3), 201–203.

*McCarthey, S. J. (2008). The impact of no child left behind on teachers' writing instruction. *Written Communication, 25*(4), 462–505.

*McGinley, W., & Kamberelis, G. (1996). Maniac Magee and Ragtime Tumpie: Children negotiating self and world through reading and writing. *Research in the Teaching of English, 30*(1), 75–113.

Miles, M. B., & Huberman, A. M. (1994). *An expanded source book: Qualitative data analysis* (2nd ed.). Thousand Oaks, CA: Sage.

Moll, L. C., Amanti, C., Neff, D., & Gonzalez, N. (1992). Funds of knowledge for teaching: Using a qualitative approach to connect homes and classrooms. *Theory into Practice, 31*(2), 132–141.

*Monte-Sano, C., & Harris, K. (2012). Recitation and reasoning in novice history teachers' use of writing. *The Elementary School Journal, 113*(1), 105–130.

*Morrow, L. M., Pressley, M., Smith, J. K., & Smith, M. (1997). The effect of a literature-based program integrated into literacy and science instruction with children from diverse backgrounds. *Reading Research Quarterly, 32*(1), 54–76.

*Muhammad, G. E. (2015). The role of literary mentors in writing development: How African American literature supported the writings of adolescent girls. *Journal of Education, 195*(2), 2–14.

*Myhill, D., & Jones, S. (2009). How talk becomes text: Investigating the concept of oral rehearsal in early years' classrooms. *British Journal of Educational Studies, 57*(3), 265–284.

National Center for Education Statistics. (2012). *The nation's report card: Writing 2011.* (NCES 2012–470). Washington, DC: Institute of Education Sciences, U.S. Department of Education.

*Nolen, S. (2001). Constructing literacy in the kindergarten: Task structure, collaboration, and motivation. *Cognition and Instruction, 19*(1), 95–142.

*Norris, E., Mokhtari, K., & Reichard, C. (1998). Children's use of drawing as a prewriting strategy. *Journal of Research in Reading, 21*(1), 69–74.

**Olinghouse, N. G., Graham, S., & Gillespie, A. (2015). The relationship of discourse and topic knowledge to fifth graders' writing performance. *Journal of Educational Psychology, 107*(2), 391–406.

*Pantaleo, S. (2009). An ecological perspective on the socially embedded nature of reading and writing. *Journal of Early Childhood Literacy, 9*(1), 75–99.

Peréz, B. (2004). Literacy, diversity, and programmatic responses. In B. Peréz & T. L. McCarty (Eds.), *Sociocultural contexts of language and literacy* (2nd ed., pp. 3–24). Mahwah, NJ: Taylor & Francis.

**Peterson, S. (2000). Fourth, sixth, and eighth graders' preferred writing topics and identification of gender markers in stories. *The Elementary School Journal, 101*(1), 79–100.

*Peterson, S., & Ladky, M. (2001). Collaboration, competition and violence in eighth-grade students' classroom writing. *Reading Research and Instruction, 41*(1), 1–17.

Pluye, P., Gagnon, M. P., Griffiths, F., & Johnson-Lafleur, J. (2009). A scoring system for appraising mixed methods research and concomitantly appraising qualitative, quantitative and mixed methods primary studies in mixed studies reviews. *International Journal of Nursing Studies, 46*(4), 529–546.

Purves, A. C. (1992). Reflections on research and assessment in composition. *Research in the Teaching of English, 26*(1), 108–122.

*Ranker, J. (2007). Designing meaning with multiple media sources: A case study of an eight-year old student's writing processes. *Research in the Teaching of English, 41*(4), 402–434.

*Read, S. (2005). First and second graders writing informational text. *The Reading Teacher, 59*(1), 36–44.

**Reynolds, G., & Perin, D. (2009). A comparison of text structure and self-regulated writing strategies for composing from sources by middle school students. *Reading Psychology, 30*(3), 265–300.

*Roth, K., & Guinee, K. G. (2011). Ten minutes a day: The impact of interactive writing instruction on first graders' independent writing. *Journal of Early Childhood Literacy, 11*(3), 331–361.

**Sadoski, M., Willson, V., & Norton, D. (1997). The relative contributions of research-based composition activities to writing improvement in the lower and middle grades. *Research in the Teaching of English, 31*(1), 120–150.

*Schneider, J. J. (2001). No blood, guns, or gays allowed!: The silencing of the elementary writer. *Language Arts, 78*(5), 415–425.

*Schneider, J. J. (2003). Contexts, genres, and imagination: An examination of the idiosyncratic writing performances of three elementary children within multiple contexts of writing instruction. *Research in the Teaching of English, 37*(3), 329–379.

*Schultz, K. (1997). Do you want to be in my story? Collaborative writing in an urban elementary classroom. *Journal of Literacy Research, 2*(2), 253–287.

Siegel, M., & Rowe, D. W. (2011). Webs of significance: Semiotic perspectives on texts. In D. Lapp & D. Fisher (Eds.), *Handbook of research on teaching the English and language arts* (pp. 202–207). Hoboken, NJ: Taylor & Francis.

*Silby, A., & Watts, M. (2015). Making the tacit explicit: Children's strategies for classroom writing. *British Educational Research Journal, 41*(5), 801–819.

*Sipe, L. (1998). Transitions to the conventional: An examination of a first grader's composing process. *Journal of Literacy Research, 30*(3), 357–388.

*Sutherland, J. A., & Topping, K. J. (1999). Collaborative creative writing in eight-year-olds: Comparing cross-ability fixed role and same-ability reciprocal role pairing. *Journal of Research in Reading, 22*(2), 154–179.

*Tracy, B., Reid, R., & Graham, S. (2009). Teaching young students strategies for planning and drafting stories: The impact of self-regulated strategy development. *Journal of Educational Research, 102*(5), 323–331.

*Tracy, K. N., & Headley, K. N. (2013). 'I never liked to read or write': A formative experiment on the use of a nonfiction-focused writing workshop in a fourth grade classroom. *Literacy Research and Instruction, 52*(3), 173–191.

*Vass, E. (2007). Exploring processes of collaborative creativity: The role of emotions in children's joint creative writing. *Journal of Thinking Skills and Creativity, 2*(2), 107–117.

*Vass, E., Littleton, K., Miell, D., & Jones, A. (2008). The discourse of collaborative creative writing: Peer collaboration as a context for mutual inspiration. *Journal of Thinking Skills and Creativity, 3*(3), 192–202.

Vygotsky, L. (1978). *Mind in society: The development of higher psychological processes.* Cambridge, MA: Harvard University Press.

Vygotsky, L. (1986). *Thought and language.* Cambridge, MA: MIT Press.

*Watanabe, L. M., & Hall-Kenyon, K. M. (2011). Improving young children's writing: The influence of story structure on kindergartners' writing complexity. *Literacy Research and Instruction, 50*(40), 272–293.

**Wilson, K., Trainin, G., Laughridge, V., Brooks, D., & Wickless, M. (2011). Our zoo to you: The link between zoo animals in the classroom and science and literacy concepts in first-grade journal writing. *Journal of Early Childhood Literacy, 11*(3), 275–306.

*Wiseman, A. (2003). Collaboration, initiation, and rejection: The social construction of stories in a kindergarten class. *The Reading Teacher, 56*(8), 802–810.

*Wohlwend, K. E. (2009). Damsels in discourse: Girls consuming and producing identity texts through Disney princess play. *Reading Research Quarterly, 44*(1), 57–83.

*Zheng, B., Lawrence, J., Warschauer, M., & Lin, C. H. (2015). Middle school students' writing and feedback in a cloud-based classroom environment. *Technology, Knowledge, and Learning, 20*(2), 201–229.

*Zumbrunn, S., & Bruning, R. (2013). Improving the writing and knowledge of emergent writers: The effects of self-regulated strategy development. *Reading and Writing, 26*(1), 91–110.

PROCESS WITH A PURPOSE: LOW-STAKES WRITING IN THE SECONDARY ENGLISH CLASSROOM

Sue Verlaan and Wolfram Verlaan

ABSTRACT

Purpose — *To describe how low-stakes writing can assist teachers in eliciting greater student engagement and involvement in their own writing by focusing the stages of the writing process more on student thinking than on the surface structure of their writing.*

Design/methodology/approach — *This chapter examines some of the important research literature addressing process writing in general and low-stakes writing in particular. The authors' experiences with teaching English in the secondary classroom inform their analysis of implementing low-stakes writing assignments as part of the writing process.*

Findings — *The authors describe how using non-judgmental feedback on low-stakes writing assignments allows the teacher and students to have conversations on paper which are intended to help students explore, expand, and clarify their own thinking about a topic. By establishing a continuing conversation on paper with the students about their writing, the teacher takes on the role of "trusted ally" in the writing process, rather than the more traditional role of an arbiter of writing conventions.*

Practical implications – *Although the presumptive focus of writing instruction for the last two decades has been on the writing process, the tendency to turn the individual steps of the writing process into discrete writing products in a formulaic manner can cause many important parts of the writing process itself to be either overlooked or given short shrift. This chapter provides useful descriptions of ways in which low-stakes writing assignments can afford teachers the means by which to focus their students' attention on key portions of the writing process so that their writing products are ultimately improved.*

Keywords: Writing process; low-stakes writing; conversations on paper

WRITING: PROCESS OR PRODUCT?

Teachers make room for writing instruction by providing time to deliver writing *instructions*: what to write about, how much to write, and which form to write in. To support these instructions, class time is often devoted to traditionally teacher-directed tasks: modeling a particular process such as brainstorming either via whole-class discussion or in small group activities, guiding students through a dense passage or some subtle ambiguity or theme, and presenting lessons on grade-level appropriate vocabulary, grammar, or syntax study; the writing itself, because it has been traditionally a singular, individual activity, is usually assigned as homework.

Since the mid-1980s, writing instruction theory has been grounded in the idea that writing is itself a process, a recursive meaning-making activity with overlapping "stages" of development. As early as 1990, Cohen (1990) acknowledged that it had "become apparent to many educators that this approach of one-draft submissions discourages learners from taking their writing seriously because of its focus on instant products and on the grade that the writer receives" (p. 105). Since writing as a process was thus demonstrated, established, and printed in textbook chapters, teachers have gone dutifully about their jobs, assigning a brainstorming sheet, assigning an outline, assigning a draft, and assigning a revision, leading to the simple replacement of one with four one-draft homework submissions. Still, though preparation for each task may include whole-class or group discussions of a text or topic, the pre-writing, drafting, revision, and editing are typically given as individual assignments to be completed at home (apart from timed, on-demand essays written in class), though occasional in-class peer review work might allow for on-site editing and reworking of some sentences or paragraphs.

Process-based writing, as such, has thus shifted the grading of writing from one grade to at least four, but each of the grades remains necessarily a focus on the student writer's *product*, not *process*, each stage of the process turning into a kind of product in and of itself: the student writers' ideas, the student writers' organization, the student writers' composition, and the student writers' revision. Some teachers assign as process writing the collection of each stage of the four-step assignment, in which case students are instructed to keep each of the separate (usually one-draft) products and to hand them in as a packet for a final grade. And as online tutors have become available at local college campuses, some dual credit or otherwise college-bound English classes include as an additional step to the multi-draft writing process the submission of drafts to online tutors for targeted review and revision.

With a class of competent student writers who are already comfortable with both the process of writing and their own capacity to articulate meaningful and interesting ideas, such curricular plans often work relatively well, and the teacher may in fact be most useful to such a group of students as the arbiter of performance standards, assigning well-designed tasks meant to push particular learning boundaries and appraising the students' attempts to master particular learning objectives. But how many teachers or students see the process as more than a mere collection of a sequence of separate assignments? How many teachers or students see evidence of progress from the first to the final stage, apart from perhaps fewer misspelled words or comma splices thanks to the teacher's or a peer's review of the "first" draft? And how many teachers and students can actually specify what they might be looking for in terms of progress or improvement, if they were in fact trying to assess how a focus on a multi-draft writing process assignment might change the way students approached and completed writing tasks?

WRITING APPRAISAL: PROGRESS OR PERFORMANCE?

One of the reasons why teaching the writing process may not always work to actually elicit noticeable improvement in either the student writer's capacity for clear and meaningful written expression or willingness to work toward that capacity might be a mistaken assumption about the student's and the teacher's roles during the process. Cohen (1990) asserts that because a written piece "takes shape" as the student works on subsequent drafts, the student writer's "awareness of writing processes is heightened" (p. 105); but there is good reason to question whether just because a student writer has read and reread and had his written work reviewed that his awareness of writing as a process has in fact been "heightened." Such awareness usually comes after much longer incubation periods than one series of multiple drafts or even one semester that includes several multi-draft writing assignments. And, depending on his maturity (sometimes, but not always akin to age group) and intellectual readiness, a student may be very adept at minimizing his efforts on any particular task, including the transfer of planning thoughts into draft form or the insertion of revised sentences and paragraphs into a "final" draft.

What figures in the rest of Cohen's assertion as presumably a more important reason to use process-based writing instruction is that "the work comes to a teacher for appraisal only at the point when the writer is prepared for such appraisal. The composition has usually gone through several rounds of peer edits and self-assessment *before* it reaches the teacher for assessment" (p. 105). Here is the frequent motivation behind most of a teacher's choices in writing instruction: the demands on a teacher's time being great, especially when we include close attention to each of her student's writing ability and potential for growth, her preference for a sure and efficient mode of accounting for each student's best performance is not only understandable but necessary. The teacher's role as an appraiser of performance can keep her in the product mode of instruction in spite of any effort to convey the generative and recursive aspects of the writing process. Quite often, in order to justify their critique of a student writer's performance and teach their student writers how to spot their own errors, teachers correct or comment on most everything they notice as inadequate in a paper, which can result in feedback that is so profuse, whether in red ink or green, that a student writer may have difficulty making sense either of his strengths or how his weaknesses distract from his intended meaning.

Alternately, in the attempt to streamline their reading and scoring of student work, teachers will use rubrics either to itemize the various elements of successful performance or to describe and thereby measure the separate criteria that the assignment was designed to teach. But rubrics — even those used for formative assessment — are always by definition a type of summative evaluation of a student writer's performance and so can interrupt the very development that writing process instruction purportedly seeks. This interruption occurs for two reasons. First, the focus is on level of competency as achieved, rather than progress toward competency (the new rubrics labeled "exemplary," "proficient," and "emerging" notwithstanding); students often perceive rubrics either as final indicators or predictors of proficiency, and so may respond with either complacency, if their scores are good, or reluctance, if their scores fall short. Second, the relationship between the teacher and the student writer can become one of judge and applicant – a relationship that if not inherently antagonistic still maintains a power differential that makes development difficult (with student writer being more interested in "did I do it right?" than in "what can I do?") as much as it makes a student writer's achievement the hallmark of the exchange. (And what teacher, novice or veteran, hasn't wondered at multiple points in any grading session whether her judgment is in fact fair, or accurate, or valid?)

Too often, the text itself, the teacher's interpretation of the text (or her validation of someone else's interpretation, student or critic), or the high-stakes rubric used for benchmark performances restrict the student-as-apprentice, whose every effort to write may amount to little more than a capitulation, to whatever degree his ability allows, to the meaning embedded in the authority of the moment. He will always fall short, either in terms of content or presentation (who gets a 100 in English?); he may even look to the presence or absence of past praise as a measure of the likelihood he will score well this time. As is often the case, surface errors, marked with either a professional or teacher-made nomenclature in the margins, will command much of a teacher's appraisal. Grammatical errors remain the easiest to spot and the simplest to fix, though the several pages explaining the scoring of the on-demand essay portion of the ACT, a standardized college admissions test, includes only a one-sentence reference to grammar. A student writer needs to make sense of what his *language* is trying to do, not just his words or the surface presentation of his thoughts. When teachers focus on surface errors, so too do student writers, who can no longer focus on language as a means of communicating or expressing their thoughts. Instead, writing easily becomes a matter of which word goes next, or what should I say next. We thus run the risk of frightening student writers out of allowing themselves to think.

When teachers are appraisers of student writers' performance, communication can no longer be the primary goal; instead, ranking preempts other possible reasons for instruction. A score is considered feedback and duly reported in a grade book with or without a kind of algorithm that makes an individual score neither too heavy nor too light in the overall weighting of 100-point-based letter grades. And thus, any grade — even any evaluative comment — makes of a stage of the writing process a writing product. As Newell (2006) reports, process-oriented approaches assume "that learning is not linear and sequential but instead involves false starts and tentative explorations. Understanding will grow and change as learning progresses. Premature evaluation will short-circuit that process and stall risk-taking" (p. 236). By appraising a student writer's current stage in his process as a product — and this is what we do whether we use a grading scale, a rubric, or even a standard marginal note that judges the writing as somehow deficient — we run the risk of encouraging students to relinquish any personal investment in their own language development. As Culham (2003), the developer of the *6 + 1 Writing Traits* program ("6 + 1") recognizes, if students believe their grade will be negatively impacted by trying out a new technique, "they will be less willing to try it in the first place" (p. 278).

Culham goes on to emphasize that the 6 + 1 rubric scores "are intended to help the students see where their relative strengths and weaknesses are on a piece of work — a part of the process of learning" (p. 278). However, recognizing strengths and weaknesses is just a part of the process of learning, and often only a preliminary one. And knowing where they are on a scale is less important than knowing what to try next. Many students know their writing isn't as good as the model or as good as a peer's, but *they don't know what else to do*. While programs such as 6 + 1 become a means of identifying (as much for the teacher as the student writer) what types of strategies to use to improve a strength or eliminate a weakness, they can often be used in ways that can neglect the student writer himself. The messy process of writing can be either so personal or so unique that a student writer may have difficulty finding answers to his particular problems in the typical series of options or common evaluative phrases such programs supply.

FREEING STUDENTS TO WRITE

What can often work better for many students is to read or hear an individual response from a trusted ally — whether the teacher or a peer. A conversation about both the student writer's topic and the writing itself can begin when a student writer knows and trusts that he has an interested reader, a reader interested in more than just finding evidence of a trait or accurately scoring a piece of writing. When a student writer feels more interest in what he has to say than in how he has to say it, he can allow himself to be interested in his writing himself, and therefore invested in saying more, or in saying what he has said more clearly, and eventually, in saying so with more of his own language, ideas, and personal style. With the formality of evaluation relaxed, "writing becomes revelatory of the writer's own thinking" (Newell, p. 236). Outside the restrictions normally imposed by the impulse to correct the surface features of writing, both the student writer and the teacher are freed to work with the student writer's thoughts as they develop. Thus, ironically, it is often by delaying evaluation of a written product that a teacher can increase the scope and range of benefits historically ascribed to process writing and, once a student writer's performance has become rich with his own ideas, language, and attempts to organize his thoughts, can evaluate a far better product than she might have otherwise.

The benefits of process writing have been the subject of Language Arts research for several decades, including but not limited to the theories and subsequent teaching practices advocated by the writing-to-learn movement. Newell (2006) attributes James Britton's theories of language use with helping to establish the early roots of writing and learning theory. As early as 1970, Britton was espousing the idea that children and adolescents use language to investigate and understand their inner and outer worlds. Pradl (2004) goes on to argue that teachers' and adults' primary responsibility is "to ascertain the child's inner outlook" (p. 521). Or, as Britton (1978) characterized it: "If we listen hard enough, there may be hints of the child's view of the world in many an unexpected twist given to an utterance" (p. 36). The merits of process writing were also championed by Elbow (2000), who posited that freewriting allows us to "enter more fully into our words" through what he calls the "unfocused exploring" that can occur when we are granted "permission to pursue [a thought] on paper in an uncontrolled way wherever it wants to go, even if it digresses (as it usually does)"; he goes on to suggest that freewriting is an exceptional tool of the writing process because we "cannot find as many ideas or perceptions if [we] try to stay on one track or be organized" (pp. 117–18).

Freewriting allows student writers to meander through their own minds without worrying about the typical constraints of coherence and clarity necessary to academic writing; instead, they become almost as spectators of the thoughts they find, recording what they discover in what Elbow (2000) calls "movies of the mind" (p. 125). Elbow goes on to suggest that the benefit for student writers is that it splits the two very different tasks of articulating and clarifying thought into two separate tasks: "Freewriting shows me I can do them one at a time: just *get my mind into words*, but leave those words messy and incoherent" (italics in original, p. 130); within this messy and incoherent writing, which usually occurs in bursts of no more than 10 minutes, are qualities desirable in most writing but often absent in school writing − "the energy, the talkiness, the sense of voice, and the sense of the words' or the writer's reaching toward a reader" (p. 129). In Britton's view, there is more to writing than mere transcription of preformed thoughts into conventional standards of presentation (1970). When freed from the traditional expectations of school writing, student writers can more easily access their writing potential, using language as Britton suggested − to make sense of their worlds − and as Fishman (1997) attested − to involve themselves in their own learning by: "Introducing students to the often ungraded and informal types of composing ...[helps students] attend more to the meaning of their writing than to its formal, grammatical qualities" (p. 54). Without the penalties normally associated with taking risks, student writers will feel free enough to stay eager and involved while they "just write."

While "rightness" isn't what is at stake in freewriting, freewriting isn't completely free from expectations. In spite of there being "no such thing as uncontrolled or unplanned writing," Elbow (2000) insists that one can expect to be startled by one's own writing. "Freewriting increases the frequency of surprise ...[and] opens the doors to thoughts and feelings that startle" (p. 131). By allowing themselves to write without stopping, to write without worry, and to write without critiquing or erasing or changing the words they see materialize on their papers, student writers will find out things about their own minds that they hadn't known were there. And what "startles" a student writer may delight his teacher with something new to acknowledge, to hear and wonder about and react to, something that is uniquely the student writer's own.

Fishman (1997) notes that because of its open-ended nature, freewriting offers not only "a way to get started," but also "a way of uncovering relationships, raising new questions, and complexifying topics" (p. 60), the hallmark of good discussions. Elbow (2000) characterizes both freewriting and feedback as "narrative[s] of the mind reacting" (p. 125), which together scaffold the student writer in developing and exploring ideas, rather than just producing "good" writing. Freewriting thus offers an invaluable opportunity to "talk on paper," to have the kind of exchange conducive to creating an on-going dialogue about a perpetually transforming text in a manner characterized by Radcliffe (2012) as a "spiral of writing experiences" (p. 19). Writing is, of course, different than speech, but the benefits of having a discussion on paper is that in the very recording of one's thoughts, the teacher and student writer create a document that allows them to carry on their conversation asynchronously and retrospectively. The implication is that a student writer's first thoughts in freewriting are not the end of either the writing or the thinking.

Through her response to the freewriting, a teacher can stimulate further thought, prompting the student writer to elaborate, extend, clarify, or explain something he included in his otherwise probably messy or incoherent string of thoughts. And the teacher can allow this sort of conversation on paper to continue as long as she wants to, according to either the criteria of the writing project or the student writer's needs.

FRUITFUL FEEDBACK, FURTHER THINKING

Critical to both initiating and sustaining the kind of conversation on paper that will benefit a student writer's future academic writing is the absence of obvious evaluation. For Durst (2015), the most fruitful feedback is the facilitative response, one in which the teacher "instead of treating every piece of student writing as an occasion for evaluation ... treats the paper as if the student were trying to communicate with the teacher on an issue of personal significance" (pp. 392–393). Taking on the role of either teacher as examiner or teacher as trusted adult (Britton, 1970), a teacher determines what freewriting can lead to. As Britton (1987) notes, "The teacher's response — even where it may be brief — is responsible for maintaining the tone, and thereby the purpose, of the exchange" (p. 3). Typically, teachers read student writing as examiners, limiting their focus to writing quality, strengths and weaknesses, and what the student writer can do to make it better. Elbow (2000) suggests that a teacher can instead "*assume* value," (italics in original) asking questions common to the study of professional texts:

> What does the text say?' What does it imply or entail? What are its consequences? What does the writer assume? What is the writer's point of view or stance? Who does the text speak to? How does the text ask me to see the world? What would I do if I believed it? (p. 405)

He insists that because these questions "have no inherent connection to quality or value, ... it's not hard to answer them without saying anything about a paper's quality." (p. 405) When a teacher uses these questions to start a line of inquiry, to make a remark about a personal connection or related topic, or even just to get the student writer to continue where he left off, she will in essence be responding to the student writer's thought, or the inchoate germs of it, in a manner that prompts the student writer to continue. The teaching and learning thus happen via dialogue, one that may continue over several days, whether on yesterday's exit ticket or last week's multi-step brainstorming session, a dialogue of thoughts in response to each other, a continuous loop of feedback about ideas rather than the degrees of a student writer's correctness.

When the student writer's own thinking matters more than the clarity or correctness with which he presents it, the teacher can participate in developing the student's capacity for clear writing and complex thought by finding the questions that might nudge his thought a litter further or provide direction for what alternatives to explore, whether conceptual or syntactic: what word is the student writer really looking for, what ideas is he beginning to grapple with, or what grammatical conventions can he use to pack all of his meaning into a coherent sentence? A teacher thus does not abdicate her role as evaluator entirely; she merely makes it less of an initial concern. It is the student writer's thinking and the continued *in-process* writing he is using to get this thinking down on paper that is most important. When the teacher reads and responds more as a trusted ally than a judge, she helps the student find the voice or the idea or the words he is looking for, leading the student writer in his own development both because she knows or has designed the criteria by which the student writer will ultimately be judged, and also because she has listened and responded to the student writer's words with the intent to continue a purposeful conversation that will draw him further along.

The key to this discovery of how best to move her student writers forward is in the tenor of the conversation she establishes with each individual student writer in her classroom. As it becomes clear to student writers that they have room to use language as an exploration, not just a demonstration, of thought, that they can take risks without suffering a noticeable drop in their class average, they will be more likely to take advantage of the "free" of freewriting and thereby access what Elbow (2000) identifies as "states of increased intensity or arousal or excitement" when ideas and possibilities can come more readily to mind, "bubble up, and ... fall more directly into language (though not necessarily better, clearer, or more organized language)" (p. 127). Much of the writing-to-learn movement was grounded in theories that allowed for the false starts and generally messy process of sorting out one's experience by trying to find the right words and phrasings to articulate one's thoughts about what it might mean. According to Barnes (1976), who made some of the earliest arguments for the shift to process writing, language "is the major means by which we consciously organize experience and reflect upon it" (p. 84), two actions that require room for sorting things out before we are held accountable for using language "correctly." He distinguished two types of teachers – the Transmission teacher and the Interpretation teacher – to highlight the need for conversation, with its inevitable mis- and re-directions, in the classroom:

> The Transmission teacher sees it as his task to transmit knowledge and to test whether the pupils have received it .... For the Interpretation teacher, however, the pupil's ability to re-interpret knowledge for himself is crucial to learning, and he sees this as depending on a productive dialogue between the pupil and himself. [He emphasizes] the importance of making responses of various kinds to what is said or written, since these will support the learner's attempts to interpret. (p. 142)

For Barnes, a teacher could best guide student writers and thinkers not through her role as evaluator but through her role as audience for their oral and written attempts at meaning.

Whether as evaluator or as audience, the question a teacher poses to herself when reading a student writer's response is essentially "what does this writer understand?" The difference lies in a teacher's reactions to her own assessment. The teacher as evaluator will indicate where on the scale of proficiency a particular sampling of a student writer's work has landed, whereas the teacher as audience, while also cognizant of the student writer's proficiency, has a wider range of choices along a spectrum not just of performance criteria, necessarily, but also of the ideas and questions prompted by the student writer's response. By privileging her own non-evaluative thoughts over any inclination to judge, she lets the student writer know that it is his thoughts, not his performance, that she is interested in. Thus, the *in-process* writing, a messy, multi-phase, and sometimes surprising interpretation of one's experience via language and the response it garners, can continue.

LOWERING THE STAKES

Acknowledging what student writers are doing with language without evaluating what they have done helps the teacher and the student writer keep the writing in a state of being *in-process* so the benefits of freewriting, risk-taking, false starts, and other messy bits of writing can come to light.

Writing about his experience assigning both "low-stakes" and "high-stakes" writing, Elbow (2000) argues that academic writing noticeably improves when student writers are given ample time and occasion to write without the worry of being judged. Writing often suffers when student writers are overly aware of the high stakes of most academic assignments. In contrast, Elbow (2000) contends that when the stakes are low, student writers regularly "discover that completely unplanned, unstudied writing is often worth sharing" and are thus "more willing to read something out loud if they've just freewritten it quickly than if they've worked hard revising it" (p. 121). Because it is graded, writing usually "*feels* like an inherently high-stakes activity," even though writing is "the best possible low-stakes arena for language – for using words to learn, explore, take risks, or commune with ourselves and not have our words be evaluated"; furthermore, while the goal of low-stakes assignments "is not to produce excellent pieces," low-stakes writing is typically "livelier, clearer, and more natural – often more interesting – in spite of any carelessness and mistakes" (pp. 351–53). Rosenwasser and Stephen (2015) agree that freewriting "allows you to worry less about what you don't understand and instead start to work things out as you write" (p. 48). And because freewriting is not product-oriented like most graded schoolwork but instead participates in the process of discovery and composition, Fishman (1997) contends that it can be "a vehicle for developing student self-respect, for helping students appreciate their own ability apart from someone else's evaluation" (p. 60). The very absence of penalty and criticism ironically can elicit writing that could fare much better if critiqued.

If we believe risk-taking is central to learning and expect student writers to make any number of false starts in the various stages of the writing process, marking as insufficient their initial attempts to form thoughts and construct meaning through language they are still learning to use sends an inconsistent message. When evaluation predominates a teacher's or a peer's feedback, student writers who aren't naturally adept or fluent, or those who don't believe they can be successful when attempting formal prose, won't have a sense that what they say on paper means anything more than whether or not they completed an assignment according to instructions. And we will be back to the "tortured and tangled prose" more often found in high-stakes than in low-stakes writing. Instead, since student writers are just trying to get their "minds into words" on the paper, when teachers notice the carelessness and surface errors inevitable in any first-draft writing, they can shift their focus and respond in ways to support the thinking evident in the language without declaring it deficient in any way. Acting as a trusted ally, teachers can respond in ways that will shepherd their student writers along toward the coherence or clarity that the final writing product demands.

RESPONDING TO IN-PROCESS WRITING

For a teacher to remain non-evaluative, a student writer's surface errors and even presumed proficiency must thus remain peripheral concerns of *in-process* writing. In order to lead a student writer to clearer thinking and more accurate expression of his thoughts without outright evaluative comments, the teacher should be ready to field all sentences equally — whether good, bad, or even unintelligible — as attempts to construct or communicate meaning. Essentially, the teacher's job is to decipher what kind of intention the writing, confused as it may be *in-process*, represents. Is it intended to question or to clarify? To list or to contradict? To imitate or identify rationale? To complain or to explain? Once the teacher has deciphered a student writer's possible intention, her job is not to correct what is already on the page but to draw out what isn't quite there yet, so that the student writer can find his own way through semi-formed or otherwise incomplete thoughts to intelligible, articulate, and perhaps even more complex ideas. There are a myriad of ways a teacher can stimulate continued, deeper, and more expressive and intuitive thought from a student writer, ways that have nothing directly to do with grades or other forms of evaluation. "Tell me more," or "huh, that's interesting — why do you think this matters?" or "when else might this happen?" are examples of replies that show a student writer that what he has to say is, for the time being, more important than how he says it, even while they may in fact direct the student writer to use more conventional or formal language forms.

Cohen (1990) describes the dialog journal as currently understood as a kind of record of in-process difficulties and questions that a teacher can respond to directly, with the caveat that a teacher is "not to *correct* the language" (p.113); rather, the function of a dialog journal is to provide a record of student writer's questions and difficulties that the teacher responds to individually, with the student writer and teacher creating between them "an ongoing written dialog" (p. 113). Pradl (2004) suggests that in this manner writing functions as "part of an ongoing conversation with a peer or teacher acting as a trusted figure" (p. 523). A student writer will tend to trust a teacher when he feels she values what he has to say; he will be even more trusting if she can find the strengths and good ideas in his writing that he cannot see for himself. Though the benefits of such a journal have no doubt often been outweighed by the time constraints most teachers are under, with multiple 25+ person classes in multiple grade levels, with students who have varying degrees of writing competence, it is possible to translate the function of the dialog journal to the in-process writing itself – with the writing task itself becoming its own record of the writer's thoughts, and the teacher's in-process feedback her response. When writing tasks are made shorter ("write your first scenario that will serve as a real-life example of your thesis statement") or when teachers ask student writers which paragraph is their best, teachers can reduce the amount of time they spend with each student so that they may spend at least some time with each student writer. Not surprisingly, a brief, "live," in-process interchange between a teacher and a student writer can do a world of good in helping the student writer produce interesting and meaningful text. As the teacher is able to generate the kinds of in-process conversation – even if only in snatches of reading and response to text – the atmosphere of a class begins to support itself, with student writers exchanging ideas and writing among themselves when the teacher is busy with another student writer (Moje, 1996).

When a teacher keeps evaluation at bay, the relationship that can evolve between the student writer and his teacher via the regular and on-going conversations they have on paper can become instrumental in continuing and possibly even furthering a student writer's engagement in his own writing process. To this end, Elbow's low-stakes writing is primarily a writing-to-learn content-area strategy that allows students to explore course content without worrying about surface errors or the conventions of language. And with its combination of freedom from the risk of criticism and even self-correction that comes with freewriting and the promise of little to no penalty for work that may be somehow deficient because it is still in-process (especially important to young, struggling, or reluctant student writers), low-stakes writing also offers a solution for those teachers interested both in promoting their students' engagement with the writing process and in addressing their students' needs for demonstrable cognitive development. Elbow (2000) lists the criteria frequently used by many teachers in judging essays:

> sticking to the topic or question or assignment; getting the information or concepts right; having good ideas of one's own; reasoning carefully, giving enough arguments, evidence, and examples; organizing effectively; and making meaning clear at the sentence level. (p. 345)

and asserts "*It is possible to meet every one of these criteria and still use lots of language people call wrong*" (p. 345). Conceding that an occasional punctuation error may mar the clarity of a student writer's sentences, he suggests that teachers can "give students feedback on *all* these criteria and help them satisfy everyone ... [without] worrying about grammar, syntax, and spelling" (p. 345, emphasis in original). Of course, grammar, syntax, and spelling present the most obvious and measureable problems for student writers, and many English teachers have been conditioned by their own schooling and later trained or encouraged by their administrations to instruct via sentence level problems. But most writing problems run deeper than surface level errors, and it is difficult even for the best student writers to negotiate the rules of grammar and syntax *and* create drafts that say what they in fact want to say. When student writers try simultaneously to find meaning and to follow the rules of language, they often find themselves sacrificing meaning creation for sentence correctness.

LOW-STAKES WITH A PURPOSE: FOCUSED FREEWRITING

Low-stakes writing can be adjusted for the classroom to serve both meaning and correctness in tandem, so that neither teachers nor student writers have to make a choice of process over product or vice versa. By designing her curriculum to include a range of low-stakes writings throughout all stages of the writing process — instead of just during pre-writing — a teacher can make room for sustained in-process writing throughout the student writers' progress toward a final product. She can thereby identify, teach, and reinforce the specific skills her student writers need to achieve proficiency. Simply stated, low-stakes writing gives teachers the opportunity to build in multiple "drafts" of each stage in the writing process and to tailor the timing and sequencing of these episodes according both to what her particular class of student writers might need (Penrose, 1993) and to what they are discovering and refining as they write their ways through various iterations of *focused* freewriting.

As Cohen (1990) notes, writing is "an activity that builds on itself. The context for writing ...[is] the text that has been created so far" (p. 107). Focused freewriting, by keeping the emphasis on the expression of ideas and the using of language to learn rather than to demonstrate learning, keeps the writing *in*-process and so helps all student writers – whether young, struggling, or even competent writers addressing a new complication or genre of writing – to keep moving forward from their initial ideas. Research suggests that focused freewriting activities can show demonstrable growth between the initial drafts of a writing project and the final writing products (Li, 2007). The regular iterations of focused freewriting allow the teacher multiple opportunities to encourage or redirect her student writers along the way, instead of having to wait for revised drafts that offer both too much (because of the length of a typical assignment) and too little (because of the time between drafting and receiving feedback) chance to give instructive directions. And because it is still "free" of penalty for the inevitable errors or mis-directions of draft writing, focused freewriting is conducive to student writers forgetting for some moments about "being correct." They become more apt to derive meaning from significant details when encouraged to think about the deeper meanings of text (Morse, 2000), whether the text is the one being studied or the one they are creating as they write. Focusing instead on what they think they want to say or ask about or explore, student writers can access and sustain those elements most characteristic of professional writing but often so absent from school writing – the liveliness and voice of personal style.

Focused freewriting thus allows a teacher to keep what student writers say more important than how they say it long enough for them to pay attention to and grow interest in what they think they are saying while they attempt to figure out how to say it "better," whether more clearly, more fully, or more in line with the criteria on which they will eventually be judged. Johnston (2012) posits that "The purpose of feedback is to improve conceptual understanding or increase strategic options while developing stamina, resilience, and motivation – expanding the vision of what is possible and how to get there" (p. 48). Moreover, Li (2007) contends that when the students feel they are encouraged and supported, have a sense of purpose and direction, they will have more confidence in writing, and they will find their writing tasks easier to complete. By directing the purpose of each writing task, the teacher can set a clear intention for the writing. Instead of, for instance, providing a formula that student writers should follow in building a paragraph or an outline, teachers can provide student writers with structure by directing each subsequent focused freewriting task according to what the teacher deems important for her student writers' progress. The teacher's (or peer's) responsive, non-evaluative feedback on such purpose-specific writing tasks becomes situated in the intentional learning context, which is more important than the "quality" or "readiness" of the writing itself while the student writer is still learning how to grow his competencies.

As Emig (1977) notes, "One writes best as one learns best, at one's own pace" (p. 126). When writing tasks have specific, iterative, and sequential purposes that guide student writers' thinking and therefore learning, whether learning more about the topic or about how to say what they think they mean to say, writing will improve over time (Calkins, 2015). A teacher's focus while writing directive feedback is short term (what is the purpose of this paragraph, or this attempt at revision?) while her perspective is long term (what is the instructional purpose of the project? where is the student writer on the spectrum of improvement toward mastery of criteria by which he will be judged?). Within the larger goal of improved writing, a teacher can establish fluency, complexity, coherence — any of the criteria typically used to judge academic writing — as separate purposes for each focused freewriting, keeping in mind how each will fit into the larger writing project but communicating with her student writers in terms of their own words and ideas and needs.

Newell (2006) suggests that "different tasks focus the writer's attention in specific ways" (p. 238) — with specific goals, teachers are more likely to identify (and students more likely to identify with) separate and specific experiences of success in each writing task, experiences that student writers need if they are going to continue to invest in their own language development. When each focused freewriting assignment is task-oriented and aligned with a stated purpose, the teacher also has a means of ensuring that she is not simply giving easy grades for easy effort. The stakes may be low, but the intention is not. When low-stakes tasks have a stated, discrete purpose, the grade shifts from a mark that simply means "did you do it?" to a more intentional "did you do it according to the goals of the particular assignment?" So while the recorded grade may be a simple check mark, the feedback can address the specific "how" and "why" of the assignment's stated intention. The teacher thus guides her student writers with mini-purposes that help them conceptualize why they are doing each step: reread for what? Find what in this paragraph? Change what in my writing? Make connections how? Lengthen or shorten sentences why? Add details when? Reduce wordiness how? Repeat which words? Rethink my plan and change the order of which paragraphs? Find the right word for which idea? Adjust my style how? She teaches the elements of rhetoric and style and formal conventions by specifying the different choices writers have — what kind of details? What kind of elaboration? What mix of sentence lengths? Which rhetorical strategies? — and as student writers try out specific elements of style, they learn what fits their ideas, expanding both their sense of language and their understanding of content.

Directive, responsive feedback makes the on-going in-process exchange both purposeful and generative of continued thought. And, as with most freewriting, these *low-stakes with a purpose* assignments can be completed in short bursts of time in class, where the consequences for not participating are immediate: any student writer who doesn't complete the task according to its purpose will be a step behind his classmates as the subsequent task begins, a consequence that is often more effective than a "0" for two reasons: one, a "0" suggests the student writer can relinquish responsibility for the assignment and "just take the '0'" instead of continuing to apply himself; and two, seeing one's classmates discussing and making changes to their writing can spur a student writer to do what he needs to so he can join them. Additionally, by conducting a series of focused freewrites in class, with multiple short bursts of task-specific writing, the teacher can create opportunities for multiple points of feedback, whether from the teacher or the students themselves. Student writers thus can learn how to account both to and for each other as they engage in reading and talking about what they have written. The teacher circulates around the room during each short burst of writing and reviewing, taking advantage of multiple opportunities to read over shoulders, redirect, write brief responses, and otherwise support her student writers as they are engaged in using language to construct meaning. Because they have been guided by a specific purpose each time they write and review each other's writing, they become more and more adept at identifying and finding ways around obstacles on their own, with the possibility to direct problems to the teacher's attention when they can't solve the problem themselves.

INVITING IMPROVEMENT THROUGH ON-GOING CONVERSATIONS ON PAPER

By making the student writer's in-process text the content of the conversation, the teacher does not abnegate her role as evaluator but instead privileges her role as trusted ally, using a tone that invites further reflection or elaboration by the student writer. Conversation means on-going communication, starting with a student writer's first explorations and continuing via the teacher's replies, supplemented by mini- impromptu conferences or other brief oral exchanges, which then lead to further exploration and discovery of ideas, understanding, and points of view. The conversation on paper with a student writer need not even be primarily academic, as often questions about a student writer's experience or feelings about the content can help him identify the thought he may be falling just short of clearly expressing. The student writer is continually being prompted to further thought and to ask himself "what do I want to say? What do I want others to know or think? how will I lead others to follow my thoughts so that they come to the same conclusions?"

As the teacher writes her individual replies, whether in the margins of a student writer's draft or as a direct response to a chunk of freewriting, she can restrict the focus of her comments to one or two specific criteria. Even as the teacher attunes her replies more and more to particulars of style, audience, and performance criteria, she keeps the conversation open, giving specific prompts in the form of questions or suggestions so the student writer will know how to use the feedback to continue to move forward. As long as the writing is still considered in-process, as long as it has yet to be marked with an evaluative comment or grade, the teacher can direct her student writer to continue along a path she has discerned he needs to follow. Something as simple as "pick three of my marginal comments to respond to, either in question form or additional text in your writing" can address the student writer's need for continued purpose and instruction for next steps while it allows the teacher to direct as a whole a class of student writers with a variety of language competencies.

By thus encouraging her student writers to participate in sustained in-process writing without categorizing the writing as deficient in some way, low-stakes focused freewriting offers a means for a teacher, a peer, and even the student writer himself, to hear his voice, see his difficulties, and help him find possible ways around or through an obstacle of thought, language, or meaning construction. The conversation on paper becomes a record of speech and thought as they take place, remaining available for reference throughout the entire writing project to stimulate additional questions, ideas, and alternatives of language, or to serve as a reminder of earlier thinking that can once again be incorporated. What is most difficult about such conversation is what also makes it so valuable: it is very often "live," happening almost simultaneously sometimes, as when a teacher reads a student writer's paragraph while at his elbow, just after he has finished it and has perhaps surprised himself with his own words. If the teacher's foremost goal in any given exchange with a student writer is not to evaluate but to engage the student in the development of his language, she may not be prepared for the particular surprises in a student writer's paper, but she will at least be prepared for the fact that she may be surprised. The comfort of control via formats and formulas in directing writing progress is replaced by a mix of original if sometimes inchoate writing with "live" oral feedback in class and/or written feedback returned on a following day, both of which contribute to an authentic and responsive conversation that supports the student writer's creation or construction of meaning.

What is most important for developing student writers (struggling, reluctant, and even fairly proficient writers) is that the teacher finds ways to acknowledge and support the individual student writer's in-process writing while she directs or re-directs him so that he may improve. Via her choice to use purposeful low-stakes writings in a way that facilitates conversations on paper, a teacher can keep in the foreground the particular voice, style, and ideas that her student writer expresses in the "free" in-process writing and direct the student writer's continued focus and intellectual growth through the specific sequence of her responses. Whether a teacher focuses on fluency, coherence, logic, figurative language, or the use of abstractions or concrete details, she develops the thinking and language use a student writer might make by setting mini-purposes according to the particulars of the writing project. Minor surface errors can be quietly addressed in asides when need be, remaining, however, subordinate to the progression and coherence of a student writer's ideas; questions can help the student writer recognize what he thinks is on the page but in fact isn't, offering even a reticent student a way to continue explaining what he means; and particular phrases that carry original rhythms and emphatic evidence of voice or style can be highlighted to lend the student writer either confidence or interest in his own use of language. Using low-stakes writing, a teacher can instill in her student writer an experience of personal value, interest, and perhaps even trust in his own writing process, encouraging him to value his own writing enough to invest the time and attention he needs to make it more closely approximate his ideas about himself and his world as he deepens his ability to understand and articulate what those ideas are in the form a particular writing project requires. The teacher's foremost goal is to invite and support the student writer as a learner, one who needs time and room to fall short of this mark or another without being penalized so he can continue trying until the desired improvement is made.

REFERENCES

Barnes, D. (1976). *From communication to curriculum.* Harmondsworth,: Penguin.
Britton, J. N. (1970). *Language and learning.* London: Penguin.
Britton, J. N. (1978, May). I'm listening. *The Journal/Le Journal,* 33–36.
Britton, J. N. (1987). *Writing and reading in the classroom.* Berkeley, CA: Center for the Study of Writing, University of California, Berkeley.
Calkins, L. (2015). *Writing pathways: Performance assessments and learning progressions, grades K-8.* Portsmouth, NH: Heinemann.
Cohen, A. D. (1990). *Language learning: Insights for learners, teachers, and researchers.* Boston, MA: Heinle & Heinle.
Culham, R. (2003). *6 + 1 traits of writing: The complete guide, grades 3 and up.* New York, NY: Scholastic Professional Books.
Durst, R. K. (2015). British invasion: James Britton, composition studies, and anti-disciplinarity. *College Composition and Communication, 66*(3), 384–401.
Elbow, P. (2000). *Everyone can write: Essays toward a hopeful theory of writing and teaching writing.* New York, NY: Oxford University Press.
Emig, J. (1977). Writing as a mode of learning. *College Composition and Communication, 28*(2), 122–128.
Fishman, S. M. (1997). Student writing in philosophy: A sketch of five techniques. In M. D. Sorcinelli & P. Elbow (Eds.), *Writing to learn: Strategies for assigning and responding to writing across the disciplines* (Vol. 69, pp. 53–66). New Directions for Teaching and Learning. San Francisco, CA: Jossey-Bass.
Johnston, P. H. (2012). *Opening minds: Using language to change lives.* Portland, ME: Stenhouse.
Li, L. Y. (2007). Exploring the use of focused freewriting in developing academic writing. *Journal of University Teaching and Learning Practice, 4*(1), 40–53.
Moje, E. B. (1996). "I teach students, not subjects": Teacher-student relationships as contexts for secondary literacy. *Reading Research Quarterly, 31*(2), 172–195.
Morse, O. (2000). Access to excellence participant's manual. In *Building success: Advanced Placement Program, English and history.* New York, NY: College Entrance Examination Board.
Newell, G. E. (2006). Writing to learn: How alternative theories of school writing account for student performance. In C. A. MacArthur, S. Graham, & J. Fitzgerald (Eds.), *Handbook of writing research* (pp. 235–247). New York City, NY: Guilford.
Penrose, A. M. (1993). Writing and learning: Exploring the consequences of task interpretation. In A. M. Penrose & B. M. Sitko (Eds.), *Hearing ourselves think: Cognitive research in the college writing classroom* (pp. 52–69). New York, NY: Oxford University Press.
Pradl, G. M. (2004). Nancy Martin and James Britton: The language work of democratic learning. *Language Arts, 81*(6), 520–525.
Radcliffe, B. J. (2012). Narrative as a springboard for expository and persuasive writing: James Moffett revisited. *Voices form the Middle, 19*(3), 18–24.
Rosenwasser, D., & Stephen, J. (2015). *Writing analytically.* Stamford, CT: Cengage Learning.

LEARNING LANGUAGE AND VOCABULARY IN DIALOGUE WITH THE REAL AUDIENCE: EXPLORING YOUNG WRITERS' AUTHENTIC WRITING AND LANGUAGE LEARNING EXPERIENCES

Ewa McGrail, J. Patrick McGrail and Alicja Rieger

ABSTRACT

Purpose — *To explore the potential of conversations with an authentic audience through blogging for enriching in young writers the understanding of the* communicative *function of writing, specifically language and vocabulary use.*

Design/methodology/approach — *We situate our work in the language acquisition model of language learning, in which learners develop linguistic competence in the process of speaking and using language (Krashen, 1988; Tomasello, 2005). We also believe that language learning benefits from formal instruction (Krashen, 1988). As such, in our work, we likened engaging in blogging to learning a language (here, more broadly conceived as learning to write) through both natural communication (acquisition) and prescription (instruction), and we looked at these forms of learning in our study.*

We were interested in the communicative *function of language learning (Halliday, 1973; 1975; Penrod, 2005) among young blog writers, because we see language learning as socially constructed through interaction with other speakers of a language (Tomasello, 2005; Vygotsky, 1978).*

Findings — *The readers and commenters in this study supported young writers in their language study by modeling good writing and effective language use in their communication with these writers. Young writers also benefited from direct instruction through interactions with adults beyond classroom teachers, in our case some of the readers and commenters.*

Practical implications — *Blogging can extend conversations to audiences far beyond the classroom and make writing a more authentic endeavor for young writers. Teachers should take advantage of such a powerful tool in their writing classrooms to support their students' language study and vocabulary development.*

Keywords: Blogging; language study; vocabulary development; young writers; writing

INTRODUCTION

Language study and vocabulary development are essential components of learning to read and write (Calkins, 1994; Kirby, Kirby, & Liner, 2004). The vivid use of language and vocabulary makes writing insightful and compelling, and communication becomes effective and intentional. In contrast, poor grammar, word choice, and punctuation interfere with communication; a weak vocabulary in particular negatively impacts reading comprehension (Graves, 2000). Incorrect word choice can be embarrassing for the writer, while the use of vague or bland words may bore the reader. Simply put, language and vocabulary matter (Bruffee, 1984; Dunn & Lindblom, 2011; Elbow, 1998). Successful writers know this. They use language and words carefully and they enjoy studying language and vocabulary rules and proper usage (Dunn & Lindblom, 2011; Kittle, 2008).

Young writers, however, find grammar and vocabulary difficult to learn and enjoy (Andrews & Smith, 2011; Weaver, 1998). They also find the study of these skills of little value and application to life (Gilbert & Graham, 2010). This is because they often learn language and vocabulary in a mechanistic or automated way through "fill in the gaps" or multiple choice activities. Freeman and Freeman (2004) agreed with this sentiment when they captured the state of language instruction in schools in these words:

> [E]ven though language is a fascinating topic, the only exposure many students get to language study during their elementary and secondary years is worksheets and exercises that bore them to tears and serve little practical purpose in improving their reading and writing. (p. xi)

Students thus learn grammar and vocabulary in abstraction, that is, in isolation from the communicative context and purpose for which these tools are intended (Applebee & Langer, 2011; Gilbert & Graham, 2010; Weaver, 1998). Research has found, however, that such abstract instruction is usually ineffective, having little effect on the quality of student writing (Graham, Harris, & Santangelo, 2015). In response to this situation, Freeman and Freeman (2004) suggest that "what students need is a new approach" (p. xi) to language study.

We contend that teaching young writers strong language use and enhanced vocabulary implementation through dialogue with actual readers of student writing on blogs is an innovative approach to language study that can change this undesirable state of affairs. Accordingly, this chapter demonstrates the potential of writer–reader conversations for enriching in the young writer the understanding of the *communicative* function of writing, specifically language and vocabulary use. Our chapter draws from a year-long study of fifth-graders writing for and with an authentic audience, that is, the readers of their blog posts. The chapter concludes with practical recommendations for enhancing authentic writing and language learning experiences in the classroom.

LITERATURE REVIEW

Much of the literature that we reviewed concerning language study among young writers focused on morphological awareness and vocabulary skills. We synthesize the key findings from this literature here and make connections to our study.

Morphological Awareness

Morphological awareness refers to children's ability to recognize the structural morphemes or functional constitutive parts of words, and manipulate them to create fresh composition (Kirby et al., 2012). An example might be that of a child who intuitively recognizes what the word *playful* means, even if she has never encountered the word in that exact form. She "back-intuits" that it must describe, as indeed it does, something that is "full of play," as she recognizes the word "play", and the morpheme "ful" that is a shortened version of "full." Research has long suggested that explicit and direct instruction in morphological awareness can have positive effects of on improving student reading comprehensions skills, especially reading complex texts, advancing their spelling and vocabulary development, as well as enhancing the quality of their writing skills (Goodwin & Ahn, 2010; Kieffer & Lesaux, 2010, 2012; Kuo & Anderson, 2006; Pacheco & Goodwin, 2013).

Some scholars argue, however, that "most language learning happens naturally, without conscious effort" (Carlisle, 2010, p. 465) and that "[m]orphological awareness develops gradually, as students come to understand complex relations of form and meaning" (Carlisle, 2010, p. 466). These scholars question the need for and effectiveness of explicit and direct instruction in morphological awareness. For instance, Carlo et al. (2004) examined the effectiveness of a 15-week intervention that consisted of the use of direct instruction while teaching words and specific word learning strategies with a morphology awareness element. They discovered "only marginally significantly differential gains" (p. 196) for both English language learners and their native English-speaking peers. However, Kirby et al. (2012) found that "morphological awareness was a significant predictor of word reading accuracy and speed, pseudoword reading accuracy, text reading speed, and reading comprehension" in children from grades 1 through 3 (p. 389).

Vocabulary Development

With regard to vocabulary development, research provides strong support for explicit and systematic approaches to teaching vocabulary skills (Beck, Perfetti, & McKeown, 1982; Kame'enui, Carnine, & Freschi, 1982). For instance, Marulis and Neuman (2010), in their meta-analysis of 67 studies for the impact of direct instruction on acquisition of vocabulary skills, reported significant gains on vocabulary measures (an effect size of .88). Explanation of words and providing examples were found particularly effective forms of explicit vocabulary instruction. At the same time, research offers evidence in support of informal approaches to teaching vocabulary in the classroom as well. This is because as Seipel (2011) proposes, "a substantial amount of vocabulary is learned incidentally from context" and that informal instruction "is able to fill the instructional void left by inadequate time in classrooms for explicit vocabulary instruction" (p. 7).

In summary, while the findings acknowledge the positive role of formal and direct instruction, they also suggest substantial benefits of informal and non-traditional approaches as well. We also note that despite the benefits of traditional approaches to language study, young writers find that learning grammar and vocabulary out of context and through repetition is uninteresting (Andrews & Smith, 2011; Weaver, 1998) (Applebee & Langer, 2011; Gilbert & Graham, 2010; Weaver, 1998). Our study among fifth-graders explored the potential of blogging when it was done with an authentic purpose and with real audiences.

METHODOLOGY

Conceptual Framework

We draw on multiple perspectives to inform our work, broadly situating it in the language acquisition model of language learning, in which learners develop linguistic competence in the process of speaking and using language (Krashen, 1988; Tomasello, 2005). According to the language acquisition theory, language learning involves acquiring knowledge of language as a system, with subsystems such as phonology, morphology, syntax, semantics, and pragmatics (Krashen, 1988; Tomasello, 2005). Speakers of a language use "the full range of the subsystems" when they speak or write (Harmon & Wilson, 2006, p. 12). While the language learning process is aided by what Chomsky (1965) referred to as the language acquisition device (LAD), activated through exposure to language amid a rich linguistic context, it is also benefited by formal instruction (Krashen, 1988). In other words, rich language learning is composed of both conscious and unconscious knowledge attainment, that is, acquisition through natural communication and learning through prescriptive instruction.

Blogging with an authentic audience serves as a rich linguistic learning context, as it provides young writers with opportunities to observe language use in the context of writing produced by "expert" writers (readers and commenters). In addition, the feedback that young blog writers receive from their readers and commenters in response to their writing is a form of instruction itself about various aspects of their language and vocabulary use (e.g., grammar, syntax, and word choice) and the communicative effectiveness of these choices. As such, in our work, we likened engaging in blogging to learning a language (here, more broadly conceived as learning to write) through both natural communication (acquisition) and prescription (instruction).

We also view language learning as socially constructed, through interaction with other speakers of a language, particularly adults and more knowledgeable others (Tomasello, 2005; Vygotsky, 1978). It is through the social interaction with others that language users learn about the functions and uses of languages within specific discourses, disciplines, communities, and contexts (Gee, 1990). In addition, the socially constructed learning process in which they engage with other speakers helps young learners to understand and appreciate the relationships between language and intention, connotation and denotation, as well as overt and covert meanings (Harmon & Wilson, 2006). This is because speakers and writers make their choice of syntax and words, and use other simultaneous semiotic means of representation, such as signs, images, or symbols, to enable them to accomplish specific rhetorical goals (Ede & Lunsford, 1984; Lunsford & Ede, 2009). Given this understanding of language learning in our work, we were interested in the *communicative* function of language learning (Halliday, 1973, 1975; Penrod, 2005) among young blog writers.

Data Collection

The data set for this study consisted of elementary student writing generated in a year-long blogging project in a fifth-grade language arts classroom in a Title I school, and their readers' comments and responses, for a total of 659 single-spaced pages of blog scripts. The blog writing the students produced included personal narratives, in which students chose topics to describe themselves and their interests to their readers; persuasive writing, in which students were asked to write convincingly about a subject about which they themselves felt a conviction; and research reports, where students shared with their audiences the readings in content areas that were of particular interest to them. Much of this writing, however, consisted of "free writes" and quick posts that either invited responses from readers or that responded to comments they had received from audience members. The audience of readers came from many walks of life and parts of the world and frequently conversed textually with these young writers.

At the start of the project, we solicited audience members from the national and international educational and blogging professional communities to which we belonged. These audience members were contacted because they either maintained classroom blogs or posted regularly on educational blogs. Many retired teachers and other teachers to whom we introduced the project and explained its educational goals volunteered to read and comment on the students blogs. We also recruited graduate students enrolled in teacher education programs at our institutions. We explained the goals of the blogging project and we asked the readers and commenters to assist young writers in developing critical thinking and writing skills. Other respondents and commenters were simply members of the world audience at large who joined the existing conversations. We had a system in place allowing us to monitor incoming comments from readers and block inappropriate comments or commenters from posting on student blogs, if needed.

The teacher maintained a class blog that introduced students to blogging and its conventions, and included strategies and advice on how to develop and sustain dialogue in posts and comments, how to ask and answer questions, and how to develop one's voice in students' writing. Student blog writers were also mentored about internet ethics, that is, how to communicate in respectful and responsible ways with these larger audiences and how to employ public writing conventions, such as giving credit to others' words and not revealing personally identifying information. The class blog also provided topics for future conversations and communication with readers and commenters.

The student writers we studied were a group of ten girls and five boys – nine Caucasians, five Hispanics, and one African-American. Two students were in the gifted program and one was in the special education program. All students were new to blogging and needed to work on critical thinking and writing skills. The group reflected the school student population's ethnic and socioeconomic backgrounds, with 81% considered economically disadvantaged, based on student participation in the free or reduced lunch program. (This information was obtained from the school website.)

Data Analysis and Limitations

We employed a qualitative content analysis method (Creswell, 2007) to develop a coding scheme that included open and axial coding (Corbin & Strauss, 2008). This helped us to explore patterns in the data about vocabulary development and various aspects of language study in student writing. These patterns included categories such as inquiries about language and vocabulary use; spelling, grammar, and punctuation interventions; strategies for engaged writing; teaching new vocabulary; modeling language use; and cultural and idiosyncratic differences in language and vocabulary applications. The acquisition model of language learning (Krashen, 1988; Tomasello, 2005) and the socio-cultural perspective on the meaning making process (Tomasello, 2005; Vygotsky, 1978) informed the analysis and description of the findings reported in this work. The data were analyzed iteratively by the lead author and in consultation with the other authors, who provided an audit check (Creswell, 2007) for the initial analysis. This collective data analysis process resulted in adjustments made to the open and axial coding and led to reduction of the coding categories to two themes reported in the findings. The first finding focused on vocabulary development and the other on key aspects of language study.

Although there is much that can be gleaned from the blog writing of these young writers and about their individual and collective language learning and vocabulary development experiences, there is a limit to what can be learned from written product analysis (Dalton & Smith, 2014). Future studies should engage young writers in other forms of reflection and meta-analysis of their own writing to access the student writer perspectives on their language study learning experiences.

FINDINGS

Learning Vocabulary and Language Use through Immersion/Acquisition

The student bloggers in this study were exposed to good writing and had numerous opportunities to observe and be immersed in effective language use by experienced writers. For example, in the following response to blogger Michael's[1] story about Yoshi (a character in his fictional story), his commenter used a new word, "aghast," to describe her reaction to

Michael's unusual choice of the phrase "concentration camp" for his story about a learning camp. Michael's story began with these words, "My post today is about Yoshi. They go to a learning camp called concentration camp. They learn school stuff and they learn about Yoshi stuff ...":

> Hi Michael,
>
> When I first read your post I was aghast! I immediately thought of one definition of concentration when you said a learning camp was a concentration camp. Then I got to thinking and realized maybe Yoshi's meaning was different from what I first thought.
>
> Can you tell me what meaning concentration has when it's used for Yoshi's learning camp? Can you imagine why I might have been aghast?...
>
> Best,
>
> Lena

Another commenter, who also wondered about the unusual use of this phrase, provided a clue to the meaning of the word "aghast" in the question she posed to Michael: "Can you find out why I was startled by your reference to a concentration camp?"

Alternatively, Chara modeled for Anni how to pull in the reader with an engaging introduction to the story:

> Have you thought of starting your story more dramatically? Something like "Isabelle had always dreamed of climbing Cir Mhor [that's the name of the left-hand mountain]. Today, at last, she was on her way. The mud squelched beneath her feet and water trickled into her boots, but she didn't care." That's how I feel in that particular glen – it's like a muddy paradise as far as I'm concerned!

Dulce Maria, in turn, received this sophisticated response, which introduced her to complex syntax and specialized vocabulary concerning a tree saving call she made to the readers and commenters on her blog:

> Hi Dulce Maria,
>
> Reading your comment, I kept thinking of the Amazons, the so-called lungs of our planet, which are threatened by an incessant deforestation campaign by some "strong" corporations. I do agree with you that the consequences of cutting threes without replacing them will cost us not only changes in ways/quality of living, but also have us live a future without animals. I can't agree more with your ideas and the urgent need we have to take action soon. I was just wondering what actions could each of us take to raise others' attention to this problem. Most people are too busy to be thining of a future without trees and animals; they have to be reminded of the need to stop cutting trees and start using alternatives. Do you have any ideas for action?...
>
> Omer

Another blogger, Eddie, was introduced to phi, a complex mathematical concept, by his commenter, a high school math teacher. The teacher even offered an exercise for Eddie so that he could try out the application of the concept to real-life situations, such as in how to measure the distance between certain body parts:

> There's another special number called "e" and another one called phi (like "fly" without the "l").
>
> Phi is approximately 1.618 which seems weird I know, but it gets weirder. If you measure your height and then the distance from the ground to your belly button, then divide your height by the belly button distance it's going to be pretty close to 1.618.
>
> Measure the length of your arm (shoulder to finger tips), then measure from your elbow to your fingertips. Divide the long length by the short one ... you'll get 1.618 (Phi) again.

In addition, the commenters and readers often modeled for our young writers the use of colorful language, rich descriptions, and engaging dialogue in their own writing, as evident in this sample of prose by Victoria's commenter, who responded to Victoria's call to the readers to tell their own stories in support of wildlife, especially polar bears:

> Hi Victoria,
>
> This post made me think about another story I read in the news the other day.
>
> A 6-year-old, towheaded neighbor, George, came screaming through the front door of this lady's house. "The polar bear is getting extinct," he yelled. "It's global warming. It's killing them."
>
> The lady telling the story said her children had been talking about how the melting Arctic ice cap is reducing the bears' hunting ground, and attempts at swimming to catch seals have only led to increased drowning. Deaths are up, and the main culprit, say experts, is global warming.
>
> This lady's son told the six-year old neighbor "That's why we're getting our new car," my 6-year-old son explained to George, his best friend. "To save the polar bear."
>
> This is how the lady explained her son's reasoning: "As counterintuitive as it sounded, my son's statement was true. Global warming was the main factor in deciding to buy a fuel-efficient car when we traded in our minivan this holiday. For our children, that translated into helping the polar bear."...
>
> Mrs. C

Learning Vocabulary and Language Use through Instruction

Learning about vocabulary and language use among young writers in this study was also supported with direct instruction. Direct instruction was provided by readers and commenters and it concerned various aspects of language use and vocabulary development. Specifically, readers and commenters introduced student bloggers to new vocabulary. Providing a definition, synonym, illustration, or paraphrase were the most frequent strategies that the commenters employed to accomplish this goal. For example, Cordelia introduced Anni to two new verbs, to persuade and to eliminate [in bold], in her response to Anni's post urging schools to allow water fountains on their premises. Cordelia also was brainstorming with her the ways in which she could bring her proposal to fruition:

> What a fabulous idea! I had never even thought about having a water fountain right there on the playground. That would solve so many problems. You stated your reasons in a very organized and persuasive way. (**Persuasive means you are trying to get someone else to agree with you.**) It is obvious you had thought this out before posting .... So, you could add to your very good points about thirst and good health that an outside water fountain would also eliminate (**get rid of**) hallway misbehavior.
>
> Has your principal read your opinion on a playground water fountain? Do you think he/she would agree? Have you thought about making an appointment with the principal and presenting your persuasive speech? Think about it. Students often bring about the best changes. If you don't, who will?

A commenter from Australia, on the other hand, taught Anni not only another word for water fountains (bubblers) but also explained that the rules concerning the use of water fountains can vary across different contexts and different climates:

> In Queensland, Australia where I teach and went to school, water fountains (bubblers) are an essential! Each school has rows of bubblers outside for student use. It gets so hot here and much of our time is spent outdoors that i needed to be reminded by your entry that not all schools have the same needs. Children are strongly encouraged to drink water often at school (in and out of the classroom). I taught in Canada for a year in 1999 and was really surprised by how little water people consumed there in a day. Of course the difference in climate impacts on this.

Alternatively, the readers and commenters probed young writers' about the use of vocabulary in their own writing. To illustrate, in this post, the commenter wanted Johnny to clarify the meaning of "Runescape": "I am a little confused about what Runescape is" and she wondered if rewriting the passage with the confusing content could help: "Do you think you could maybe think about how you have written the middle part of this and see if you can make it any clearer? Then maybe I'd understand better." Although Johnny was willing to provide an explanation "Runescape is just a online game that teaches you normal skills," he did not feel a rewrite was necessary.

In addition, the readers and commenters encouraged young writers to use descriptive language and to elaborate on their ideas. For example, one commenter asked Mia to explain why she chose the adjective "peace" to describe a picture with a snowed-in house in it. Mia was happy to provide this explanation:

> I chose peace because when first you look at it. It looks white, calm, and like you will like to really want to play on it. But if you think about it and look at it again you might think of more adjectives.

In yet another example, Cordelia posed this question to Michael, a student blogger who had written an amusing story about his dog, named Sparky: "Don't you just love those sad "please pet me" eyes of a lab?" Michael was happy to supply the answer and elaborate on it as well: "My dog does the please pet me eyes to and when I am on the computer she sticks her head through the armrest and pushes my arm on her head."

Many comments focused on various aspects of language use in student blog writing, including grammar, punctuation, or spelling. For example, this commenter was helping Anni to see the difference in meaning between "their" and "there," the two words she used in her post about a family camping trip which she entitled "Mountain Sight":

> I like the ending of your story! I think there are some mistakes you can find by proofreading your paper out loud. Also, figure out the difference between homophones so you know you are using the right one. For example, there and their are different words. Can you tell me when you would use each one?

Anni did her homework and offered this explanation in response to her commenter, "You would use their when it belongs to someone and you would use there when it is talking about some where." Cordelia, on the other hand, offered this advice to Rosalinda on the meaning, spelling and pronunciation of a word she needed to describe one of her family members in her post, "Sister in Sight:"

> How very exciting! It sounds like you had TWO wonderful things come your way – a visit from your sister and a chance to be with your nephew Jonathon! A nephew is what you call your brother or sister's son. A niece is what you call your brother or sister's daughter. So, you would say that Jonathon is your nephew (pronounced like "nefew"). The "ph" makes the "f" sound.

Another commenter encouraged Mary to adopt a different approach to creating the mood in her story than through the use of the exclamation mark, "Can I suggest that instead of using multiple exclamation marks you use your language skills (which are considerable) to create the tone of voice implied?" Mary accepted the challenge and promised to take it into consideration in her future stories: "I will take your advice and stop using so many exclamation marks." Alternatively, Lena, another commenter, tried to convince Johnny that spelling matters when she challenged his spelling of his favorite instrument [gautier] in the post he entitled "What are you passionate about":

> Hi Jhonny,
>
> You really are passionate about music! It comes through when you describe all you do with music and your guitar. I agree hard work comes with passion but don't you feel great when you look at all you accomplish?
>
> One question: I wonder if you might want to check the spelling of guitar. Shouldn't a man such as yourself with such a passion for his instrument spell it correctly?
>
> Best,
>
> Lena

Although Johnny agreed with Lena, he admitted that he found the word difficult to spell, in his playful reply back to Lena: "I know but i always get it mixed up with the spelling of my instrument. But i can play it does that matter better then the spelling it?" Victoria, another, student blogger, too learned about the importance of punctuation when she received this response to her post "What is our main resources," because it was missing a full stop:

> Something that makes our writing clear is our use of punctuation. Can you see places in this post where you have run sentences together? Look at your very first sentence and see if you can spot where there should be a full stop. Then you can check the rest of the post. I'm very, very fussy about punctuation because I like clarity in writing!

DISCUSSION AND IMPLICATIONS

Learning Vocabulary and Blogging

Learning vocabulary requires seeing and using new words in rich contexts (Marulis & Neuman, 2010; Stahl & Fairbanks, 1986). Analogous to learning new words through reading, students need to be provided with opportunities to apply words to new contexts, including their own writing (Carter & Evensen, 2011). As evident in this work, blogging provided such opportunities, both when students wrote about the aspects of their learning that involved new concepts and when they invited the use of new terminology to describe their learning. Readers introduced bloggers to new ideas and specialized vocabulary.

As students blogged about ideas that were interesting to them individually, they became more deeply involved in the processing and learning of the attendant words (Stahl & Fairbanks, 1986). More importantly, they often received feedback from their readers and commenters, confirming the correctness of, or signaling the issue with their usage and indicating how to fix it. The process itself served as "new instruction, rather than informing the student solely about correctness" (Kulhavy, 1977, p. 212). Vocabulary development through blogging in our work with the young writers thus depended on active and contextualized engagement with new words (Padak, Newton, Rasinki, & Newton, 2008).

Young writers also benefited from learning through their interactions with adults beyond classroom teachers, in this case some of the older readers and commenters. Specifically, these commenters, about whom we knew little (because they were an unselected "real world" group) appeared to be a combination of undergraduate and graduate students, teachers and retired teachers, based on their limited self-description. They often asked for clarification of specific words in the students' writing or introduced them to new vocabulary in their comments and responses. Because they were from different countries, they also educated the young writers about the difference in word choice and usage across cultures and linguistic contexts. As such, the young writers were learning vocabulary in an ideal communicative context (Applebee & Langer, 2011; Gilbert & Graham, 2010; Weaver, 1998). More importantly, they had the opportunity to discover for themselves that there is more to vocabulary and usage than looking up new words in the dictionary to learn their meanings. The context of the word and the readers' background on the subject matter, too.

Language Study and Blogging

The readers and commenters in this study supported young writers in their language study by modeling good writing and effective language use in their communication with these writers. As such, their responses to student blogging served as exemplars for these young writers.

In light of genre theory, the writing samples served as "the functional model of language, revealing the way in which a particular culture manages to coordinate different and recurrent language resources to construct particular meanings that are valued within the specific cultural context" (Cao & Guo, 2015, p. 2613). These writing samples thus taught the young writers in this study about the communicative purpose and function of language and about the rhetorical tools and strategies that were available to them in support of their own rhetorical and communicative goals (Halliday, 1973, 1975; Penrod, 2005).

Such subtle and enriching goals have not always been sought after in contemporary American writing practice in schools. Recent studies have shown that the most frequent writing assignments involved completing worksheets and writing short responses, as opposed to writing for a real-life purpose and an authentic audience (Applebee & Langer, 2011; Gilbert & Graham, 2010). Our rich international blogging investigation has shown promise in overcoming some of these challenges by providing young writers with real world counterparts and sympathetic foreign English language practitioners with whom to negotiate meaning and structure.

Another way the readers and commenters supported young writers in improving their writing craft was through direct instruction on the matters of language use in their blog writing. As evident in our data, the purpose of such instruction was not merely to help the young writers fix language issues in their writing; most inexperienced writers experience problems such as run-ons, fragments, misused words, bland prose, poor grammar, punctuation, and spelling mistakes (Gilbert & Graham, 2010). Rather, it is to help them understand how these problems affect their readers and can interfere with comprehension (Graves, 2000). As a result of this greater awareness, they can begin to sense how such issues compromise the communicative power of the words and language they use in their writing.

Implications

Based on this work, we see several implications for teachers and their classroom practice. First, teachers should use student writing as the context for helping students build their vocabulary and practice language use. Second, students should be given the opportunity to write daily about what they are learning in content area classes, and not only in the language arts classroom. Content area readings and lessons expose students to the concepts and discourses unique to specific disciplines (e.g., deforestation or population increases, two topics that were explored by the student bloggers in our study). Opportunities to think and write about these and similar ideas will help young learners to study new concepts and acquire the vocabulary and syntax to describe them. The writing activities that are ideal for such explorations are report writing, "explaining to another" writing and "take a stand" writing.

Thirdly, teachers should engage student writers in genre analysis that will help them to learn about the linguistic and functional features of different genres of writing (e.g., persuasive argument vs. exposition). A part of such instruction should include teaching specialized vocabulary used in different genres to communicate ideas to readers. Teachers should conduct genre analysis in either a whole-class or small group discussion format, with the teacher serving as the leader or having students lead their peers to facilitate such analysis. Genre models and specialized vocabulary lists can come from the content area material students read in their other classes or from exemplar writing produced by teachers, or other writers and commenters. These latter stakeholders are experts in the subject matter and who can also show students how to write effectively using specialized terminology in the genres under analysis.

Bamford and Krisco's (2003) book, *Making facts come alive: Choosing and using nonfiction literature K-8* is a great resource that offers texts and activities that are ideal for reviewing with young writers. The book contains the key conventions, syntax, vocabulary, and visual display features in nonfiction genres on topics from across the content areas. The text also provides the learning tools to introduce young writers to discipline-based thinking and reasoning (Beck & Jeffery, 2009) characteristic of the writing produced by scientists, historians, and literary critics. It also has sections on discipline-based discourse (e.g., analytic exposition) which scholars use to express their disciplinary thinking. We believe that genre analysis and genre writing should be taught both in writing classes and across the curriculum to prepare young writers for the demands of academic writing and the common core curriculum requirements.

Finally — and perhaps most importantly — teachers should provide students with a real audience with which to engage in written conversations about their learning. The audience might be their immediate peers or peers in other classes at the same or another school, parents or even other community members. As illustrated in this work, blogging can extend conversations to audiences far beyond the classroom and make writing an authentic endeavor for young writers. Teachers should take advantage of such a powerful tool in their writing classrooms to support their students' language study and vocabulary development.

NOTE

1. We use pseudonyms for student bloggers and respondents in our data reporting. We also preserve the numerous idiosyncratic spellings of our young authors and their respondents.

REFERENCES

Andrews, R., & Smith, A. (2011). *Developing writers: Teaching and learning in the digital age*. New York, NY: Open University Press.

Applebee, A. N., & Langer, J. A. (2011). A snapshot of writing instruction in middle schools and high schools. *English Journal, 100*(6), 14–27.

Bamford, R. A., & Krisco, J. V. (2003). *Making facts come alive: Choosing and using nonfiction* literature K-8. Norwood, MA: Christopher Gordon Publishers.

Beck, I. L., Perfetti, C. A., & McKeown, M. G. (1982). Effects of text construction and instructional procedures for teaching word meanings on comprehension and recall. *Journal of Educational Psychology, 74*, 506–521.

Beck, S. W., & Jeffery, J. V. (2009). Genre and thinking in academic writing tasks. Journal of *Literacy Research, 41*, 228–272.

Bruffee, K. A. (1984). Collaborative learning and the "conversation of mankind". *College English, 46*(7), 635–652.

Calkins, L. M. (1994). *The art of teaching writing*. Portsmouth, NH: Heinemann.

Cao, C., & Guo, S. (2015). Genre analysis and advanced English teaching. Theory & Practice in *Language Studies, 5*(12), 2613–2618.

Carlisle, J. F. (2010). Effects of instruction in morphological awareness on literacy achievement: An integrative review. *Reading Research Quarterly, 45*(4), 464–487.

Carlo, M. S., August, D., McLaughlin, B., Snow, C. E., Dressler, C., Lippman, D. N., … White, C. E. (2004). Closing the gap: Addressing the vocabulary needs of English-language learners in bilingual and mainstream classrooms. *Reading Research Quarterly, 39*(2), 188–215.

Carter, J. B., & Evensen, E. A. (2011). *Super-powered word study*. Gainesville, FL: Maupin House Publishing.

Chomsky, N. (1965). *Aspects of the theory of syntax*. Cambridge, MA: MIT Press.

Corbin, J. M., & Strauss, A. L. (2008). *Basics of qualitative research: Grounded theory procedures and techniques* (3rd ed.). Los Angeles, CA: Sage.

Creswell, J. W. (2007). *Research design: Qualitative, quantitative, and mixed methods approaches* (3rd ed.). Thousand Oaks, CA: Sage.

Dalton, B., & Smith, B. E. (2014). Teachers' lesson design as remix: Composing with internet resources and a smart authoring tool. In R. E. Ferdig & K. E. Pytash (Eds.), *Exploring multimodal composition and digital writing* (pp. 116–134). Hersey, PA: IGI Global.

Dunn, P. A., & Lindblom, K. (2011). *Grammar rants: How a backstage tour of writing complaints can help students make informed, savvy choices about their writing.* Portsmouth, NH: Heinemann & Boyton/Cook.

Ede, L., & Lunsford, A. (1984). Audience addressed/audience invoked: The role of audience in composition theory and pedagogy. *College Composition and Communication, 35*(2), 155–171.

Elbow, P. (1998). *Writing with power: Techniques for mastering the writing process* (2nd ed). Oxford: Oxford University Press.

Freeman, D. E., & Freeman, Y. S. (2004). *Essential linguistics: What you need to know to teach reading, ESL, spelling, phonics, and grammar.* Portsmouth, NH: Heinemann.

Gee, J. P. (1990). *Social linguistics and literacies: Ideology in discourses: Critical perspectives on literacy and education.* London: Farmer Press.

Gilbert, J., & Graham, S. (2010). Teaching writing to elementary students in grades 4-6: A national survey. *The Elementary School Journal, 110*(4), 494–518.

Goodwin, A. P., & Ahn, S. (2010). A meta-analysis of morphological interventions: Effects on literacy achievement of children with literacy difficulties. *Annals of Dyslexia, 60*(2), 183–208. doi:10.1007/s11881-010-0041-x

Graham, S., Harris, K. R., & Santangelo, T. (2015). Research-based writing practices and the common core: Meta-analysis and meta-synthesis. *Elementary School Journal, 15*(4), 498–522.

Graves, M. (2000). A vocabulary program to complement and bolster a middle-grade comprehension program. In B. Taylor, M. Graves, & P. van den Broek (Eds.), *Reading for meaning: Fostering comprehension in the middle grades.* Newark, DE: International Reading Association.

Halliday, M. A. K. (1973). *Explorations in the functions of language.* London: Edward Arnold.

Halliday, M. A. K. (1975). *Learning how to mean.* London: Edward Arnold.

Harmon, M. R., & Wilson, M. J. (2006). *Beyond grammar: Language, power, and the classroom.* New York, NY: Routledge.

Kame'enui, E. J., Carnine, D. W., & Freschi, R. (1982). Effects of text construction and instructional procedures for teaching word meanings on comprehension and recall. *Reading Research Quarterly, 17,* 367–388.

Kieffer, M. J., & Lesaux, N. K. (2010). Morphing into adolescents: Active word learning for English-Language learners and their classmates in middle school. *Journal of Adolescent & Adult Literacy, 54*(1), 47–56.

Kieffer, M. J., & Lesaux, N. K. (2012). Effects of academic language instruction on relational and syntactic aspects of morphological awareness for sixth graders from linguistically diverse backgrounds. *The Elementary School Journal, 112*(3), 519–545.

Kirby, D., Kirby, D. L., & Liner, T. (2004). *Inside out: Strategies for teaching writing* (3rd ed.). Portsmouth, NH: Heinemann.

Kirby, J. R., Deacon, S. H., Bowers, P. N., Izenberg, L., Wade-Woolley, L., & Parilla, R. (2012). Children's morphological awareness and reading ability. *Reading and Writing, 25,* 389–410. doi:10.1007/s11145-010-9276-5

Kittle, P. (2008). *Write beside them: Risk, voice, and clarity in high school writing.* Portsmouth, NH: Heinemann.

Krashen, S. D. (1988). *Second language acquisition and second language learning.* Upper Saddle River, NJ: Prentice Hall.
Kulhavy, R. W. (1977). Feedback in written instruction. *Review of Educational Research, 47*(2), 211–232.
Kuo, L. J., & Anderson, R. C. (2006). Morphological awareness and learning to read: A cross-language perspective. *Educational Psychologist, 41*(3), 161–180.
Lunsford, A., & Ede, L. (2009). Among the audience: On audience in an age of new literacies. In M. E. Weiser, B. M. Fehler, & A. M. González (Eds.), *Engaging audience: Writing in an age of new literacies* (pp. 42–73). Urbana, IL: NCTE.
Marulis, L. M., & Neuman, S. B. (2010). The effects of vocabulary intervention on young children's word learning: A meta-analysis. *Review of Educational Research, 80*(3), 300–335.
Pacheco, M. B., & Goodwin, A. P. (2013). Putting two and two together: Middle school students' morphological problem-solving strategies for unknown words. *Journal of Adolescent & Adult Literacy, 56*(7), 541–553.
Padak, N., Newton, E., Rasinki, T., & Newton, R. M. (2008). Getting to the root of word study: Teaching Latin and Greek word roots in elementary and middle grades. In A. E. Farstrup & S. J. Samuels (Eds.), *What research has to say about vocabulary instruction* (pp. 6–31). Newark, DE: International Reading Association.
Penrod, D. (2005). *Composition in convergence: The impact of new media on writing assessment.* Mahwah, NJ: Lawrence Erlbaum.
Seipel, B. E. (2011). *The role of implicit learning in incidental vocabulary acquisition while reading.* Unpublished Dissertation, University of Minnesota, MN.
Stahl, S. A., & Fairbanks, M. M. (1986). The effects of vocabulary instruction. *Review of Educational Research, 56*(1), 72–110.
Tomasello, M. (2005). *Constructing a language: A usage-based theory of language acquisition.* Cambridge, MA: Harvard University Press.
Vygotsky, L. (1978). *Mind in society.* London: Harvard University Press.
Weaver, C. (Ed.). (1998). *Lessons to share on teaching grammar in context.* Portsmouth, NH: Heinemann.

UNDERSTANDING A DIGITAL WRITING CYCLE: BARRIERS, BRIDGES, AND OUTCOMES IN TWO SECOND-GRADE CLASSROOMS

Jessica S. Mitchell, Rachael F. Thompson, and Rebecca S. Anderson

ABSTRACT

Purpose — *To describe how the digital writing experiences of two collaborating second-grade classrooms are representative of a digital writing cycle that includes barriers, bridges, and outcomes. Additionally, this chapter aims to link theory and practice for teachers working with an increasingly younger generation of multimodal learners by connecting teacher reflections to New Literacies perspectives.*

Design/methodology/approach — *The current study is informed by multiple perspectives contributing to New Literacies research. These perspectives blend the traditional disciplines of literacy and technology while recognizing both the growing use of digital tools and the new skills and dispositions required for writing. This chapter uses multiple data points to present (1) how the teachers approached implementation of digital writing tools, (2) how students responded to the use of digital writing tools, and (3) how the digital-related writing experiences aligned with key tenets of New Literacies research.*

Findings — *The authors present student barriers for full participation with corresponding bridges implemented by teachers to help students navigate in the digital writing classroom. Each finding is supported with examples from student and teacher interviews as well as classroom observations and artifacts. The chapter concludes with a "lessons learned" section from the perspective of the teachers in the study with each tenet supporting a New Literacies perspective by addressing key considerations of multimodal environments such as the importance of early opportunities for teaching and learning with new literacies, the need to help inexperienced students bridge technical skill gaps, and the benefit of social relationships in the digital community.*

Practical implications — *By adapting findings of the study to a digital writing cycle, this chapter discusses how guiding principles of New Literacies research reflects classroom practice, thereby granting current and future teachers a practical guide for bridging theory and practice for implementing digital writing experiences for elementary students in multimodal environments.*

Keywords: New literacies theory; digital writing; multimodal learners

Meet Ms. Mason, a second-grade teacher for twenty years. Recently, she has noticed something different about her students. More and more, Ms. Mason observes excited conversations among her students who watch web-based videos on YouTube. When she discovers these videos, she is surprised to learn that children are the stars of their own channel with millions of viewers "tuning in" to watch. Ms. Mason wonders how these larger social practices are impacting students as writers in her classroom, especially when, although students appear to have outside access to streaming media, they appear to struggle when working with what she thinks should be "basic" technology skills in the computer lab at school. When experiencing these situations, Ms. Mason has even more questions about how to prepare students with foundational writing development in an increasingly digital society. These questions leave Ms. Mason wondering if she is missing an important piece in her curriculum – a piece that could help her students to circumvent barriers for positive outcomes in the digital writing classroom.

The above illustration demonstrates a potential challenge for teachers who are seeking ways to incorporate digital writing into their early writing curriculum. As students gain access to digital tools at increasingly younger ages, teachers can struggle with what counts as literacy and how best to prepare students for success in the 21st century. According to Rowe, Miller, and Pacheco (2014):

> To become effective twenty-first century communicators, children need early opportunities to explore ways of combining print, images, and other modalities to create interesting and effective digital texts. While young children are often offered opportunities to be consumers of electronic games and digital stories, we believe that it is also important to give them opportunities to be active designers of digital content. (p. 300)

In order to provide opportunities for students to practice 21st century communication skills, writing teachers must meet the challenge of guiding student learning in more complex environments than traditional print (Leu, Kinzer, Coiro, Castek, & Henry, 2013). Noting these charges, the authors worked conjunctively with two second-grade teachers who were interested in "bridging" early writing development with digital writing experiences during each step of the writing process. The study was guided by these questions: (a) How did the teachers utilize digital writing tools? (b) How did the digital-related writing practices impact student writing? (c) How did students perceive the use of digital tools for their writing?

PERSPECTIVES

This study is informed by multiple perspectives contributing to New Literacies research (Kress, 2003; Leu et al., 2013; New London Group, 1996). These perspectives blend the traditional disciplines of literacy and technology while recognizing both the growing use of digital tools and the new skills and dispositions required for writing (Lankshear & Knobel, 2006; Leu et al., 2013). As O'Brien and Scharber (2008) explain:

> Digital literacies are here to stay – they are at the core of new literacies. It behooves each of us to seriously consider how best to weave together old, new, and future literacies so that young people leave school literate in the ways of school and in the ways of the world. (p. 68)

For our study, we specifically adapt the lowercase new literacies principles that Leu, Zawilinski, Forzani, and Timbrell (2014, p. 350) offer to guide instruction in various contexts: (a) begin teaching and learning new literacies as early as possible; (b) use new literacies to help the last student become the first; (c) teach online search skills since these are important to success in the new literacies of online research and comprehension; (d) use online reading experiences to develop critical thinking skills and a generation of "healthy skeptics"; (e) integrate online communication into lessons; (f) when online tools are blocked, use the word "pilot" to create new instructional opportunities in your classroom; (g) use performance-based assessments for evaluating students' ability with new literacies; (h) use Internet reciprocal teaching in one-to-one computing classrooms; (i) prepare students for their future by using collaborative online learning experiences with classroom partners in other parts of the world; and (j) recognize that a New Literacies Journey is one of continuous learning.

LITERATURE REVIEW

As traditional research on teaching young children to write has highlighted the typical phases of literacy development and the appropriateness of literacy instruction to match such developments (Purcell-Gates, 1996), there is evidence to support a need for monitoring the evolution of writing with young children in a new "digital" age. For example, research suggests young children not only bring a variety of oral and written experiences into the classroom (Hart & Risley, 1995), but also a variety of technology experiences (Hare, Howard, & Pope, 2002). Although more tech-savvy students are coming to school with advanced computer skills (Bennett, Maton, & Kervin, 2008; Gu, Zhu, & Guo, 2013), special populations such as English Language Learners with linguistic barriers and economically disadvantaged students with material barriers for out-of-school participation have raised concern for educators and researchers alike (Mossberger, Tolbert, & Stansbury, 2003). As a result, there is a need for research related to primary grade students and the impact technology has on the development of their literacy skills. Additionally, although there is ample information concerning the way adolescents participate in online culture, there is less evidence indicating how younger students participate digitally with their peers or larger social circles (Sweeny, 2010).

Digital Literacies in Elementary Classrooms

Although we may not fully understand how the types of technology experiences young children bring into their classrooms impact their literacy development, a variety of disciplines have reached a general consensus that technology largely has been integrated as an engagement factor to provide stimuli for students (Shin, Sutherland, Norris, & Soloway, 2012). Additionally, a growing field of research addresses young children's classroom usage of specific devices including 1:1 laptop usage and hand-held devices such as iPads (Murray & Olcese, 2011). However, Bogard and McMackin (2012) argue more research is needed to understand how writing digitally influences the development of young writers. By understanding the differences between composing online and with paper, we provide further evidence for studying the effects digital writing has on young children.

Process Approach to Digital Writing in Elementary Classrooms

Traditional writing research corroborates the effectiveness of process writing (Elbow, 1981; Flower & Hayes, 1981) as both a developmentally appropriate approach for teaching young children to write as well as one conducive to an effective literate environment (Graves, 1983; Moffett, 1981; Pritchard & Honeycutt, 2007). Process writing is particularly effective at the elementary level because it takes into account the developmental concerns of young children and helps to provide ample opportunities for students to write while considering an authentic purpose (Neuman, Copple, & Bredekamp, 2000). A few recent studies have explored the convergence of digital writing with young students through a process approach (Anderson, Mitchell, Thompson, & Trefz, 2014; Bogard & McMackin, 2012; Rowe et al., 2014). However, there still remains a need to understand the complexities of a variety of young student experiences with digital process writing.

Opportunities and Challenges in Digital Literacy Classrooms

Digital writing evolves and changes by its nature. From the inclusion of video, images, and other media in the definition of the word "text" (Kress, 2003) to expanded opportunities to connect to a variety of audiences

(Palmquist, 2003), the changing nature of digital writing presents both opportunities and challenges for classroom educators working with young children. Peterson-Karlan (2011) discusses some of the benefits of digital writing:

> Technology-supported writing can advance all phases of writing – planning, transcribing, editing, and revising using tools. But technology also enables writing in new ways. Technology provides new sources for and means of obtaining information (e.g., the Internet, search engines) and enables sharing, editing, and collaboration among writers, teachers, and peers. (p. 41)

However, research has also demonstrated that although more classrooms are documenting the positive uses of technology integration for young children, negative aspects have been associated with these efforts, too. For example, teachers have reported several barriers to technology integration such as availability of technology, unreliability of technology, and lack of support in technology integration (Duhaney, 2001). Particularly, more research is needed to understand how teachers overcome such barriers (Foley & Guzzetti, 2012). As Forzani and Leu (2012) contend, this research is timely because "new literacies instruction not only is necessary and appropriate for young children, but it will define their future" (p. 421).

METHODOLOGY

Context and Participants

This qualitative case study (Yin, 2014) took place in two second-grade classrooms in a K-5 laboratory school of a large, urban university. In Classroom A, students included: (a) nine boys and eight girls; (b) seven students whose parents were employed by the university with ten students enrolled from the community; (c) six students who performed above grade level, nine students who performed at grade level, and two students who performed below grade level on a school-wide literacy assessment tool; and (d) seven students who self-identified as a member of a minority population. In Classroom B, students included: (a) nine boys and eleven girls; (b) ten students whose parents were employed by the university with ten students enrolled from the community; (c) eight students who performed above grade level, ten students who performed at grade level, and two students who performed below grade level on a school-wide literacy assessment tool; and (d) six students who self-identified as a member of a minority population. Additionally, all students from each classroom reported some type of Internet access at home, and there were no English Language Learners identified in this study.

Both teachers in the study had taught five years at the laboratory school, had a mounted SMART Board in their classroom, and frequently used the school's rotating cart with 15 laptops. Additionally, each class had weekly access to the university's technology lab. As a result of the growing technology emphasis in the laboratory school, the two elementary teachers consulted with the university research team to help plan and implement digital writing tools into their existing social studies curriculum. Students followed a process writing approach and researched, planned, and wrote either narrative, expository, or persuasive texts to advocate for an endangered animal of their choice. As a culminating event, students displayed their writing on laptops to parents and other students, and they collected donations for the World Wildlife Fund.

The research team consisted of a professor, an instructor, and two doctoral students from the university's literacy program. The instructor served as a non-participant observer. One of the researchers served a dual role as both a teacher in the study and a doctoral student under the leadership of the literacy professor. All members of the team had worked together on previous research studies.

Data Collection

Data were collected over 10 weeks from each teacher in the study and included the following: (a) pre-survey questionnaire regarding background teaching experiences; (b) ten classroom observations with field notes; (c) four 30-minute interviews inquiring into the teachers' technology uses; and (d) weekly lesson plans and teaching artifacts. Data collected from the 37 students included: (a) a survey related to their digital writing experiences; (b) a reflection sheet about the digital writing tools used that week; (c) online writing artifacts produced by six focal students from each classroom including two high, two moderate, and two with minimal level technology expertise based on their self-reporting from the initial survey; (d) five classroom observations with field notes; and (e) four 20-minute interviews with each focal student.

Data Analysis

Using categorical aggregation (Creswell, 2012), analysis proceeded by searching for patterns across multiple sources. These patterns were organized into two categories: affective versus cognitive representations of student learning. Affective categories included preferences, interests, and attitudes. Cognitive categories included knowledge, skills, and abilities. These categories were refined through ongoing conversations and by continually returning to the data set for confirmation. Finally, the analysis proceeded into naturalistic generalizations related to the barriers, supports, and outcomes for student learning. An effort was placed on triangulating findings (Lincoln & Guba, 1985) by the researchers analyzing individually and meeting weekly with the research team for peer rating checks.

FINDINGS

We identified three variables of digital writing that influenced students' learning in these two second-grade classrooms: (a) barriers, (b) bridges, and (c) outcomes.

Student Barriers in Digital Writing Classrooms

At the onset of the study, students in both classrooms experienced barriers for full participation in the digital writing classroom. According to the data, two specific barriers included: (a) the diverse technology background experiences of students, and (b) the cognitive overload experienced by the students.

Diverse Background Experiences of Students
As both teachers in the study explained, students needed differentiated technology instruction as their diverse background experiences provided an initial barrier for students to fully participate in the digital writing classroom. For example, one student who lacked the technology knowledge needed to save her work explained: "I had a hard time because every time I would get back, I would have to do it all over and I kept clicking save and it would just like disappear." By not understanding how to save her work, this student trailed behind her peers because she continually restarted her story. Another student expressed confusion when she lacked the

prerequisite search skills needed to find clip art for her story: "I needed help, like I didn't know what to put in Kidspiration." Yet another student expressed: "Sometimes when I'm using Google, it's hard to find answers to the questions that I asked the computer." Again, as these students did not possess the same knowledge for online searches as some of their peers, they lagged behind the class. Not surprising, Teacher A noted: "The students with the most technology experience are further along in the process than others." Similarly, the participant observer wrote: "One student had 12 pages of her book completed at one point during the project, whereas another student was still working in Google Docs on the first draft," and she also noted that special arrangements were made to accommodate these discrepancies: "Out of the eight pairs, four had finished and four were not finished. The teacher clapped to end the lesson and told those students who were not finished they could finish after lunch."

Thus, the variety of technology background experiences created initial barriers for participation in the digital writing classroom. Most of these barriers presented logistical complications as students needed special arrangements for additional time to finish their digital writing products.

Cognitive Overload Experienced by Students

According to the data, students not only experienced barriers initially based on their background experiences, but they also frequently experienced cognitive overload related to both their technical and writing skills. When presented with multiple processing demands, such as typing on the keyboard and spelling unfamiliar words, some students recognized their need for assistance and sought help, but others appeared to face a wall and "shut down" instead. For example, a student who naturally "sought" help for her problems explained: "We were typing when we did the project, but I like need help with typing, finding the letters, stuff like that and like do the exclamation marks because you just can't type in the exclamation marks." Another student was observed asking help from a peer: "Sam, can you help me? I don't know how to do this one bit!" By contrast, another student who "shut down" and did not seek help for problems was described by the non-participant observer: "In the entire class time, this student did nothing on his eBook, but talked to and watched the person beside him."

The need for quick redirection and assistance escalated this finding. One student explained: "When you raise your hand they can tell that you need help and then they'll come over and help you." Meanwhile, the non-participant observer explained: "Lots of questions arise, lots of hands raised — A new digital tool is being introduced and with a 1:17 teacher—student ratio, it's a little hard ..." Similarly, another day the non-participant observer noted: "At one point, there were 13 students off task because of either not typing or hands raised waiting for assistance." It was also found that while some students seemed engaged in the writing project, others were less so, which also contributed to students' being off task: "I did notice that during this time that the four students not doing narrative stories were having a hard time staying on task. They were investigating text size, fonts, color, etc." Thus, many students in the classroom, regardless of their ability level or technological expertise, experienced barriers when persevering through the digital writing process.

In summary, there was a clear cycle identified with student barriers and digital writing. Whenever new digital tools were introduced, students with limited technology skills experienced cognitive overload, needing peer and teacher support to respond to processing demands. Some students, without support, were unable to work through the technical and cognitive overload, while others became distracted by other students or the multiplicity of options such as font or design options. In the following section, we discuss how the teachers offered bridges to these student barriers.

Teacher Bridges in Digital Writing Classrooms

As the teachers in the study responded to the needs of their students, they incorporated bridges to help students cross barriers in two major ways: (a) incremental introduction of digital tools following a process writing approach, and (b) the implementation of social support structures to accommodate student needs.

Incremental Introduction of Digital Tools Following a Process Writing Approach
A major bridge for students was their teachers' ability to locate and link user-friendly tools to each stage of the writing process. Some examples of the tools utilized were: (a) YouTube and BrainPOP videos to generate online discussion for prewriting on Chatzy; (b) Kidspiration to organize thoughts for prewriting and drafting; (c) Google Docs for drafting, revising, and editing; (d) Kidblog for peer feedback on drafts; (e) WikiSpaces as a hub for links and examples provided by the teacher; and (f) StoryJumper,

Barriers, Bridges, and Outcomes in a Digital Writing Cycle 147

Prezi, and Windows Movie Maker for publishing. In the following interview selection, Teacher A described the tools she previously used to teach writing prior to the current study:

> The main way we've used technology [in the past] in the classroom is just with our six or seven classroom computers and the students have used Microsoft Word to type and some different websites for research projects so usually, I'm selecting the websites that they go to.

As the teachers progressed in the project and implemented a process approach, both teachers and researchers noted a more thorough approach to planning and implementing technology into the classroom. For example, the same teacher who had previously only used Microsoft Word noted: "I know I am learning how to use this, too, and I think to myself, I need more practice with this digital tool in order to explain it to them and assist my students." At the end of the project, both teachers were able to reflect on the process and explain how and why they implemented digital writing tools. When asked to explain which tools were implemented and why, teachers noted some of the benefits of linking a different tool with each step of the writing process. For example, one teacher noted the benefits of Kidspiration as a graphic organizer tool because it helped students "organize and kind of get their very beginning thoughts." Also, the teachers' noted their own preferences for using the classroom blog in the revision stage because they valued that their students "commented on each other's writing and gave feedback for revising."

In sum, while initially the scope of this project may have appeared daunting for both the teachers and students in the classroom, following a process writing approach and introducing digital tools in a corresponding fashion served as a bridge for students to accommodate the needed skills to complete the digital writing product.

Implementation of Social Support Structures

According to students, the digital tools allowed them to give and receive instant peer feedback from classmates which affected their writing in a positive manner: "Some of my friends, the people that I put in the story, they read over it and said, 'Tiffany you need a period right there' or 'Tiffany you need an exclamation mark' or stuff like that." One student communicated how she perceived others felt about her writing based on the help they solicited from her: "I'm good at it and I type faster and I can tell that really, I'm good at it and other people think I am too because they will ask for my help." Another student explained how the online feedback worked: "We would review on their KidBlog the comments others left for them and revise their draft." This finding was also noted in the researchers' notes: "The class seemed very eager for this part of the writing process. They appeared to enjoy reading other's drafts." Thus, providing opportunities for peer feedback in digital writing allowed a positive environment for students to consider other opinions while revising and editing their drafts.

In sum, as the teachers introduced a different tool for each stage of the writing process, students were able to work collaboratively with one another as peer feedback served as a social support structure that was embedded into the academic context.

Outcomes in Digital Writing Classrooms

According to the data, there were two outcomes in these second-grade digital writing classrooms: (a) increased engagement by students, and (b) expanded perspectives of writing achievement by teachers.

Increased Engagement by Students
At the beginning of the study, focal students with low levels of technology experience reported that they would rather write with pencil and paper, but changed to preferring writing with digital tools as the project continued. This is evidenced in the following progression of one student's interview:

Interview One:

I would rather write with paper and pencil ... Because I'm faster at it ... Because, pencil and paper, I'm more used to it than computers and I don't play computers that much.

Interview Two:

Because if you use [a computer] more you could get faster and more used to it.

Interview Three:

Like on computers when you type something it's actually not messy at all and sometimes when I write, it's kind of messy ...

As illustrated in this interview, technology allowed students to polish their products to communicate their ideas to an audience. The more students used the tools, the more proficient they became, and the more their preferences for the tools increased. Additionally, according to the data, student engagement with technology increased as students progressed into the unit of study. For example, after students formulated their ideas about concerns related to endangered animals, they became active participants by creating a project-based solution and soliciting participation for their project through writing with a variety of multimodal representations such as pictures, videos, and hyperlinks which they presented to their school as well as posted online. During this experience, students were able to choose their own modality of writing. Some chose to create a digital narrative in StoryJumper, others wrote and produced a persuasive commercial in Windows Movie Maker, and some created an informative Prezi with facts about endangered animals. In addition to choosing their own modality, students appreciated the choices available within each digital tool. One student using Prezi commented that he could either "search for real pictures or you could have like cartoon pictures for it." Another student said, "I like the Story Jumper ... it was fun when you got to look at everything you could choose from." Thus, by providing students with choice, both in writing modality and within each digital tool, students became more invested in their digital writing products (see Fig. 1 for an example of a student writing sample in StoryJumper). Their engagement with the task allowed them to express their confidence in writing as they progressed with increasing proficiency.

Fig. 1. Example of Student Writing in StoryJumper.

Expanded Perspectives of Writing Achievement by Teachers
As the teachers viewed student products and engagement with the digital writing process, their own perspectives of student expectations for digital writing was expanded. During Teacher A's pre-project interview, she explained how she previously evaluated writing in her classroom using a rubric:

> We have a rubric that's based on the six traits of writing and so it goes into ideas and organization and then mechanics, voice and still having your own voice and some variety in there, so I use this framework with the writing objectives.

In her final interview session, this teacher discussed what students learned from this project and indicated a shift in her thinking about what was important in evaluating student writing:

> I think they [students] obviously learned a lot of content about the endangered animals, so that's the most obvious thing, but I think they learned a lot about using the computers and navigating. I think being able to use Google Docs and just general Cloud storage and saving files is a really big skill for them in the age that we live in, and how to log in, you know, just general technology navigation. They definitely learned collaboration and effective communication, you know, sometimes they would read something or write something that they thought made sense to them and then they'd have a buddy read it and it didn't make sense, so they'd have to kind of go back and consider the best way to communicate that with somebody else.

Indeed, by implementing digital tools into the classroom, the teachers expanded their own perspectives regarding the importance of digital writing. From their experiences, the teachers reported the importance of not only preparing students for being better writers, but also preparing students to communicate digitally through collaboration.

In conclusion, the barriers for student learning included their diverse technology experiences and the cognitive overload they experienced. These barriers were circumvented by the bridges offered by teachers, including an incremental approach to digital writing and the placement of social support structures. Finally, as student engagement increased in the classroom, students improved their digital writing products, impacting the teachers' perceptions of success in digital writing classrooms. A salient conclusion in this study is the apparent cycle between the student barriers, teacher bridges, and outcomes for both students and teachers. As illustrated in Fig. 2, an increased frequency of student barriers

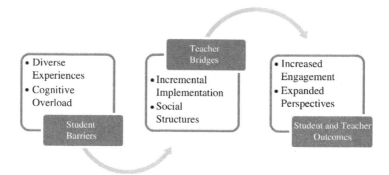

Fig. 2. The Cycle between Barriers, Bridges, and Outcomes in Two Second-Grade Digital Writing Classrooms.

impacted the teachers' responses. By implementing bridges as a response to those barriers, student engagement increased and teachers expanded their perspectives.

DISCUSSION

Our discussion centers around five lessons learned as reported by the two second-grade teachers in this study who used digital writing tools during a process writing approach project. In addition to the teachers' final reflections, we offer links between student barriers and teacher bridges, and make connections to the new literacies principles (Leu et al., 2014) that are guides to successful student outcomes.

Lesson One: Teaching in a Digital Literacy Context Starts with Early Practice

Teacher Reflection: Expect to sweat. Seriously. With each digital tool that was introduced, I felt like I was running around the room helping with the various issues that popped up. Logging into the computer, learning how to copy and paste, and using a laptop mouse pad were common barriers that students needed help with.

Teachers can bridge these early digital barriers by providing daily opportunities for students to engage in digital writing. Additionally, teachers can create a plan to utilize classroom assistants, parent volunteers, and even older students while teachers help students with writing content. As new literacies theory reminds us, although there are stresses and challenges with young children learning how to use digital tools, it is important to, "begin teaching and learning new literacies as early as possible" (Leu et al., 2014, p. 350).

Lesson Two: Teaching in a Digital Writing Classroom Encourages Teachers and Students to Learn Together

Teacher Reflection: You don't have to be an expert, students learn fast. After 1–2 class periods with each tool, the students learned the tricks of each digital tool faster than I did. As they became the experts, students were able to offer peer assistance and feedback easily while I could focus on the students needing more support.

Teachers can bridge the diverse experiences and cognitive overload that students experience when using new digital tools by using "new literacies to help the last student become the first" (Leu et al., 2014, p. 351). In other words, students who struggle academically might be an accomplished techie, capable of providing leadership, guidance, and support in the digital classroom.

Lesson Three: Teaching in a Digital Writing Classroom Requires Collegial Support

Teacher Reflection: Use your colleagues. Having other teachers that you can talk to about what worked, what didn't work, and what you would do differently next time helps tremendously. Some digital tools need direct instruction before you use them, others don't. Use other teachers to find their own successes and challenges and share yours with them. Don't be afraid to collaborate with teachers in other grade levels and content areas, many digital tools cross all boundaries.

As Leu et al. (2014) posits, a "New Literacies Journey is one of continuous learning" (p. 359). Teachers can learn how to bridge student barriers by having support systems of colleagues who share experiences and insights with using digital writing tools.

Lesson Four: Teaching in a Digital Writing Classroom Impacts Teacher Planning and Instruction

> Teacher Reflection: It takes time to incorporate digital tools, but it is time well spent. Making time for digital writing tools took away from other content areas. To maximize this time, I integrated social studies standards into the writing process.

Thus, when teachers teach writing in the content areas, they provide bridges to time intensive barriers associated with learning new digital tools. Furthermore, content area writing encourages teaching online search skills that enable students to succeed in the new literacies of online research and comprehension (Leu et al., 2014).

Lesson Five: Teaching in a Digital Writing Classroom Creates an Engaging Cycle

> Teacher Reflection: The excitement is epidemic when using digital tools. After finding digital tools and planning instruction, I was excited to share them with the students. The students were just as excited to use them. They wrote some of the most detailed stories of the year during this digital writing project and many spent free time writing with the digital tools for fun. Watching the students get that excited to write for an outside audience made me even more excited to find additional digital tools for them to use.

Consistent with a new literacies principle, teachers can bridge student barriers with positive outcomes by preparing "students for their future by using collaborative online learning experiences with classroom partners in other parts of the world" (Leu et al., 2014, p. 358). By connecting to audiences beyond the immediate classroom context, both teachers and students are eager to investigate more ways to improve their writing products.

In this study it was a normal cycle for students to experience barriers, receive support, and have positive outcomes with their writing. When teachers embrace this digital writing cycle, they create classrooms in which students understand that while barriers are always connected to learning new technologies, there are also instructional and social bridges in place to help them learn and be successful writers. As researchers, our primary challenge is to identify new and ongoing bridges that will constantly evolve as new literacies continue to grow, change, and expand. Then perhaps teachers such as Ms. Mason will have a clearer path for helping her students connect their personal interests to their academic success in today's digital writing classrooms.

REFERENCES

Anderson, R. S., Mitchell, J. S., Thompson, R. F., & Trefz, K. D. (2014). Supporting young writers through the writing process in a paperless classroom. In R. S. Anderson & C. Mims (Eds.), *Handbook of research on digital tools for writing instruction in K-12 settings* (pp. 337–362). Hershey, PA: Information Science Reference.

Bennett, S., Maton, K., & Kervin, L. (2008). The "digital natives" debate: A critical review of the evidence. *British Journal of Educational Technology, 39*(5), 775–786.

Bogard, J. M., & McMackin, M. C. (2012). Combining traditional and new literacies in a 21st-century writing workshop. *The Reading Teacher, 65*(5), 313–323.

Creswell, J. W. (2012). *Qualitative inquiry and research design: Choosing among five approaches*. Thousand Oaks, CA: Sage.

Duhaney, D. C. (2001). Teacher education: Preparing teachers to integrate technology. *International Journal of Instructional Media, 28*(1), 23–30.

Elbow, P. (1981). *Writing with power: Teaching for mastering the writing process*. New York, NY: Oxford University Press.

Flower, L., & Hayes, J. R. (1981). A cognitive process theory of writing. *College Composition and Communication, 32*(4), 365–387.

Foley, L. M., & Guzzetti, B. J. (2012). Using do-it-yourself media for content teaching with at-risk elementary students. In P. J. Dunston, S. K. Fullerton, C. C. Bates, K. Headley, & P. M. Stecker (Eds.), *61st yearbook of the literacy research association* (pp. 276–288). Oak Creek, WI: National Reading Conference, Inc.

Forzani, E., & Leu, D. J. (2012). New literacies for new learners: The need for digital technologies in primary classrooms. *The Educational Forum, 76*(4), 421–424.

Graves, D. H. (1983). *Writing: Teachers and children at work*. Exeter, NH: Heinemann.

Gu, X., Zhu, Y., & Guo, X. (2013). Meeting the "digital natives": Understanding the acceptance of technology in classrooms. *Educational Technology & Society, 16*(1), 392–402.

Hare, S., Howard, E., & Pope, M. (2002). Technology integration: Closing the gap between what preservice teachers are taught to do and what they can do. *Journal of Technology and Teacher Education, 10*(2), 191–203.

Hart, B., & Risley, T. (1995). *Meaningful differences*. Baltimore, MD: Paul Brookes.

Kress, G. (2003). *Literacy in the new media age*. London, UK: Routledge.

Lankshear, C., & Knobel, M. (2006, April 11). *Blogging as participation: The active sociality of a new literacy*. American Educational Research Association, San Francisco, CA (pp. 3–13).

Leu, D. J., Kinzer, C. K., Coiro, J., Castek, J., & Henry, L. A. (2013). New literacies: A dual level theory of the changing nature of literacy, instruction, and assessment. In D. E. Alvermann, N. J. Unrau, & R. B. Ruddell (Eds.), *Theoretical models and processes of reading* (6th ed., pp. 1150–1181). Newark, DE: International Reading Association.

Leu, D. J., Zawilinski, L., Forzani, E., & Timbrell, N. (2014). Best practices in new literacies and the new literacies of online research and comprehension. In L. M. Morrow & L. B. Gambrell (Eds.), *Best practices in literacy instruction* (5th ed., pp. 343–364). New York, NY: Guilford Press.

Lincoln, Y. S., & Guba, E. G. (1985). *Naturalistic inquiry*. Beverly Hills, CA: Sage.

Moffett, J. (1981). *Active voice: A writing program across the curriculum*. Montclair, NJ: Boynton/Cook.

Mossberger, K., Tolbert, C. J., & Stansbury, M. (2003). *Virtual inequality: Beyond the digital divide.* Washington, DC: Georgetown University Press.

Murray, O., & Olcese, N. (2011). Teaching and learning with iPad, ready or not? *TechTrends: Linking Research and Practice to Improve Learning, 55*(6), 42–48.

Neuman, S. B., Copple, C., & Bredekamp, S. (2000). *Learning to read and write: Developmentally appropriate practices for young children.* Washington, DC: National Association for the Education of Young Children.

New London Group. (1996). A pedagogy of multiliteracies: Designing social futures. *Harvard Educational Review, 66*(1), 60–93.

O'Brien, D., & Scharber, C. (2008). Digital literacies go to school: Potholes and possibilities. *Journal of Adolescent & Adult Literacy, 52*(1), 66–68.

Palmquist, M. (2003). A brief history of computer support for writing centers and writing-across-the-curriculum programs. *Computers and Composition, 20*(4), 395–413.

Peterson-Karlan, G. (2011). Technology to support writing by students with learning and academic disabilities: Recent research trends and findings. *Assistive Outcomes and Benefits, 7*(1), 39–62.

Pritchard, R. J., & Honeycutt, R. L. (2007). Best practices in implementing a process approach to teaching writing. In S. Graham, C. A. MacArthur, & J. Fitzgerald (Eds.), *Best practices in writing instruction* (pp. 28–49). New York, NY: Guilford Press.

Purcell-Gates, V. (1996). Stories, coupons, and the "TV guide:" Relationships between home literacy experiences and emergent literacy knowledge. *Reading Research Quarterly, 31*(4), 406–428.

Rowe, D. W., Miller, M. E., & Pacheco, M. B. (2014). Preschoolers as digital designers: Composing dual language eBooks using touchscreen computer tablets. In R. S. Anderson & C. Mims (Eds.), *Handbook of research on digital tools for writing instruction in K-12 settings* (pp. 279–306). Hershey, PA: Information Science Reference.

Shin, N., Sutherland, L. M., Norris, C. A., & Soloway, E. (2012). Effects of game technology on elementary student learning in mathematics. *British Journal of Educational Technology, 43*(4), 540–560.

Sweeny, S. M. (2010). Writing for the instant messaging and text messaging generation: Using new literacies to support writing instruction. *Journal of Adolescent & Adult Literacy, 54*(2), 121–130.

Yin, R. K. (2014). *Case study research: Design and methods* (5th ed.). Thousand Oaks, CA: Sage.

CLASSROOM WRITING COMMUNITY AS AUTHENTIC AUDIENCE: THE DEVELOPMENT OF NINTH-GRADERS' ANALYTICAL WRITING AND ACADEMIC WRITING IDENTITIES

Susan S. Fields

ABSTRACT

Purpose − *To describe the role one classroom writing community played in shaping students' understandings of the analytical writing genre; and to discuss the impact the community had on students' developing academic writing identities.*

Design/methodology/approach − *While research has demonstrated the impact of classroom writing communities on student writing practices and identities at the elementary level (Dyson, 1997) and for secondary students engaged in fiction writing (Halverson, 2005), less is known about the role classroom writing communities may play for secondary students who are learning to write in academic discourses. This chapter explores the practices of one such classroom community and discusses the ways the community facilitated students' introduction to the discourse of analytical writing.*

Findings — *The teacher turned the classroom writing community into an authentic audience, and in so doing, he developed students' understandings of the analytical writing genre and their growing identities as academic writers. First, he used the concept of immediate audience (i.e., writing to persuade real readers) as the primary rationale for students to follow the outlined expectations for analytical writing. Second, he used inquiry discussions around student work (i.e., interacting with other members of the writing community) to prepare students for a future audience of prospective independent school English classrooms.*

Practical implications — *By turning the classroom writing community into an authentic audience through inquiry discussions, teachers can develop students' deep and flexible understandings of a potentially unfamiliar writing genre. Furthermore, by employing the classroom writing community as a support for moving students through moments of struggle, teachers implicate students' expertise as academic writers, thereby facilitating their willingness to take on academic writing identities.*

Keywords: Classroom writing community; authentic audience; literary analysis; academic writing identity; diverse adolescents

Recently, literacy organizations and researchers have made numerous calls to involve secondary students in authentic writing endeavors (Council of Chief State School Officers & National Governors Association, 2010; Hillocks, 2011; Yancey, 2009; Purcell-Gates, Duke, & Martineau, 2007). Typically, these calls focus on the nature of writing tasks, but the role of a classroom writing community may be equally as important. That is, when students write in a community that acts as an authentic audience, organized around common writing practices and shared expectations, the experience has the potential to not only impact students' writing development but also reinforce their membership in a particular writing community (Atwell, 1998; Calkins, 1986; Magnifico, 2010). Brokering membership into that community may motivate students with diverse linguistic backgrounds to take up the rhetorical conventions of an academic genre that is unfamiliar to them and ultimately facilitate their willingness to identify as academic writers (Magnifico, 2010).

In this chapter, I describe the instructional practices in which a ninth-grade teacher, Mr. Campbell, engaged with his students during a literary analysis unit to create a writing community. I show how Mr. Campbell conducted inquiry discussions around students' writing as a springboard for further instruction in the analytical writing genre. I argue that the classroom community's interactions around their peers' writing allowed students to negotiate both their understanding of genre-specific features as well as their writing identities in the communities of their current and future writing classrooms.

THEORETICAL FRAMEWORK: UPTAKE OF DISCOURSE THROUGH A COMMUNITY OF PRACTICE

Wenger's (1998) work on *communities of practice* and Gee's (1996) notion of *Discourse* serve as guiding frameworks for this chapter. These frameworks facilitated analysis of the ways in which the ninth-grade classroom writing community apprenticed students into the Discourse of the classroom and the analytical writing genre. Wenger (2010) describes communities of practice (also referred to as discourse communities; Gee, 1996) as "groups of people who share a concern or a passion for something they do and learn how to do it better as they interact regularly" (p. 180). Mr. Campbell's writing classroom was a community of practice oriented around the writing of analytical essays through collaborative inquiry discussions and a shared repertoire of resources. In this chapter, I refer to this particular community of practice as the "classroom writing community." Furthermore, students in Mr. Campbell's class were learning to write analytical essays in a way that would prepare them for success in the independent school classrooms and postsecondary institutions they aspired to attend in the coming years. I refer to these communities of practice as the "wider discourse communities."

As such, this investigation considered how students were learning the Discourse (Gee, 1996) of the classroom, of the analytical writing genre, and of their future school contexts. Gee's notion of Discourse refers to "ways of being in the world" (p. 190). Beyond the features of academic language, the Discourse of academic writing includes a combination of shared expectations, values, behaviors, and goals (e.g., treating writing as a process rather than a one-off attempt at a final draft). Those who are developing their academic writing identities, then, are working to acquire a common Discourse identifiable by a certain combination of behaviors. As Magnifico (2010) articulates, "[Novices] must take up the norms of communication and interaction as their own, mastering how the community understands and uses particular skills and particular forms in particular situations" (p. 173). In other words, to take up the identity of an expert academic writer, a novice needs to internalize genre expectations and goals, as well as develop a sense of how their rhetorical choices impact audiences in various contexts.

The notion of writing community as authentic audience (Magnifico, 2010) served as a guiding framework for viewing how students were taking up the new Discourse and developing their academic writing identities. First, the classroom writing community was an immediate audience in that students were "writing for readers" (p. 176). Real readers (i.e., Mr. Campbell and other students) read students' writing and were either swayed by their arguments or not. As such, this investigation considered the students' interactions with each other to understand how they were developing as analytical writers. Secondly, the writing communities of students' prospective independent school classrooms and beyond were a future audience. Students' discussions about writing were regarded as attempts to try on the identity of an academic writer – an identity that would prepare them for these future writing communities. By examining the ways students collaboratively learned about analytical writing, this investigation sought to understand how "writer[s] [bid] for membership ... by taking part in ... common writing practices" (p. 176). Through analysis of students' interactions with these two audiences, this study sought to understand how they negotiated their understanding of genre-specific features and their growing identities as academic writers.

RESEARCH QUESTIONS

While research has demonstrated the impact of classroom writing communities on student writing practices and identities at the elementary level (Dyson, 1997) and for secondary students engaged in fiction writing (Halverson, 2005), there is less known about how classroom writing communities may be used to facilitate the development of secondary students who are learning to write in academic genres. This chapter explores the role one such classroom community played in inducting students into the discourse of analytical writing. Specifically, during the *Of Mice and Men* unit, Mr. Campbell introduced students to the analytical writing genre and guided them to write their first five-paragraph analytical essay. In this chapter, I set out to address the following research questions:

1. *During the first three classes of the Of Mice and Men unit, what role did the classroom writing community play in shaping students' understandings of the analytical writing genre (most specifically, the thesis statement)?*
2. *What impact did the classroom writing community have on students' academic writing identities?*

METHODS

Setting

This investigation took place at an independent day school, Hilltop Academy,[1] over the course of the 2014–2015 school year. Situated in a large northeastern city, the Academy selects a group of 20 culturally and linguistically diverse adolescents to undertake a 14-month program between eighth and ninth grades, such that they are on track to gain admission to elite, competitive high schools. In essence, students "repeat" their eighth grade year to fill what the school terms an "education gap" to increase the likelihood of admissions to these institutions. In the service of this larger goal, the Academy's English instructional program engages the students in the same curriculum as these elite high schools, a curriculum that incorporates challenging, contextualized literacy experiences.

The English program consisted of two classes: a 60-minute literature/grammar class that met daily (termed "English class" by the school) and a 60-minute writing class that met twice a week (termed "writing class" by the school). Each class was taught by separate teachers who taught two sections of their respective classes and coordinated lessons together. The investigation in this chapter focuses on one section of the writing class. While the writing class covered analytical, descriptive, narrative, and research report writing, I focus particularly on the analytical writing unit because research has shown that competence in the analytical genre supports the future professional trajectories of adolescents (Fahnestock & Secor, 1991; Hillocks, 2010).

The 12-week analytical writing unit included the writing of three analytical essays that were coordinated with three of the novels being read and discussed in the English class – *Of Mice and Men* (Steinbeck, 1937); *To Kill a Mockingbird* (Lee, 1960); and *The Bluest Eye* (Morrison, 1970). This chapter reports on data from the first subunit on *Of Mice and Men*. The subunit had two main goals: (1) introduce the genre of analytical writing; and (2) guide students through the writing of their first analytical essay. This subunit spanned four weeks for a total of eight classes.

Participants

Mr. Campbell
Mr. Campbell, the teacher of the writing class, was a white male in his thirties. Previous to his two-year tenure at Hilltop, he had taught high school English at independent schools for six years.

Students
All 20 students from the 2014–2015 cohort participated in the study. Upon completion of their eighth grade year in public, charter, and parochial school contexts in the northeastern city's urban areas, the students applied, interviewed, and gained admission to Hilltop. They ranged in age from 14 to 15 years old, and their ethnic backgrounds included Afro-Caribbean, African American, Hispanic-American, and White.

Sula
Sula was one of the 20 students in the class who attended Hilltop Academy during the 2014–2015 year. In this chapter, I use samples of her work to illustrate broader patterns I observed in the class. Sula was 14-years-old at the time of the study, identified as Hispanic-American, and spoke both English and Spanish at home.

Researcher Role

During observations of classroom activity, I assumed the role of participant-observer (Patton, 2002). As participant, I sat at a table with the students and, from time to time, shared an interpretation I had on a novel or answered a question about an author's moves. As an observer, I typed field notes and asked questions of participants when I needed clarifying information. Important also to my role was that I did not share the cultural and linguistic backgrounds of the majority of students I observed. I am a white woman who grew up in an English-speaking household.

Data Sources

Classroom Observation Field Notes
I conducted observations of all writing classes during the four-week *Of Mice and Men* subunit in order to document the nature of the instructional approach to the analytical writing unit and students' responses to it. During classroom observations, I took descriptive, handwritten notes in a bound notebook; I typed and expanded these notes within several hours of the observation (Emerson, Fretz, & Shaw, 2001).

Interviews
I conducted three interviews with eight focal students over the course of the school year (24 total interviews), which allowed me to hear directly from students about their experiences in the writing class. Furthermore, I conducted three interviews with both the English and writing teachers (six total interviews) in order to learn how they described their instructional approaches, as well as to gain insight into how they viewed students' reading and writing development over the course of the year. For this chapter, I drew upon the first two interviews with the writing teacher and focal students in order to understand their experiences before and during the *Of Mice and Men* unit.

Student Work
I collected outlines, notes, rough drafts, and final drafts of students' analytical essays on *Of Mice and Men*. These ongoing work samples were collected in order to document how the students were incorporating lessons into their writing and how their writing was developing.

Data Analysis

I used inductive thematic analysis (Braun & Clark, 2006) to analyze the field notes and student work. The method, which emphasizes describing repeated patterns among the data (i.e., codes) and analyzing across codes for themes, allowed me to document commonalities in the classroom discourse, as well as in the development of students' analytical writing and academic writing identities.

Analyses of field notes and teacher interviews indicated several patterns in the classroom discourse used to induct students into the discourse of analytical writing. This chapter reports primarily on one of those patterns: the classroom writing community as an authentic audience.

Analyses of student work and student interviews supplemented the field notes analysis by helping me see if and how students were taking up the classroom discourse on analytical writing in their written work and in their reported descriptions of the unit. In order to analyze student work, I determined the degree to which students' thesis statements reflected the outlined expectations. The thesis statements fell into one of four categories: strong interpretation, interpretation, almost interpretation, and no interpretation. This chapter reports on one student's thesis statement from the category of strong interpretation. I chose to explicate Sula's work because it illustrates the positive impact the classroom community had on shaping some students' understandings of the analytical writing genre.

OVERVIEW: BUILDING THE CLASSROOM WRITING COMMUNITY AS AN AUTHENTIC AUDIENCE

Analysis indicated that Mr. Campbell turned the classroom writing community into an authentic audience, which in turn, impacted students' developing understandings of the analytical writing genre, as well as their identities as academic writers. He connected the day-to-day work during the *Of Mice and Men* unit to two important audiences: first, he wanted students to write clear essays that convinced the immediate classroom writing community of their literary interpretations. Second, he encouraged students to write in ways that aligned with the wider community of sophisticated, academic writers (i.e., those of their future independent schools and beyond). These two practices helped to attune students to the discourse of analytical writing both in the context of their immediate and prospective writing classrooms.

Writing for Immediate Audience

In every lesson, Mr. Campbell explained why adhering to the expectations for analytical writing was important to the immediate audience. Specifically, he encouraged the students to write essays convincing enough so that he and the other students in the class would be won over by their individual interpretations of the novel.

Mr. Campbell told students on the first day of the unit that the purpose behind learning the five-paragraph essay format was to "[help] you deliver your idea convincingly or persuasively." As such, the classroom writing community gauged the effectiveness of an essay by the degree to which the essay clearly convinced the students of its main argument (or literary interpretation). When students read a model analytical essay, for example, Mr. Campbell asked them if they were convinced of the argument and if so, he questioned, "How does she [the writer] convince us?" Mr. Campbell used students' answers as a springboard for discussing the role of evidence and analysis in body paragraphs. In subsequent classes, Mr. Campbell asked students to apply the emerging standards to evaluations of each other's writing (i.e., Are the quotes convincing you? Does the writer have enough evidence to back up her claim? Do the explanations of evidence prove the point of the essay?). The expectations for writing an analytical essay were recorded on a checklist that students referred to throughout the unit (see Fig. 1). These discussions attuned students to the needs of their audience. Adhering to the expectations of analytical writing (i.e., developing an original literary interpretation and supporting it), then, was not about simply checking off items on the list to make a certain grade – they were the means by which students convinced their fellow classmates of their arguments.

Mr. Campbell also pointed out the multiple ways writers' rhetorical choices can enhance or detract from their arguments. In framing discussions on standard grammar, genre conventions, and sentence structure, Mr. Campbell urged students not to think about these topics as "a bunch of rules" but as "ways to emphasize and add style to your writing." For example, adding complex sentences to a paragraph "allows you to express more complex ideas" and communicates to the reader "you're capable of sophisticated thinking." On the other hand, carelessly misspelling an author's name can communicate that you are "perhaps not trustworthy," which he described as potentially turning the reader off of your argument. Mr. Campbell communicated the specific ways language can sway the reader one way or the other. Beyond organizing an overall compelling

---

Essay Checklist

Introduction

____ My intro contains a hook sentence.

____ My intro names the author and title and sets the stage for my thesis.

____ My intro contains a thesis statement that makes an argument or interpretation.

Body Paragraphs

____ Each of my body paragraphs contains a clear topic sentence.

____ Each of my body paragraphs contains a direct quotation.

____ Each of my body paragraphs provides an explanation of how the quotation supports my thesis.

[...]

Fig. 1. Excerpt of the Analytical Essay Checklist.

essay, he reminded students that these choices at the sentence level (e.g., writing in standard grammar and with sentence variety) held importance too. This was important because those choices could strengthen the effectiveness of students' communication to their audience.

Mr. Campbell's practice of sharing student writing (i.e., the essays of both former and current students) contributed to the classroom writing community's role as an audience with a set of shared expectations and goals. This sharing happened during what I call inquiry discussions, whereby Mr. Campbell used students' questions and/or observations on others' texts to guide their understandings of the analytical genre features. Some were more guided than others, but these inquiry discussions were the means by which students normed each other to the discourse of analytical writing.

Preparing for a Future Audience

Inquiry discussions also served to orient students to the writing communities of their future independent school classrooms and beyond.

Mr. Campbell explained that if students learned to write analytical essays according to the format he outlined (i.e., introductory paragraph with arguable thesis statement; body paragraphs with carefully chosen evidence; and concluding paragraph), they would be prepared for long-term success in independent school English classrooms and elsewhere (which was the explicit goal of Hilltop). This format was "what most English teachers will expect from you in high school," he said. Mr. Campbell also referenced several graduates of Hilltop who had reported to him how prepared they were to write analytical essays in their new contexts. Essentially, Mr. Campbell communicated that brokering membership in this classroom writing community equaled membership in students' future independent school writing communities.

In the following section, I outline the specific topics and texts Mr. Campbell used in the inquiry discussions to introduce students to analytical writing. Intertwined throughout the section is a two-part case study highlighting the impact of the instructional sequence on the development of Sula's thesis statement.

INTRODUCING ANALYTICAL WRITING

Mr. Campbell used the following instructional sequence to introduce students to the genre of analytical writing (see Table 1), as well as prepare them to write their first five-paragraph analytical essay on *Of Mice and Men*. These introductory classes oriented students to the expectations and goals of analytical writing – specifically, crafting an effective thesis statement – that then governed the activity of the classroom writing community for the rest of the 12-week unit.

Class One: Guided Inquiry/Crafting a Thesis Statement

Mr. Campbell referred to this class as "the most important writing class of the year" because students would learn the "foundations for writing an analytical essay."

Viewing of the Equalizer Trailer to Define Interpretation of a Literary Work
During the first 10 minutes of class, Mr. Campbell introduced the concept of interpretation by inviting students to comment on an interpretation of

Table 1. Introductory Instructional Sequence for the Analytical Writing Unit.

	Method of Instructional Delivery	Topics	Texts
Class One *(Monday)*	Direct instruction and guided inquiry	a. What is an interpretation? b. Structure of a five-paragraph analytical essay c. Composing thesis statement (process)	1. *Equalizer* movie trailer (Fuqua, 2014) 2. *Old Man and the Sea:* A Love Story? (Former student, 2009)
Class Two *(Friday)*	Inquiry discussion	a. Review criteria of effective thesis statement b. Workshop students' thesis statements	*Of Mice and Men* thesis statement handout
Class Three *(Monday)*	Rough draft of analytical essay due		

The Old Man and the Sea made by two characters in a scene from a movie. Importantly, the class had read and analyzed the Hemingway novella together the summer prior, so they had recently informed opinions on the text. The movie was *The Equalizer* with Denzel Washington and Chloe Grace Moretz, and in the scene, the two characters – a man and teenage girl – dialog about the meaning of the story *The Old Man and the Sea*. Prior to viewing the scene, Mr. Campbell prepared students for the discussion that was to follow, "There's going to be some literary analysis in this preview, and I want to see if you agree or disagree with it." Following their viewing of the movie preview, students exchanged ideas about whether or not they agreed with the man's interpretation of *The Old Man and the Sea*.

Mr. Campbell used their discussion to define interpretation and explain why it is important to be able to make one:

> In order to make an interesting interpretation in a paper, you want to come up with some kind of thesis or argument that you can try to prove. Even though he's having banter with the girl at the bar, what he's doing is making an interpretation of the book that stands out to him. [...] [It's an] interesting way to think about reading, too. When you're reading things, you should try to think about the meaning – why the book matters – and how that meaning is conveyed. [...] Ultimately, you want to arrive at some big interpretation that you can argue in a paper.

Mr. Campbell defined an interpretation as an "argument that you can try to prove" and explained that the interpretation was what would guide the writing of their essays. He also emphasized that reading analytically, thinking about "why the book matters," would be an important preparation to writing analytical essays. Mr. Campbell captured students' attention with a familiar pop culture reference (i.e., *The Equalizer* scene) and used it to provide an authenticity for taking this kind of stance on reading and writing.

Using a Former Student's Model Essay to Frame Expectations and Goals for Writing
For the next 30 minutes, Mr. Campbell outlined the structure of the five-paragraph analytical essay by guiding an inquiry discussion around a model essay. The essay on *The Old Man and the Sea* had been written by a former student who attended the independent school Mr. Campbell worked at prior to his tenure at Hilltop. His use of this model essay communicated to students that someone the same age was doing what was expected of them and doing it well. The students and he read the essay out loud paragraph-by-paragraph, discussing the components of effective introductory, body, and concluding paragraphs.

While at times Mr. Campbell offered moments of direct instruction, he mostly guided the students in an inquiry of the essay (e.g., What do you notice in the body paragraph? How does she help convince us of her idea?) and used their observations to name the important features of the discourse. Mr. Campbell stressed that this model essay could serve as a resource for the rough draft they were to compose on *The Of Mice and Men* in two days. He told students they could "emulate the structure," "not the idea" of the essay.

Using Guided Inquiry to Discuss the Composing Process
Then, Mr. Campbell outlined the four criteria (the "what") that defined an effective thesis statement (see Table 2). He called for students' thesis

Table 2. Criteria for an Effective Thesis Statement.

Criteria for Effective Thesis Statement
1. Clear
2. Arguable
3. Enough for three body paragraphs
4. Able to support with textual evidence

statements to go beyond plot summary to "[make] an original, insightful argument." Furthermore, he explained that the "crystal clear" thesis statement should be "not too big" and "not too small": broad enough to "branch into three different body paragraphs" but specific enough that the argument was transparent to the reader. Moreover, Mr. Campbell explained that students must be able to secure enough evidence in the novel to support the thesis statement.

Mr. Campbell also modeled the thinking steps (the "how") involved in turning a student observation into an effective thesis statement (see Table 3). For homework that night, all students were to try composing the thesis statement for their analytical essay on *Of Mice and Men*. In order to prepare them for this task, he led three students through a guided inquiry until each had the rough draft of a thesis statement they could use for their analytical essay. I explicate one of these conversations in the following case study illustration.

Table 3. Steps to Conduct an Inquiry Discussion on Composing a Thesis Statement.

Instructional Move	Purpose	Example
1. Start with what is familiar and interesting to the students	Engage students and validate their contributions	– When you were reading, what were some of the things you were most interested in? – What captivated you about the book? – What questions did you have after reading the book?
2. Provide students with an appropriate heuristic (or interpretive framework)	Move students from thinking about making an observation toward an arguable statement	*Of Mice and Men* uses Lennie's mind to show ____.
3. Ask follow-up questions, as needed	– Prompt students to think about why their initial idea matters (i.e., answering the "so what?" question) – Cue students to think beyond the text toward the bigger meanings the author intends to communicate	– What does your idea point out about other characters? – What does your idea point out about society?

Sula Case Study Part I: The Composing Process through Guided Inquiry

The case study proceeds in two parts. (Part II follows on page 173.) The purpose of the illustration is to trace the ways the classroom writing community shaped the thesis statement of one student, Sula, over the course of the first two classes in the *Of Mice and Men* unit. Mr. Campbell began by using guided inquiry to usher Sula from expressing a mere interest ("The mind of Lennie always interested me") toward making an arguable statement ("Lennie's mind shows how cruel other people are in the book"). He used a series of increasingly complex questions (see Table 3) to move Sula to this end point.

The guided inquiry began when Sula expressed confusion over how to start the process of composing a thesis statement. Mr. Campbell had been identifying the criteria of a successful thesis statement when Sula admitted, "I just sit completely baffled at my computer ... like how do I start? I don't know how to unravel the ideas in my head." First, Mr. Campbell invited Sula to connect with the novel as a starting point for developing her thesis ("When you were reading, what were some of the things you were most interested in?"). Mr. Campbell's move afforded Sula the opportunity to talk about an aspect of the novel that was both interesting and familiar to her. His request also communicated to Sula that she already brought something of value to the table. Sula did not hesitate to offer her observation, stating that Lennie's childlike mind was what captured her attention ("Like Lennie's mind ... wasn't ... on track with his age, so the mind of Lenny always interested me.")

The discussion continued for several more exchanges. First, Mr. Campbell paired a heuristic ("*Of Mice and Men* uses Lennie's mind to show _____") with more guided inquiry to move Sula's thinking, but her response ("*Of Mice and Men* uses Lennie's mind to show [...] how Lennie couldn't control his impulses") was not yet arguable. Then, he posed several questions to further push her idea from observation to argument: he inquired about the role Lennie's mind plays in the book ("What does it point out about things that other characters believe in?") and outside of the book ("What does it point out about society?"). He prompted Sula and the class to think beyond the events in the text to the bigger reason the author might have chosen to write such a character. Mr. Campbell pushed Sula, and the struggle began to pay off, as she extended her observation in the following exchange:

> Mr. Campbell: [...] Why do you think John Steinbeck wrote a character who has this limited mind or who is really innocent and doesn't really understand things the way George does?
>
> Sula: To show – like the what's it called – to show the opposite of how real people act, like how some people can kill, like having the total instinct to kill, or how like how Lennie didn't want to, or to show the comparison between Lennie's world and the real world because Lennie's world is totally la-la land and everyone's else world is complex and real.

Sula asserted that Steinbeck uses Lennie's mind "to show the opposite of how real people act," and in his subsequent response, Mr. Campbell revoiced her statement in clearer language, "to show something about how cruel other people are in the book." For homework that night, Sula composed an introductory paragraph, which ended in a thesis statement representing the thinking that had transpired during class [bold text added to emphasize thesis statement]:

> Children often have the mentality that nothing in the world can hurt them. Adults, on the other hand, seem to expect the worst from others. In John Steinbeck's *Of Mice and Men*, Steinbeck uses two characters to display this idea. Lennie has been portrayed with the mind of a child, when in reality he is a man. **With his personality, the novel shows the world through Lennie's eyes.** *Of Mice and Men* **uses Lennie's mind to show how cruel other people are in the book.**

Following this discussion, Mr. Campbell repeated the guided inquiry with two other students, and he invited students who wanted similar guidance to meet with him one-on-one during study hall later that week.

While he led the inquiry in *this* class, Mr. Campbell turned more of the inquiry over to the students in the *next* class. In class two, students in the classroom writing community asked questions about and provided feedback on each other's thesis statements.

Class Two: Inquiry Discussion/Thesis Statement Workshop

During the thesis statement workshop, students submitted their statements for the classroom writing community's review. The workshop ran much like a critique in an art class would. First, Mr. Campbell distributed a handout containing every student's thesis statement (students had submitted them to him the night before via Google Docs). Next, one by one, students read their statements out loud to the class. Their peers then jumped in to offer critiques based on the aforementioned four criteria. Finally, students used the feedback, as they saw fit, in their writing of the full rough draft. Sula's presentation during the workshop had the impact of further revising her thesis statement.

Sula Case Study Part II: Revising During the Thesis Workshop

Sula put her introductory thesis statement to the ultimate test of effective communication: convincing the audience of her peers that the statement was clear, arguable, and capable of supporting three body paragraphs. Mr. Campbell explained that the community's feedback was important to ensuring they had enough of a statement to build an entire paper around (as they were to write the full five-paragraph essay for homework that weekend). When the time came for Sula to present her introductory paragraph to the class, she realized that what made sense to her may not have been as clear to her audience. The classroom community helped to revise Sula's thesis statement for a third time (see Table 4).

In the following exchange, it was Sula's turn to read (see Sula's introductory paragraph on page 19), and several students had to negotiate the meaning of her statement before providing feedback. In particular, two students Dylan and Anita expressed confusion that Sula's introductory paragraph had set the reader up to learn about *two* characters with a childlike mind ("Steinbeck uses two characters to display this idea") but only mentioned *one* ("*Of Mice and Men* uses Lennie's mind to show how cruel other people are in the book") in the thesis statement. Cyrus and Kianna maintained that including more characters in the first half of the thesis statement would run contradictory to Sula's main argument. Kianna, in particular, understood the message of Sula's thesis and clarified it for Anita and Dylan.

> Dylan: I think even though you said that there were two characters used to represent this, it only shows one. So basically, it just shows how Lennie is portrayed in the

Table 4. Development of Sula's Thesis Statement over the First Three Classes.

	Class One	Class Two	Class Three
Thesis statement drafts	*Of Mice and Men* uses Lennie's mind to show how Lennie couldn't control his impulses	*Of Mice and Men* uses Lennie's childlike mind to show how cruel other people are in the book	*Of Mice and Men* uses Lennie's childlike mind to show how cruel Curley, Crooks, and George are in the book

children-like mentality, but we don't know anything about George or, like, any of the other characters. So I think you should probably add something else to it to make it a little more detailed.

...

Cyrus: [...] Dylan said that she should add more characters, but that would contradict the point of this ....

Anita: I would just say you should [...] add George into it, because you said the two characters, so in my head I'm thinking the [...] two main characters [...]

Kianna *(interrupting Anita)*: But the writing isn't about George, it's about Lennie.

Anita: [...] But your supporting paragraphs is *(sic)* about how cruel others are to him. There are times when George is cruel to Lennie [...]

Kianna: But her writing is about how Lennie's childlike mind shows how cruel the other people are. So, it's not just about George and Lennie, it's about Lennie. And then in her body paragraph, *(directly addressing Sula)* are you going to explain situations ....

When directly addressed by Kianna, Sula entered the discussion for the first time to clarify that her thesis statement was indeed trying to show something specific about Lennie's mind. After several minutes of absence from the discussion, Mr. Campbell stepped in to guide students' observations toward a clear, actionable takeaway for Sula.

Mr. Campbell: The one thing that Sula could specify a little bit more – we could know which characters. She could say Steinbeck uses Lennie's child-like mind to show how cruel – and then she could name three characters.

In sum, Dylan and Anita questioned the clarity of the relationship between Sula's introductory paragraph and her thesis statement, Kianna corrected Anita's misunderstanding about the message of the thesis statement, and Mr. Campbell suggested that her statement more specifically set up the essay for three body paragraphs. As a result of the feedback, Sula changed her thesis statement to read, "*Of Mice and Men* uses Lennie's childlike mind to show how cruel Curley, Crooks, and George are in the book." The final product – a more specific, arguable thesis statement than her initial observation – represented the collaborative thinking of the classroom writing community.

Summary

The findings from this study demonstrate that the use of inquiry discussions were the means by which students interacted with two audiences — their immediate and future classroom writing communities. These inquiry discussions, characterized by the following features, were an effective instructional tool in supporting students' developing understandings of the analytical writing genre and their growing writing identities:

a. Inquiry discussions moved from teacher-guided to student-led.
b. Inquiry discussions used relevant texts (i.e., scene from *The Equalizer*, former student's model essay) to introduce genre conventions.
c. Inquiry discussions used students' observations as the basis for crafting literary arguments.

The discussions provided students with a shared repertoire (i.e., common vocabulary, resources, and expectations) that the classroom community would come back to again and again in the coming months as they developed as analytical writers.

DISCUSSION: DUAL ROLE OF AUDIENCE

Mr. Campbell turned the classroom writing community into an authentic audience in two main ways. First, students wrote *to* an immediate audience — the teacher and students in front of them (i.e., the classroom writing community). Second, students wrote in anticipation of the future academic communities to which they aspired for membership (i.e., independent schools, universities, and professional networks). The dual role of classroom community as authentic audience impacted students' development for the following reasons:

- When students were readers of each other's work, they learned the impact their rhetorical choices had on effective communication (i.e., writing clear, compelling, arguable thesis statements) and learned how to support each other during moments of struggle.
- When students interacted with each other around the discourse of analytical writing using student-centered topics and texts as starting points, they built meaningful understandings of an unfamiliar discourse.
- When the classroom writing community interacted in this way, they were collectively bidding for membership in their future academic communities, thereby supporting their identity development as academic writers.

Classroom Community: Rhetorical Choices, Effective Communication, and Support

During the thesis statement workshop, students were beginning to understand how their particular rhetorical choices and reasoning landed on the ears of real readers. Mr. Campbell and the students provided feedback on the clarity, logic, and arguability of the presenters' statements. When confusion over Sula's thesis statement occurred, for example, students engaged in a process of questioning and challenging each other until they reached new understandings. Sula made revisions to the specificity of her thesis statement as a result of the audience's response. Over time, students began to anticipate the voices of these real readers when composing thesis statements. For Sula and the other students, this meant that when on their own, they were motivated to answer to these voices and write in ways that persuaded future readers (i.e., the classroom writing community) of their literary arguments. Indeed, research demonstrates that when writers envision a specific audience reading their work, they make revisions to better meet their rhetorical goals (Bereiter & Scardamalia, 1987; Flower & Hayes, 1981). The classroom community performed this role of immediate audience: students were beginning to make particular rhetorical choices in order to more effectively communicate to their peers.

Simultaneously, the classroom writing community was beginning to serve as a resource for completing difficult writing tasks. The students applied the criteria for effective thesis statements to evaluate Sula's work. As such, students were beginning to adopt "ways of doing and approaching things that [were] shared among members" (Bullmaster-Day, 2015, p. 2). A framework was set for future writing workshops (in this class and beyond), whereby students could support one another and provide mature feedback during the challenging practice of writing analytical essays.

Wider Discourse Communities: Meaningful Interactions and Writing Identities

Students in Mr. Campbell's class were writing to an immediate audience, but they were also writing to a future audience beyond the students and teacher in front of them. Given that membership in this classroom writing community equaled membership in students' future independent school writing communities, students were writing *to* the community of all former, current, and future academic writers who have successfully navigated independent schools and professional networks. Students' interactions around writing (i.e., crafting personally relevant thesis statements; offering and receiving feedback; sharing resources) were collective bids for membership into these wider discourse communities.

By turning the inquiry over to the students, Mr. Campbell implicated the students' expertise as analytical writers, and students rose to the occasion by working through moments of struggle and taking strong stands on feedback to each other's work. Throughout the discussion with Sula, for example, Mr. Campbell modeled the specific steps (i.e., heuristic and thinking questions) involved in crafting a successful thesis statement. Following those steps, however, was not a guarantee that the process was easy and straightforward. Sula struggled to fill in the blank of the heuristic to make her thesis statement arguable. Mr. Campbell followed up with targeted feedback and questions, refusing to supply Sula with a possible answer. Over time, moments of productive struggle (Bullmaster-Day, 2015) like this have the capacity to "build deep conceptual understanding and procedural fluency that transfers to new situations" (p. 2). The struggle was productive for Sula because she had to engage the critical thought processes needed to think beyond the text. As such, Mr. Campbell was not the only bearer of knowledge or the only one permitted to be critical of others' work in this classroom – the students were, too. Students were working through moments of struggle and developing the identities of the writers Mr. Campbell expected them to become: effective communicators capable of making sophisticated interpretations of literature.

Furthermore, students were developing as academic writers through texts and topics that were meaningful to them. Too often, students experience in-school writing tasks as far removed from their interests and values (Moje, Overby, Tysvaer, & Morris, 2008), but in this class, Mr. Campbell grounded discussions in several student-relevant frameworks (e.g., scene from *The Equalizer* and a former student's model essay). He used these frameworks to explicitly introduce the discourse of analytical writing in a way that resonated with students.

Moreover, starting the inquiry about thesis statements from students' observations about the novel (rather than in response to a given prompt) allowed students to build interpretations that were relevant to them. While Mr. Campbell helped Sula refine her initial idea, the idea remained hers throughout the discussion. He leveraged what she already knew and cared about (i.e., her observation about Lennie) in the service of learning a new academic skill (i.e., making an arguable statement). For culturally diverse students, in particular, completing the analytical essay to strict expectations may not only be a negotiation of discourse patterns and behaviors but of one's identity, or sense of self (Gee, 1996). Students, therefore, need to be explicitly taught the features of the genre but in ways that do not dismiss students' cultural and linguistic backgrounds (Delpit, 1995). In Mr. Campbell's class, students were beginning to develop the skills and identities of academic writers, but it was through texts and topics that were meaningful to them.

INSTRUCTIONAL IMPLICATIONS: STUDENT-CENTERED PRACTICES

The findings from this study point to the following implications for secondary teachers to consider as they teach their students to write essays in a new academic genre:

1. *Use student-grounded frameworks to develop understandings of a new discourse.*
   It is important to use student-grounded frameworks to develop students' understandings of a new discourse, like writing analytical essays. Research has demonstrated that instructional contexts using student contributions as access points for acquiring formal literate practices can have the impact of validating and promoting their academic identities (Lee, 1993). As such, teachers can nurture students' developing academic writing identities by honoring and leveraging their contributions.
2. *Move students from teacher-guided to student-led inquiry discussions while demanding active student participation throughout.*
   Ultimately, for inquiry discussions around student writing to work, the students need to participate in the bulk of the reacting and responding to writing. Studies on classroom talk show that when students actively participate in sustained, elaborated discussions, they develop deeper, more meaningful understandings of a topic (e.g., Nystrand, 1997). Accordingly, teachers in writing classrooms could give students ample opportunities to respond to writing. That being said, giving over the inquiry to the students, rather than relying on direct instruction or modeling, requires more instructional minutes. The teacher has to follow the discussion where students lead him, and that takes more time

than delivering a tight lecture or modeling the steps in a process. In the current era of standardized testing, pressures on teachers to stick to a timeline are significant. As such, some teachers might not be able to devote the time needed to let students jointly construct understanding in this way. It is important to understand, however, that when students engage in more of the inquiry around learning a new discourse, they may be more likely to acquire the adaptive, enduring writing skills and the independence of mind they need to thrive in postsecondary contexts.

CONCLUSION

This chapter set out to describe the role one classroom writing community played in shaping students' understandings of the analytical writing genre; and to discuss the impact the community had on students' developing academic writing identities. The role of a classroom writing community has been deemed important for the writing development of culturally diverse learners (Dyson, 1997). Interacting with writing communities may encourage students with diverse cultural and linguistic backgrounds to take up the rhetorical conventions of formal writing genres and grow their identities as academic writers. The results of this study demonstrate that by turning the classroom writing community into an authentic audience through inquiry discussions, Mr. Campbell developed students' deep and flexible understandings of a new academic discourse and facilitated students' willingness to take on academic writing identities. Specifically, Mr. Campbell conducted inquiry discussions around students' thesis statement drafts as a springboard for further instruction in crafting literary interpretations. The classroom community's reactions to their peers' writing allowed students to negotiate both their understanding of genre-specific features as well as their identities in their current and future school communities.

NOTE

1. In order to protect the identities of research subjects, all names of places, teachers, and students have been changed to pseudonyms.

REFERENCES

Atwell, N. (1998). *In the middle: New understandings about writing, reading, and learning.* Portsmouth, NH: Boynton.
Bereiter, C., & Scardamalia, M. (1987). The psychology of written composition. Hillsdale, NJ: Erlbaum.
Braun, V., & Clark, V. (2006). Using thematic analysis in psychology. *Qualitative Research in Psychology, 3,* 77–101.
Bullmaster-Day, M. L. (2015). *Productive struggle for deeper learning.* [White paper.] Retrieved from WeAreTeachers: http://www.weareteachers.com/docs/default-source/triumph-learning-lessons/triumph-learning-productive-struggle-white-paper.pdf. Accessed on April 1, 2016.
Calkins, L. M. (1986). *The art of teaching writing.* Portsmouth, NH: Heinemann.
Delpit, L. (1995). *Other people's children: Cultural conflict in the classroom.* New York, NY: The New Press.
Dyson, A. H. (1997). *Writing superheroes: Contemporary childhood, popular culture and* classroom literacy. New York, NY: Teacher's College Press.
Emerson, R. M., Fretz, R. I., & Shaw, L. L. (2001). Participant observation and fieldnotes. In P. Atkinson, A. Coffey, S. Delamont, J. Lofland, & L. Lofland (Eds.), *Handbook of ethnography* (pp. 352–368). London: Sage.
Fahnestock, J., & Secor, M. (1991). The rhetoric of literary criticism. In C. Bazerman & J. Paradis (Eds.), *Textual dynamics of the professions: Historical and contemporary studies of writing in professional communities* (pp. 76–96). Madison, WI: University of Wisconsin Press.
Flower, L., & Hayes, J. (1981). Plans that guide the composing process. In C. Frederiksen & J. Dominic (Eds.), *The nature, development and teaching of written communication* (pp. 39–58). Hillsdale, NJ: Lawrence Erlbaum Associates, Inc.
Fuqua, A. (Director). (2014). *The Equalizer* [Motion picture]. United States: Village Roadshow Pictures.
Gee, J. P. (1996). *Social linguistics and literacies: Ideology in discourses* (2nd ed.). London: Falmer.
Halverson, E. R. (2005). InsideOut: Facilitating gay youth identity development through a performance-based youth organization. *Identity: An International Journal of Theory and Research, 5*(1), 67–90.
Hillocks, G. (2010). "EJ" in focus: Teaching argument for critical thinking and writing: An introduction. *The English Journal, 99*(6), 24–32.
Hillocks, G. (2011). Teaching argument writing, grades 6–12: Supporting claims with relevant evidence and clear reasoning. Portsmouth, NH: Heinemann.
Lee, C. D. (1993). *Signifying as a scaffold to literary interpretation: The pedagogical implications of a form of African-American discourse.* (NCTE Research Rep. No. 26). Urbana, IL: National Council of Teachers of English.
Lee, H. (1960). *To kill a mockingbird.* New York, NY: Warner.
Magnifico, A. M. (2010). Writing for whom? Cognition, motivation, and a writer's audience. *Educational Psychologist, 45*(3), 167–184.
Moje, E. B., Overby, M., Tysvaer, N., & Morris, K. (2008). The complex world of adolescent literacy: Myths, motivations, and mysteries. *Harvard Educational Review, 78*(1), 107–154.

Morrison, T. (1970). *The bluest eye*. New York, NY: Holt, Rinehart, and Winston.

National Governors Association Center for Best Practices, Council of Chief State School Officers. (2010). Common core state standards for English language arts & literacy in history/social studies, science, and technical subjects. Washington, DC: National Governors Association Center for Best Practices, Council of Chief State School Officers.

Nystrand, M. (1997). *Opening dialogue: Understanding the dynamics of language and learning in the English classroom*. New York, NY: Teachers College Press.

Patton, M. Q. (2002). *Qualitative research and evaluation methods*. Thousand Oaks, CA: Sage.

Purcell-Gates, V., Duke, N. K., & Martineau, J. A. (2007). Learning to read and write genre-specific text: Roles of authentic experience and explicit teaching. *Reading Research Quarterly, 42*(1), 8–45.

Steinbeck, J. (1937). *Of mice and men*. New York, NY: Bantam.

Wenger, E. (1998). *Communities of practice: Learning, meaning, and identity*. Cambridge: Cambridge University Press.

Wenger, E. (2010). Communities of practice and social learning systems: The career of a concept. In C. Blackmore (Ed.), *Social learning systems and communities of practice* (pp. 179–197). London: Springer Verlag and the Open University.

Yancey, K. B. (2009). Writing in the 21st century: A report from the national council of teachers of English. Urbana, IL: National Council of Teachers of English.

ENGAGING STUDENTS IN MULTIMODAL ARGUMENTS: INFOGRAPHICS AND PUBLIC SERVICE ANNOUNCEMENTS

Emily Howell

ABSTRACT

Purpose – *To present the instructional activities of an intervention enacted in two formative experiment studies. The goal of these studies was to improve students' argumentative writing, both conventional and digital, multimodal.*

Design/methodology/approach – *This chapter provides the instructional steps taken by high-school teachers as they integrated multimodal argument projects into their classroom, describing the planning and instructional activities needed to teach students both the elements of argument and the practice of digital, multimodal design.*

Findings – *The author discusses the practical pedagogical steps and considerations needed to have students create digital, multimodal arguments in the form of infographics and public service announcements. Students were engaged in the creation of these arguments; however, practical considerations are discussed for both task complexity and the merger between digital and conventional writing.*

Practical implications — *Research suggests that integrating digital tools and multimodality into classrooms may be needed and valued, but practical suggestions for this integration are lacking. This chapter provides the needed pedagogical application of digital tools and multimodality to academic instruction.*

Keywords: Argument; multimodality; infographic; public service announcement

One needs to look no further than the 2016 presidential debates to see arguments that go beyond the linguistic mode of communication. In a recent Republican debate, the moderator challenged the candidates' linguistic claims using a montage of visual video evidence that seemed counter to their claims (Jackson, 2016). Furthermore, this debate also illustrates that arguments are social, not just cognitive in nature (Newell, Beach, Smith, & VanDerHeide, 2011). In other words, there are cognitive elements of argument such as the claims and evidence that structure argument, but arguments are also social, developed in specific contexts using tools attuned to that context. Candidates were aware of their audience and the tools of their culture most capable of reaching this audience. They conveyed their arguments not only through a variety of modes, such as their words and gestures on stage, but also tools such as microphones, cameras, and social media. Candidates were attuned to their audience engaging in this debate not only via television, but in a more communal way through social media (Pfeiffer, 2015). For example, those watching the debate were not isolated, even if they watched the debate from home, because they may have also been following the debate through Twitter with the hashtag, or searchable link, #GOPDebate. Candidates had to consider not only how to logically structure their responses, but how to convey those responses socially, effectively using the tools and context to attempt to make their message continue virally, pleasing an audience who was assessing the quality of their arguments as they made them.

This example illustrates the need for students to be able to critique and construct arguments that include the multimodality increasingly afforded to them via digital tools (Kress, 2003). Although current literature acknowledges the need for argument to account for the visual nature of our lives (Birdsell & Groarke, 2004), most research on argument focuses on the elements of argument, how these elements are developed logically, and how statements can best represent this logic (Newell et al., 2011). However, argument is not just about logically forming statements based upon a linguistic mode; instead, it is also a set of social practices that involves design choices including which modes to use to convey information and which tools to use to meet that design. Students today may employ linguistic, visual, physical, spatial, and audio modes to achieve their argumentative purpose (Andrews, 1997; Birdsell & Groarke, 2004; Bowen & Whithaus, 2013; Hocks, 2003). Professional organizations have called for teachers to use such digital tools and multimodality as an integrated part of their curriculum (International Reading Association [IRA], 2009; National Council of Teachers of English [NCTE], 2005, 2008). At the same time, argument has increasingly become a central focus in both educational standards and assessments (Council of the Chief State School Officers [CCSSO] & the National Governors Association Center [NGAC], 2010; National Center for Education Statistics [NCES], 2012; Smith, Wilhelm, & Fredricksen, 2012). Thus, how can teachers integrate the teaching of multimodality and argument instruction into their classrooms?

In this chapter, I will present two types of multimodal arguments high-school students constructed: infographics and public service announcements (PSAs). In two formative experiments (Reinking & Bradley, 2008), I worked with three high-school English teachers as we investigated the implementation of an intervention aimed at improving argumentative writing, conventional and digital, multimodal. Based upon these studies (Howell, 2015; Howell, Butler, & Reinking, 2014), I will describe the students' multimodal argument projects, both infographics and PSAs, providing teachers with practical guidance for integrating concepts of multimodality into their classroom. Such guidance is missing from current research, especially as it pertains to applying concepts of design and multimodality to specifically academic content, such as argumentative writing (Graham & Benson, 2010; Jocius, 2013). After discussing how these projects were implemented, I will describe their implications for students and considerations that might be made when integrating digital tools and multimodality into argument instruction.

INFOGRAPHICS AS ARGUMENT

An infographic is an abbreviation of the term *information graphic* and "uses visual cues to communicate information" (Lankow, Ritchie, & Crooks,

2012, p. 20). Although infographics became popular in the 1930s (Lankow et al., 2012), these representations of information are increasingly significant, as competition for audience has increased in an age in which everyone is an author (Yancey, 2009), and this medium allows authors to communicate information quickly and creatively. Infographics are prevalent in digital spaces such as online news websites and social media platforms like Facebook, Pinterest, and Twitter (Lazard & Atkinson, 2015); due to this prevalence, they provide a relevant format for students' arguments.

Whithaus (2012) found in his study of scientific reports for elements of the Toulmin form of argument (1958/2003) that a model of argument may be needed that can account for visual and numeric evidence rather than just linguistic. Infographics may be an ideal space for students to create arguments as they provide a consolidated opportunity for students to consider claims and evidence for those claims by combining linguistic and visual modes. Further, Lazard and Atkinson (2015), in two controlled experiments with a total of 528 participants between the ages of 18 and 80, found that when issues were presented via an infographic, which combines text and images, people thought more critically about those issues than when presented with the same information with just text or a visual illustration. Thus, teaching students to critique and write information for an infographic may help them to more deeply understand both the concept of argument and the content of their arguments.

Another consideration for using infographics that I found in the studies that serve as the basis for this chapter (Howell, 2015; Howell et al., 2014) is that integrating multimodality into curriculum can be a complex task that requires students to learn aspects of digital tools, concepts of multimodal design, as well as elements of conventional writing. Thus, multimodal composing can be at times overwhelming, although engaging, for students who may have various levels of familiarity with technology (Bennett, Maton, & Kervin, 2008) and may have little experience with conventional writing (Applebee & Langer, 2013) let alone digital, multimodal composing. Thus, the consolidated nature of an infographic may alleviate some of the tension that occurs with the novelty of attempting multimodal arguments.

Planning for Students to Create Infographics

I worked with three teachers as we implemented an intervention in high-school classrooms with the goal of improving students' conventional and digital, multimodal arguments. During the first stage of the intervention, two of these teachers had their students create infographics that developed arguments. These teachers allowed the students to work in groups and create arguments that were pertinent to their content. The ninth-grade teacher I worked with was teaching the novel *Tuesdays with Morrie* (Albom, 1997) with her college-preparatory students. Thus, she had students create an infographic in which they argued over the legality of euthanasia, as the main character in this novel, Morrie, has to deal with his own mortality during his battle with Amyotrophic Lateral Sclerosis (ALS).

This unit took seven weeks to implement, but that time entailed instruction on the elements of argument, aspects of design and multimodality, the functionality of various digital tools, and working through stages of the writing process such as drafting, revision, and publication of the infographics. The tenth-grade teacher focused her unit on infographics on the novel *To Kill a Mockingbird* (Lee, 1960). In reading this classic text, the students were discussing themes of prejudice as it pertained to age, race, and gender. The students chose one of these prejudices and made an argument for how it occurred in current times versus the time frame of the novel. This unit occurred over six weeks, but, once again, this teacher was covering the same variety of skills as the ninth-grade teacher.

Instructional Activities

Elements of Argument

The teachers in these studies based their definition of argument on the Toulmin (1958/2003) model of argument, which is common to composition classrooms (Lunsford, 2002). This model consists of six fundamental components: (1) *claims* or assertions that must be proven by the argument, (2) *data* or evidence that supports the claim, (3) *warrants*, statements that explain how the datum support the claim, (4) *qualifiers*, words that specify the degree to which the arguer thinks the data support the claim, such as the word "probably," (5) *rebuttals*, statements of condition of which the warrant would not apply, and (6) *backing* or statements needed to support the warrant (Toulmin, 1958/2003). However, we limited our instruction of arguments to the elements of argument that Toulmin (1958/2003) deemed necessary to have an argument: claims, data or evidence, and warrants or explication of the evidence. Limiting the elements of argument initially introduced to students may help students focus on the essential elements of argument and prevent them from becoming overwhelmed by what can be a challenging academic task, composing arguments.

The teachers began their instruction of this unit by introducing the language of argument and defining each of the terms, claims, evidence, and warrants or elaboration of evidence. The students then practiced these terms with an activity in which they had to become detectives and solve a crime (Wilhelm, 2014). The students looked at a picture of a crime and had to make a claim arguing for what happened in the picture. Their arguments were based on evidence from the same picture and their explication of how that evidence supported their claim (their warrants). After this activity, students then examined a television commercial online for the claim, evidence, and warrants in that commercial (see Smith et al., 2012). Both of these introductory activities not only introduced the structure of argument, but also introduced arguments that were not limited to a linguistic mode. The first being the picture in the crime, in which most of the students' evidence was visual, and the second being the television commercial, which included linguistic and visual evidence among other modes. Students then practiced making their own advertisements, making arguments to sell different products (see Smith et al., 2012), using not only text, but also a variety of modes to make their first multimodal argument. To make these arguments digitally, students used Glogster EDU (edu.glogster.com) a tool that will be discussed subsequently (see also Howell, Reinking, & Kaminski, 2015).

During this discussion of not only the structure of argument (claims, evidence, and warrants), but also using multimodality to express arguments, it seems important to explicitly draw comparisons between arguments relying upon text alone and those using a multimodal design. Students need this discussion to help them transfer their learning about the elements and design of argument between their conventional writing and their multimodal, digital design. Attention may also need to be directed to how other skills of argumentation also compare between conventional and digital, multimodal texts. For instance, in these studies the teachers had to teach students not only documentation of print sources, such as parenthetical citation and a references page, but also how to document more multimodal evidence, such as pictures and video clips. Students may not be familiar with where to find evidence that is more visual and how this evidence can be used in accordance with copyright laws. To give students the opportunity to use visual images as evidence in their arguments, we introduced them to Google Images (https://images.google.com/) and the search tools available through this search engine that enable students to select usage rights that are copyright friendly. Websites such as morgueFile (https://www.morguefile.com/) that allow students to search for images with limited restrictions on usage and collections of images purchased by school media centers are also valuable resources for students to obtain images.

Multimodal Composing and Digital Tools
Once students learned the definitions of the elements of argument, understood that arguments could also be designed multimodally, analyzed a model of multimodal argument for these elements, and practiced creating their own multimodal argument, we started the writing process of creating their infographics. Many teachers assume that arguments begin with creating a thesis or a claim; however, students need to examine the evidence before they can decide which perspective of a topic to argue (Hillocks, 2010). Thus, students began examining evidence pertaining to the topic they selected for their infographic. This process was both collaborative and multimodal.

First, the students worked in groups on a Google Doc (http://www.google.com/docs/about/), an online tool that allows for document creation and sharing, exploring different topics. Each topic included sources of information that also provided several models of writing from linguistic-based sources, such as articles, to more multimodal sources, including television interviews and online infographics. For instance, the tenth graders interested in the topic of prejudice based upon age looked at infographics, such as one from *Forbes* website (Miller, 2012) that discussed hiring Millennials, and they also viewed documents that were more text-based, such as a newspaper article on age discrimination. Students not only explored this evidence collaboratively, but they also discussed their perspective based on the evidence examined and how they might represent that evidence multimodally. Fig. 1 shows part of the Google Doc the students exploring the age prejudice topic completed to prepare the argument for their infographic.

Next, students were given several models of infographics as multimodal arguments. We intentionally chose infographics as sources for each topic as this not only gave the students information for the content of their arguments and allowed them to see sources displaying this information multimodally, but it also provided them an opportunity to see how these texts were being used in authentic contexts. Gallagher (2006) discussed the importance of using models of writing, "Having our students closely examine real-world writers helps them to see the craft behind good writing" (p. 84). Hicks (2013) extended this discussion in terms of digital writing linking the exploration of multimodality in digital texts with building students' purpose and creativity. Thus, these models were important to help students see the craft in digital argumentative writing, both in how to

Is Age Prejudice Better or Worse Now as Compared to the 1930s?

Directions:

1. Write down evidence from the sources above for each side of this issue.

Better	Worse
E1:	E1:
E2:	E2:
E3:	E3:
E4:	E4:

2. Select a side, and write your claim below:

3. Write your claim, evidence, and explanation of that evidence in the chart below (This time only use the evidence for your side):

Claim:	
Evidence (What makes you say so?)	Elaboration/Warrant (So What?)
E1:	W1:
E2:	W2:
E3:	W3:

4. What evidence about age prejudice was in the novel?

5. Compare and contrast what you found in the novel with what you found in the sources above.

6. What images and symbols would be important in representing your side of this issue?

7. What colors might you use to represent your side of the issue and why?

8. What types of music might represent your side of this argument and why?

9. How might you use space and layout to convey your argument?

Fig. 1. Examination of Topic.

structure the elements of their arguments and how to use multimodal design to convey this structure. We also provided students a variety of infographics when we introduced directions for how they would compose an argument via an infographic. For these models, we chose the most popular infographics from a popular digital tool for creating infographics, Piktochart (see http://piktochart.com/top-10-best-infographics-of-2013/).

Engaging Students in Multimodal Arguments 191

After showing students several such models of infographics, we discussed with students the design elements of infographics. The NLG (1996) suggested in their discussion of *multiliteracies* that literacy must account for a new variety of texts, technologies, and modes of representation. Their pedagogy of multiliteracies included overt instruction or explicitly teaching elements of design including the modes available to students and how they might use these elements to express meaning (NLG, 1996). Thus, we gave students examples of how they might use different design elements in their infographics including the following: images and graphics, hyperlinks, audio files, colors, fonts, shapes, use of space, and how the elements might be used effectively together. As the multimodal design was just as important as effectively structuring their arguments, students were assessed on how they structured their arguments, their design, and their ability to explain their design. See Fig. 2 for an example of an infographic created by ninth-grade students. This figure shows students asserting a claim at the center of the infographic and supporting that claim with evidence from research sources, such as the Gallup poll, and quotations from the novel *Tuesdays with Morrie*. In addition, these students used teardrop

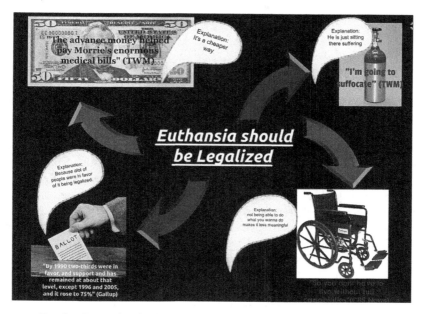

Fig. 2. Example of Infographic Created by Ninth-Grade Students.

shapes to highlight elaboration of evidence and labeled their elaboration with the heading *Explanation*.

An important consideration in this project was deciding which digital tools to use with the design of students' multimodal arguments. The digital divide was once defined as those who had access to technology and those who did not; however, now that technology use is becoming more pervasive, this concern is changing from one of access to one of use (Jenkins, Clinton, Purushotma, Robison, & Weigel, 2006). Educators must ensure that technology use is encouraging equitable participation and creation with digital tools rather than simply ensuring its inclusion in the classroom as "*more* technology use isn't inherently good" (Pollock, 2016, p. 39, emphasis in original). Thus, we focused on selecting tools that were accessible, that afforded multimodality, and that students would use repeatedly so as to build their technological expertise. There are many free tools available online that specifically focus upon creating infographics, such as Easel.ly, Infogram, Piktochart, and Smore among others (see Yearta & Mitchell, 2016 for a review of these tools).

However, we wanted to use tools that would also be beneficial to students in creating their PSAs. Thus, we chose Glogster EDU, which is an online website in which students can create online, multimodal posters and which students had already used in the aforementioned creation of advertisements. This website is one that allows teachers to control the functionality for students (i.e., whether or not students publish online or just for their classmates) and also mimics the functionality of social media platforms with which students may have familiarity. For instance, students can easily share their posters online, and they select different modes – including audio, linguistic, and visual – with the click of an add button that may remind students of sites such as Facebook and Instagram. As described previously, the students also used Google Docs to examine models of arguments and collect evidence for their infographic topic. Both of these tools, Glogster EDU and Google Docs, were used again with the PSA. Such repetition seems valuable because even though research has suggested that adolescents today are inherently technologically savvy (see Prensky, 2001 for his definition of digital natives), we found that students often lacked technological skills especially when using digital tools for academic purposes. This finding is supported by those such as Bennett et al. (2008) who suggested that students vary in their technological knowledge, debunking the myth of the digital native. Thus, the frequency with which students will use digital tools may be an important factor when considering which tools to integrate into classroom instruction.

PUBLIC SERVICE ANNOUNCEMENTS AS ARGUMENT

PSAs were the second type of multimodal argument studied. The Ad Council (2016) explained the objective of PSAs: "to raise awareness or change behaviors and attitudes on a social issue." I was first inspired by an article by Selfe and Selfe (2008) to use PSAs as a vehicle to allow students to explore argument and multimodality with an assignment in which there are prevalent authentic examples and through which students could explore a social issue of their choosing. While Selfe and Selfe (2008) focused upon the pedagogical need to incorporate multimodal projects such as the PSA, authors such as Hatfield, Hinck, and Birkholt (2007) suggested that PSAs are an ideal model exemplifying that the rhetorical realization of arguments often extends beyond the linguistic mode. This belief aligns with the intervention in these studies entailing cognitive instruction of the elements of argument and the social practice of designing arguments using the tools appropriate for the context of the argument (see Newell et al., 2011). For example, Hatfield et al. (2007) discussed that those creating a PSA to raise money for UNICEF for former child soldiers had to not only realize what claims they wanted to make and how to structure their arguments, but also had to be aware of the social practice of these arguments. In this case, their audience in African countries had become saturated, and therefore apathetic, with images of child suffering. In an attempt to overcome this apathy, the authors of this particular PSA used Smurfs, the cartoon characters, instead to portray visual evidence for a linguistic claim. Hatfield et al. (2007) argued that because PSAs, such as the UNICEF PSA, overtly make a claim and provide reasons for that claim that can be consciously analyzed by an audience, they should be considered visual arguments. In this study, students developed multimodal arguments through their creation of a PSA in which students examined models of PSAs, researched evidence on a social topic, and published their PSA via a website.

Planning for Public Service Announcements

I worked with a ninth- and tenth-grade teacher over the course of seven (in tenth grade) and eight weeks (in ninth grade) to implement units in which students argued a position on a social issue via a PSA. In the ninth grade, the teacher implemented the PSA with the students' study of the novel *Of Mice and Men* (Steinbeck, 1937). The students chose from a list of social issues occurring in the novel, examined evidence on that issue in both the novel and in research from current times on that issue, and argued a position on that issue. In the tenth grade, the teacher implemented the PSA as a unit focused on argumentation without also including a study of literature. Her students selected a social issue of interest, researched that issue at both the state and national level, and published a PSA in which they advocated a position on this issue.

Instructional Activities

Elements of Argument
Similar to the infographic assignment, the teachers began this unit exploring models of argument. Students began looking at conventional arguments in newspaper editorials and analyzing those editorials for how the authors included the elements of argument: claims, evidence, and elaboration of that evidence. Students then explored models of PSAs using sources they accessed through a Google Doc. Students explored PSAs in the form of online posters and videos made by the American Heart Association (see http://www.localheart.org/branding/VideoContentAssets/GeneralVideosPSAEssenceVideos/General-Videos-PSAEssence-Videos_UCM_465825_Sub HomePage.jsp) and the Ad Council (see http://www.adcouncil.org/Our-Campaigns). They also studied PSAs in the form of a website by analyzing issues conveyed by The More You Know website (see http://www.themoreyouknow.com/topics/). Students were asked to analyze these PSAs for the elements of argument, how these elements were conveyed, whether they found the PSAs effective and what, if anything, they might emulate from these PSAs in their own arguments.

Hillocks (2010) argued that although most teachers begin argument instruction with instructing students on writing a thesis statement or claim, argument instruction should, instead, begin with an examination of evidence. To encourage such examination we began with having students explore three possible topics and the evidence available for those topics before they chose an issue and began to consider the claim they would develop for that issue. Fig. 3 shows the assignment that provided the scaffold for this exploration of evidence. This figure also demonstrates that along with examining potential topics and evidence for those topics, we encouraged students to consider how to present these arguments multimodally as the second question for each topic asked students to explore how they might gather evidence for their arguments that was multimodal. Once students chose their topic for their PSA, they explored this issue using

Name:_____
Class Period:_____
Directions:
1. Go to the library homepage and go to the search engines we have discussed.
2. Take some time to look through issues of interest. Or, you can look up issues that are also at the bottom of this packet as social issues.
3. Think about which issues you would like to develop a public service announcement for via a website. Remember, you will spend a lot of time on this project, so make sure to choose something that has relevance and interest to you.
4. "PSAs are generally developed for one of three reasons: to prevent a behavior from starting; to stop a behavior (cessation); or to encourage adoption of a new behavior" (Atkin, 2001). Try to pick a topic that you could make an argument about-something that has multiple sides, and an issue where you could pick a side and propose a solution.
5. As you look at sites that contain possible social issue topics, please consider the following questions and take notes accordingly. Pick three issues that you are most interested in and answer the following questions for each issue.

Topic 1:_____
1. Why is this topic interesting and relevant to you?
2. What types of information, including text, video, images, etc., will you be able to find on this topic?
3. Will you be able to find information on this topic that is both national and local in scope?
4. How will you take a stance on this topic (Make sure there are legitimately multiple sides.)?
5. Is this topic appropriate for the audience? Who is your audience?

Topic 2:_____
1. Why is this topic interesting and relevant to you?
2. What types of information, including text, video, images, etc., will you be able to find on this topic?
3. Will you be able to find information on this topic that is both national and local in scope?
4. How will you take a stance on this topic (Make sure there are legitimately multiple sides.)?
5. Is this topic appropriate for the audience? Who is your audience?

Topic 3:_____
1. Why is this topic interesting and relevant to you?
2. What types of information, including text, video, images, etc., will you be able to find on this topic?
3. Will you be able to find information on this topic that is both national and local in scope?
4. How will you take a stance on this topic (Make sure there are legitimately multiple sides.)?
5. Is this topic appropriate for the audience? Who is your audience?

Fig. 3. Exploring Issues and Evidence for PSA.

a database available at their library and worked collaboratively to gather evidence about their chosen issues, which they shared via Google Docs.

Multimodal Composing and Digital Tools

Once students had completed the previously described steps of prewriting including examining conventional and multimodal models of argument, exploring different social issues, deciding upon their topic and gathering evidence for that topic, they began to draft their PSAs using Google Sites (see https://www.google.com/sites/overview.html). This tool was chosen because it was easily accessible to students through their school email account and allowed for students to create a multimodal website. The students also used Glogster EDU once again, but this time they used it to create one component of their overall argument, which was embedded in their website. For instance, the tenth-graders created a Glogster EDU poster about a component of their social issue at the state level, and the ninth-graders created their online poster about how their social issue applied to the novel *Of Mice and Men*. See Fig. 4 for an example of a portion of a ninth-grade student's PSA in which the student argued for the importance of the agriculture industry with evidence organized in columns, images to support this evidence, as well as hyperlinks for sources of this information.

They then embedded this component into their Google website, which reflected their overall argument. Breaking the PSA website into several different projects was intended to scaffold this task, which was complex for students as it demanded a variety of new academic learning: argumentative writing, multimodal design, and using digital tools for academic content. Further scaffolding, such as providing students with templates for how they might design their website and handouts for how to operate each digital tool were important to help students navigate their digital, multimodal design. One of the findings of the studies related to these instructional activities was that teachers might focus on controlling task elements of multimodal projects so that they do not become overwhelming to both their teaching and the students' learning.

POTENTIAL BENEFITS FOR STUDENTS EXPLORING MULTIMODAL ARGUMENTS

The ninth-grade teacher enacting this intervention summed up some of the benefits for students learning argument through digital, multimodal composing: "I think they had more creativity, and they were able in their minds to get a structure and a design. And, they could see the big picture before they started." The students seemed to be engaged in their design of arguments and learned the elements of argument through the multimodal design of argument. Further, prior to this intervention students did not seem to know that arguments could entail other modes beyond that of the

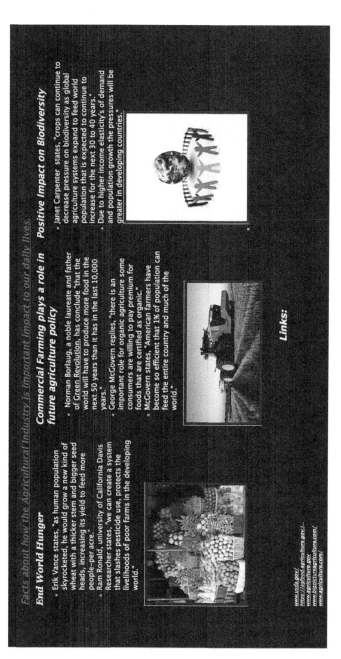

Fig. 4. Portion of Ninth-Grade Student PSA Website.

linguistic, suggesting that they did not recognize that popular mediums of argument, such as infographics and PSAs, included elements of argument. Thus, this intervention seemed to expand their understanding not just of the elements of argument, but also the design of arguments. They demonstrated this learning in their successful creation of both infographics and PSAs in which they argued various perspectives pertaining to a variety of social issues. Jenkins et al. (2006) suggested that instruction of such new forms of writing and publishing such forms in a digital world is necessary because today, "The young people are creating new modes of expression that are poorly understood by adults, and as a result they receive little to no guidance or supervision" (p. 17).

Yet, these benefits were not without some challenges. For instance, in my experience with these assignments, students were not experienced with using digital tools for academic purposes and encountered some frustration as they learned to design using digital tools and multimodality. Teachers may need to provide needed scaffolding and control task elements of these assignments so that students' engagement in these activities does not become dampened by task complexity. In addition, although students may achieve in these tasks important 21st century skills called for by organizations such as the International Literacy Association (previously known as IRA, 2009) and the National Council of Teachers of English (NCTE, 2005, 2008), teachers should not assume that students' digital writing of arguments will immediately transfer to their conventional writing. Rather, both digital and conventional writing instruction may be necessary for students to be competent, effective citizens in a digital world that increasingly affords multimodal forms of communication. In fact, Jenkins et al. (2006) suggested that a renewed focus be placed on conventional literacies even as one explores new forms of communication.

This intervention and the series of instructional practices it entailed included the conventional teaching of argument, based upon students learning claims, evidence, and elaboration of that evidence. Yet, it combined this instruction with students learning to use digital tools and design arguments using the multimodality these tools offered. However, Newell et al. (2011) described research investigating such practices as limited. The studies that examined this intervention are beginning to address this need, but further research is necessary. Interventions that effectively merge conventional and digital forms of composing as well as the cognitive and social practices of argument need to be studied in varied contexts until they become what Grossen (1996) described as "polished stones" or "instructional procedures that have been revised and refined by different teachers until they work so reliably, they are polished to a shine" (p. 27). Further, teachers need to understand the complexities of integrating such interventions, including factors that enhance or inhibit their implementation, any unanticipated outcomes, and how these factors vary across learning ecologies (Cobb, Confrey, diSessa, Lehrer, & Schauble, 2003; Gravemeijer & Cobb, 2006; Reinking & Bradley, 2008).

REFERENCES

Ad Council. (2016). *Frequently asked questions*. Ad Council website. Retrieved from http://www.adcouncil.org/About-Us/Frequently-Asked-Questions#What's%20the%20difference%20between%20a%20commercial%20and%20a%20PSA?

Albom, M. (1997). *Tuesdays with Morrie: An old man, a young man, and life's greatest lesson* (1st ed). New York, NY: Doubleday.

Andrews, R. (1997). Reconceiving argument. *Educational Review*, *49*(3), 259–269. doi:10.1080/0013191970490305

Applebee, A. N., & Langer, J. A. (2013). *Writing instruction that works: Proven methods for middle and high school classrooms*. New York, NY: Teachers College Press.

Atkin, C. (2001). *Public service announcement: How can we make them effective*. The Health Communication Unit. Centre for Health Promotion, Toronto. Retrieved from http://kabodian7.pbworks.com/f/Atkins_Effective_PSAs_ContentFeb01_Format_aug.03.pdf

Bennett, S., Maton, K., & Kervin, L. (2008). The digital natives debate: A critical review of the evidence. *British Journal of Educational Technology*, *39*(5), 775–786. doi:10.1111/j.1467-8535.2007.00793.x

Birdsell, & Groarke. (2004). Toward a theory of visual argument. In Handa, C. (Ed.), (2004). *Visual rhetoric in a digital world: A critical sourcebook* (pp. 309–320). NY: Bedford/St. Martin's.

Bowen, T., & Whithaus, C. (Eds.). (2013). "What else is possible": Multimodal composing and genre in the teaching of writing. *Multimodal literacies and emerging genres* (pp. 1–13). University of Pittsburgh Press.

Cobb, P., Confrey, J., diSessa, A., Lehrer, R., & Schauble, L. (2003). Design experiments in educational research. *Educational Researcher*, *32*(1), 9–13.

Council of Chief State School Officers [CCSSO] & the National Governors Association Center [NGAC]. (2010). *Common core state standards for English language arts and literacy in history/social studies, science, and technical subjects*. Washington, DC: National Governors Association. Retrieved from http://www.corestandards.org/ELA-Literacy

Gallagher, K. (2006). *Teaching adolescent writers*. Portland, ME: Stenhouse Publishers.

Graham, M. S., & Benson, S. (2010). A springboard rather than a bridge: Diving into multimodal literacy. *English Journal*, *100*(2), 93–97.

Gravemeijer, K., & Cobb, P. (2006). Design research from a learning design perspective. In J. van den akker, K. Gravemeijer, S. Mckenney, & N. Nieveen (Eds.), *Educational design research* (pp. 17–51). New York, NY: Routledge.

Grossen, B. (1996). Making research serve the profession. *American Educator*, *20*(3), 7.

Hatfield, K. L., Hinck, A., & Birkholt, M. J. (2007). Seeing the visual in argumentation: A rhetorical analysis of UNICEF Belgium's Smurf public service announcement. *Argumentation and Advocacy*, *43*(3–4), 144–151.

Hicks, T. (2013). *Crafting digital writing: Composing texts across media and genres*. Portsmouth, NH: Heinemann.

Hillocks, G. (2010). Teaching argument for critical thinking and writing: An introduction. *English Journal*, *99*(6), 24–32.

Hocks, M. E. (2003). Understanding visual rhetoric in digital writing environments. *College Composition and Communication*, *54*(4), 629–656.

Howell, E. (2015). *Creating arguments using a multiliteracies approach: A formative experiment*. All dissertations. Paper 1582.

Howell, E., Butler, T., & Reinking, D. (2014, December). Multimodal arguments, technology, and social issues: A formative experiment. Paper presentation given at the 2014 Literacy Research Association (LRA) Conference, Marco Island, FL.

Howell, E., Reinking, D., & Kaminski, R. (2015). Writing as creative design: Constructing multimodal arguments in a multiliteracies framework. *The Journal of Literacy and Technology*, *16*, 2–36.

International Reading Association [IRA]. (2009). *New literacies and 21st century technologies* (Position statement). Newark, DE: International Reading Association. Retrieved from http://www.reading.org/Libraries/position-statements-and%20resolutions/ps1067_New Literacies21stCentury.pdf

Jackson, D. (2016, March 4). 11th GOP debate: Highlights from Detroit. *USA Today*. Retrieved from http://www.usatoday.com/story/news/politics/onpolitics/2016/03/03/live-republicans-detroit-debate-trump-cruz-rubio-kasich/81275106/

Jenkins, H., Clinton, K., Purushotma, R., Robison, A., & Weigel, M. (2006). Confronting the Challenges of Participatory Culture: Media Education for the 21st Century. White Paper. MacArthur Foundation.

Jocius, R. (2013). Exploring adolescents' multimodal responses to the kite runner: Understanding how students use digital media for academic purposes. *The Journal of Media Literacy Education*, *5*(1), 310–325.

Kress, G. R. (2003). *Literacy in the new media age*. New York, NY: Routledge.

Lankow, J., Ritchie, J., & Crooks, R. (2012). Introduction. *Infographics: The power of visual storytelling* (pp. 11–24). Hoboken, NJ: Wiley.

Lazard, A., & Atkinson, L. (2015). Putting environmental infographics center stage: The role of visuals at the elaboration likelihood model's critical point of persuasion. *Science Communication*, *37*(1), 6–33.

Lee, H. (1960). *To kill a mockingbird*. Philadelphia, PA: Lippincott.

Lunsford, K. J. (2002). Contextualizing toulmin's model in the writing classroom: A case study. *Written Communication*, *19*(1), 109–174. doi:10.1177/074108830201900105

Miller, M. (2012). Why you should be hiring millenials (infographic). *Forbes*. Retrieved from http://www.forbes.com/sites/mattmiller/2012/07/03/why-you-should-be-hiring-millennials-infographic/#502ac5f537f8

National Center for Education Statistics. (2012). *The nation's report card: Writing 2011 (NCES 2012–470)*. Washington, DC: Institute of Education Sciences, U.S. Department of Education.

National Council of Teachers of English [NCTE]. (2005). *NCTE position statement on multimodal literacies*. Retrieved from ncte.org/positions/statements/multimodalliteracies

National Council of Teachers of English [NCTE]. (2008). *The NCTE definition of 21st century literacies (Position statement)*. Retrieved from http://www.ncte.org/positions/statements/21stcentdefinition

New London Group [NLG]. (1996). A pedagogy of multiliteracies: Designing social futures. *Harvard Education Review*, *66*, 60–92.

Newell, G. E., Beach, R., Smith, J., & VanDerHeide, J. (2011). Teaching and learning argumentative reading and writing: A review of research. *Reading Research Quarterly*, *46*(3), 273–304.

Pfeiffer, D. (2015, September 15). How social media is revolutionizing debates. *CNN*. Retrieved from http://www.cnn.com/2015/09/15/opinions/pfeiffer-social-media-debates/

Pollock, M. (2016). Smart tech use for equity. *The Education Digest*, *81*(8), 39–41.

Prensky, M. (2001). Digital natives, digital immigrants part 1. *On the Horizon*, *9*(5), 1–6.

Reinking, D., & Bradley, B. A. (2008). *On formative and design experiments: Approaches to language and literacy research*. New York, NY: Teachers College Press.

Selfe, R. J., & Selfe, C. L. (2008). "Convince me!" valuing multimodal literacies and composing public service announcements. *Theory into Practice*, *47*(2), 83–92.

Smith, M. W., Wilhelm, J., & Fredricksen (2012). *Oh yeah?! Putting argument to work both in school and out*. Portsmouth, NH: Heinemann.

Steinbeck, J. (1937). *Of mice and men*. New York, NY: Penguin.

Toulmin, S. E. (1958/2003). *The uses of argument*. New York, NY: Cambridge University Press.

Whithaus, C. (2012). Claim-evidence structures in environmental science writing: Modifying Toulmin's model to account for multimodal arguments. *Technical Communication Quarterly*, *21*(2), 105–128.

Wilhelm, J. (2014, September). *Teaching argument : Writing as a form of inquiry across the grades and disciplines*. Workshop presented at argument in-service for Upstate Writing Project, Greenville, SC.

Yancey, K. B. (2009). *Writing in the 21st century*. Urbana, IL: National Council of Teachers of English. Retrieved from http://www.ncte.org/library/NCTEFiles/Press/Yancey_final.pdf

Yearta, L., & Mitchell, D. (2016). Infographics: More than digitized posters. *Reading Matters*, *16*, 66–69. Retrieved from http://user-23310503727.cld.bz/RM-Winter-2016-FLIP1

THE USE OF GOOGLE DOCS TECHNOLOGY TO SUPPORT PEER REVISION

Jessica Semeraro and Noreen S. Moore

ABSTRACT

Purpose — *To investigate sixth-grade students with learning disabilities and their use of Google Docs to facilitate peer revision for informational writing.*

Design/methodology/approach — *A qualitative case study is used to examine how students used Google Docs to support peer revision. Constant comparative analysis with a separate deductive revision and overall writing quality analysis was used.*

Findings — *The findings indicate that students used key features in Google Docs to foster collaboration during revision, they made improvements in overall writing quality, their revisions focused on adding informational elements to support organization of their writing and revisions were mostly made at the sentence level, and students were engaged while using the technology.*

Practical implications — *We postulate that the use of peer revision coupled with Google Docs technology can be a powerful tool for improving student writing quality and for changing the role of the writing teacher during revision. The use of peer revision should be accompanied with strong explicit instruction using the gradual release of responsibility model so that peer tutors are well-trained. Writing teachers can use Google Docs to monitor and assess writing and peer collaboration and then use this knowledge to guide whole and small-group instruction or individual conferences.*

Keywords: Writing; learning disabilities; technology; peer revision; adolescents

With the adoption of the Common Core State Standards (CCSS), writing and technology have become two crucial components of all subject areas (CCSS, 2016). Further, writing and technology are becoming intertwined. In order to be considered ready for college and the workplace, it is imperative that students learn to utilize technology to facilitate the writing process and to produce high-quality writing (CCSS, 2016).

Given the importance of writing in school, everyday life, and the workplace, students must learn to write cohesively for a variety of audiences and purposes (NCTE, 2004; The National Writing Project, 2015). Without this capability, students will encounter many challenges inside and outside of school. However, many students today are finishing high school without the literacy skills that they need to succeed in college and the workforce (The Alliance for Excellent Education, 2015). Writing presents many challenges for students because it is a complex process. One of the most challenging aspects of the writing process for students is revision (Graham, MacArthur, & Fitzgerald, 2013), but revision is necessary because it improves writing quality and it gives students a space in which to practice and learn about writing (MacArthur, 2012).

Writers with learning disabilities face particular challenges regarding writing. They often have low motivation to write and they struggle to engage in cognitive processes that successful writers use: creating goals, drafting, organizing, evaluating, and revising (MacArthur, 1996). Indeed, students with learning disabilities often struggle to adequately and accurately evaluate their own writing, problem solve, and refine the structure, style, and organization of a writing piece and these areas are all required for successful revision (MacArthur, 2012).

Students with learning disabilities need explicit instruction and writing practice, but without motivation for writing, they do not elect to write extensively. Therefore, building motivation to write should be a primary goal for educators (Brouwer, 2012). One way to motivate students is to use technology (Purcell, Buchanan, & Friedrich, 2013). In addition to being motivating, technology has also proven to be a useful tool for supporting writing development. For example, word processors can support the revision process (Graham et al., 2013). Since new technologies are constantly being introduced in the classroom and in our students' lives and because technology is emphasized in the CCSS, educators need to discover how new and readily available technologies, such as Google Docs, can support learning in general and students' writing and motivation to write in particular. The purpose of the current study is to understand how middle school students with learning disabilities engage in peer revision using Google Docs while writing an informational text.

REVIEW OF LITERATURE

Developing writers often face challenges when revising due to their limited task schemas for revision (McCutchen, 2006). For example, they often focus on editing their spelling, punctuation and grammar, rather than making global revisions to content or organization (MacArthur, 2012). Fortunately, there are ways teachers can support students' learning about revision. Teacher feedback and conferencing are two main ways to help students, but these are time consuming methods and result in less overall feedback and practice for students due to student−teacher ratios (MacArthur, 2012).

Peer revision can be a solution to these issues. First, it can be an efficient way to provide more frequent feedback and assistance to students and this feedback can be helpful when peers are trained to provide quality feedback and to work cooperatively (Beach & Friedrich, 2006). Secondly, peer revision is one way to reduce writers' cognitive load, to compensate for deficits in the task schema, and to help orchestrate the complex process of revision. Peers can help evaluate each other's writing and provide direction for revision (Beach & Friedrich, 2006; Graham & Perin, 2007). Third, peer revision provides an opportunity for student writers to experience a real audience, which demonstrates to students the social nature of language (Pritchard & Honeycutt, 2006). This is important because much of the writing completed in school is done for evaluation or for a very limited audience (i.e., teacher; Britton, Burgess, Martin, McLeod, & Rosen, 1975). Peer response is one way of foregrounding the importance of audience in writing in the context of a classroom. Further, theory suggests that writing for an audience may have salutary effects on students' writing (DiPardo & Freedman, 1988).

Technology can facilitate peer revision with real audiences. Research also indicates that when technology is used during the writing process, students' revisions and writing improves (Graham et al., 2013). The remainder of this review will focus primarily on peer revision and Google Docs technology since both bodies of literature directly inform the current study.

PEER REVISION

Vygotsky's theory of cognitive development as the result of social interaction within a person's zone of proximal development comprises the theoretical underpinnings of peer assisted learning (PAL) (Topping & Ehly, 1998). PAL is "the acquisition of knowledge and skill through active helping and supporting among status equals or matched companions. PAL is people from similar social groupings, who are not professional teachers, helping each other to learn and by so doing, learning themselves" (Topping & Ehly, 1998, p. 1). Peers can be students of the same age and ability or students of differing ages and abilities; they can be paired or in small groups. Assistance can range in intensity for peers in the helping role. Both the helper peers and the peers being helped are assumed to be learning through the interactive process of PAL. Peer revision is a PAL activity for writing.

Recent reviews of writing instruction have identified peer revision as effective. Hillocks' (1986) study identified peer revision as an effective pre, during, and postinstructional activity. However, he found that a combination of peer interaction with teacher instruction was most successful. In their meta-analysis on effective writing instruction for adolescents, Graham and Perin (2007) assert that peer assistance when writing has a strong, positive impact on writing quality. Finally, Beach and Friedrich (2006) assert that peer feedback has proven effective in enhancing the overall quality of high school and college students' writing. Together, Hillocks (1986), Graham and Perin (2007), and Beach and Friedrich (2006) provide strong evidence for the effectiveness of peer revision at a broad range of grade levels.

Despite its effectiveness, peer revision is difficult to implement in writing classrooms and poor implementation negatively impacts results. Effective training methods for tutors and tutees include direct instruction, modeling, and supervised practice on skills such as giving and receiving timely and appropriate feedback, providing and receiving explanations, and asking questions (Chapman, 1998). In addition, training students to use specific evaluation criteria for writing has proven effective (Hillocks, 1986). Instruction on the use of concrete evaluation criteria can focus on students applying rubrics to their own writing, to their peers writing, to other writing samples, or to a combination of these.

Peer Revision and Adolescents

Olson (1990) examined the effects of peer revising as a complementary activity to whole-group revision instruction on the amount and type of revisions and overall writing quality of 93 sixth-grade students. Students were assigned to one of four conditions: revision instruction, revision instruction and peer review, peer review, or control. Students in the revision instruction conditions received five direct instruction lessons on specific revision strategies for adding, deleting, substituting, paraphrasing, and rearranging. Students in the peer revision conditions received feedback on their writing from a peer partner and also provided feedback to a partner's writing. Students submitted a preinstructional writing sample prior to the study. Then, on the last week of instruction, students wrote an initial draft, revised the draft with or without peers depending on the condition to which they were assigned, and wrote final drafts. The before and after instruction initial drafts and the final drafts of students were evaluated for revision behavior and overall personal narrative writing quality. Results indicate that students in the revision instruction conditions made the most content revisions (i.e., substitutions and additions) whereas students in the control condition made the most surface level revisions. In addition, students in the revision instruction conditions revised the most between the first and second draft than during the final revision. However, students in the revision instruction and peer review condition had papers with significantly higher total writing quality and rhetorical quality than all other groups. The results illustrate that revision instruction alone is not as effective as it is with peer support; on the other hand, peer revision by itself is not as effective as when it is paired with direct instruction on specific revision criteria or techniques.

MacArthur, Schwartz, and Graham (1991) examined the effects of a peer editing strategy that included instruction on specific evaluation criteria on students' overall writing quality, amount, type, quality of revisions made, and knowledge about writing and revision. Fourth, fifth, and sixth-grade students' with learning disabilities were the main participants in the study. The peer editing strategy was designed to support both cognitive and social aspects of writing. Specific revision strategies comprised the cognitive support and a structure for listening and responding comprised the social support. More specifically, the strategy included two structured meetings between two peers. During the first meeting, each peer took a turn reading his writing aloud while his peer listened and read along. After the author read aloud, the listener told the author what he liked best about the writing. Finally, the listener reread the author's paper again to himself and noted if something in the writing was unclear and identified places where the author could add more details or information. Both students in the pair played both roles. After receiving feedback, students made revisions to their writing independently. Next, the students met to discuss the revisions they made and to edit each other's writing using a checklist. The students trained in the peer editing strategy group were compared to students in a control group which continued regular classroom activities consistent with the writing workshop approach. Overall, results illustrate that students in the experimental group improved the quality of their writing, made more revisions, and made less spelling and punctuation errors. Further, although students in the control group made more revisions when revising alone, they did not make more substantive revisions or improve the overall quality of their writing more than the control group. Metacognitive interviews revealed no difference between the experimental and control groups.

Stoddard and MacArthur (1993) used a similar peer editor strategy with seventh- and eighth-grade students with learning disabilities. Peers were asked to listen to the author read her writing aloud, tell the author what she liked best about the writing, re-read the author's paper and make notes on the draft using revision questions, and discuss suggestions with the author. Revision questions included specific evaluation criteria about the extent to which the author provided the key parts of an essay (beginning, middle, end), a logical ordering of ideas, adequate details, and clarity. A multiple probe design across pairs was used to assess the effects of instruction. Writing was assessed using several measures: number of words, percent of spelling, capitalization and punctuation errors, number and types of revision, overall quality of final drafts, and change in quality between drafts. Results indicated that after instruction all students made more substantive, successful revisions. In addition, following instruction, second drafts were rated better in quality than first drafts. Moreover, the overall quality of final drafts increased from baseline to post-tests. Overall quality was defined as content, organization, and style. Finally, gains were maintained at one and two month maintenance testing and generalized to independent production of handwritten compositions.

Similarly, Prater and Bermúdez (1993) studied the effects of a peer response strategy in which fourth grade, limited English proficient students used specific evaluation criteria to provide feedback on each other's writing. In a pretest post-test quasiexperimental design, intact classes of students were assigned to one of two groups: small group condition and individual condition. Students in the small group condition met in heterogeneous groups of four to five students (i.e., students with limited English proficiency and native English speakers). Students in the small group condition met for three consecutive weeks. They met to select writing topics and to share their first drafts. When sharing their drafts, students followed a procedure modeled by the teacher. The procedure included the author reading aloud his writing to the group, group members telling the author places they liked, the author asking for help on a particular area, and group members telling the author parts of the piece that they wanted to know more about or that they wanted to be clearer. Students were instructed to be specific when commenting by referring to specific parts of the text. Thus, the evaluation criteria utilized in this study was: readers' likes, need for more information or detail, and clarity. During the three-week intervention, students in the control group worked individually on three self-selected topics. Their teachers provided spelling and grammar correction. ANCOVAs were used to assess the effects of the intervention at post-test, after adjusting for pretest scores. The analyses indicate no significant differences between groups on overall quality of writing; however, the mean for the experimental group was slightly higher than the mean for the control group. Significant differences in the fluency measures (i.e., number of words and idea units) were found to favor the experimental group. The authors believe that the lack of significant results on overall writing quality is likely due to the short intervention or the need for more direct instruction in the rubric used for evaluation.

REVISING AND GOOGLE DOCS TECHNOLOGY

Technology can be integrated into writing instruction to assist students with revision (Graham et al., 2013; Harper, 1997). Google Docs is a web-based word processor that allows students to type, insert text features, share work with teachers/classmates online, work simultaneously with others, and receive feedback through virtual comments. Due to its collaborative features, Google Docs can be used to facilitate peer revision. However, research on its use is just beginning.

Suwantarathip and Wichadee (2014) analyzed the influence of Google docs on college students' collaborative writing. The participants in this study were split into two groups. The first group met face-to-face to complete a collaborative writing assignment and the second group completed the assignment online using Google Docs. Results indicated that Google Docs had a greater impact on the students' writing and motivation. In particular, students said the following: they enjoyed using the technology, it was simple to use, and collaboration was easy. In addition, more feedback and comments were provided with the technology than without.

Lin and Yang (2013) explored the influence of Google Docs on English Language Learners in Taiwan. This study was conducted with 44 first-year college students who were not English majors. They were partnered with one of 11 e-tutors who were English majors. E-tutors gave students feedback through Google Docs. The students completed 12 writing tasks throughout the study. Student writing, reflection logs completed by the teachers and students, group interviews, and classroom observations were analyzed. Overall, there was an increase in English language skills, and the e-tutors learned throughout the process as well. Google Docs also had a positive impact on the feelings students had towards English language learning. Finally, students also saw an increase in their personal communication skills.

Finally, Krajka (2012) examined the influence of web 2.0 online collaboration tools on university students who were learning English. Students were placed in pairs and used online collaborative writing environments to complete writing tasks. Throughout the process, students were observed and interviewed. Overall, the results revealed that the participants had positive attitudes towards using Google Docs and Moodle. Google Docs could facilitate collaborative writing because it was easy for students to share documents and compare drafts. Overall, educators and students found these tools useful for teaching language skills, motivating learners, and creating enriching learning experiences.

RESEARCH QUESTIONS

Peer revision, if implemented well, can be an effective method for helping adolescents improve their writing. Further, research on Google Docs suggests that it can be a useful tool for teaching writing. However, very few studies examined the use of Google Docs to support writing. This research focused mostly on ELLs and university students and on motivation and ways students used the technology. The current study aims to fill a gap in the literature by examining middle school students with learning disabilities and their use of Google Docs to facilitate peer revision. In addition, this current study analyzes the writing and revision activity of the students using Google Docs and this type of analysis was not seen in previous research with this technology.

The research questions that guide this study are as follows: (1) How does the use of Google Docs technology during peer revision influence sixth-grade writers with learning disabilities?; (2) How do students use the technology to support and revise their writing?; (3) What are the characteristics of the writing they produce on Google Docs?; and (4) Does the use of technology influence students' motivation for writing?

METHOD

The study took place over the course of an eight-week period in a classroom in a public school located in the Northeastern part of the United States. The eight-week period marked the length of an informational writing unit in the classroom where the data were collected. Seven sixth-grade students with learning disabilities who received instruction in a resource room English class were selected to be the participants. Five of the students were 11 years old and two of the students were 12 years old. In addition, three of the students were females while four were males. Standardized testing scores indicated that the students were not performing well in the area of writing.

At the beginning of the study, all students were given an informational pre on-demand assessment without any instruction on informational writing. Next, the students began a unit on informational writing. Students learned about the informational genre during instruction and composed their own informational process piece on Google Docs. Then, students were taught two peer revision strategies: identifying informational elements in a partner's writing and asking questions when more information was needed. The teacher used direct instruction, modeling, and guided practice to introduce and reinforce how to use each strategy. In addition, students received notes on the importance of revision and the purpose of each strategy. At the revision stage, students shared their writing piece virtually on Google Docs with one partner. Then, they used the peer revision strategies to provide feedback through Google Docs on their partner's writing. During this time, students also conferenced one-on-one with the teacher about informational elements, suggestions made to the students, and student concerns. After students gave and received feedback, they made revisions to their writing.

Once this process piece was complete, the students completed an informational post on-demand writing piece to demonstrate the learning they retained about informational writing. In addition, students were interviewed about their revision process after completing the entire unit. Specifically, students were asked to discuss changes they made to their writing, explain why they did or did not make the revisions, review the feedback they gave to their partner and why they gave that feedback, and share their opinions on Google Docs.

DATA ANALYSIS

Multiple data sources were collected during the course of the study to ensure triangulation (Mathison, 1988). The data collected included: all student writing samples, student interviews, field notes and reflective journal, peer feedback, and conference notes. Data were analyzed using constant comparative analysis (Strauss & Corbin, 1990). In addition, a separate deductive analysis of students' writing and revisions was conducted using coding schemes developed in previous studies (Moore & MacArthur, 2012). The pre on-demand and post on-demand writing pieces were scored for overall quality and informational elements using a holistic and primary trait rubric respectively. The process piece was also scored using the holistic and primary trait rubrics. The holistic rubric used was the PARCC research simulation task rubric that focused on reading comprehension and written expression and knowledge of language and conventions (PARCC, 2015). The primary trait rubric evaluated writing in six areas specific to the informational genre: thesis, content, organization, evidence, text features, and knowledge of language and conventions. Students earned a point for each trait utilized. Revisions made during the process piece were also coded for the following categories: type, operation, purpose, informational element, and overall quality.

Two trained raters scored the writing. The first author coded and scored all writing for overall quality and informational elements using the holistic and primary trait rubrics respectively. The first author also coded and scored all revisions for the process piece. The second author scored 50% of all of the writing at each stage. Inter-rater agreements for the pre-on demand writing were 98% for holistic and 97% for primary trait. For the process piece, inter-rater agreement ranged from 97% to 100% agreement on revision coding, 99% for holistic, and 97% for primary trait. Finally, for post on-demand, interrater agreement was 99% for holistic and 98% for primary trait.

RESULTS

Five major themes frame this study. Each theme will be explored in more depth below.

Students Used Highlighting and Virtual Comments to Facilitate Peer Revision

Students used key features available in Google Docs during peer revision to practice and reinforce concepts learned during instruction. Three features were utilized the most because they supported instruction: peer sharing of writing, highlighting, and virtual comments.

After sharing their writing with their partners, peers used font colors to color-code the elements of an informational writing piece and comment on what was missing. If a student was missing an element, his/her peer partner would create a comment identifying the missing piece. For instance, one student commented to his/her partner, "Where is your closing?" While students were utilizing the color-coding strategy to analyze and evaluate their peer revision partner's organization, students verbalized strengths and challenges that their partners encountered with the organization. For instance, one student stated, "She needs to work on her closing sentences. One isn't finished and another isn't even there," and another student evaluated, "She wasn't missing anything!" Student interviews also revealed how students were using Google Docs features. One student explained how the color-coding marks her partner gave helped her add details. She stated, "I added important details I was missing. I had to add a topic sentence to my first body paragraph because it was missing and a closing sentence to another paragraph because I needed it to close it up."

Students also used the comment feature to ask their partners questions about their writing. Student questions helped peers elaborate points. During a student–teacher conference, one student explained, "He [his partner] needs to say more. What if I don't know what this looks like?" Another student posted a comment on her peer's writing piece asking, "What does this look like?" During the student interview, she explained that her partner needed to add details so she can picture what she was saying.

Students Learned Evaluation Criteria

A second theme that emerged from the data was that students were learning evaluation criteria for informational texts through peer revision. For example, an analysis of students' revisions shows they were focused mostly on adding informational elements to their writing. See Table 1 for revision analysis. In addition, an analysis of students' peer comments and color-coding during peer revision revealed that students were accurately

Table 1. Frequency of Student Revisions.

Student	A (%)	B (%)	C (%)	D (%)	E (%)	F (%)	G (%)
Type							
Word	40	9	18	14	0	9	9
Phrase	0	55	18	14	40	36	55
Sentence	60	36	64	71	60	55	36
Operation							
Add	60	91	73	100	100	36	82
Delete	0	9	0	0	0	27	0
Substitute	40	0	27	0	0	36	18
Purpose							
Give new information	0	9	18	14	10	0	9
Clarify	40	18	36	29	10	27	27
Elaborate	0	18	18	57	10	18	18
Organize	40	36	18	0	10	27	9
Emphasize	0	0	9	0	10	0	9
Delete	0	9	0	0	0	27	0
No purpose	20	9	0	0	0	0	27
Informational element							
Organization	40	36	27	0	40	64	28
Content	40	55	18	71	40	18	73
Evidence	0	9	55	29	20	18	9
Language and conventions	20	0	0	0	0	0	0
Quality							
Success	20	91	82	100	100	100	9
No success	60	9	9	0	0	0	55
No change	20	0	9	0	0	0	36

evaluating peer's writing for informational elements. For instance, one student understood that organization is an important aspect of informational writing; therefore, the student indicated that his partner needed to make his topic sentence more general rather than give a specific example in order to focus on the topic of the paragraph.

When the students were interviewed about their revision process, they were able to discuss the characteristics they were looking for when evaluating a partner's writing. This further demonstrated their knowledge of the informational genre. For example, one student explained how he gave his partner feedback that allowed him to better organize his writing, add more information, elaborate, and clarify. He discussed how he did this by mostly asking questions.

Finally, during the interviews, students were able to explain the revisions they made and why they made those changes. Their responses show they were developing a general evaluation criteria for good writing. One student explained, "I deleted sentences that did not make sense to what I was saying. I deleted words to clear up my sentences, and I eliminated sentences. I also added details to show more about what I was saying." Another student stated, "I was missing a lot, and I got to fix it. Now it is better. I also got to learn a little more on a subject." Finally another student said, "I added important details that I was missing," "I had to add more information to be more specific. People who go there would want to know what I added," and "I had to add more to clarify."

Students Focused on Adding Additional Details during Revision

Student revisions were coded according to type, operation, purpose, informational element, and quality. While coding revisions, a third theme emerged. Student revisions were mostly additions at the sentence level for the purpose of giving new information, clarifying, elaborating, and organizing. In addition, the majority of their revisions were rated successful.

A major trend across students' revisions was that they were adding informational elements for the purpose of improving organization. For example, in response to a peer comment, "You need a closing sentence," one student added a closing sentence to wrap up the paragraph. In another case, a peer wrote the comment, "In this body paragraph, you need a topic sentence" and this prompted his partner to add a topic sentence to organize her body paragraph.

A second trend was that students were adding details to improve content. In response to the peer question, "Why did they choose that? Did they have something better?" his partner added a sentence to provide more information for the reader. In an interview, another student stated, "I added information to be more specific," and one more student explained, "I added to clarify and show differences."

Students Improved the Quality of their Writing

A fourth theme that emerged from the analysis was that students improved their overall writing quality. After peer revision, all of the students showed an improvement in the quality of their writing on both holistic and primary trait ratings (see Tables 2 and 3 for scores). Students performed better on the process piece than the pre and post on-demand writing assessments. However, students performed better on the post on-demand piece than on the pre on-demand writing piece. On the post on-demand, students wrote lengthier essays, followed the format of an informational writing piece, and elaborated more by adding details to their writing. These three factors contributed to the students' ability to write higher quality essays than on the pre on-demand piece.

Table 2. PARCC Holistic Writing Scores.

	A (%)	B (%)	C (%)	D (%)	E (%)	F (%)	G (%)
Pre on-demand	40	33	56	65	60	48	40
Pre process piece	54	56	67	75	69	52	58
Post process piece	83	81	88	90	88	81	83
Post on-demand	80	80	81	92	85	80	83

Table 3. Primary Trait Scores.

	A	B	C	D	E	F	G
Pre on-demand	1/6	3/6	3/6	3/6	3/6	2/6	2/6
Pre process piece	3/6	3/6	4/6	5/6	4/6	3/6	3/6
Post process piece	5/6	5/6	6/6	6/6	6/6	4/6	4/6
Post on-demand	4/6	3/6	5/6	5/6	5/6	3/6	4/6

Students were Motivated to Write and Revise using Google Docs

Finally, the last theme to emerge from the data was that Google Docs positively influenced students' motivation to write and revise. Students demonstrated motivation for writing by asking if they could continue to work on their writing outside of class. In addition, after Google Docs was introduced to the students, they came to class asking to write on the computer.

Students also appeared to be motivated by the revision strategies and use of Google Doc features. For example, while students were color-coding their partners' writing, one student explained, "I can't wait to see if I was missing anything." Then, when the students were asking each other questions as comments, another student stated, "I want to see what I can answer."

Collaboration also motivated students to revise. When it came time to "share" papers, one of the students stated, "I can't wait to see what my partner said." Motivation related to collaboration was also seen during the interviews. One student explained, "I liked to get feedback because I got to fix and change what I wrote to make it better." Another student stated, "I wanted to revise because I saw I was missing a lot of stuff, and I wanted to make it better." Students were also motivated to revise because Google Docs revealed that partners accepted the feedback by revising their writing. For example, a student asked, "Why do they change colors?" and the writer added the answer to clarify why the animal changed colors. Collaboration was essential to help each other improve their writing on Google Docs.

DISCUSSION

Google Docs has proven to be a useful tool that motivates writers, but very little research on the use of Google Docs to support writing and peer revision has been conducted. This study aimed to contribute to research in this area. Overall, the findings indicated that Google Docs facilitated peer revision and was motivating for students. Further, students were able to learn about evaluation criteria for writing, apply it during revision, and improve the quality of their writing. In a transfer task, they maintained their learning.

However, it is not clear from this study if students would have been just as successful in a face-to-face setting with the instruction in peer revision they received. Future research should analyze the differences in motivation, revisions, and writing quality of students using face-to-face environments and online environments during peer revision. This study also indicated that students were successful during revision when working with a peer revision partner. Peer revision reduced the amount of teacher feedback that was needed before final copies of writing were published for their writing folders. However, this study did not examine the difference between student writing with peer feedback and teacher feedback. Further research should examine teacher feedback on Google Docs versus peer feedback on Google Docs.

Recommendations for Teachers

This study points to several recommendations for teachers interested in using Google Docs to support peer revision. First, we recommend that teachers use explicit, strategy instruction on peer revision strategies prior to students working together during peer revision. Instruction should include clear explanations of the strategies, a rubric for informational writing, teacher modeling of the strategies, and guided practice. In addition, it should include teacher scaffolding so students understand the purpose of revision. As in previous research, we believe that this step impacted students' abilities to give feedback and revise their writing

A second consideration for teachers implementing this strategy is how they will modify their own role. Peer revision can decrease a teacher's workload in terms of giving feedback because students are providing this for each other. However, teachers must monitor peer feedback and students' use of revision strategies to ensure students are on-task and giving thoughtful feedback. Google docs allows teachers to monitor peer activity virtually. Because comments are saved, teachers can also read through all conversations to ensure feedback is appropriate and helpful. Instead of providing written feedback on student writing, teachers can use their time to read and reflect more deeply on student writing and peer feedback and craft minilessons that address classroom trends. Alternatively, teachers can conference with students about their writing, their feedback to peers, or other issues that arise during peer revision.

CONCLUSION

In an age where writing and technology are intertwined and ubiquitous, students should be given opportunities to write with technology and to explore how technology can facilitate writing. Google Docs has proven to be a powerful tool that helps facilitate peer revision for informational writing. This technology provided students with an online work environment that promoted collaboration. In turn, the students' overall writing quality improved. Educators should consider utilizing Google Docs in order to supervise writing instruction, assess students' writing and peer feedback, and continue to nurture students' writing development.

REFERENCES

Beach, R., & Friedrich (2006). Response to writing. In C. A. MacArthur, S. Graham, & J. Fitzgerald (Eds.), *Handbook of writing research* (pp. 222–235). New York, NY: The Guilford Press.

Britton, J., Burgess, A., Martin, N., McLeod, A., & Rosen, H. (1975). *The development of writing abilities: 11–18*. London: MacMillan Education.

Brouwer, K. L. (2012). Writing motivation of students with language impairments. *Child Language Teaching and Therapy, 28*(2), 189–210. doi:10.1177.0265659012436850

Chapman, E. S. (1998). Key considerations in the design and implementation of effective peer-assisted learning programs. In K. Topping & S. Ehly (Eds.), *Peer-assisted learning* (pp. 67–85). Mahwah, NJ: Erlbaum.

Common Core State Standards. (2016). *About the standards*. Retrieved from http://www.corestandards.org/about-the-standards/

DiPardo, A., & Freedman, S. W. (1988). Peer response groups in the writing classroom: Theoretic foundations and new directions. *Review of Educational Research, 58*, 119–149.

Graham, S., MacArthur, C. A., & Fitzgerald, J. (Eds.) (2013). *Best practices in writing instruction* (2nd ed.). New York, NY: The Guilford Press.

Graham, S., & Perin, D. (2007). *Writing next: Effective strategies to improve writing of adolescents in middle and high school*. Washington, DC: Alliance for Excellent Education.

Harper, L. (1997). The writer's toolbox: Five tools for active revision instruction. *Language Arts, 74*(3), 193–200.

Hillocks, G., Jr. (1986). *Research on written composition: New directions for teaching*. ERIC Clearinghouse on Reading and Communications Skills and the National Conference on Research in English Urbana, IL.

Krajka, J. (2012). Web 2.0 online collaboration tools as environments for task-based writing instruction. *Egitim Bilimleri Fakultesi Dergisi, 45*(2), 97–117.

Lin, W., & Yang, S. C. (2013). Exploring the roles of google.doc and peer e-tutors in English writing. *English Teaching, 12*(1), 79-n/a.

MacArthur, C. A. (1996). Using technology to enhance the writing processes of students with learning disabilities. *Journal of Learning Disabilities, 29*(4), 344–354.

MacArthur, C. A. (2012). Evaluation and revision processes in writing. In V. W. Berninger (Ed.), *Past, present, and future contributions of cognitive writing research to cognitive psychology* (pp. 461–483). London: Psychology Press.

MacArthur, C. A., Schwartz, S. S., & Graham, S. (1991). Effects of a reciprocal peer revision strategy in special education classrooms. *Learning Disabilities Research and Practice, 6,* 201–210.
Mathison, S. (1988). Why triangulate? *Educational Researcher, 17*(2), 13–17.
McCutchen, D. (2006). Cognitive factors in the development of children's writing. In C. A. MacArthur, S. Graham, & J. Fitzgerald (Eds.), *Handbook of writing research* (pp. 115–131). New York, NY: The Guilford Press.
Moore, N. S., & MacArthur, C. A. (2012). The effects of being a reader and of observing readers on fifth grade students' argumentative writing and revising. *Reading and Writing, 25,* 1449–1478.
Olson, V. B. (1990). The revising processes of sixth-grade writing with and without peer feedback. *Journal of Educational Research, 84*(1), 22–29.
PARCC. (2015). Retrieved from http://parcc.pearson.com/resources/practice-tests/english/Grade6-11-ELA-LiteracyScoringRubric-July2015.pdf
Prater, D. L., & Bermúdez, A. B. (1993). Using peer response groups with limited English proficient writers. *Bilingual Research Journal, 17*(1–2), 99–116.
Pritchard, R. J., & Honeycutt, R. L. (2006). The process approach to writing instruction: Examining its effectiveness. In C. A. MacArthur, S. Graham, & J. Fitzgerald (Eds.), *Handbook of writing research* (pp. 275–290). New York, NY: Guilford Press.
Purcell, K., Buchanan, J., & Friedrich, L. (2013, July). *The impact of digital tools on student writing and how writing is taught in schools (Pew Research Center).* Retrieved from http://www.pewinternet.org/files/old-media//Files/Reports/2013/PIP_NWP%20Writing%20and%20Tech.pdf
Stoddard, B., & MacArthur, C. A. (1993). A peer editor strategy: Guiding learning-disabled students in response and revision. *Research in the Teaching of English, 27*(1), 76–103.
Strauss, A. L., & Corbin, J. M. (1990). *Basics of qualitative research: Grounded theory procedures and techniques.* Newbury Park, CA: Sage.
Suwantarathip, O., & Wichadee, S. (2014). The effects of collaborative writing activity using google docs on students' writing abilities. *Turkish Online Journal Of Educational Technology – TOJET, 13*(2), 148–156.
The Alliance for Excellent Education. (2015). Retrieved from http://all4ed.org
The National Writing Project. (2015). *Writing is essential.* Retrieved from http://www.nwp.org/cs/public/print/doc/about.csp
Topping, K., & Ehly, S. (Eds.). (1998). *Peer-assisted learning.* Mahwah, NJ: Erlbaum.
Writing Study Group of the NCTE Executive Committee. (2004). NCTE beliefs about teaching of writing.

A FRAMEWORK FOR LITERACY: A TEACHER−RESEARCHER PARTNERSHIP CONSIDERS THE "C-S-C PARAGRAPH" AND LITERACY OUTCOMES

Christopher W. Johnson

ABSTRACT

Purpose − *To describe the role of teaching "the paragraph" in furthering literacy goals. The study considers one concept, the Claim-Support-Conclusion Paragraph (CSC) as a curricular and pedagogic intervention supporting writing and academic success for the marginalized students in two classrooms.*

Design/methodology/approach − *While this study corresponds to a gap in the literature of writing instruction (and paragraphing), it takes as its model the development of comprehensive collaborations where researcher-scholars embed themselves in the real practices of school classrooms. A fully-fledged partnership between researcher, practitioners, is characteristic of "practice embedded educational research," or PEER (Snow, 2015), with analysis of data following qualitative and case study methodology.*

Findings — *Practice-embedded research in this partnership consistently revealed several important themes, including the effective use of the CSC paragraph functions as a critical common denominator across rich curricular choices. Extensive use of writing practice drives increased literacy fluency for struggling students, and writing practice can be highly integrated with reading practice. Effective writing instruction likely includes analytic and interpretive purposes, as well as personal, aesthetic writing, and teaching good paragraphing is intertwined with all of these genres in a community that values writing routines.*

Practical implications — *Greater academic success for the marginalized students in their classroom necessitates the use of a variety of scaffolds, and writing instruction can include the CSC paragraph as a means to develop academic literacies, including argumentation. Collaborative and innovative work with curriculum within a PEER model may have affordances for developing practitioner and researcher knowledge about writing instruction.*

Keywords: Writing; writing instruction; paragraphing; adolescent literacy; practice-embedded educational research (PEER)

INTRODUCTION

The Classroom

In a school media center, hunched over a desktop computer screen, Jess considers the question: "Am I a weirdo?" His assignment concerns eccentricity and society, and right now he's working on his third draft. He's just been called out by peer editors and teacher for failing to connect his self-description to assigned readings. Navigating two screens and a Xeroxed handout, he's struggling with revision. On his desk is a copy of John Stuart Mill's On Individuality, *and he's skimming that for a new quotation. On his screen is the paper itself and a website open to the results of a personality survey. It gives him insight into his own tendencies toward introversion or extroversion. He glances at notes written on his messy first draft. He pauses, reads live feedback in Google docs from his social studies teacher, and plunges back into his writing.*

The Problem

Amid ever-increasing calls for students to be "college-ready," literacy researchers and secondary educators have renewed attention on reading and writing with evidence and argumentative rigor. When teachers of writing consider writing for academic purposes, instruction in the structure and rhetoric of paragraphing is often a priority (Noden, 2011; Tyre, 2012). Given that assessment data and research (NAEP, cited in Applebee & Langer, 2013) suggest that many American high school students write relatively little, and given that much writing students complete is brief, it is not surprising to see practitioners turn to the paragraph as exemplar and starting point for academic writing. Meanwhile, although a review of recent literature reveals ample scholarship about "college writing," "argumentative writing," and "argumentative reasoning using evidence," manuscripts about the teaching of paragraphing are sparse. It is time to update the discussion of teaching paragraph structure to secondary students, particularly as scholars call for a renewal of academic interest in how we write, what good writing looks like, and how teachers learn to teach writing (Kiuhara, Graham, & Hawken, 2009; Newell et al., 2011; Noden, 2011; Pinker, 2014; Sword, 2012).

This chapter will consider an outwardly simple question: What is the role of teaching "the paragraph" in furthering literacy goals? The concept of the Claim-Support-Conclusion paragraph (C-S-C) is a curricular and pedagogic intervention supporting academic writing in one Midwestern U.S. secondary school, and it is central to literacy instruction in the two classrooms at the heart of this study. Two teachers understand that to encourage greater academic success for the marginalized students in their classroom, a variety of scaffolds are required, and the teaching of the CSC paragraph is a common scaffold integrated with others. The teachers operationalize this intervention by layering supports and scaffolds into instruction, and then they "send" the students out for the rest of the school day, including the other required courses of instruction. School data suggest that this "framework for literacy" is a success, with many struggling students securing a secondary diploma.

WHAT DO WE KNOW?

Writing to Learn, Writing to Argue

A truism of literacy discourse is the notion that writing practice supports deeper learning and greater argumentative skills. How writing does so, to what extent, and under what circumstances, remain questions ripe for further investigation (Graham & Hebert, 2011; Langer & Applebee, 1987; Newell et al., 2011). Nearly four decades ago, Applebee (1981) surveyed the current state of writing in American classrooms, noting that the writing process was the new emphasis of American pedagogy, with writing "product" falling somewhat by the wayside. For at least forty years, this seesawing conflict between "process" and "product" has defined writing pedagogy, sometimes dividing writing teachers into warring camps.

Whatever one's orientation toward writing, research has consistently suggested that American students get too little writing instruction, write too little, write infrequently in analytical modes, and receive writing instruction from teachers who are sometimes unfamiliar with many evidence-based approaches to writing, or even the rhetorical and linguistic factors at work in writing (Applebee, 1981; Applebee & Langer, 2011, 2013). Recently, research suggests that while writing practices have increased, instruction in research-based writing is still problematic, and too few students write in sustained ways, particularly using analytical or interpretive approaches (Applebee & Langer, 2011, 2013). Others have found similar results. Kiuhara et al. (2009) surveyed a national sample of secondary teachers ($N = 361$) and saw improvement relative to Applebee's (1981) observations, but plenty of reason for continued concern about writing in secondary schools. Their findings and recommendations suggest the importance of writing about content so as to show knowledge of a domain, writing multiple paragraphs, and increasing the frequency of analysis and interpretation. Most importantly, the survey revealed that among teachers who did use writing in their classroom, they used evidence-based writing practices infrequently, and rarely for periods of great duration (Kiuhara et al., 2009). In a review of evidence-based practices supporting CCSS-era instruction, Troia and Olinghouse emphasize the role of extra writing time, planning for writing, drafting, editing, extensive use of word processing, writing in response to text, feedback, vocabulary instruction in supporting student achievement; in addition, they noted that a weaker evidence base influences instruction in several areas: vocabulary, inquiry, the teaching of revision and editing, and grammar usage instruction (2013).

Several research projects have ambitiously tackled the relationship between writing and other modes of learning. Bangert-Drowns, Hurley, and Wilkinson (2004) created a school-based writing to learn study highly relevant to this study. They analyzed data on the relationship between writing-to-learn interventions and academic achievement in their meta-analysis of writing for academic outcomes. 75% of studies showed a positive, causal relationship between writing interventions and enhanced academic outcomes, as compared to other, conventional instructional routines not emphasizing writing. Their analysis of 48 interventions offered evidence that more writing, focused writing, and writing routines contributed to enhanced effects, particularly when writing instruction emphasized metacognitive awareness of how learners think about writing processes. Significantly, increased treatment length was a critical factor in effect size. Interestingly, and especially relevant for this study of focused instruction in paragraphing, was the strong evidence that longer writing assignments were not necessarily effective in themselves; focused, highly contextualized writing assignments appeared to have greater traction in producing positive academic outcomes (Bangert-Drowns et al., 2004).

Graham and Hebert (2011) looked specifically at the role of writing in promoting better reading. Their meta-analysis of dozens of studies concludes that writing skill does aid reading comprehension, more writing improves reading, and specific instruction in written technique (rhetoric) also improves reading. Newell et al. (2011) conducted a review of research on reading and writing toward argumentative ends, analyzing studies published between 1985 and 2011. Central to their findings is a call for research integrating cognitive and social models of writing. They also highlight the importance of argument as a process unfolding over time in dialogic, discursive ways, and they acknowledge the reality that it is critical to build the knowledge base of teachers charged with teaching rhetoric.

Rhetoric

The "C-S-C Paragraph" has an unclear history. No "Wikipedia" entry exists for this topic, and search engine searches produce many "instructional how-tos" from college and secondary settings, but few references to a research base. Searches of academic databases produce few results, and those are topics related to composition and rhetoric in generic terms, usually with reference to the use of the "five-paragraph model" of composition, or in some cases, Toulmin's model of argument (Lunsford, 2002).

Likely, the C-S-C Paragraph is anchored in classical rhetorical traditions of thesis and support in argumentation. Clearly, it also bears close relation to the five-paragraph essay as assigned by generations of English and composition teachers, being a microcosm of the notions of thesis and support described in such models (Booth, Colomb, & Williams, 2008; Miller, 2010; Noden, 2011; Nunes, 2013). As described by the teachers in this study, it is essentially a visual or graphic model, with a claim sentence in first position, evidentiary and transition sentences in the body position, and a concluding (summarizing) sentence in the final position. The effect of such paragraphing is that of a whole, coherent, and cohesive piece of rhetoric what Pinker (2014) calls an arc of coherence, and what Joseph Williams argues is the central concern of good style in writing, "... the cumulative effects of topics" (p. 51, 1990).

Adolescent Literacy, Social Practice, and Situated Learning

We know a great deal about addressing literacy gaps for PK-3 learners, but less about the gaps that develop for early adolescent and young adults making their way in complex social terrain (Moje et al., 2004; Perin, 2013; Snow & Biancarosa, 2003). Many students complete high school without writing skills central to college or workplace success, producing a disconnect between high school writing, college writing, and productive literacy in a digital economy (Denecker, 2013; Kress & Selander, 2011). Despite focusing on a skill phenomenon, the paragraph, this study remains committed to a notion of literacy as an ecological phenomenon with social dimensions (Barton, 2007), where literate acts happen not at isolated skills, but as part of communities of discourse, social practice, and varied modes of literate production (Barton, 2007; Gee, 1989).

The notions of funds of knowledge and "third space" discourse are critical to this study, given the emphasis on knowing the home-out-of-school lives of the students that the teachers in this study exhibit (Moje et al., 2004; Moll, Amanti, Neff, & Gonzalez, 1992). In this theoretical framework, learners make the most of the discourse space provided where there nonschool lives meet traditional academic discourse. A model of practice, as theorized by Lave and Wenger (1991), in which learners are apprenticed to practices and skills deemed central to a particular community, also obtains where struggling learners are invited into academic performance via a community and varieties of scaffolding.

Methodology

This study of writing pedagogy and curriculum took place within the context of unique program in a Midwestern high school located in a semirural county. LET, or *Light at the End of the Tunnel*, is a literacy-driven intervention administered by the Special Education Coordinator of the district, but targeted at students not receiving special services and at risk for not graduating. District documents describe LET as "... available to high school students as an alternative and relevant English and Social Studies class that offers credit recovery with the expectations of work ethic, attendance, and respect." Notably, the dropout rate at the high school is 1.3% − low by national and state standards. In a recent year, 2014, 93.3% graduated from high school. Statewide proficiency in reading is 59.5% in 2015, and 60.4%, slightly above state averages. Literacy proficiencies are highlighted in a mandated "World's Best Workforce Plan College and Career Readiness Plan," with goals for college and career readiness the major goal. In a Midwestern high school with a typical semirural demographic profile, the school is modestly diverse: Native American 17.0%; Hispanic 2.5%; Asian-Pacific 1.6%; Black not Hispanic 1.0%; White not Hispanic 77.9%. Eligibility for Free and Reduced Lunch is significant, at 37.8% of district students.

When this longitudinal study of a classroom began in 2012, it was envisioned as an educational case study (Merriam, 1998; Stake, 1995). Given the importance of sociological and discourse phenomena at work in an intimate setting of fewer than 15 people, it has tended toward educational ethnography (Wolcott, 1994). Today, a robust partnership between researcher, practitioners, and to some degree, students, is characteristic of what Snow (2015) labels "practice embedded educational research," or PEER, where classroom teachers and the researcher learn from each other through a structured, supported, and sustained research-practice partnership (Donovan, Snow, & Daro, 2013). Practice-Embedded Educational Partnerships originate in the pressing concerns of practitioners (Donovan, Wigdor, & Snow, 2003), rather than in a traditionally envisioned problem derived from theory or a gap in the literature. Nevertheless, the present study on paragraphing does correspond to a gap in the literature of education and literacy − an absence of treatments of the efficacy and implementation of paragraph level teaching and learning for academically marginalized students.

For the current study, data sources include student work, student and teacher interviews, field notes of writing lessons, curricular materials, and practice-based discussions with the teachers about the interface between secondary academic writing and college-career readiness. In this chapter, all names are pseudonyms. Analysis moved along lines common to ethnographic, qualitative, and discourse analysis, with coding, memos, and the development of core themes (Denzin & Lincoln, 1998; Wolcott, 1994).

FINDINGS

Curriculum and the C-S-C: Teachers' Pedagogical Journeys

Each school year, teachers in the LET program have complete freedom as they choose new topics and themes for curricular development and implementation. They do not use traditional textbooks, they do not "teach to tests," and they resist any version of canned curriculum. Nevertheless, they are committed to creating redundancies and critical structures: a constant emphasis on writing, an exploration of many rich, varied, and provocative texts, and the use of primary sources, whether websites, documentaries, cinematic features, or historical artifacts. One teacher (Joe) insists that the topics selected for LET are "a vehicle for literacy," and this vehicle is intended to attract the kids, be relevant to them, and give them exposure to the world. In recent years, topics/themes have included eccentricity, sustainability, fast-food, and war, all taught with an eclectic assortment of primary source texts, from Gladwell's *David and Goliath* (2013) to Krakauer's *Into the Wild* (1997).

The teachers emphasize that topic selection flows from *the reality that these kids don't fit in* — they are in LET because they have perennially struggled in school, and exist at both social and academic margins because of difficult home lives, mental illness, poverty, and transience. The teachers remind us that the students know they're different, and these topics offer them windows into questions of their own identity. The teachers make considerations for geography, culture, and the local economy, and a writing assignment is as likely to involve some local culture relevance (such as hunting, or Bakken oil field employment), as it is one or more demanding source texts. Analysis of student paragraph writing samples suggest that most were developed with evidence from real life rich description by the students of the challenges, hardships, realities, and dreams that they experience in their home lives.

The curricular development is intertextual, with a variety of texts that have the effect of talking to each other. It could also be understood as multimodal (Kress & Selander, 2011) as students are asked to understand the structure (and production) of texts within different, often contrastive modes of genre. Indeed, each year students experiment in one or another new genres – from their own graphic novel production to newspaper publication. The C-S-C paragraph is a stabilizing factor within this rich milieu, offering structure and discipline. The texts are rich and demanding. Many are at Lexile levels (MetaMetrics, 2016) more typical of AP or college level texts: Emerson on Thoreau (1862), John Stuart Mills on Liberty (1869). The richness of texts provokes a kind of interplay that can be captured in the C-S-C structure – claims about big ideas, support from multiple sources.

Professional collaboration is a daily reality, with prompts, texts, and tasks negotiated between two teachers, and sometimes, with the professor. The two teachers are in constant contact with each other – pushing, pulling, critiquing each other's work, and at times, playing "good cop, bad cop" in motivational theater with the students. Students' writing is for an audience of at least two teachers, often three, including the researcher, and also subject to peer reading.

When the researcher first encountered this classroom emphasis on writing at the level of paragraphing, he was ambivalent about the routinizing of prescriptive writing pedagogy. Subsequent observation revealed more to the story. Samples of curricular materials, including frequent study guides, offer a preponderance of higher order activities where students explore connections, textual detail, and evidence of important concepts. Teaching and learning has an orientation toward close reading, evidence, watching, and listening closely for nuance. Writing is often in response to quotations, with student oral dialogue about passages, read-alouds of students' own words and reactions, and rereading. In one class period, a student makes sense of *David and Goliath* (Gladwell, 2013). He reads a quote aloud, disfluently, but with conviction. Jerry says, "I picked it because I think a lot of people are like that they come out strong but they're not, really." Others agree orally, and take notes in a dialogic, interactive process.

In typical classroom routines, consideration of a text involves notetaking, annotation, and questions for consideration, followed by the writing prompt. Writing prompts are never generic; instead, they always "index" a text or literate modality in some important way, and, importantly, they tend to privilege the ways that texts speak to individual lives. The mind-map of "THE MAN" is one such indexing move contingent on "text to life connections." This graphic organizer consists of a comical sketch of a human figure with lined spaces for important evidentiary detail about the character. A writing prompt followed student engagement with the Emerson text in a class read-aloud and subsequent completion of the graphic organizer. Joe describes the organic, responsive development of a writing prompt this way:

> The prompt was less structured. It began with the painfully slow whole class close read of Emerson's bio. The Pre-writing activity was a "THE MAN." The *theme* we promoted was to answer ... "Thoreau did/did not march to his own drum."

Here, curriculum, pedagogy, and student lived experience converge. Fairly early in the year, one student, an 18-year-old attempting to salvage his senior year and graduation, responded as shown in Fig. 1 to the prompt.

The Iconoclast

First, Thoreau rejected the idea of money. For example, when he started working at his father's pencil company he designed a new pencil that was approved by chemists and artists from Boston. When he returned home, his friends congratulated him and told Thoreau that his future was set. Thoreau denied this chance of making it rich by making more of those pencils and said "Why should I? I would not do again what I have done once."....He never had just one job; he worked for a few days to get the money he needed. For instance, Thoreau was a man of many talents, yet he never stayed with one occupation. "He declined to give up his large ambition of knowledge and action for any narrow craft or profession, aiming at a much more comprehensive calling, the art of living well." Moreover, Thoreau did not require a lot of money because he lived a minimalistic lifestyle. "He chose to be rich by making his wants few, and supplying them himself." He lived on what he needed, not what he wanted. When he did want something he made it himself. When Thoreau was at dinner parties and was asked which dish he wanted, he simply replied "the nearest....In conclusion, Thoreau was against the idea of making a lot of money and buying a lot of things. He would much rather live a more simple life without the stress of money.

Fig. 1. Thomas' C-S-C Paragraph Response to "THE MAN" Prompt/(Abridged).

This sample takes us from Emerson's description of Thoreau — the original prompt — to a student's consideration of personal finance in Thoreau's philosophy. Implied in the sample is the careful consideration of Thoreau via "THE MAN" exercise in annotation. Importantly, this sample is not divorced from student "funds of knowledge," (Moll et al., 1992). A month earlier, in a gut-wrenchingly honest essay, the same young man spoke of his own family's struggle to make ends meet, from derelict cars to house siding pocked by hail storms.

Even as they teach paragraphing with relentless drive, the two teachers in this classroom privilege relationships in their classroom, relationships built on getting to know young people, their contexts, the people they rely on, or in some cases, can't rely upon. Steve, who wrote this prompt, is routinely emphatic about two things:

> One, you've got to know these kids, you've got to get them to know that you are there for them ... every day, and *they've got to show up* . Two: When I was teaching Social Studies ten years ago, I was struck by the inability of learners to get past the short one answer or sentence in response to a question. They couldn't organize their thoughts in writing. I wanted more ... what I call "meat."

In this young man's response, there is "meat," striking for honesty, clarity of detail, and a kind of specificity with evidence. Given the history that this student (like others in the class, and in other years) has had with traditional school assignments, it is striking.

Examples like this suggest affordances and successes, particularly as they offer integration of student personal funds of knowledge and demanding texts in the academic milieu, the so-called "third space" (Moje et al., 2004; Moll et al., 1992). Allowing for this space necessitates a flexible, responsive set of teaching moves. At times the curriculum might be envisioned one way by the teachers, and it gets changed by the student's (or students') "wiring." At the level of a paragraph, this can mean a transformation of a writing assignment so that what students produce is incomprehensible. A not uncommon phenomenon is the paragraph where a student writes on both sides of an issue, making first one point, and then another, using contradictory evidence. This is where C-S-C fits in — kids who have "great ideas, but need for structure," to cite Joe. Staying with the plan of "teaching the C-S-C" becomes very important, but calibrated responses are also vital. Students may "not be ready to write yet," as their thinking about a topic has not developed to the point that writing in paragraphs would be productive. Other times, after writing, they need more work on the structure in response to an editor's demand that their writing be coherent.

A flexible curriculum — one that allows for fresh starts, revisiting, repeating, or slowing down — is critical to the development of clear and coherent writing in learners who have rarely produced it before this course.

Kevin offers that his orientation toward writing changed over several years of his own education, experimentation with forms, and the mentorship of teacher educators, writing instructors, and local writers. Today he sees the C-S-C as a tool for building skill as a writer, for responsible treatment of evidence, clarity in argument, and learner agency in communicating with the world. His commitment is personal: He names a former school principal turned student-teacher supervisor who pressed on him the need to help students write with clarity, precision, and structure in order to communicate. It was transformational, he said, and it jibed with later instruction he received about the importance of clear logic in composing college-ready compositions for the local university. Joe relates a kind of helpless naiveté about teaching writing, a naiveté that changed with the implementation of the structural scaffold of C-S-C instruction in a number of English courses at the school. He saw students' writing change, and he wanted "in on the game." He was a convert, and while he's watched his own children learn how to write in other ways in other settings, he's committed to the role of such rhetorical structure in supporting unskilled writers who struggle to make written sense of complex knowledge.

Scaffolding and the C-S-C: Toward the Visual

Within the LET classroom, C-S-C instruction is a deliberate intervention for greater literacy fluency. The scaffolding of the C-S-C is closely integrated with a variety of supports for close, analytic, and interpretive reading: Graphic organizers, study guides, double entry journals, sustained annotation have become *de rigeur* (Fisher & Frey, 2014). Such annotation reinforces the reality that "coverage" of topics is never the focus in this setting. How topics lead to big questions, important words, as in academic language — these are the emphases. There is a constant, spiraling dialogic emphasis on the interplay of varied sources and the evidence they provide. This enriches topic development, but also *models* the interplay of claims and evidence within argumentative discourse generally, and expository writing specifically. Consistent with Williams' and Colomb's theorizing on topic strings, discussions often explore all the ways that a topic can be related to other phenomena, but then the discussion has to come back to the original topical string (Williams & Colomb, 1990).

C-S-C is the big scaffold, though, and instruction is designed, layered, and adjusted toward student success at the level of the paragraph. Joe acknowledges "... these students can't write," and sees C-S-C as necessary for reengagement with the rudiments of clear communication in writing. Kevin argues that the C-S-C curriculum may be analogized to basketball.

> I was coaching kids in a recent tournament, and this kid throws a one-handed pass, and the first time he does it, it works, and then, second time, he does it again, and it's intercepted. I pull him aside, and I say, no .... You're not going to do that again; you need to throw two-handed passes. They see the pros do it, but they're not ready. That's true for these students, too, they need structures to get ready to argue. Joe agrees: "I like that analogy."

Instruction often focuses on a concept the teachers call "workable parts." At the paragraph level, this includes student understanding of rhetorical purposes of particular sentences within a paragraph — claims, transitions, evidence, conclusions. Instruction varies, with direct instruction used in some contexts, interactive exercises with Smartboard technology, and adaptations for particular topics or classes. The concept of "workable parts" is often extended down to the level of the sentence, with focused attention of the varieties of grammar moves that make sentences flexible and adaptable. Often, students write simple sentences, but work on paragraphing includes specific scaffolding to introduce sentence variety, and C-S-C forces engagement with issues of transition in sentences.

"Workable Parts" are presented to students through a series of visual scaffolds. As in the graphic organizer "THE MAN," a variety of graphic and visual aids support writing instruction. One of the teachers, Joe emphasized that visual scaffolds are important to this routine. He calls himself a visual learner, and he stresses that what works for him often works for struggling writers. In his observation, students who are weaker writers need visual models "to see what is being asked of them." In one striking example, Joe holds up his hand, and he outlines how the parts of the hand — fingers, tendons, knuckles, fingernails — work for him as a visual analogy to the parts of a paragraph, for example, a fingernail on the second finger may be the placeholder for a transitional phrase using a subordinating conjunction. Fig. 2 depicts one template (abridged for this chapter) used by the teachers to scaffold the learning of transitions in paragraphs.

Fig. 3 offers another iteration on this scaffold. Students employ this scaffold to analyze a piece of writing produced by another writer, sometimes in close reading, but more frequently, in active editing of the writing of a fellow classmate. This scaffold is routinely scaffolded with

Workable Parts

Claim: _____

Transition 1: _____ Support Statement 1: _____

_____

Facts, Details and examples to S1: _____

_____

Transition 2: _____ Support Statement 2: _____

Facts, Details and examples to S2: _____

Transition 3: _____ Support Statement 3: _____

Facts, Details and examples to S3: _____

Transition to Conclusion: _____ Concluding Statement: _____

Fig. 2. The Workable Parts Scaffold for a C-S-C Paragraph (abridged for this chapter).

color display on a Smartboard, direct instruction, interactive partner work using the color-coded processes, culminating in student editing and read-alouds.

With this instruction, learners become more responsive to transitions in writing at two levels. First, they consider the level of content and evidentiary choice, and second, they gain facility with sentence structures (varieties of conjunctions, syntactical moves) that offer fluent argument in a paragraph. In an interview, a student noted that

> ... getting transitions right is important ... and if you can't do that, more writing won't make for a better grade. You've got to get the structure right, and then you can do more ... Yea ... they like that, but not if you don't understand the structure.

These templates do not function as static desk-work. In the classroom, students and teachers routinely read samples of work aloud. There is frequent commentary on good sentences, with public kudos given. In summative

Editing Sheet: Editor's Name _____

1. **Workable Parts**

    Required Materials:
    Red, blue, green, purple pencils

    Deconstruct CSC structure:
    1. Circle the Claim sentence with red.
    2. Circle the Concluding sentence with red.
    3. Put away the red pencil.
    4. Locate all transitional words/phrases and circle them with green.
    5. Put away the green pencil.
    6. Circle Support Statement #1 with blue. Write "S1" in blue at statement's start.
    7. Circle Support Statement #2 with blue. Write "S2" in blue at statement's start.
    8. Circle Support Statement #3 with blue. Write "S3" in blue at statement's start.
    9. If there are more than three Support Statements, continue in same fashion.
    10. For each support statement, underline all details, examples, etc. in blue.
    11. Put away blue pencil.
    12. Locate all in-text citations and circle each with purple, then put pencil away.

2. Edit the paper for mechanics, spelling, etc. Use editing symbols. Comment on each issues related MLA Format: margins, header, spacing, indents, and fonts.

3. Specific issues related to word choice, sentence structure, punctuation, etc.

4. Is the paragraph focused or should some material be deleted as unrelated?

Fig. 3. Working Parts Editing Sheet with Color Coding.

assessments, more sophisticated sentences and structures are noted as the teachers read student work, and problems with transitions and sentence variety frequently catalyze teacher feedback on drafts and final work.

Written Production and the C-S-C: Routinizing High Expectations

Core to LET teaching and learning is a sense of community. This classroom merges process and product, not always smoothly, efficiently, or even with beauty, but both happen, and they happen again and again during nine months of instruction, consistent with research that suggests that best writing outcomes are repeated, of significant duration, and dependent on analytic thinking, interpretation, and careful reading (Graham & Hebert, 2011). Students write routinely, but much of the discussion of what will go into writing happens in an almost intimate situation – there is none of the "here is a writing assignment and it's due in two weeks" routine observed by the researcher in numerous secondary classrooms.

As Lave and Wenger (1991) describe, this is an apprenticeship, particularly when students are new to the program in September, or mid-year in January. In several class sessions, both teachers and students talked about expectations for samples of paragraphing in response to recent readings. The talk was clear, forceful, and even abrasive. "No sloppy, disjointed, rambling writing, you hear?" And as students say, "No ... You can't do that; they won't accept that in LET .... You gotta do the structure." Students tease their teachers about the endless demand for samples of writing, but a quiet work ethic belies their objections: many classroom periods are characterized by writing in notebooks, at computer screens, or alternatively, by students reading their work aloud to one another.

As both teachers emphasized in their discussions with the researcher, they strive for balance between writing that is reliant on information, evidence, and analysis, and writing that is connected to description and narration based on students' lived experiences. One reading strategies prompt suggests an additional layer to the outward emphasis on skill in paragraphs. Highlighted in a set of guideposts for successful reading are the terms *efferent* and *aesthetic*, paraphrasing Rosenblatt's theory of responses to reading (1978). Counter to examples in the literature (Applebee & Langer, 2011, 2013; Graham & Hebert, 2011; Newell et al., 2011), these students produce many pages of writing within multiple genres and they do metacognitive work about the demands of reading and writing in different genres. Examples from the data routinely included 10 samples of student work between three and five pages in length, double-spaced and word-processed, and samples of paragraphing were routinely produced between two and four times weekly. One student wrote a 6 1/2 page essay during the second week of class, notable from students who are behind in credits in the very courses which most frequently demand writing compliance and proficiency – English and Social Studies.

Kevin and Joe focus on writing with purpose when students are ready to write, and adjust timing to match student readiness to engage in complex thinking and writing about a topic. Sometimes they plan for writing to happen in period one on Monday, but after assessing students' readiness at that time, they alter course – debriefing or engaging in dialogue about material, and then writing during the second period, or even the next day. In daily classroom schedules, they employ a balanced combination of classroom writing (handwriting), and word processing. While they routinely have a computer lab available, they avoid technology in the regular classroom, focusing on texts, dialogue, scaffolds for reading, video clips, and quiet writing. One teacher makes extensive use of Google Docs for editorial process, sharing comments and critiques in live editing sessions that include the professor. The other teacher uses printed drafts almost exclusively for tactile, immediate, personal response, noting, "I've got to feel it, hold it ... respond in person."

Throughout, there's a focus on pride, quality control, and accountability. Confrontation about sloppy, late, or incomplete work is not uncommon, and is usually resolved by teacher and students digging in to work with renewed energy. The atmosphere bespeaks trust, a work ethic, and a drive toward professionalism, including MLA citation, care with evidence, and thoughtful reading and interpretation. Here we see a snapshot sample of such work, where a student (Calinda) concludes a paragraph about Thoreau's way in the world.

> ... Henry David Thoreau was opposite. He was opposite of friends. He was opposite of family. He was opposite of neighbors and townspeople. He was opposite of writers. He was opposite of the law. Henry David Thoreau was opposite.

Calinda's writing growth was striking – the year began with a reluctant writer who didn't see herself as at all skillful, as her teacher Kevin shared:

> When Calinda first entered LET, she was quiet in class and reluctant to share ideas on paper. We did quite a bit of journaling and sharing. Once Calinda felt comfortable with classmates, she began sharing her ideas more in class; this also transferred to her writing. The narratives and responses became longer, more detailed, more open. By the time we moved to more formal C-S-C/Argumentative essays, she seemed to have a sense of pride and confidence in her ideas and her ability to express them in writing ... Calinda worked hard to make her writing stand out ....

Clearly, teaching paragraphing, while a staple of this classroom, is not as key as teaching students. Calinda's response after two months suggests a flowering, an engagement, and a willingness to open her thoughts to pen and paper, and as both she and her teachers related in interviews, a new pride in her writing identity.

DISCUSSION AND IMPLICATIONS

Practice-embedded research in this partnership consistently revealed several important themes. First, the C-S-C paragraph functions as a critical lever within a rich curriculum that drives toward increased literacy fluency for struggling students. As recent literature suggests, success in this classroom is built upon extensive writing, writing for analytic and interpretive purposes, and writing that connects texts to lives to audiences (Moje et al., 2004; Newell et al., 2011). Second, the teachers and researcher have developed scaffolding for teaching deeper reading and writing, with many of the current practices recent in origin, and highly correlated with evidence-based practices. Visual learning modalities have become critical to the implementation of these practices, and now occupy prominent and routine positions in instruction. Thirdly, an atmosphere of literate production *as routine* characterizes this community of practice (Lave & Wenger, 1991), and, while the "paragraph" is a common denominator, student writers habitually engage in an array of writing tasks across genres. Finally, this study describes a unique ecology of literacy (Barton, 2007), in which adults and students learn together from each other's experiences. This partnership generally, and the investigation of the paragraph, specifically, represent a type of teaching at risk in an age of mandated standardized and test-driven instruction. These teachers and partnership resist a deskilling, formulaic literacy curriculum (Luke, 1998), even as they emphasize skills that some would call a "dinosaur," archaic, or too "traditional." The practices in these classrooms offer one example of critical literacy, integrating as they do the life stories of marginalized students, provocative, demanding texts, and focused, sustained writing instruction for students who now find themselves about to graduate from high school.

REFERENCES

Applebee, A. (1981). Looking at writing. *Educational Leadership, 38*(6), 458–462.
Applebee, A., & Langer, J. (2011). "EJ" extra: A snapshot of writing instruction in middle schools and high schools. *The English Journal, 100*(6), 14–27.
Applebee, A., & Langer, J. (2013). *Writing instruction that works: Proven methods for* middle and high school classrooms. New York, NY: Teachers College Press.
Bangert-Drowns, R., Hurley, M., & Wilkinson, B. (2004). The effects of school based writing to learn interventions on academic achievement: A metaanalysis. *Review of Educational Research, 74*(1), 29–58.
Barton, D. (2007). *Literacy: An introduction to the ecology of language*. Malden, MA: Blackwell.
Booth, W., Colomb, G., & Williams, J. (2008). *The craft of research*. Chicago, IL: University of Chicago Press.
Denecker, C. (2013). Transitioning writers across the composition threshold: What we can learn from dual enrollment partnerships. *Composition Studies, 41*(1), 27–50.
Denzin, N., & Lincoln, Y. (1998). *Collecting and interpreting qualitative materials*. Thousand Oaks, CA: Sage.

Donovan, Snow, & Daro (2013). The SERP approach to problem-solving research, development, and implementation. In *Design based implementation research: Theories, methods, and exemplars*. SERP Institute. Retrieved from http://serpinstitute.org/publications.html

Donovan, M. S., Wigdor, A. K., & Snow, C. E. (Eds.). (2003). *Strategic education research partnership*, The National Academies Press. Retrieved from http://www.nap.edu/catalog/10670.html

Emerson, R. W. (1862). Thoreau. *The Atlantic Monthly*, August. Retrieved from http://www.theatlantic.com/magazine/archive/1862/08thoreau/306418/

Fisher, D., & Frey, N. (2014). Scaffolded reading instruction of content area texts. *The Reading Teacher, 67*(5), 347–351.

Gee, J. (1989). What is literacy? *Journal of Education, 171*(1), 18–25.

Gladwell, M. (2013). *David and Goliath: Underdogs, misfits, and the art of battling giants*. New York, NY: Little, Brown, & Company.

Graham, S., & Hebert, M. (2011). Writing to read: A Meta-analysis of the impact of writing and writing instruction on reading. *Harvard Educational Review, 81*(4), 710–744.

Kiuhara, S., Graham, S., & Hawken, L. (2009). Teaching writing to high school students: A National survey. *Journal of Educational Psychology, 101*(1), 136–160.

Krakauer, J. (1997). *Into the wild*. New York, NY: Anchor Books.

Kress, G., & Selander (2011). Multimodal design, learning, and cultures of recognition. *Internet and Higher Education, 15*, 265–268.

Langer, J., & Applebee, A. (1987). *How writing shapes thinking: A study of teaching and learning*. Urbana, IL: NCTE.

Lave, J., & Wenger, E. (1991). *Situated learning: Legitimate peripheral participation*. Cambridge: Cambridge University Press.

Luke, A. (1998). Getting over method: Literacy teaching as work in new times. *Language Arts, 75*(4), 305–313.

Lunsford, K. (2002). Contextualizing Toulmin's model in the classroom: A case study. *Written Communication, 19*(1), 109–165.

Merriam, S. (1998). *Qualitative research and case study applications in education*. San Francisco, CA: Jossey-Bass Publishers.

MetaMetrics. (2016). *The Lexile framework: Matching readers with texts*. Retrieved from https://lexile.com/

Miller, J. (2010). Speaking my mind: Persistence of the five-paragraph essay. *The English Journal, 99*(3), 99–100.

Mills, J. S. (1869). Of individuality, as one of the elements of well-being. In *On liberty*. Retrieved from http://www.bartleby.com/130/3.html

Moje, E., Ciechanowski, K., Kramer, K., Ellis, L., Carillo, R., & Collazo, T. (2004). Working toward third space in content area literacy. *Reading Research Quarterly, 39*(1), 38–70.

Moll, L., Amanti, C., Neff, D., & Gonzalez, N. (1992). Funds of knowledge for teaching: Using a qualitative approach to connect homes and classrooms. *Theory Into Practice, 31*(2), 132–141.

Newell, G., Beach, R., Smith, J., VanDerHeide, J., Kuhn, D., & Andriessen, J. (2011). Teaching and learning argumentative reading and writing: A review of the research. *Reading Research Quarterly, 46*(3), 273–304.

Noden, H. (2011). *Image grammar: Teaching grammar as part of the writing process* (2nd ed.). Portsmouth, NH: Heinemann.

Nunes, M. (2013). The five-paragraph essay: Its evolution and roots in theme writing. *Rhetoric Review, 32*(3), 295–313.

Perin, D. (2013). Literacy skills among academically underprepared students. *Community College Review, 41*(2), 118–136.

Pinker, S. (2014). *The sense of style: The thinking person's guide to writing well.* New York, NY: Viking.

Rosenblatt, L. (1978). *The reader, the text, the poem: The transactional theory of literary response.* Carbondale, IL: Southern Illinois University Press.

Snow, C. (2015). Rigor and realism: Doing educational science in the real world. *Educational Researcher, 44*(9), 460–466.

Snow, C., & Biancarosa, G. (2003). *Adolescent literacy and the achievement gap: What do we know and where do we go from here? Advanced Literacy Funders Meeting Report.* New York, NY: Carnegie Foundation.

Stake, R. E. (1995). *The art of case study research.* Thousand Oaks, CA: Sage.

Sword, H. (2012). *Stylish academic writing.* Cambridge, MA: Harvard University Press.

Troia, G., & Olinghouse, N. (2013). The common core state standards and evidence-based educational practices: The case of writing. *School Psychology Review, 42*(3), 343–357.

Tyre, P. (2012). The writing revolution. *Atlantic Monthly*, October. Retrieved from http://www.theatlantic.com/magazine/archive/2012/10/thewritingrevolution/309090/

Williams, J., & Colomb, G. (1990). *Style: Toward clarity and grace.* Chicago, IL: University of Chicago Press.

Wolcott, H. (1994). *Transforming qualitative data: Description, analysis, and interpretation.* Thousand Oaks, CA: Sage.

POWERFUL WRITING INSTRUCTION: SEEING, UNDERSTANDING, AND INFLUENCING PATTERNS

Marla Robertson, Leslie Patterson and Carol Wickstrom

ABSTRACT

Purpose — *Our purpose in this chapter is to examine the implementation of a set of lesson frameworks to set conditions for teachers to deal with the complex challenges related to writing instruction in a high-stakes testing environment. These lessons provided a flexible framework for teachers to use in tutorials and in summer writing camps for students who struggle to pass the state-mandated tests, but they also build shared understandings about writing as a complex adaptive system.*

Design/methodology/approach — *We look to two sources for our theoretical framework: the study of complex adaptive systems and research-based writing instruction. In the chapter we summarize insights from these sources as a list of patterns that we want to see in powerful writing instruction. The analysis presented here is based on open-ended interviews of 17 teachers in one of the partner districts. The results of an inductive analysis of these transcripts is combined with a summary of 9th and 10th grade test results to inform the next iteration of this work.*

Findings — *Our findings suggest a shift toward patterns that imply shared understandings that writing and writing instruction require dialogue, inquiry, adaptability, and authenticity. These lesson frameworks, rather than limiting teacher's flexibility and responsiveness, provide just enough structure to encourage flexibility in writing instruction. Using these frameworks, teachers can respond to their students' needs to support powerful writing.*

Practical implications — *This set of lesson frameworks and the accompanying professional development hold the potential to build coherence in writing instruction across a campus or district, as it builds shared understandings and practices. We look forward to further implementation, adaptation, and documentation in diverse contexts.*

Keywords: Writing lesson frameworks; complex adaptive systems

> Writing is powerful. Whether it's a little girl hiding from the Nazis in an attic, or Amnesty International writing letters on behalf of political prisoners, the power of telling stories is usually what causes change.
>
> Erin Gruwell, *The Freedom Writers Diary*

Writing is powerful. Erin Gruwell (1999) and her students confirm what we have learned from many writers, teachers, and students. Writing has the power to change individual lives, and those individuals, in turn, can write to change the world. That is why we teach literacy, and that is why we work with colleagues in our local National Writing Project site — the North Star of Texas Writing Project — to support powerful writing instruction in as many classrooms, campuses, and districts as we can.

We have learned that teachers and administrators face overwhelming challenges in their efforts to help students become powerful writers. The basic challenge is that classrooms and schools are infinitely complex systems. Each student and each teacher brings a unique set of identities, background experiences, dispositions, and skill sets. Policy mandates, community expectations, and scarce resources shape instructional options in diverse ways. Especially in high schools, we find that the urgency to pass the state-mandated tests too often overshadows all other goals. This high-stakes testing environment is a particularly complex challenge for immigrant students who are not only settling into life in an unfamiliar culture, but who are learning English. In addition, the educational landscape is continually changing. New policies, shifting demographics, and emerging technologies are just a few of those changes.

Administrators often try to reduce this complexity and uncertainty by standardizing instruction across classrooms and grade levels. In many schools, we hear an emphasis on uniformity — in phrases like "fidelity of implementation." Unfortunately, these efforts often result in practices that privilege low-level skills and test preparation over what Erin Gruwell (1999) calls "the power of telling stories." We argue that in these complex systems, powerful writing teachers must somehow make sense of this chaos and find ways to respond to individual students in the midst of curriculum mandates and high-stakes testing regimes.

As colleagues in North Star of Texas Writing Project, we have attempted to respond to this challenge by designing a set of lesson frameworks and professional development that provides both structure and flexibility to negotiate the complex systems where teachers and students work together. Our goal was to provide enough structure to help teachers build their repertoire of instructional tools for developing powerful student writing, yet enough flexibility to modify instructional plans in response to student needs. The intent was not to standardize writing instruction, but to offer lessons to provide concrete help for teachers who are searching for ways to support student writers in tutorials and in summer writing camps, to accelerate students' writing progress in time for the upcoming test. We call them "lesson frameworks," to emphasize that we encourage teachers to adapt and modify them to meet students' needs.

Our central question in this work is about how to use a set of lesson frameworks and accompanying professional development to set conditions for teachers to deal with complex challenges related to writing instruction. Does this approach, rather than standardizing instruction, set the conditions for a system-wide, adaptive reading/writing/learning systems in which teachers become more flexible decision-makers and in which their student writers build confidence, fluency, and flexibility?

In this chapter, we first explain insights from the study of complex adaptive systems (CAS) that inform our work. We next describe the lesson framework and its underlying rationale. Then we summarize patterns of student and teacher outcomes that we have seen over three years of implementation in three different districts, with our conclusions and implications for further research and practice.

BUILDING CAPACITY IN COMPLEX ADAPTIVE SYSTEMS

To help teachers and administrators set conditions for self-sustaining writing instruction on their campuses, we look to the study of complexity (Holland, 1998) and human systems dynamics (Patterson, Holladay, & Eoyang, 2013). We have found these insights relevant for writing teachers and their administrators:

- Learning, teaching, and literacy are all CAS which are inherently diverse, interconnected, recursive, and unpredictable.
- Over time, patterns of thought and behavior emerge from the interactions within a complex adaptive system.
- Agents in these systems (teachers and students, for example) can learn to see the emerging patterns, understand how those patterns are generated, and take action to influence the interactions and, perhaps, to shift the patterns.

Our first insight is that learning, teaching, and literacy are all CAS which are inherently diverse, interconnected, recursive, and unpredictable. One way to visualize how a CAS works is illustrated in Fig. 1. Components and people interact in particular settings, and system-wide patterns of behavior and patterns of thinking emerge.

That leads to our second insight useful to writing teachers. Those patterns, over time, influence the subsequent interactions, which, in turn, amplifies and strengthens those patterns. For example, in a high-stakes testing environment where the focus is on right and wrong answers, "compliance" may emerge as a predominant pattern. When compliance becomes a dominant pattern, it discourages creativity and risk-taking, the hallmarks of powerful writing. In other classrooms, however, we see creativity and risk-taking as repeating patterns which, in turn, encourage more of the same. Fig. 2 illustrates that insight.

Powerful Writing Instruction

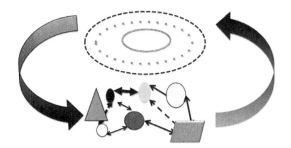

A CAS is a collection of agents (people, groups, ideas) that interact so that system-wide patterns emerge, and those patterns subsequently influence the agents' interactions.

Fig. 1. Definition and Illustration of Complex Adaptive System (Dooley, 1996).

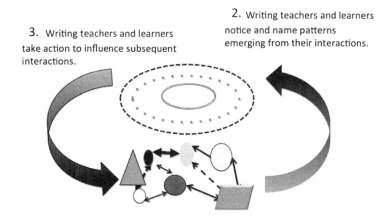

3. Writing teachers and learners take action to influence subsequent interactions.

2. Writing teachers and learners notice and name patterns emerging from their interactions.

1. Writing teachers and learners interact with one another, with texts, and with ideas via the *Finding True North* lesson cycle.

Fig. 2. A Complex Adaptive Process at Work in a Literacy Classroom.

In our classroom observations, interviews, and informal conversations with effective writing teachers over the course of several years (Wickstrom, Araujo, Patterson, Hoki, & Roberts, 2011; Wickstrom, Patterson, & Isgitt, 2012), we have noticed a number of recurring patterns emerging in these classroom systems. We have come to see these patterns as essential to any learning community, but they are especially useful as we envision classroom communities where powerful writing instruction is happening. In professional development sessions, we often explain these patterns to teachers and ask them to choose three or four patterns that seem most relevant or useful to their students, and we invite them to name other patterns they want to see in the work of their students. We have found it useful to use these patterns retrospectively, to reflect on our experiences. We have also found the patterns useful to envision the instruction we want to see in our classrooms or across our campuses. Table 1 lists and explains the patterns of instruction we have found most supportive of powerful writing instruction. These are patterns we want to generate in our classrooms. These serve as aspirational patterns grounded in our experience and in the published literature. We do not, however, claim that this is an absolute or comprehensive list, nor do we claim that one instructional program will inevitably cause these patterns to appear.

Our third insight is that agents in these systems are not passive recipients, objects, or victims in the system. They are agents. They hold the potential to "see, understand, and influence patterns" in a complex adaptive system, and, therefore, they hold the potential to shape the interactions, which can then shift the patterns. We frame this process as "Adaptive Action" — a recursive inquiry action cycle through which we continually ask three questions: What is happening?, So what does it mean?, and Now what shall we do about it? These three deceptively simple questions help us see, understand, and influence the patterns emerging from various systems where we live and work (Eoyang & Holladay, 2013). Fig. 3 is a simple representation of Adaptive Action.

These three insights undergird our development of lesson frameworks to help build system capacity to support student writers in complex systems. We encourage teachers to observe their students closely, to listen to their perspectives, and to look carefully at their writing products to see what strengths and targets for growth are emerging. We support them as they reflect on these observations and generate instructional options. If fact, each lesson framework concludes with questions, encouraging teachers to think about their students' responses, to adapt, and to plan the next step.

We engage in Adaptive Action as well. We have developed and continually modify these lesson frameworks and the accompanying professional development in response to specific district needs and teacher feedback. The goal is to help teachers implement flexible, research-based practices in thoughtful and responsive ways, with the hope that teachers will take the lessons and adapt them for their own situation and needs.

Table 1. Aspirational Patterns of Instruction in Writing Classrooms and Communities.

Aspirational Pattern	Description	Supporting Research
Empathy We try to empathize with the experiences of others	Empathy is the capacity to take the perspective of others; to imagine how they might think and feel. This applies to colleagues and classmates, as well as authors and characters in books, films, etc.	Etzioni (2014), Mraz and Hertz (2015), Rifkin (2009)
Inquiry We stand in inquiry as teachers and learners	Inquiry drives our instruction and our learning. We define inquiry as turning judgment into curiosity, defensiveness into self-reflection, conflict into shared inquiry, and assumptions into questions Eoyang and Holladay (2013)	Ballenger (2009), Cochran-Smith and Lytle (2009), Dewey (1910), Harvey and Daniels (2015), Short, Harste, and Burke (1996), Wells (1999), Wickstrom (2013)
Dialogue We teach and learn by engaging in dialogue in which everyone has a voice	Open dialogue that invites all participants' voices is critical to learning. Students and teachers engage in this dialogue through multiple modes, media, and genre (listening, speaking, reading, writing, viewing, and representing)	Freire (2000), Tharp and Gallimore (1988), Ritchart, Church, and Morrison (2011), Vygotsky (1978)
Authenticity We read, write, and represent honest messages for real purposes and audiences	Authenticity means that the students see reading and writing as a way to participate in (and influence) the world beyond the classroom. This means, when possible, that teachers offer relevant topics that build on students' interests and background knowledge, opportunities for student choice, and real audiences for their writing and other products	Cammarota (2008), González et al. (1993), Lee (2007), Newkirk (2014)
Apprenticeship We work side-by-side; sometimes teaching and sometimes learning from others	Students are literacy apprentices. Teachers demonstrate and explain their reading and writing strategies as well as their discoveries.	Gallagher (2011, 2015), Kittle (2008, 2012), Tharp and Gallimore (1988)

Table 1. (*Continued*)

Aspirational Pattern	Description	Supporting Research
	Teachers invite students to learn from mentor texts and to participate in conferences about what they are reading and writing. Students are invited to share their expertise with others. Teachers gradually move students toward independence	
Re-visioning We continually reflect on our work; when useful, we adapt and revise our thinking and our messages to be both true and useful	Re-visioning goes beyond "fixing" what is wrong to wondering, imagining, and creating new possibilities for thought and action. Writers, readers, and teachers use feedback to envision what is possible in their words, stories, lives, communities, and world	Anderson and Dean (2011), Dweck (2007), Eoyang and Holladay (2013), Messner (2011), Mraz and Hertz (2015)
Deep content learning We are learning essential concepts and principles relevant to multiple disciplines	Deep content learning in school is typically defined by the standards and curriculum. Outside of school, content is related to authentic work in multiple contexts, about a wide range of topics	Elish-Piper, L'Allier, Manderino, and Di Domenico (2016), Hirsch (2010), Rainey and Moje (2012)

DEVELOPING THE LESSON FRAMEWORKS AND TEACHER SUPPORT

In the summer of 2012, a partner district invited our local National Writing Project site *were invited* to develop a set of lessons for high school students as preparation for retaking the state assessment. Some of the target students had failed the test(s) more than once, and had already been exposed to the format and language used in the tests. We assumed that these students needed to learn some basic writing strategies for expository and/or persuasive writing (depending on which tests they would be taking), but we also knew that they needed to build confidence in their power as writers.

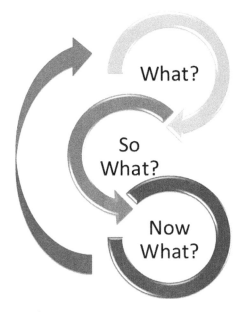

Fig. 3. Adaptive Action – An Inquiry Cycle Focusing on Complex Adaptive Systems.

Our previous work with teachers and students had convinced us to invite students to take an inquiry stance as they engaged in research-based writing routines and practices, always with an effort to provide authentic purposes and audiences (e.g., Patterson, Wickstrom, Roberts, Araujo, & Hoki, 2010). We take a sociocultural stance toward literacy teaching and learning, emphasizing the role of joint participation and apprenticeship (Lave & Wenger, 1991). Johns (1997) called this approach "socio-literate" – one in which learners are "constantly involved in research into texts, roles, and contexts and into the strategies that they employ in completing literacy tasks in specific situations" (p. 15).

These lesson frameworks, entitled *Finding True North: A Lesson Framework for Powerful Writing Instruction* (*FTN*), set up a series of guided inquiry (Adaptive Action) cycles through which students think and write about their personal experiences, study mentor texts, and write authentic messages (see Fig. 4). As many researchers and practitioners advise, the teacher observes students carefully, documenting their progress and mediating for the group and for individual students as necessary (e.g., Anderson, 2011; Atwell, 2015; Burke, 2013; Gallagher, 2011). This lesson cycle is not

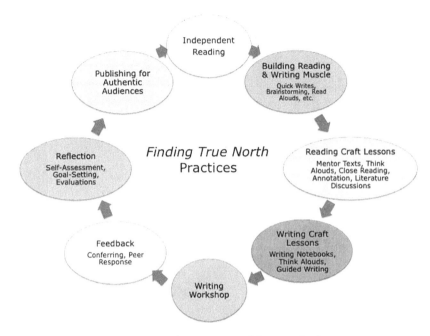

Fig. 4. Finding True North Lesson Cycle.

original with us, of course; we have combined familiar components of reading and writing workshop approaches to develop the representation in Fig. 3 – a picture of this approach which teachers have found useful. Our professional development emphasizes that this cycle is not a rigid, linear sequence of activities, but a recursive, flexible, and adaptive process. We know that administrators and teachers are reluctant to use this kind of open-ended literacy instruction with students who are at risk of not passing high-stakes tests so we remind teachers that this fluid, inquiry-based instruction meets the needs of all learners regardless of their performance levels or previous academic experiences.

Since 2012, teams of our writing project Teacher Consultants have worked with three different districts to develop and customize this series of lesson frameworks designed to engage student writers in this cycle using mentor texts, writer's notebooks, and a culminating essay for publication. These lessons focused on narrative, expository or persuasive essays. After piloting the initial version in a summer writing camp in 2012, we have revised and added to the lessons several times for particular district needs (for after-school tutorials, as the core curriculum for reading courses, or as supplementary lessons for mainstream English classes). As teachers implement these lesson frameworks, we always work with them in one- or two-day professional development sessions and in coaching conversations. We focus on the implementation of the lessons, but we know that these particular lessons – no matter how effective they are – will not make students powerful writers. To set conditions for powerful writing we need teachers who can adapt and extend the lesson cycles as appropriate for their students. We coach teachers in their efforts to respond to particular student needs and to integrate mentor texts from their curriculum. We also work with administrators when possible, always attempting to build capacity to sustain this work after we are no longer in the picture.

The structures and processes at the center of *FTN* were deliberately designed to work in CAS. The insights about complex systems explained above informed each iteration of the lesson frameworks, the professional development support, and our relationships with the partner districts. As professional development consultants, we thought about the patterns we wanted to see in these classrooms, and we tried to set conditions for interactions among the teachers and students that would generate those patterns.

WHAT HAPPENED? SEEING AND DOCUMENTING THE PATTERNS

What evidence do we see about whether these lessons cycles are building powerful student writers? In the following summary of findings, we focus on one school district, which we call Stargazer ISD (SISD). We have sustained a working relationship with this district since 2012. During 2015, a research team interviewed 17 teachers who had participated in this district's *FTN* initiative. We used a semistructured interview (adapted from Wilson-Grau & Britt, 2012), and we conducted an inductive analysis of seven transcripts from teachers representing a range of teaching assignments. The codes generated in that initial analysis were used to analyze the remaining interviews. The following outcomes are based on that analysis, in addition to conversations with district leaders. In the following section we summarize outcomes from both students and teachers.

We present the findings in three parts: the patterns in student changes reported by the teachers; the patterns in teacher changes reported in their interviews; and the patterns in the test data reported by the district. For each identified pattern, we offer evidence, either from the interviews or from the tests.

These findings, of course, represent the perceptions of seventeen teachers and student performance on a limited number of tests. The patterns we describe here are useful, but we do not claim that these findings can be generalized beyond these cases.

Patterns in Teacher Reports of Student Changes

In the interviews, these teachers identified some clear patterns in the changes they had seen in their students. Some of the teachers reported more dramatic changes than others, and some emphasized one or more of these patterns over the others, but these five patterns emerged as predominant:

1. Confidence as writers

> So once I feel really confident teaching, I think that they feel really confident writing and a lot of them, if they're hesitant writers it's because they don't know where to start or they don't know what a good answer looks like or they don't know if theirs will be right. Once we let go there's no one right answer in English class and they have these strategies to really understand what needs to go in their writing, they've been confident. (JH)

> I think for the first time in a long time, I had students who said to me "I didn't think I could do this." But at the end of the year we did a big, long research paper, which required them to write 2–3 pages of information. (JH)

2. Enthusiasm and engagement

> Well, because I have the Pre-AP kids they pretty much like to read and write. Most of them do to a certain extent but I have seen more passion with it .... They are more engaged. (BB)

> Their attitudes completely change! Even the ones that really love it, love it more by the end because they can do it better and they can do it deeper and it means more to them. (JH)

> ... they've always been willing to write, but now they're excited. I guess it is a change in attitude if they're excited about writing. Instead of just being willing to, they're happy to sit down and do it. They were excited about being able to put their voice down. (PV)

> ... they (students) enjoyed the writing. They did not at first. They did not. They question "why are we in this class? Why are we doing this much writing? Why are

we doing something different than all of the other English classes?" But at the end of the year in their own reflections they said that they enjoyed the writing the most. (HG)

3. Adaptability and persistence

> They (students) are a lot more willing to try, and they get into the habit of writing daily or almost daily with the quick writes .... even if you are not great at it, you can get better in this class. (KW)

> We write everyday so just building stamina for writing has been a huge improvement. (JH)

> They write a lot – they write a LOT – and so in the end they've learned what their triggers are so they know when the anger's coming now, or when the depression is coming or when a bipolar swing (manic-depressive episode) is coming. They know when it's coming. So when they can feel that coming, they get their journals out and write what they're doing, and then they process through the anger, and then they come out on the other side. And that journal is sitting there waiting for them to continue where they started. (PV)

4. Authenticity

> I would say the quality of writing has gotten better. I see more authenticity and (students) give authentic opinions and (they know) that it is okay to have, you know, unique opinions. (BH)

> I think they have embraced revising a little bit more. You know, they don't seem as hesitant to do the revising. I think they have been able to get back into their writing. Whenever you do anything that is process the kids have a stronger ownership so they are more dedicated, when it gets a little tougher, to do the revisions and editing. (BB)

> So we come in and we read and we write and that's who we are in this class ... (KW)

5. Proficiency in writing

> Their planning is much more purposeful. I see that they are using these protocols – define it, remember it, connect it, so what? They are writing about what they know, not making it up because they know that we can tell when they make it up, and because of that all of their essays are organized because they are based on the ideas they generated. (RS)

> Some of them were really able to get down a response and they were proud of the writing they had done. When we got their STAAR test results back they were super shocked. I was shocked at some of them. I thought "Wow this is pretty awesome. In the past you might not have done so well." I think their scores on their tests helped them, the North Star tutorials and the practices and resources helped bump their writing. (JH)

We were getting a lot of 0s and 1s [not passing scores on the state test] and now we are getting more 2s and I actually had one of my SPED kids get a 3 [2 and 3 are passing scores on the state test]. (SG)

Patterns in Teacher Reports of Their Changes

Not only did teachers report that their student writers made progress, but they also talked about changes in themselves and in their colleagues. Every teacher mentioned particular tools from the lesson frameworks, such as writer's notebooks, mentor texts, and writing conferences. They also mentioned particular prewriting techniques for developing expository and persuasive essays, explaining that many students internalized these procedures and were using them in their independent writing.

Given our interest in facilitating teachers' adaptive instruction in general, we were also interested in what the teachers said about shifts in their general understandings about writing and writing instruction. We saw these patterns in their shifting practices:

1. Confidence and agency

> Well, I've gained confidence because I know what a good answer requires. I know the different parts without it being too formulaic where the students are just plugging in different words or different sentences to make their essay look exactly like mine, or their short answer questions look exactly like mine. (JH)

> I feel that the training kind of reminded me – let's do what is right for the kids. (BB)

2. Enthusiasm for writing and the teaching of writing

> I think I had a renewed enthusiasm for writing instruction. At the high school level they have been so focused on the product even when they slip in some process. ... You know for me it was almost like a little refresher course, like a shot in the arm. (BB)

> I'm a better writer because I write more often and I revise more often and I'm doing it because my kids need to see me do it, which before I wouldn't do it because I didn't think my kids needed to see it. And I have to prove to them that it's okay to go back and look at something you've already written and revise it instead of making huge mistakes and correct those mistakes- I had to prove to them that that's okay and through that process of proving it to them, I've proven it to myself. (PV)

3. Adaptability and flexibility

> I think that it has definitely allowed me to grow as a teacher too and broaden my thoughts of what my kids can do. Because before ... I don't know that I would have helped them to the same level because they're resource kids but now I do. (JH)

> I think when something is effective and true it works for whatever level the child is. (BB)
>
> So I'm a better writer, a better person by the fact that I'm listening more. The kids need to tell me things and I need to listen and I've learned that through this. Better teacher, that just goes back to being more in tune with what the kids want and need. (PV)

4. Authenticity and relevance

> I have had a couple students who were writing their own book and they have had 5 chapters of their novel that they have written. Once they are done, they will be able to publish what they have written on Walkpad (app) for free and then if it goes viral, they will be contacted by a publisher. (BH)
>
> Modeling has gotten a lot more ... We have our own writer's notebooks; we write during the quick write time; we share our writing so that the students feel confident sharing their own. (KW)
>
> I think the biggest thing that has changed is the way that I interact with my kids when it comes to writing, the type of conferencing that we do, and what that looks like. So now more than ever, I conference with my kids probably more than I do even teaching the specific skill of writing that we are working on that week. (CK)

5. Proficiency in writing instruction

> As the teacher, I really liked that I could just insert different pieces, texts, and do the same activities. I liked that they were like protocols, like this is not just an isolated activity. So that inferencing carousel, I used that multiple times throughout whenever we would read a short story, that was almost always a protocol to kind of get our brains working, and the students loved it, and they got to collaborate, and it forced them to think which for them to love thinking is a big deal. (RS)
>
> I think it has definitely allowed me to grow as a teacher too and broaden my thoughts of what my kids can do because before [this experience] I would have just assumed. I don't know that I would have helped them to the same level because they are resource kids ... (JH)
>
> Well, I've gained confidence because I know what a good answer requires. I know the different parts without it being too formulaic where the students are just plugging in different words or different sentences to make their essay look exactly like mine ... so it ... helped me to know exactly what they need to help them to answer a question well and write well. (NH)

Patterns in Student Outcomes on the Test

Both district leaders and teachers are convinced that the *FTN* initiative has had positive effects on student learning. Of course, this is one among several initiatives within this district (e.g., independent reading, cooperative learning strategies, project-based learning) so it is not possible to tease out direct influences on student scores. The data suggest that our work has been one of several contributing factors.

E. Simpson, district Secondary Language Arts Coordinator, shared the following data (personal communication, March 28, 2016). In the fall of 2013, a year after the initial implementation of the lesson frameworks,

- The 9th Grade Center where teachers abandoned tutorials and pullouts, choosing instead to integrate these lessons as their mainstream English instruction, was the highest scoring campus in the district.
- A 9th–10th grade campus, the second most economically disadvantaged population in the district (56.8% Free and Reduced Lunch), scored the highest in the district for 10th grade reading.

In addition, a report of the progress of 140 students in the 2014 summer writing camp (provided for students who had failed the test one or more times before) provides more specific information:

- The percent of English I (9th grade) students who "Met Standard" was only 6% less than the district average (including students taking the test for first time).
- The English I average essay score of campers was 3% above the district average.
- For English learners, the percent of campers who "Met Standard" was 2% above the district average.
- The percent of English II (10th grade) campers who "Met Standard" was 4% higher than the district average.
- The English II campers' essay score average was 4% higher than the district average.
- For English learners at the camp, scores were 12% above the district average.

Also in this district, the number of students retaking the high school tests decreased significantly from 2014 to 2015. For the English I test, 750 students had to retake the test in 2014, but only 273 had to retake the test in 2015, which is a reduction of 63.6% – almost two-thirds. For the English II test, the number fell from 473 to 240, which is a reduction of approximately 50%.

Certainly this is progress that any district would welcome. Although these trends deserve further study, they have definitely sustained the district leaders' interest in continuing our partnership.

Summary of Findings

The interviews of teachers in one partner district suggest that the patterns that teachers report in students and themselves in have shifted toward more enthusiasm, confidence, adaptability, authenticity, and proficiency. Not only do we see positive movements in these areas, but patterns in test scores also suggest that students are becoming better readers and writers. This happened, not by mandating a standardized instructional package, but when we invited the teachers into Adaptive Action – to follow the lesson frameworks, to observe their students, and to adjust and modify and adapt in response to student needs. One of the teachers explained it this way:

> I feel like the Finding True North lessons ... are like training wheels .... they give you this lesson cycle and you learn how to do them, and you learn the cycle, and you learn this way of teaching, and then it is like you take the training wheels off. And then you are building your own lessons based off of that same cycle–the same cycle of learning. (HG)

SO WHAT? NOW WHAT?

The central question in this chapter is whether a set of lesson frameworks and accompanying professional development support might set conditions for writing teachers to adapt their instruction to meet the complex needs of their students, in spite of the high stakes tests. We invited teachers to use them and to engage in cycles of Adaptive Action:

- What am I doing in these lessons to support student writers?
- What are the various student responses?
- So what do these student responses mean for next steps?
- Now what support do the students need next?
- Now what more do I need to learn about writing and writing instruction to support my students?

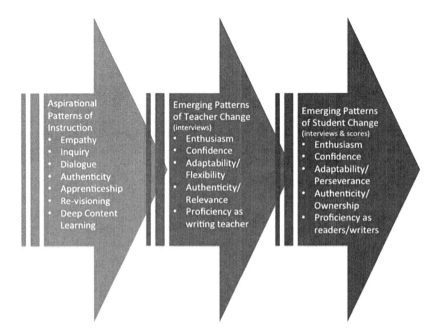

Fig. 5. Aspirational Patterns of Instruction and Emerging Patterns in Teacher and Student Change.

We were surprised and encouraged when the patterns from interviews and test data resonated with the aspirational patterns of instruction inherent in the lesson framework design, as Fig. 5 illustrates.

Although these patterns were strong, we are careful not to claim a direct causal link between these lesson frameworks and particular changes in teachers or students. We know that teachers' work moves forward within complex networks of multiple curriculum and professional learning initiatives. These findings can remind teachers, administrators, and professional learning consultants to look closely at the multiple overlapping and layered CAS involved in writing instruction, to watch as particular patterns emerge, and to set conditions for teachers and students to continue the productive and generative patterns that emerge when powerful writers are at work (Fig. 6).

Erin Gruwell (1999), in the quote that opens this chapter, tells us that powerful writing can cause change. Through our *Finding True North* partnership with writing teachers, we have learned something else — that seeing,

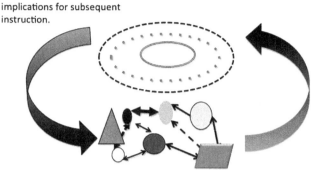

Fig. 6. A Complex Adaptive Process at Work in the *Finding True North* Partnership.

understanding, and influencing patterns in complex systems can also contribute to change. By noticing and naming these patterns, we can help our students tell their powerful stories.

REFERENCES

Anderson, J. (2011). *10 things every writer needs to know*. Portland, ME: Stenhouse Publishers.
Anderson, J., & Dean, D. (2014). *Revision decisions: Talking through sentences and beyond*. Portland, ME: Stenhouse Publishers.
Atwell, N. (2015). *In the middle: A lifetime of learning about writing, reading, and adolescents*. Portsmouth, NH: Heinemann.
Ballenger, B. P. (2009). *The curious writer*. New York, NY: Pearson Longman.
Burke, J. (2013). *The English teacher's companion*. Portsmouth, NH: Heinemann.
Cammarota, J. (2008). *Revolutionizing education: Youth participatory action research in motion*. New York, NY: Routledge.
Cochran-Smith, M., & Lytle, S. (2009). *Inquiry as stance: Practitioner research in the next generation*. New York, NY: Teachers College Press.
Dewey, J. (1910). *How we think*. Boston, MA: D.C. Heath & Co.
Dooley, K. (1996). A nominal definition of complex adaptive systems. *The Chaos Network*, *8*(1), 2–3.
Dweck, C. (2007). *Mindset: The new psychology of success*. New York, NY: Ballantine Books.

Elish-Piper, L., L'Allier, S., Manderino, M., & Di Domenico, P. (2016). *Collaborative coaching for disciplinary literacy: Strategies to support teachers in grades* (pp. 6–12). New York, NY: The Guildford Press.

Eoyang, G., & Holladay, R. (2013). *Adaptive action: Leveraging uncertainty in your organization.* Stanford, CA: Stanford Press.

Etzioni, A. (2014). We need empathy, too. In *Essays on character & opportunity: Center on children & families: The character & opportunity project* (pp. 42–44). Washington, DC: Brookings.

Freire, P. (2000). Pedagogy of the oppressed, 30th anniversary edition. New York, NY: Bloomsbury Academic.

Gallagher, K. (2011). *Write like this: Teaching real-world writing through modeling and mentor texts.* Portland, ME: Stenhouse Publishers.

Gallagher, K. (2015). *In the best interest of students: Staying true to what works in the ELA classroom.* Portland, ME: Stenhouse Publishers.

González, N., Moll, L. C., Floyd-Tenery, M., Rivera, A., Rendon, P., Gonzales, R., & Amanti, C. (1993). *Teacher research on funds of knowledge: Learning from households.* Educational Practice Report: No. 6. Tucson, AZ: Center for Research on Cultural Diversity and Language Learning, University of Arizona. Retrieved from http://www.ncela.gwu.edu/pubs/ncrcdsll/epr6.htm. Accessed on January 1, 2007.

Gruwell, E. (1999). *The freedom writers diary: How a teacher and 150 teens used writing to change themselves and the world around them.* New York, NY: Broadway Books.

Harvey, S., & Daniels, H. (2015). *Comprehension and collaboration, revised edition: Inquiry circles for curiosity, engagement, and understanding.* Portsmouth, NH: Heinemann.

Hirsch, S. (2010). Mastering new standards will require teams to dig into deep content learning. *Journal of Staff Development, 31*(5), 72.

Holland, J. H. (1998). *Emergence from chaos to order.* Oxford: Oxford University Press.

Johns, A. M. (1997). *Text, role, and context: Developing academic literacies.* New York, NY: Cambridge University Press.

Kittle, P. (2008). *Write beside them: Risk, voice, and clarity in high school writing.* Portsmouth, NH: Heinemann.

Kittle, P. (2012). *Book love: Developing depth, stamina, and passion in adolescent readers.* Portsmouth, NH: Heinemann.

Lave, J., & Wenger, E. (1991). *Situated learning: Legitimate peripheral participation.* New York, NY: Cambridge University Press.

Lee, C. (2007). *The role of culture in academic literacies: Conducting our blooming in the midst of the whirlwind.* New York, NY: Teachers College Press.

Messner, K. (2011). *Real revision: Author's strategies to share with writers.* Portland, ME: Stenhouse Publishers.

Mraz, K., & Hertz, D. (2015). *A mindset for learning: Teaching the traits of joyful, independent growth.* Portsmouth, NH: Heinemann.

Newkirk, T. (2014). *Minds made for stories: How we really read and write informational and persuasive texts.* Portsmouth, NH: Heinemann.

Patterson, L., Holladay, R., & Eoyang, G. (2013). *Radical rules for schools: Adaptive action for complex change.* Circle Pines, MN: Human Systems Dynamics Institute.

Patterson, L., Wickstrom, C., Roberts, J., Araujo, J., & Hoki, C. (2010). Deciding when to step in and when to back off. *The Tapestry Journal, 2*(1), 1–18. Retrieved from http://tapestry.usf.edu/journal/v02n01.php

Rainey, E., & Moje, E. B. (2012). Building insider knowledge: Teaching students to read, write, and think within ELA and across disciplines. *English Education, 45*(1), 71–90.

Rifkin, J. (2009). *The empathic civilization.* New York, NY: Jeremy P. Tarcher.

Ritchart, R., Church, M., & Morrison, K. (2011). *Making thinking visible: How to promote engagement, understanding, and independence for all learners.* San Francisco, CA: Jossey-Bass.

Short, K., Harste, J., & Burke, C. (1996). *Creating classrooms for authors and inquirers* (2nd ed.). Portsmouth, NH: Heinemann.

Tharp, R. G., & Gallimore, R. (1988). *Rousing minds to life: Teaching, learning, and schooling in social context.* New York, NY: Cambridge University Press.

Vygotsky, L. (1978). M. Cole, V. John-Steiner, S. Scribner, & E. Souberman (Trans). *Mind in society: The development of higher psychological processes.* Cambridge, MA: Harvard University Press.

Wells, G. (1999). *Dialogic inquiry: Towards a sociocultural practice and theory of education.* New York, NY: Cambridge University Press.

Wickstrom, C. (2013). Inquiry can be transformative: From "I will make him write" to "He will learn to write". In S. Szabo, L. Martin, T. Morrison, & L. Haas (Eds.), *Literacy is transformative* (pp. 255–274). Louisville, KY: Association of Literacy Educators and Researchers.

Wickstrom, C., Araujo, J., Patterson, L., Hoki, C., & Roberts, J. (2011). Teachers prepare students for careers and college: "I see you," therefore I can teach you. In P. J. Dunston, L. B. Gambrell, C. C. Bates, S. K. Fullerton, V. R. Gillis, K. Headley, & P. M. Stecker (Eds.), *60th literacy research association yearbook* (pp. 113–126). Oak Creek, WI: Literacy Research Association.

Wickstrom, C., Patterson, L., & Isgitt, J. (2012). One teacher's implementation of culturally mediated writing instruction. In P. J. Dunston, S. K. Fullerton, C. C. Bates, K. Headley, & P. M. Stecker (Eds.), *61st literacy research association yearbook* (pp. 322–334). Oak Creek, WI: Literacy Research Association.

Wilson-Grau, R., & Britt, H. (2012). *Outcome harvesting.* Cairo: Ford Foundation.

FOURTH GRADERS AS RESEARCHERS: AUTHORS AND SELF-ILLUSTRATORS OF INFORMATIONAL BOOKS

Anita Nigam and Carole Janisch

ABSTRACT

Purpose — *To facilitate teacher–researcher collaboration in order to implement an informational writing research project using the framework of Browse, Collect, Collate, and Compose embedded within the writing workshop.*

Design/methodology/approach — *This study was conducted using a qualitative (Merriam, 1998) method of inquiry, more specifically, case study research design. A researcher and a practitioner came together to explore problems related to authentic use of expository genre and collaborated to help fourth graders write informational books.*

Findings — *The development of an authentic informational book was in contrast to the inauthentic purposes whereby students studied expository writing as preparation for statewide testing of student writing achievement.*

The study advocates the usage of authentic literacy contexts where students can enjoy writing for personal purposes.

Practical implications — *Collaboration between classroom teachers of writing and researchers contributes to the theoretical and practical knowledge base of the teacher and researcher. Overall literacy development is enhanced when students read and write out of their own interest. Students use trade books as mentor texts to compose and create their informational books. The value of seeing fourth graders as researchers and making an informational book serves the authentic purpose of writing.*

Keywords: Informational research project; authentic writing; teacher; researcher collaboration

> I felt the research project really helped the students see how to do authentic writing and be able to tie everything they learned all through the year into an authentic manner ... and I felt this will be a good way to end writing [instruction]... they can do this [kind of writing] for life. (Ms. Smith, Classroom Teacher)

In times of standardized testing, few classroom teachers recognize the powerful nature of teacher and students as collaborators in the construction of knowledge (Cowie, Ortel-Cass, Moreland, Jones, Cooper, & Taylor, 2010). What happens when students research topics, constructing knowledge in a way that empowers them such that they become experts, and, in turn, teach others about their selected topics? Students engaged in the foregoing bring various perspectives, have access to views of their peers who are their real audience, and offer valuable insights to each other from their respective world views. Understanding and seeing informational books produced by budding researchers reveals their collaborative construction of knowledge. In the present study, students researched topics in which they were interested, gathered data, organized it, wrote the prose, and became the proud owners of self-created and illustrated informational books. Focusing attention on students as researchers with self-chosen topics, we examined the question: What did the students learn about research following the phases outlined for the development of the informational writing project?

THEORETICAL FRAMEWORK

The principal theoretical frameworks influencing the instructional practices of classroom teachers of writing are Socio Constructivism (Barnard & Campbell, 2005) and writing as a process (Graves, 1983). Socio Constructivism, more than any other theoretical framework, supports the writing process (Barnard & Campbell, 2005) and with an accompanying number of concepts, for example, community of writers, mentor texts, conferencing, sharing, and revision, that comprise the process. Driven by this theoretical framework, a teacher's schedule of teaching should include teacher instruction which provides scaffolding, often in the form of teacher modeling. Vygotsky (1978) opined that human learning is social in nature and that sociocultural interactions are central to learning. Individuals use social, cultural, and psychological tools to learn and regulate their daily interactions, and language is the most important tool for regulating these daily interactions. Conceptual and social learning occurs through dialog within the Zone of Proximal Development (ZPD), which is defined as follows:

> The distance between the actual developmental level as determined by independent problem solving and the level of potential development as determined by problem solving under adult guidance or in collaboration with more advanced peers. (Vygotsky, 1978, p. 86)

Writing Process

Graves (1983) has provided foundational information for writing as a process that informs the work presented here. Fundamentally, he opined that teachers need to hold to the belief that when children have the time and opportunity to write, they can and will write. More specifically, he, among others, supports the use of writing workshop for classroom instruction to address the concepts of the writing process (Calkins, 1986; Graves, 1983). Writing workshop is a participative approach in which students are encouraged to select writing topics of personal interest from their everyday lives, engage in conversation about their writing with real audiences, and through this engagement come to understand conventions of written English. Teacher and peer conferencing closely guide the students through this endeavor (Jasmine & Weiner, 2007). The notion of a community of writers, as a concept of the writing process, plays out in writing. Graves (1983) suggests that teachers need not be expert writers while writing with children, but the sharing of ideas and writing progress among peers and teachers facilitates students' learning and growing as writers. Moreover, searching for meaning together establishes a healthy environment. Graves further suggests that "modeling provides many opportunities for choice and for a wide range of development within the classroom (p. 49)." Murray, Newkirk, and Miller (2009) echo the benefits of the notion of a community of writers: "Writing is contagious. It is almost impossible to resist the desire to write in your own voice, of your own concerns, when you are part of a supportive writing community" (p. 20).

PERSPECTIVE

According to Maloch and Zapata (2011), there are two reasons for including the use of informational texts in primary classrooms. First, tapping into the curiosity of youngsters' informational texts fulfills the need to provide real world experiences. Furthermore, as students chose their topics of interest, Caswell and Duke (1998) found that the engagement aspect enhanced overall literacy development as students followed and read materials of interest to them. Second, a study by Harvey (2002) revealed that informational texts are the most widely read texts beyond classroom textbooks. However, reading informational texts does not automatically translate into writing. According to Harvey (2002), "we are not modeling nonfiction writing with authentic well written examples" (p. 15).

In spite of the importance of informational texts, the issues surrounding helping children to become writers of nonfiction stem from unrealistic classroom expectations. After reading and writing primarily narrative texts in the earliest grades, students in third and fourth grades are often asked to write formal reports in an expository mode (Harvey, 1998). Additionally, fourth-grade students are required to read, comprehend, and write informational texts even though research shows that they have not had many classroom experiences dealing with informational genres related to writing purposes (Duke, 2000; Kamberelis & Bovino, 1999; Moss & Newton, 2002). The expectation is that the students read source materials and write about what they have understood in ways that display their understanding of the material. In actuality, students often write "fact based, encyclopedia-like rehearsals of surface knowledge rather than write reports" (Read, 2005, p. 36) that fully integrate several sources and their prior knowledge

(Cazden, 1993). According to Reutzel, Larson, and Sabey (1995), "the leap from children's generally well-developed, interesting, and well-written expressive writing in the intermediate grades to the seemingly unfamiliar expository writing arena, is often one of duty without comprehension" (p. 98).

Classroom attention to informational writing requires an understanding that authentic nonfiction writing is rich and full of voice (Harvey, 2002). Calkins (1994) talks about inviting youngsters to research things they know and care about because that provides authentic entryways into research. According to her, when children research their interests, they can develop these into passions, hobbies, and inculcate a sense of mission. Moreover, these research interests generate intensity and an absorption. Read (2005) offers another piece of the research writing process for very young writers by elaborating on the need for first graders to use talk to generate research writing ideas. Lily and Fields (2014) recommended photography for teaching informational writing whereby fourth-grade students used photographs clicked by them to promote their research and thinking. Photographs brought intensity and passion to their interests and to their informational writing.

However, more research is needed on authentic nonfiction writing (Duke, Purcell-Gates, Hall, & Tower, 2006). In 2010, Duke made an urgent appeal for U.S. educators to introduce practices and policies that introduce informational texts early in classrooms in a widespread manner. Not only should a teacher introduce informational texts through features such as vocabulary and text features, but also foster real world connections through informational texts. A number of literacy researchers (Graves, 1989; Harris, Graham, Friedlander, Laud, & Dougherty, 2013) have developed frameworks for helping students write informational books. The study reported here used a framework for informational writing and within writing workshop. One fourth-grade teacher and her students used a framework of "Browse, Collect, Collate, and Compose" to write personal informational text and in an authentic context as opposed to the customary writing practices which constituted the preparation for statewide testing.

METHODOLOGY

This study was conducted using a qualitative method of inquiry (Merriam, 1998). More specifically, case study research design was used which offers the researcher an opportunity to construct a more descriptive picture of the happenings in the setting, thus providing everybody with "a slice of life" (Erlandson, Harris, Skipper, & Allen, 1993, p. 31) from the phenomenon under study. In the case study reported here, a researcher and a practitioner explored authentic use of the expository genre and writing informational texts. The practitioner, Ms. Smith (pseudonym), was not comfortable using the genre and as related to writing. Following conversations between Ms. Smith and Anita (the researcher), the latter provided a framework for implementation of informational text writing, Ms. Smith indicated her willingness to try the four-phase framework with the students in her fourth-grade classroom.

Participants

Ms. Smith taught at a low SES Title 1 elementary school in the southwestern high plains of the United States. She was identified as an effective teacher of writing instruction (having taught for 14 years and 10 of them as a writing teacher). Her fourth-grade classroom students represented a diverse population of 18 students: 1 Anglo, 3 African American, and 14 Hispanic. Ms. Smith had been interacting with the students from the beginning of the semester on a daily basis in all the subjects and therefore had a thorough knowledge of their writing capabilities.

Data Sources and Collection

Multiple data sources for the study included semistructured interviews (teacher and students) and questionnaires before the research project began and upon its completion. Other data sources included students' work during the different phases of research (browse, collect, collate (organize), and compose) and final copies of students' informational books. Work on the informational writing research project took place 2–3 days per week and across the weeks from April 1 to May 23.

Data Analysis

In qualitative research, analysis is an ongoing process from the time the study begins. It does not happen chronologically but happens simultaneously and data collection and analysis influence each other. Anita transcribed the interviews and noted down the categories that emerged.

Similarly with questionnaires and students' research work, she jotted down the categories that emerged throughout the process. She used the constant comparative method and noted the common categories that emerged across all data sources. After the transcripts were read independently, Anita and the second author worked to reach a consensus on the themes. The six themes somewhat overlapped but in general focused on the research process: increased schema for research, appeal of writing with a self-selected topic, enhancement of composing through captured personal images, computer use provides incentive, and developed sense of community.

CLASSROOM WRITING CONTEXT

The students first learned about the framework for the informational writing: browse, collect, collate (organize), and compose. Writing workshop became the basis for the last procedure, composing, and included drafting, revising and editing, conferencing, publishing and author's chair, mentor texts, modeling, and read alouds.

Browse, Collect, Collate, and Compose

The four research phases, we collectively termed as "Writers in the Making," were outlined for the students: (1) Explore widely for information about your choice of topic for your book: browse through books, check the internet, observe the surroundings, and check authors' websites such as www.seymoursimon.com, (2) Collect the information: make notes on note cards as you read, and collect pictures and photographs, (3) Collate (organize) the information: decide sequencing of information, arrange photographs, provide headings and subheadings, and include access features (table of contents and chapter titles, glossaries, sidebars, inserted information, bibliographies, author's notes, photographs, diagrams, maps, tables), (4) Compose: provide an introduction and an ending, and above all write in your own words.

Considerable time was spent on the first stage of browsing as it was an important stage and the rest of the processes depended on it. Anita and the classroom teacher emphasized the need to search widely for interesting information; students had ample time, about six weeks, for browsing and exploring. Students were free to switch topics if something caught their interest during this phase.

In the collect phase, students logged information on their note cards for their chosen topic. The note cards represented interesting information they wanted to keep. Additionally, students were instructed to click photographs and collect pictures to supplement information in their books. Using the *Red-Eyed Tree Frog* by Cowley, Anita introduced close-up photography as done by Nic Bishop in the Cowley book. Students also had the choice of creating their own illustrations. In the context of this phase, Ms. Smith and Anita discussed Peter Siper's *People*, which is an oversized picture book and includes drawings of ears and eyes in the many shapes and colors which they can appear. The photographs of Donna Jackson in her *In Your Face: The Facts About Your Features* were observed. Eric Carle's *Very Hungry Caterpillar* with its illustrations made with tissue paper collage was also discussed. One of the fourth-grade students, Veronica (pseudonym), was excited and wanted to make a book on cats and wished to include both illustrations and photographs.

The collate (organize) phase became part of the compose phase which is described in the next section and within the discussion of writing and writing workshop.

Elements of Writing Workshop and Writing

Students began the compose phase with a draft of their writing following the collect and collate phases. In the collate phase students organized their note cards of collected information according to categories and subcategories. Headings for the categories — and in some cases, headings for the subcategories — were created. Subsequently, students wrote the first draft. Students wrote paragraphs for each category — and in some cases paragraphs for each subcategory — and included pertinent information noted on the cards. Headings introduced the paragraphs. Students wrote hurriedly and without careful attention to capitalization or punctuation — the goal was to write so as to convey the information logically and coherently. To give license to drafting and validate the ongoing process of writing, Ms. Smith used her "rough draft" stamp and carefully stamped the same on every student's paper.

Revising and Editing
Students upgraded their drafts and within the compose phase of the informational research writing. The draft paragraphs under each heading and subheading were revisited through conferencing which is discussed in a

subsequent section. The emerging informational book was provided an introduction, a title, a table of contents, and an index. Students were provided guidance for including as many access features as needed or appropriate. Finally, students added their author's bio to the informational books.

Conferencing
Students completed their final drafts with the teacher's and the researcher's help given during conferencing. Ms. Smith realized that it was the conferencing aspects of writing workshop that gave students an awareness of what they had written. The awareness was a beginning step for understanding how they might revise or modify the content of their informational book to better relate the content to the reader. Ms. Smith reported the specific and individual feedback facilitated students' growth as writers. Similar benefits accrued from peer conferencing. Ms. Smith believed in some respects peers were more helpful because they were the real audience as opposed to the instructional stance of a teacher. She also believed that students were more excited to write for their peers and in turn, do her proud and impress her. Whole class conferencing was also used so students could share their ideas and receive feedback from more than one or two persons.

Publishing and Author's Chair
The students word processed their final copies after incorporating the feedback received during the conferencing. Word processing was done to give the informational books a more professional approach. At the end of the school year, author's chair was implemented, and students read favorite parts to the teacher, researcher, and their peers.

Mentor Texts, Modeling, and Read Alouds
These components are discussed not in direct relation to the writing process but in support of it. They were important components of the project whereby the fourth-grade students conducted their research and wrote their informational books.

Use of Mentor Texts. Mentor texts are intended to help students become aware of author's craft (see Ray, 1999) and consider how they might emulate the writing of more expert writers — as well as gain content information. Ms. Smith and Anita flooded the classroom with nonfiction trade books borrowed from the school and university libraries including recommendations made by Bamford and Kristo (2003). Ms. Smith began by discussing books familiar to the students. Additionally, students were shown websites of authors, for example, Seymour Simon. Together the entire class browsed through his e-book on butterflies. Students also consulted *Volcanoes, Spiders, and Lightning* — three additional Simon books. Anita informed students of upcoming experiences for the process: what it is like to be an author, how to select a topic of interest, how to select an author whose writing style they would like to follow, what constitutes a cover page, what illustrations or research to consider, and the steps of publishing. Ms. Smith asked the class to recall the visit of an author to the school and how he described his writing of a book on snakes. Videos from http://www.readingrockets.org were also used to further examine writer's craft. Students were excited about the idea of research.

Teacher Modeling. Ms. Smith wrote her own informational book and modeled each of the four phases as they applied to her own writing. For example, she talked through her "browsing" and her thinking for selecting her writing topic (her new Labrador dog). She continued with thinking aloud for her rough draft, revising and editing, and the publishing of the final writing. Ms. Smith believed that teachers need to model their expectations for student's writing, that is, compose along with their students and thus join in the "community of writers."

Reading Aloud. Ms. Smith and Anita frequently opened the 50-minute classroom session with a read aloud and a discussion of a nonfiction book (e.g., *Here is the Tropical Rainforest* by Dumpy, *Spiders* by Gibbons, and *A Desert Scrapbook* by Wright-Frierson). Although students may have gained information from these books and relative to their topic, the purpose was to examine and emulate the author's style of writing and presentation, choice of media, illustrations, choice of cover page, and access features (e.g., acknowledgments, index, glossary, preface, bibliography, author's notes).

OUTCOMES FOR STUDENTS

The informational research project and the writing associated with it are discussed relative to the themes: increased schema for research, appeal of writing with self-selected topic, enhancement of composing through captured personal images, computer use provides incentive, and developed sense of community.

Increased Schema for Research

Students learned that writing is done for authentic purposes such as the mentor text author might do as opposed to writing practice to do well on a writing test. The research process was long and tedious but with moments of pleasure when the students discovered new information. Students came to internalize the meaning of the four phases of the framework. For example, "browsing" informational books and websites just to become familiar with information was not a general practice prior to the project. Students came to think of browsing as just "looking for stuff [information]" to determine what might be available and what might catch their attention for "collecting."

Appeal of Writing with a Self-Selected Topic

At the prompting of the researcher and teacher, many students chose a topic of interest and realized the interest sustained their work through all the phases. For example, Veronica chose the topic of "cats" because she had them for pets. She wanted to read more about them and photograph them. She was writing about something from her everyday life and eagerly expanded the ideas through activities such as reading the mentor texts or other available texts about cats. In essence, the self-selected topic was a source of motivation for staying with the writing. Ms. Smith was astonished at students' display of eagerness to engage with the books that were aligned with student topics and that were made available for reading and consulting. Alice (pseudonym), a reluctant reader and writer, became a participant in the project, and although she had minimal information, she was engaged.

Enhancement of Composing through Captured Personal Images

Introduction of cameras and photography enabled students to take photographs related to their topics as an out-of-school activity (in some cases, their very first photographs). For example, Matt (pseudonym) who worked on information for the Komodo Dragon, went to a pet store and took a picture of an actual dragon's photograph. He and others wove meaningful texts around the pictures, that is, composing through images captured. These compositions were in sharp contrast to the state achievement test compositions they wrote.

Computer Use Provides Incentive

When Ms. Smith announced that students who finished their informational writing project could word process the final piece, there was class jubilation. She was surprised that everybody was keen to use the computers. Students were intrigued by the power of technology and in part, the use of technology helped to sustain effort and time demanded by the project. Ms. Smith believed the schools needed to make students technology savvy and saw the benefits of its use for writing:

> Because of technology, the presentation of [the book] was so much better. And I guess just knowing how to work on a computer ... that was nice ... they used it for typing, presentation, and research. Just knowing how to open a file and saving a file [was good]. I think the learning was phenomenal.

Developed Sense of Community

As the book making involved a number of tasks such as drawing illustrations, choice of media, clicking photographs, and word processing, students offered help to each other, thus establishing a community of writers. Because a number of decisions needed to be made such as the choice of the cover page, how to match the text and the illustrations, which access features to include, students sought out each other for help. Moreover, all the conferencing between teacher and students and peer conferencing generated ideas for writing. This community of writers also evolved so when a student finished a task, he/she was eager to help and offer expertise − and in reciprocal fashion. For example, Veronica was not good at illustrating while Rose (pseudonym) could do it. However, finding information for a topic was difficult for Rose. The girls helped each other. Thus, a sense of community was created in the class whereby students were confident and did not hesitate to interact with each other.

DISCUSSION

The informational writing research project was a product of researcher and practitioner conversations and discussions. Ms. Smith looked at the guidelines and decided to implement the project because she believed it would nurture expository writing for her students and help her think of different ways to implement expository writing, that is, the use of the framework of browse, collect, collate, and compose. She believed the project was an important step in students being independent writers as they worked on topics they selected, used the phases of research, and wrote informational books. Students needed to realize that writing is not only related to testing purposes and the 16 line testing format, but also involves authenticity including choice of topic. Duke (2010) defines authentic as using real world information for writing. Yopp and Yopp (2012) define informational text as a type of nonfiction text that promotes information about the natural or social world.

The informational writing research project was a success, in great part, because the topic selection lay in the hands of the students. As the topics were self-selected, students took ownership for them. Graves (1983) states that if they chose topics wisely, they take ownership, show mastery and control of subject matter, and are proud of their achievements. The topics selected tapped the youngsters' curiosity and provided the much needed real world experiences with reading and writing (Maloch & Zapata, 2011). According to Caswell and Duke (1998), the engagement aspect improved their overall literacy development as students followed and read materials of interest to them.

With selection of personal topics and sustained engagement, students worked well independently. There was an intensity and an absorption evident in students' behavior (Calkins, 1994). The authentic writing was in sharp contrast to the writing pieces produced in response to the writing prompts as preparation for the statewide writing assessments. These fourth graders seemed to have understood what real writers do; we know that children have taken hold of the craft if they write and rewrite to suit their "intended meaning" and take ownership of their writing. Revision is an important part of the process as students make pertinent choices and retain ownership of their drafts (Atwell, 1998).

The excitement of clicking their first photographs and working on creating illustrations generated enthusiasm. "Reading and writing can be highly active modes for self-exploration and self-construction" (Graves, 1999, p. 34). According to Lily and Fields (2014), using photography and writing as composition processes helps students' linguistic and visual competencies. As students worked on their informational writing research project, Ms. Smith worked with the students to get the right focus while clicking photographs to include in their informational books. At the same time, word processing was useful to the students. According to Applebee and Langer (2009), "the use of word-processing software has a positive effect on the development of writing abilities, and particularly so for underachieving students (p. 6)." Cooper states that students in the poorest schools have the least access to internet at home, and if we do not make an effort at school for bringing them this necessary skill, much needed in the 21st century, the students are likely to be left behind.

A most heartening aspect of the project, was the class becoming a close knit community where each participant learned about the growing funds of facts about each other's topics and at the same time helped and modeled for each other. Going through the research process brought out different talents within the students who formed a community and helped each other in various tasks depending on where their expertise lay. There was talk and peer conferencing which helped generate writing ideas (Read, 2005).

The research project was not without issues and challenges during the implementation. Reading capabilities and dispositions were factors that were not addressed adequately. Some students were not inclined to read and asked their peers for the information they needed. Joseph (pseudonym) had chosen the topic piranhas which was not available on net tracker.com so he used Google and would not read the information given. Rose was an ELL (English Language Learner) and found it difficult to focus on one topic because of her limited English vocabulary. She changed her topic from one about African wild dogs to dolphins to rabbits and then puppies. She finally did her work on dolphins when paired up with another student, Kate (pseudonym), who was also working on dolphins and porpoises, which was a good approach considering that Rose's English reading and writing was limited. In contrast, there were several students who excelled as readers, who loved reading and were totally engrossed in reading and writing. Even Alice (pseudonym) although a below average reader enjoyed reading on her topic and did a great writing project on whales.

Although the purpose of this chapter is to discuss student outcomes, the impact of the project on the teacher is worthy of mentioning. Seeing the framework of browse, collect, collate (organize), and compose made Ms. Smith see expository writing and more specifically the teaching of expository writing in a significantly different perspective. She talked about her improved self-efficacy in the teaching of expository texts:

> I definitely feel more confident in teaching expository differently to kids after understanding it in a better way. It helped me see different ways to teach them research, and they ENJOYED it. They dug into it and it was a long process and they were okay with that. So that was good.

Ms. Smith felt that her strong belief of making students become independent writers was closer to attainment as the result of the expository writing research project.

CONCLUSION

This study advocates the use of authentic literacy contexts where students can enjoy writing for personal purposes. In the art of teaching writing, Calkins (1994) argues that "youngsters need invitations to research things they know and care about" (p. 189). The self-selection of a topic also helped the students maintain an inquiry stance toward writing and lent to a strong link between voice and subject. The educational importance of this study lies in the potential the research project holds for effective teaching of expository genre and shaping the thinking about the process fourth-grade students need to experience in becoming effective researchers and writers.

REFERENCES

Applebee, A. N., & Langer, J. A. (2009). What is happening in the teaching of writing? *English Journal, 98*(5), 18–28.
Atwell, N. (1998). *In the middle: New understandings about writing, reading, and learning.* Portsmouth, NH: Heinemann.
Bamford, R. A., & Kristo, J. V. (2003). *Making facts come alive: Choosing and using nonfiction literature K-8.* Norwood, MA: Christopher-Gordon Publishers, Inc.
Barnard, R., & Campbell, L. (2005). Sociocultural theory and the teaching of process writing: The scaffolding of learning in a university context. *The TESOLANZ Journal, 13,* 76–88.
Calkins, L. M. (1986). *The art of teaching writing.* Portsmouth, NH: Heinemann.
Calkins, L. M. (1994). *The art of teaching writing.* Portsmouth, NH: Heinemann.
Caswell, L. J., & Duke, N. K. (1998). Non-narratives as a catalyst for literacy development. *Language Arts, 75,* 108–117.
Cazden, C. B. (1993, May). A report on reports: Two dilemmas of genre teaching. Paper presented at the Working with Genre Conference, Sydney, Australia. (ERIC Document Reproduction Service No. ED 363593).
Cowie, B., Ortel-Cass, K., Moreland, J., Jones, A., Cooper, B., & Taylor, M. (2010). Teacher–researcher relationships and collaborations in research. *Waikato Journal of Education, 15*(2), 265–273.
Duke, N. K. (2000). 3.6 minutes per day: The scarcity of informational texts in first grade. *Reading Research Quarterly, 35*(2), 202–224.
Duke, N. K. (2010). The real world reading and writing U.S. children need. *Phi Delta Kappan, 91*(5), 98–71.
Duke, N. K., Purcell-Gates, V., Hall, L. A. H., & Tower, C. (2006). Authentic literacy activities for developing comprehension and writing. *The Reading Teacher, 60*(4), 344–355.
Erlandson, D., Harris, E., Skipper, B., & Allen, S. (1993). *Doing naturalistic inquiry: A guide to methods.* Newbury Park, CA: Sage.

Graves, D. (1983). *Writing: Teachers and children at work*. Portsmouth, NH: Heinemann.
Graves, D. (1989). *Investigate nonfiction*. Portsmouth, NH: Heinemann.
Graves, D. (1999). *Bring life into learning*. Portsmouth, NH: Heinemann.
Harris, K. R., Graham, S., Friedlander, B., Laud, L., & Dougherty, K. A. (2013). Bring powerful writing strategies into your classroom: Why and how. *Reading Teacher*, 66(7), 538–542.
Harvey, S. (1998). *Nonfiction matters: Reading, writing, and research in grades* (pp. 3–8). York, ME: Stenhouse.
Harvey, S. (2002). Nonfiction inquiry. Using real reading and writing to explore the world. *Language Arts*, 80, 12–22.
Jasmine, J., & Weiner, W. (2007). The effects of writing workshop on abilities of first grade students to become confident and independent writers. *Early Childhood Education Journal*, 35(2), 131–139.
Kamberelis., G., & Bovino, T. D. (1999). Cultural artifacts as scaffolds for genre development. *Reading Research Quarterly*, 3(4), 138–170.
Lily, E., & Fields, C. (2014). The power of photography as a catalyst for teaching informational writing. *Childhood Education*, 2(90), 99–106.
Maloch, B., & Zapata, A. (2011). "Dude, it's the Milky Way!": An exploration of students' approaches to informational text. In P. J. Dunston, L. B. Gambrell, K. Headley, S. K. Fullerton, P. M. Stecker, V. R. Gillis, & C. C. Bates (Eds.), 60th yearbook of the literacy research association (pp. 322–335). Oak Creek, WI: Literacy Research Association, Inc.
Merriam, S. (1998). *Qualitative research and case study applications in education*. San Francisco, CA: Jossey-Bass Publishers.
Moss, B., & Newton, E. (2002). An examination of the informational text genre in basal readers. *Reading Psychology*, 23(1), 1–13.
Murray, D., Newkirk, T., & Miller, L. C. (2009). *The essential Don Murray: Lessons from America's greatest writing teacher*. Portsmouth, NH: Heinemann.
Ray, K. W. (1999). *Wondrous words: Writers and writing in the elementary classroom*. Urbana, IL: National Council of Teachers of English.
Read, S. (2005). *First and second graders writing informational text*. Newark, DE: International Reading Association.
Reutzel, D. R., Larson, C. M., & Sabey, B. L. (1995). Dialogical books: Connecting content, conversation, and composition. *The Reading Teacher*, 49, 98–109. Retrieved from http://www.readingrockets.org/
Vygotsky, L. S. (1978). *Mind in society: The development of higher psychological processes*. Cambridge, MA: Harvard University Press.
Yopp, R. H., & Yopp, H. K. (2012). Young children's limited and narrow exposure to informational text. *The Reading Teacher*, 65(7), 480–490.

Children's Literature Cited

Carle, E. (1979). *A very hungry caterpiller*. New York, NY: Harper Collins Publishers.
Cowley, J., & Bishop, N. (1999). *Red-eyed tree frog*. New York, NY: Scholastic Press.
Dumpy, M. (1997). *Here is the tropical rainforest*. New York, NY: Hyperion Books.
Gibbons, G. (1993). *Spiders*. New York, NY: Holiday House.

Jackson, D. (2004). *In your face: The facts about your features.* New York, NY: Penguin Young Readers Group.
Siper, P. (1998). *People.* New York, NY: Doubleday Books for Young Readers.
Simon, S. (2006). *Volcanoes.* New York, NY: Harper Collins Publishers.
Simon, S. (2006). *Lighting.* New York, NY: Harper Collins Publishers.
Simon, S. (2007). *Spiders.* New York, NY: Harper Collins Publishers.
Wright-Frierson, V. (2002). *A desert scrapbook.* Hong Kong: Aladdin Paperbacks.

SENIORS, SCHOLARS, RESEARCHERS: USING AN INQUIRY APPROACH TO WRITING THE RESEARCH PAPER

Sarah M. Fleming

ABSTRACT

Purpose — *This chapter presents a description of a pilot course for 12th-grade students in research methods and writing, using Guided Inquiry Design to develop students' critical literacy and information literacy skills.*

Design/methodology/approach — *Using a practitioner inquiry methodology, this teacher research study makes use of qualitative data to examine student perspectives and experiences, teaching artifacts and student work samples. The research seeks to identify ways students practice critical literacies when engaged with inquiry learning, as well as the characteristics of a classroom learning community designed to support students' experiences in inquiry learning.*

Findings — *Teachers of research-based writing are encouraged to adopt a guided inquiry approach to their instruction in which they flip the script on the thesis statement, allow for an almost uncomfortable amount of exploratory reading, put the focus on the process instead of the product, and form a guided inquiry team with the school librarian.*

Practical implications — *This chapter serves as a resource for practicing teachers, teacher researchers, and teacher educators assisting new teachers in embedding critical inquiry skill development in student writing.*

Keywords: Critical literacy; writing process; writing teachers; guided inquiry

EARLY BIRDS ARE INQUISITIVE

It's still dark out at 6:45 am on this cold, Thursday morning in February. I make my way from the car and into the building, noting that most of the school buses haven't even left for their morning runs yet. As I fumble with my keys, the door in front of me suddenly swings open, and a chipper "Here you go, Ms. F!" nearly bowls me over.

I follow my student down the hall, past dark and empty classrooms, to the heart of the building — the library. The lights are switching on as we push through the doors, and I see my colleague Jane pulling tables together in the center of the room. Three more students help her push chairs back and reorganize the space so as to create a makeshift conference table. Book bags are flung to the floor, the coffees come out, and someone produces a box of bagels, inciting a frenzied scramble among the seven students (two are still missing, notorious latecomers). I settle into my seat and arrange my stuff — Chromebook out, opened to our online classroom, a fresh page ready for note-taking. Jane sits down next to me, her cup of tea in hand.

"So," I start. "How's it going?"

Everyone talks at once, a blurred mix of zombie-like groans and emotional outbursts. It's one of those mornings, I see. Forty-five minutes and a dozen questions later, nine seniors rush off to their first-period class, and I'm left to recover from the intellectual bedlam that was our weekly seminar.

PURPOSE OF THIS CHAPTER

The purpose of this chapter is to present a description of a pilot course implemented during the 2015–2016 school year for 12th-grade students in inquiry-based research methods and writing. The course was designed in response to a growing suspicion that many students received insufficient or inconsistent instruction in doing research for written assignments, and the fear they were heading off to college without the skills necessary to do college-level research papers and projects. While full analysis of the course's implementation is not yet complete, preliminary analysis suggests findings about adolescent literacies and writing instruction relevant to this volume.

In this chapter, I first discuss the context in which this new class, the Senior Scholar Research Seminar, is situated, including an overview of the school's demographics and learning culture. I acknowledge my position as a teacher researcher, and I make note of the relationship between practitioner inquiry as a research method (Cochran-Smith & Lytle, 1993, 2009) and the critical pedagogy at work when instructing students to practice their research and writing using an inquiry approach (Fecho & Allen, 2003; Freire, 2000). Next I present an outline of the Senior Scholar Research Seminar course as a curriculum implemented in the 2015–2016 school year, and I highlight specific assignments designed to develop students' information and critical literacies. Then, I present an overview of the Guided Inquiry Design framework as the model my coinstructor and I used to structure the course (Kuhlthau, Maniotes, & Caspari, 2012). I conclude this chapter by discussing the significance of developing classroom spaces that function as inquiry communities in order to foster students' critical inquiries (Harvey & Daniels, 2015; Kincheloe, 2005), and I present suggestions for implementing such inquiry-based writing instruction in more traditional English class settings.

THE SCHOLARS' CONTEXT

The Senior Scholars Research Seminar was implemented as a pilot course during the 2015–2016 academic year at East Valley High (pseudonym) in upstate New York, a small, suburban school graduating approximately 145 students each year. The student body is racially homogeneous; 89% of students identify as white, 4% as black or African American, 3% as Hispanic or Latino, 2% as Asian or native Hawaiian, 2% as multiracial, and less than 1% as American Indian or native Alaskan. 16% of students are considered to be economically disadvantaged, 14% of students are identified as having disabilities, and 1% are identified as being limited English proficient.

Research participants for this study were drawn from 12th-grade students enrolled in the Senior Scholar Research Seminar class. Students were recruited into this class from presentations I made in their junior-year social studies classes in which I reviewed the course's tentative design, purpose, and methods for assessment. While some students expressed interest, many voiced concern about fitting it into their schedule during the already busy senior year. Many of the students who did register were involved with the library as members of the high school book club, therefore they had already established working relationships with Mrs. Jane Miller (a pseudonym), the librarian.

I am a mid-career high school English teacher, currently in pursuit of my doctoral degree in English Education. I teach at the same high school I attended many years ago, and my role as a researcher is complicated by the multiple identities I wear on a regular basis: teacher, student researcher, colleague, alumna. Even before pursuing my degree, my understanding of my teacher identity was influenced by the memories of sitting in the same classrooms and walking the same halls. While my research benefits in multiple ways from such closeness to the context and participants under study, I have had to manage my methods for data collection and analysis carefully to account for my subjectivity and the ethical implications of teacher research (Zeni, 1998).

Another unique component to both the pilot course and the study conducted therein is the position of the high school librarian as a collaborator and coresearcher. Jane's involvement was enormously significant, from collaborating with me on lesson design, technology for online instruction, and managing the Scholars' workspace. She acted as a second instructor to the Scholars, giving them greater opportunities for idea generation and feedback. She also gave me the chance to speak on my observations, questions and concerns about the class and the research, helping me to account for my position in the study and to name occasions when my biases might interfere with a more objective understanding of the data and context.

INQUIRY AS STANCE

Practitioner inquiry is viewed by some as being theoretically critical (Cochran-Smith & Lytle, 2009), in that it empowers teachers and gives them voice and authority by privileging teachers' voices and valuing their contributions to existing scholarship. Such inquiry disrupts the authority traditionally held by educational researchers, much like what happens when students engage in similar inquiry learning experiences – it disrupts the norms of power, authority, and establishment held by classroom teachers, school administrators, and the larger institutional school culture. For example, Fecho and Allen (2003) explain that "many teachers who take inquiry stances on their practice embrace the concept of classroom as a place where language, literacy, and power intersect in ways that can be enabling or stunting. Accordingly, these teachers seek to understand what it means to teach and research language and literacy in ways that call attention to these political and power issues" (p. 234). In other words, when teachers engage in practitioner inquiry, their classrooms may also operate as communities of critical inquiry.

Cochran-Smith and Lytle (1993, 2009) address the need for teacher researchers to engage in "inquiry as stance" as Fecho and Allen do. In *Inquiry as Stance: Practitioner Research for the Next Generation* (2009), the authors speak on the critical tradition from which practitioner inquiry derives, noting that it and its various subsets (such as teacher research, participatory action research, and self-study), are all part of a larger design embracing classroom teachers as valued, authoritative knowledge producers alongside those in the academy: for example, "practitioner research legitimates practitioners' knowledge and emerging theoretical frameworks by interrogating and in many cases helping to dismantle the easy oppositions of science and craft, formal and practical, and theory and practice" (p. 112). Practitioner inquiry complicates and pushes back against such dichotomous thinking. I would argue that when teachers engage in practitioner inquiry, they have an opportunity to invite their students to participate in inquiry of a critical nature – that students should also engage in "inquiry as stance" and see their knowledge construction as valued and legitimate.

INQUIRY LEARNING, CRITICAL LITERACY, AND CRITICAL CONSTRUCTIVISM

The inquiry learning at work in this course is dependent upon students' development of their critical literacy skills and their work as critical constructivists. Theorizing constructivism as being critical demands that the knowledge produced by students must be in response to an understanding of and refusal to accept social, political, and educational inequities (Giroux, 2006; Ladson-Billings, 1995, 2014). Paolo Freire is credited with theorizing education that demands teaching for social justice and for the empowerment of the marginalized (Freire, 2000). To do otherwise, Freire explains, is to actively engage in the oppression of marginalized peoples: "any situation in which some individuals prevent others from engaging in the process of inquiry is one of violence. The means used are not important; to alienate human beings from their own decision-making is to change them into objects" (p. 85). In the case of young people who are prevented from taking a more active and powerful role in their learning, or in the construction of their own knowledge, Freire suggests that "problem-posing education does not and cannot serve the interests of the oppressor. No oppressive order could permit the oppressed to begin to question: Why?" (p. 86). In other words, Freire argues that the manner in which teachers teach is a direct reflection of the ways in which they view young people, and that teachers' pedagogy moves along a continuum from actively seeking to repress them through highly controlled and deliberately scripted instruction, to bolstering them through empowering and inquiry-driven experiences.

Teachers who work from a critical pedagogy and who employ critical constructivism in their literacy instruction and curriculum see their role as prompting students to think about their learning, knowledge production, and subsequent communication and action as being potentially restricted by those with greater political power and social control; Hynds (1997) explains that teaching from this position "call[s] into question why all voices are not given equal respect, and recognize[s] that teaching and learning are always political acts" (p. 255); and, that:

> As teachers, we need to become even more active than before, helping students to see literacy not as a window on experience, but as a form of social action. This means creating classrooms where, in Willinsky's terms, students can "make their mark" as opposed to existing within "institutions given to marking them." (p. 269)

When engaged in the instruction of research-based writing, teachers have the chance to engage in such acts of critical pedagogy and to invite their students to learn as critical constructivists. Rather than implement structures for teaching research that position the teacher as the ultimate keeper of knowledge, decision-maker and power-wielder, or replicate the rigid, task-oriented research paper unit they experienced (Maniotes, 2014), teachers can instead model for and guide students in an inquiry process that demands students use research and writing to push back against an unjust educational paradigm.

RESEARCH REBOOT: CREATING A CULTURE OF INQUIRY

Rose's characterization (all participant names are pseudonyms) of her previous experiences with research for school assignments speaks of what was clearly a trend among the Scholars:

> In most classes, research assignments tend to lack any real research. We were mostly just doing them to find sources that we can cite and put into a project. Because, most of the topics are kind of vague and general ... it's not a bad thing, it's pretty typical for school. But, it's not — you get an assigned topic, you have to research that topic, and you have to research it like the teacher tells you to ... you don't really gain any deeper understanding of the topic. Or, like, look at the information in a new way. It's encouraged, but it's not, generally ... a major part of the assignment. (Rose, video reflection, January 21, 2016)

During the initial recruitment for the course and again early in the fall semester, students spoke with excitement about wanting to take the course so that they could do the independent inquiry project during the spring semester (when they would be able to focus on their selected topic of study). A few seemed impatient and wanted to launch into their inquiries right away. While this excitement was infectious and certainly made Jane and me feel optimistic about the course, we had designed the course specifically so that students would engage first in learning tasks designed to complicate their understanding of the research process, and namely their previous experiences or expectations for selecting topics or identifying purposes for research. One student, Aiden, was quick to point out during the weekly seminar that the Scholars weren't ready to do the independent project just yet, that first they "had to learn how to learn" (memo, October 16, 2015).

Throughout the course, the Scholars spoke and wrote about their previous, and quite similar, experiences with doing research for school assignments. Aiden confessed that "for papers, your thesis was practically given to you" (video reflection, January 25, 2016). Emily discussed the "cutthroat" nature of the research process, and the lack of choice allowed in what they studied or how they did it (video reflection, January 25, 2016). Liz claimed that the paper was "pretty much to be sure you could cite things" (video reflection, January 28, 2016) and Joanna suggested that the focus was on "the exact number of paragraphs or number of sources you had to have" (video reflection, January 25, 2016). Karin explained that research had been to "copy and paste, sorta, [to] just find information that somebody already had, and then, spit it out again" (video reflection, January 28, 2016).

We designed this course working with such student preconceptions, having heard similar comments from students in previous years. Our intention was to create a classroom space that, by engaging students in personally meaningful, academically challenging, and theoretically critical work, would motivate and inspire students to respond differently to their experiences with research.

COURSE STRUCTURE

The course was designed in a two-semester format (see Appendix A). In the first semester, students would engage in a hybrid course that met both asynchronously in a virtual classroom and in real time during a face-to-face weekly seminar (as described in the introductory anecdote). The course was designed this way to enable students to take it despite conflicts within their schedule; it was thought that if the course was offered partially online, students could still take the course even if it conflicted with another single-section course. Our suburban school is quite small, graduating less than 150 students a year, so our teaching staff is limited and we often cannot offer multiple sections of classes outside the core curriculum, which can make it very challenging for our students who wish to take more electives. In this hybrid format, students were required to complete assignments and participate in online discussions in the virtual classroom, as well as more traditional assignments to complete in the library during their own time. The assignments and required work sessions were meant to be the equivalent of a full-credit, 5-day a week 40-min class.

In the second semester, the course design took on more of an independent study model, one in which students would manage their time based upon process deadlines for completing an independent inquiry project. The class would still meet once a week in a face-to-face seminar, and the online classroom would still be used for periodic group discussions and for assignment submission and information dissemination, but the nature of the course was much more self-directed and relied upon the students learning to manage their own work and deadlines. These assignments were scaffolded tasks designed to help the students move along the research process, in anticipation of producing and presenting a final text to represent their thinking and learning (see course design in Appendix A). For example, the Scholars were invited to answer a conference call for proposals, for which they had to prepare a formal document outlining their intentions for research (see Appendix B). This assignment was modeled after the conference proposals I have written as a graduate student, and it asked students to address the following: their purpose for the project as guided by their research question; a plan for the research methods they would employ; a discussion of the types of media resources they would consult and/or data they would collect; a potential theoretical lens through which they would focus their thinking; and finally, an explanation of their intended audience for their work.

The semester concluded with a grand event to showcase the students' work, the Senior Scholar Inquiry Symposium. This conference gave students the opportunity to share their inquiry projects with family, friends, teachers and community members. The Scholars gave 30-minute presentations in breakout sessions, followed by 10 minutes for questions from the audience. The conference also included a panel discussion at which the Scholars answered additional questions about the class, their respective inquiry processes and experiences. In order to share this approach with other students and faculty, we designed the conference to include a poster session as well for underclassmen who submitted posters detailing inquiry-based projects of a smaller scale done earlier in the year for class assignments. These underclassmen were solicited also using a call for poster submissions, shared with teachers Jane and I knew who were implementing research projects and assignments that more closely aligned with the guided inquiry framework rather than traditional research processes, or that engaged in inquiries of a critical nature such as human rights or social justice issues addressed in social studies classes. This gave attendees additional opportunity to see the kind of critical work that was or could be happening at various grade levels and content areas.

After the symposium, Scholars worked to complete or revise their final research papers and conference with us about their writing and revision process. The students also completed a self-evaluation assignment using open-ended questions and rubric-based criteria and submitted it to the online classroom. The year concluded with a celebratory event for just the Scholars, Jane and me, a necessary social closure filled with stories, jokes, food and grand ambitions for the coming year.

GUIDED INQUIRY DESIGN

The structure of the course, learning activities, and assignments were initially designed in accordance with Guided Inquiry Design, a framework for implementing inquiry learning (Kuhlthau et al., 2012, 2015). Kuhlthau, Maniotes, and Caspari, a collaborative team of researchers multiply positioned as teacher leaders, classroom teachers, literacy specialists, and information media specialists, developed their specific model of Guided Inquiry Design as a framework for teachers and librarians who want to implement inquiry-based learning in their curriculum, and specifically within pre-existing research assignments. The authors explain that in order for teachers to implement guided inquiry, the classroom must "be transformed into a collaborative culture around learning" (2012, p. 1).

The Guided Inquiry Design (Kuhlthau et al., 2012) process has eight phases:

1. Open – invitation to inquiry, open minds, stimulate curiosity
2. Immerse – build background knowledge, connect to content, discover interesting ideas
3. Explore – explore interesting ideas, look around, dip in
4. Identify – pause and ponder, identify inquiry question, decide direction
5. Gather – gather important information, go broad, go deep
6. Create – reflect on learning, go beyond facts to make meaning, create to communicate
7. Share – learn from each other, share learning, tell your story
8. Evaluate – evaluate achievement of learning goals, reflect on content, reflect on process (pp. 2–6)

While there is much to consider in implementing a Guided Inquiry approach to student learning and research, one of the most significant elements in considering the process as outlined above is that the students aren't expected to truly know their selected topic until halfway through the process; they only make decisions about their project's direction in response to their inquiry question in Phase 4: Identify, after having first spent a great deal of time reading, searching and exploring about the potential topic. This contrasts with what is common practice in high school classrooms when it comes to research papers and projects, when students are being given the topic, the question, the specific resources to use in constructing the research-based report, and the standard format in which to present it (Donham, 2014; Maniotes & Kuhlthau, 2014).

While teachers often construct the driving question that student inquiry seeks to answer, students in the Guided Inquiry Design model are encouraged to develop their own inquiry question, provided with appropriate, scaffolded assistance by the classroom teacher and librarian team. The distinction may seem subtle, but it's really quite significant. From my perspective, when learners are given the time to explore their interests and to read deeply about their subject, they learn how to construct an inquiry question and a subsequent research plan that aligns much more faithfully with constructivists' understanding of experiential and discovery learning. And, when learners are given the support they need to research the topics most interesting and personally relevant to themselves and their communities, they are more likely to engage in work that speaks of a critical constructivist approach to learning. Why? Because when given the opportunities to engage in learning that demands they critically interrogate the words and the world around them (Freire, 2000), when given the critical literacy skills and critical constructivist thinking with which to do so, and when given the space, autonomy, and voice to do it, students exercise their power with inquiry addressing the inequities they witness and experience (Hynds, 1997; Kincheloe, 2005).

This Guided Inquiry framework was used to design the Senior Scholar pilot course, informing both the organizational structure of the course (see Appendix A), as well as the process by which students conducted their independent inquiry projects (see Table 1).

CREATING A SPACE FOR CRITICAL INQUIRY

Perhaps the most noteworthy aspect of this experimental course is the need to understand it as operating as an "inquiry community." The class is atypical in many ways, such as in its asynchronous meeting format and its multidisciplinary content. However, at this stage Jane and I are inclined to understand the success of the course as primarily dependent upon its being positioned within the library, in its own space – a glassed-in room formerly designated as Jane's office, both visible to other students working in the library's common area and secluded from that common area, delineating a special status for those students within. I also use this term "space" in reference to multiple ways of being and interacting in the class – the physical space the class occupies during weekly seminars and when engaged in independent work, the social space the students created and shared with Jane and me, and the digital space in which the students' work extends. Having to navigate these multiple spaces proved to be a challenge for many of the Scholars, and they spoke of the difficulty of having to resolve conflicts with one another resulting from working in such close quarters. For example, the Scholars quickly realized that one of the privileges of having such designated, student-directed, space meant that they would have to account for

Table 1. Guided Inquiry Design in the Senior Scholar Research Seminar, as adapted from Kuhlthau et al. (2015).

Inquiry Phase	What is it?	What does it Mean for the Scholars' Inquiries?
Open	Invitation to inquiry; open minds; stimulate curiosity	Provocative journal and current events news articles, videos, podcasts that stimulated ideas for research, built critical literacy skills (TEDtalks, news re: #blacklivesmatter, e.g.)
Immerse	Build background knowledge; connect to content; discover interesting ideas	Scholars discuss, question, reflect upon the sampled texts, using both open teacher-created prompts and eventually student-created prompts; students consider the "what/how/why we know" of texts, and why it matters to them individually and their school community
Explore	Explore interesting ideas; look round; dip in	Students read widely and deeply around their initial ideas of interest; keep running record of their search process (visual maps, keyword lists); share findings with other students in discussion; students complete "biblioquests" – assignments for guided practice in information literacy
Identify	Identify inquiry question; pause and ponder; decide direction	Students draft/design a guiding question for their inquiry; Students respond to formal call for research proposals; students outline potential research process and conference with instructors
Gather	Gather useful information; go broad; go deep	Students engage in independent inquiry – dedicated time for intensified reading, note-taking; experiment with digital tools for note-taking and cataloging bibliographic data; securing sources via interlibrary loan and academic journals outside school databases
Create	Create to communicate; reflect on learning; go beyond facts – interpret and extend	Students prepare annotated bibliographies to report research progress; students design, produce, and rehearse presentations using digital tools and public speaking skills; construction of a formal research paper suitable for conference/journal submission (15–25 pgs., APA)
Share	Learn from each other; share learning; tell your story	Students present their inquiries at the Senior Scholar Symposium (student research conference) in 40-min sessions for other students, teachers, administrators, and parents; demonstrate inquiry process to peers through visual presence in the HS library
Evaluate	Evaluate achievement of learning goals; reflect on content; reflect on process	Continual self-reflection with each major assignment; students maintain reflective research blogs; self-evaluation after the symposium; instructor feedback in individual conferences; P/F grading system for the course

each other's needs in that shared space; while some might prefer to talk or have music on while they work, others prefer silence. Scholars also found it uncomfortable at times to manage challenging conversations in person and online, noting a need to respect each other's different ideas, while still feeling safe to share their perspectives and ask difficult questions.

Another unique component of the Scholars' class is the method by which students are assessed. The course is graded using a Pass/Fail system, allowing the instructors to place more emphasis on feedback and revision rather than on scoring for averaged grades. While students receive credit for the course, they do not have to worry about how their performance might adversely affect their GPA, as Joanna explained it: "we were able to take risks and not have it totally tank our averages" (video reflection, January 25, 2016). Instead of scoring student work using a numerical or letter-grade scale, I counted all work as complete or incomplete, and then I gave the students both verbal and typed narrative feedback, using rubrics and criteria lists. More significantly, the students engaged in self-assessment of each major assignment, and we would conference together and share our assessments. Students received a "Pass" for the course if they completed the assigned work and demonstrated growth in their reflective writing and self-assessments (e.g., if they spoke with greater and more nuanced understanding of inquiry as a process and not a task-oriented set of standardized steps, or if they applied their experiences to their thinking about future research projects in college). It must be noted, however, that such detailed and personalized feedback is only possible with such a small group of students; of course I would find it incredibly difficult to do so with a class of 25–35 students.

Ultimately the establishment of a classroom environment that operates as an inquiry community meant something very important to the Scholars – they came to see it as a "safe space." For several of them, that meant what the term implies in the LGBTQ community: a space that provides a safe refuge for queer youth. For others that meant a place to talk more openly about their beliefs and values, or to "just be themselves" away from a clique-y, judgmental student body. Scholars expressed appreciation at being able to read, talk, and write about issues left unaddressed in their other classes, namely issues about difference, such as race, gender, class, sexuality, and ability. This, combined with the multiple opportunities to practice critical thinking and analysis in varied spaces without the fear of grades or "getting the right answer" hanging over their heads, invited students to practice their critical literacies when negotiating various texts and exposed them to the concept of adopting inquiry as a stance by which they could read, interact with, and potentially resist or push back against norms of privilege and power.

APPLICATION TO THE CLASSROOM

At this stage, preliminary analysis of the data has only just begun; more formal analysis will take place in the following summer and school year. However, it is possible to offer a few practical, pedagogical suggestions for teachers and researchers considering the implementation of such a design or the inclusion of such elements into their regular classes for writing instruction. As such, I would make the following recommendations.

Flip the Script on the Thesis Statement

Teachers should not have students write thesis or purpose statements until after they've done several days of exploratory reading and identification of a research question. This might seem fairly straightforward but in my own experience it's still quite common to have students script out thesis statements (and even identical thesis statements) at the beginning of a research project. This results in students searching for evidence to fit what they've already decided upon, rather than let their thesis or purpose statement be guided by their inquiry.

Allow for More (Uncomfortable) Time to Read Widely and Deeply

I suspect that for classroom teachers, this is the most difficult aspect of inquiry learning. Time is precious, and giving multiple days over to loosely structured reading is a very scary notion. However, many a well-intentioned research project can and have been derailed by the students' rush to find sources as quickly as possible and to complete index cards or source sheets (the modus operandi at many schools). If students are to learn how to select topics and design meaningful and effective research questions, then they will need to sit in that uncomfortable space of "I don't know" and practice designing research questions in smaller, scaffolded increments. Also, if they're not frantically looking for "the right answer" to the pre-established thesis, then they will be more likely to consider ideas they encounter in that wide and deep reading, or in following down leads that come from the questions they ask with each new resource. Emily experienced this when moving through the Immersion, Identify, and Gather phases of her inquiry, when she "notic[ed] small gaps in [her] research" and that once she addressed these gaps, "new questions pop[ped] up and more research [got piled] on;" Emily concluded that post with a resounding "I love it!" (online blog, May 5, 2016). Guiding students to experiment with various forms of note-taking or concept mapping at this stage, to document their search process before committing to a research purpose, reinforces for students that the messy, individualized process of inquiry is both typical and appropriate.

Put the Focus on the Process, not the Product

Despite the title of this chapter, research-based writing does not and should not focus entirely on THE RESEARCH PAPER. Just as much, if not more, emphasis should be placed on what the students are doing along the guided inquiry process, and they should be engaged in conversation about how and why they're doing it. This is often difficult to square with philosophies of assessment and grading, which traditionally place higher value on the final paper. However, there are other means by which teachers can measure, score, and provide meaningful feedback that allow for greater attention to the process. For example, students write memos (in this case, in online blogs or discussion forums) reflecting upon their process at each benchmark of the inquiry, submitting both the work to be graded and the memo detailing their understanding of what the work accomplished. In one instance, Aiden explained in his research blog that he "wish[ed he] had kept more organized and thorough notes on the sources [he] gathered," but since he was "in such an immersive phase [he] was not thinking ahead enough," and that "at least [he] will know for next time" (online blog, March 18, 2016). Such introspective memos also allow the teacher to gather evidence of what the students are reading, learning, and thinking in the spaces in between producing text or meeting deadlines.

Form a Guided Inquiry Team with Your Librarian

I have been fortunate to work with a gifted library media specialist who sees her role as supporting her teaching colleagues as much as it is to support the students. Jane enabled me to take risks as a classroom teacher, and she supported me while I worked through (and continue to do so) this process. While I brought my instructional expertise and research background to the table, she brought her incredible knowledge and experience about information literacy. I would strongly recommend that any teacher interested in complicating the notion of how to engage in more purposeful and personally meaningful research assignments start with a shared reading of Kuhlthau et al. (2015) *Guided Inquiry: Learning in the 21st Century*.

FINAL THOUGHTS

The work presented here is still in its early stages; formal analysis must still occur, and a second iteration of the course in the coming school year will provide multiple opportunities for further theorizing, data collection, and analysis. Writing about the work we've done at such an early stage might be considered risky by some, but as a teacher researcher who acknowledges the very cyclic and ongoing nature of data-driven assessment characteristic of classroom instruction, I would suggest that this conversation started months ago and will only continue with each succeeding manuscript I prepare. Whenever you engage with this resource, dear researcher, I encourage you to reach out to me so that we might engage in the critical dialog, however it might have evolved by then. In the meantime, remember: the inquisitive bird gets the worm. We'll see you in the library.

REFERENCES

Christensen, L. (1999). Critical literacy: Teaching reading, writing and outrage. In C. Edlesky (Ed.), *Making justice our project: Teachers working toward critical whole language practice* (pp. 209–225). Urbana, IL: National Council of Teachers of English.

Cochran-Smith, M., & Lytle, S. L. (1993). *Inside/outside: Teacher research and knowledge.* New York, NY: Teachers College Press.

Cochran-Smith, M., & Lytle, S. L. (2009). *Inquiry as stance: Practitioner research for the next generation.* New York, NY: Teachers College Press.

Donham, J. (2014). Inquiry. In V. H. Harada & S. Coatney (Eds.), *Inquiry and the common core: Librarians and teachers designing teaching for learning* (pp. 69–82). Santa Barbara, CA: Libraries Unlimited.

Fecho, B., & Allen, J. (2003). Teacher inquiry into literacy, social justice, and power. In J. Flood, D. Lapp, J. R. Squire, & J. M. Jensen (Eds.), *Handbook of research on teaching the English language arts* (2nd ed., pp. 232–252). Mahwah, NJ: Lawrence Erlbaum Associates, Publishers.

Freire, P. (2000). *Pedagogy of the oppressed* (30th anniversary ed.). New York, NY: Continuum.
Giroux, H. (2006). *America on the edge: Henry Giroux on politics, culture and education*. New York, NY: Palgrave MacMillan.
Harvey, S., & Daniels, H. (2015). Comprehension and collaboration: Inquiry circles for curiosity, engagement, and understanding (Rev. ed.). Portsmouth, NH: Heinemann.
Hynds, S. (1997). *On the brink: Negotiating literature and life with adolescents*. New York, NY: Teachers College Press.
Kincheloe, J. (2005). *Critical constructivism primer*. New York, NY: Peter Lang.
Kuhlthau, C. C., Maniotes, L. K., & Caspari, A. K. (2012). *Guided inquiry design: A framework for inquiry in your school*. Santa Barbara, CA: Libraries Unlimited.
Kuhlthau, C. C., Maniotes, L. K., & Caspari, A. K. (2015). *Guided inquiry: Learning in the 21st century* (2nd ed.). Santa Barbara, CA: Libraries Unlimited.
Ladson-Billings, G. (1995). Toward a theory of culturally relevant pedagogy. *American Educational Research Journal*, *32*(3), 465–491.
Ladson-Billings, G. (2014). Culturally relevant pedagogy 2.0: a.k.a. the remix. *Harvard Educational Review*, *84*(1), 74–84.
Maniotes, L. K. (2014). Guided inquiry design and the common core. In V. H. Harada & S. Coatney (Eds.), *Inquiry and the common core: Librarians and teachers designing teaching for learning* (pp. 69–82). Santa Barbara, CA: Libraries Unlimited.
Maniotes, L. K., & Kuhlthau, C. C. (2014). Making the shift: From traditional research assignments to guided inquiry learning. *Knowledge Quest*, *43*(2), 8–17.
Zeni, J. (1998). A guide to ethical issues and action research. *Educational Action Research*, *6*(1), 9–19.

APPENDIX A

Table A1. Senior Scholar Research Seminar – Course Design.

Fall Semester	Spring Semester
Guiding Question	*Guiding Question*
What is my relationship with learning?	How do I take ownership of my inquiry?
Topics/Themes	*Topics/Themes*
Learning theories, critical literacy, information literacy, social inequities	Independently selected
Weekly Classwork	*Independent Classwork*
Google Classroom group discussions, written reflections	Google Classroom responses
Biblioquests	Research Blogs
Weekly readings, related assignments	Source reading, note-taking, organizing
	Presentation preparation
Assessments	Assessments
Autoethnography	*Annotated Bibliography*
Multimodal representation of students' exploration into previous learning experiences and preferences	List of sources with brief descriptions and rationales for their inclusion/exclusion
Self-Assessment	*Project Map/Plan; Rough Draft*
Written evaluation of the autoethnography product, guided by reflective questions and criteria-based rubric	Student-selected visual representation of the paper/presentation's structure, prewriting, drafting of sections
Collaborative Critical Inquiry	*Visual Aids & Presentation Rehearsal*
A group inquiry designed to practice information literacy and inquiry design	Construction of presentation tools (slides, handouts, web-based platform, notecards); deliver presentation to Scholar audience for critical friends feedback
Group Assessment	*Presentation*
Group review and feedback in response to the collaborative project	30-minute prepared presentation at conference
Research Proposal	*Final Paper*
Formal call for project request, including research question, research plan, data sources, and projected significance	Research paper (requirements determined by the Scholars) suitable for submission to an undergraduate conference or as a journal article

APPENDIX B: EAST VALLEY* SENIOR SCHOLAR RESEARCH SYMPOSIUM 2016 CALL FOR PROPOSALS

Critical Inquiries for Critical Communities

Saturday, May 21st, 2016

Theme Description
In discussing Brazilian educator Paulo Freire's idea of critical dialog, Christensen (1999) explained that, "beyond illumination, students must use the tools of critical literacy to dismantle the half-truths, inaccuracies, and lies that strangle their conceptions about themselves and others. They must use the tools of critical literacy to expose, to talk back to, to remedy any act of injustice or intolerance that they witness" (p. 55). In keeping with this understanding of what it means to be critical thinkers and researchers, the symposium invites proposals from Scholars using an inquiry stance to interrogate an issue of significance to their learning community, as defined by one's classroom, school, neighborhood, and/or culture. Such critical inquiries work in conjunction to drive our education away from the banking system of teaching and learning (Freire, 2000), and instead toward the creation of schools as critical communities, spaces in which learners collaborate in questioning the existing paradigms of knowledge and power. Critical inquirers ask, whose truth matters? And, how can we contribute? In so doing, critical inquirers seek to better their communities by engaging in a truly democratic dialog, one nurtured by purposeful research and reflection.

Proposal Guidelines
Proposals for conference papers and presentations should address the following:

A. Your study's purpose or rationale
   a. a description of the issue, context, circumstance, and/or problem
   b. a driving question(s) that your research seeks to answer
B. Perspectives or theoretical framework
   a. this depends upon your topic and subject matter; for example, if you're studying something about literature, are you being informed by a certain critical theory – like poststructuralism or queer theory?

If you're studying a social phenomenon, are you being influenced by a psychological or sociocultural theory?
   b. this places your research into a larger context, or discussion, about your topic and research question(s) – what's going on in the existing conversation?
C. Methods or techniques
   a. this is the discussion of HOW you will conduct your research – how you intend to seek data/information to help you answer your research question
   b. this should align with the academic expectations for your topic
   c. this should also explain WHY you're choosing these methods
D. Data sources
   a. list the informational/secondary sources you will consult (texts, databases, journals, online resources)
   b. list the social sources you will use (participants) and the type of data you will collect (as outlined in methods above – interview, observation field notes, survey, etc.); discuss access & permission
E. Preliminary implications of the research
   a. you're conjecturing here – based upon your preliminary reading in your OPEN, IMMERSE and EXPLORE inquiry phases, what do you expect to find?
   b. why is this worth exploring?
F. Interest or connection to the audience
   a. why is your research of interest to other people – and especially to the East Valley audience?
   b. how does your study fit with the overall conference theme?
G. Research plan & timeline
   a. explain what time in your school day/evening-weekend schedule you are committing to the completion of this project
   b. provide a brief outline of your research plan that addresses: your collection of data, analysis of data, writing, revising, and producing your written text & presentation

Submission Requirements
All proposals should be submitted as a single PDF file. Excluding the reference list or additional tables or figures, the proposal should be no more than 750 words and should be formatted according to APA guidelines. Proposals must be submitted electronically no later than 11:59 PM EST, Thursday, February 11th, 2016, to the Google Classroom.

APPENDIX C

Table C1. Senior Scholar Independent Inquiry Projects — Titles & Abstracts.

Aiden	Rose
The Gay Gift: How Gay Men and the Gay Sensibility Have Contributed to Mainstream American Society In this presentation, I answer two questions. The first being, "How do we conquer the social injustice of the classroom?" and the second, "How have Gay men and the Gay sensibility as a whole contributed to mainstream American society and culture?" My project uses versatile presentation methods that will leave the audience shivering with antici ... pation	*Gender: Through the Eyes of Media* In this presentation, I will explore American gender norms as portrayed through popular media, how they developed though history, and the contrasting gender norms of India and Sweden. In addition, I will also explore the gender roles in a popular American subculture; Superhero fans, and how they both contrast and conform to traditional American gender norms
John	Emily
Statsball: An Analysis of Statistics in Baseball America's Pastime and math. A perfect combination. Although this is true, the question is if numbers tell the whole story. Can baseball be based wholly on numbers or is there more to it? Can anything be based completely on numbers? The drive of this inquiry is to explore the methods of statistical analysis and how these statistics can and cannot be applied. Baseball, business, education, and politics: America and its numbers all evaluated through its pastime	*In The Minds of You, Me and a Killer* Serial killers ... you can´t turn off the TV or change the channel. Your eyes are glued to the horrific and gruesome deeds that are displaying on your TV right now. But why can you not look away? Why do Hollywood and the American people cling to the topic of serial killers and glorify these people to levels of actors, professional athletes, and musicians? Maybe we cling to them because we hope they are different
Joanna	Elizabeth (Liz)
Fiction Addiction: A Psychological Inquiry This inquiry questioned whether the behaviors of readers and book fandoms have addictive properties. In order to answer this question, it required comparing the behaviors and symptoms of drug addicts to readers. Finally, this inquiry involved research on the Internet's influence on addiction, fandoms, and readers as a whole	*The Good and the Bad* This presentation explores the idea of there being (or not) a truly good or truly bad person. Along with this, the idea of being able to tell if someone is truly good or bad (or at least slightly good or slightly bad) is explored. This project revolves around topics such as (and also not limited to) psychology, biology, sociology, and neurology.

Table C1. (*Continued*)

Karin	Samantha (Sam)
Asexuality and Attraction This presentation will challenge the conventional beliefs regarding relationships and the nature of attraction. With a focus on the Asexual community, we see how it is possible to detangle sexuality from the other aspects of relationships. We will also discuss the Asexual community itself, and why awareness and teaching about the community can aid society as a whole	*The Dragon Age of Sexism: Inequality in Gaming* As a woman, it's always frustrated me that video games are made by men, for men, even though many women play the exact games that convey women poorly. This presentation will explore sexism in video games with an emphasis on the lack of female "heroes"
Kristen	
Hunger Games Redux How does media and culture influence high school students' body image? This presentation will examine the connection between media in many forms and self-image including how students deal with the issue.	

AUGMENTING ACADEMIC WRITING ACHIEVEMENT FOR ALL STUDENTS

Wally Thompson, Debra Coffey and Traci Pettet

ABSTRACT

Purpose — *Writing is an act of expressive communication achieved through the medium of print. It is but one of three modes of linguistic communication. The other expressive mode is speaking, while listening and reading comprise the two receptive modes. The purpose of this chapter is to present the impact of a study in which students read and discussed expository poetry. Then they exchanged ideas relating to scientific concepts in the poems with students in a different group via pen pal letters. We analyzed these pen pal letters over four weeks to determine the influence of writing opportunities in an atmosphere rich in all four aspects of linguistic communication, involving authentic communication between students and within a community of learners.*

Design/methodology/Approach — *Six of Brod Bagert's unpublished poems concerned with science concepts were read by students in Collaborative Discover Groups (CDG) in two third-grade classes. After the groups discussed the poems, a mini-lesson on one of the Six Traits of Writing followed, and the students responded individually to a teacher-generated prompt related to the specific poem. The responses were in the form of pen pal letters to students in another class who had just read the same poem, received the same teacher-directed mini-lesson, and had had a similar discussion in their respective CDG. The data gleaned from these letters provide information demonstrating the effect of emphasizing all linguistic facets synergistically in a social, communicative setting. Both the processes and the findings will be discussed.*

Findings — *Analysis of the pen pal letters third-grade students wrote over four weeks showed the following patterns. (1) There was an increase in the discursive nature of the writing. (2) The incidence of rhetorical questioning, using $A + B = C$ reasoning, and evaluative thinking was present in the fifth set of letters, and not in the first. Additionally, the number of sentences per letter increased from the first to the fifth, and the number of words per letter increased from approximately 50 words per letter to 75 words per letter. It appears that the linguistically synergistic communicative processes employed in this study are reflected in the increased sophistication and communicative nature of these writings.*

Practical implications — *The data revealed the importance of including the sociocultural tenants in the classroom, emphasizing that reading, writing, speaking, and listening are all a part of the same phenomenon. Together they strengthen and support each other.*

Keywords: Collaborative; synergistic; mini-lessons; sociocultural communication; effective classroom writing instruction

Opportunities for creative and interactive teaching are exploding, yet curricular expectations often make teachers feel limited in what they can accomplish in the real world of teaching. Teachers often wish for the powers of a superhero as they strive to meet the expectations of parents, students, and administrators. They may participate in team meetings and still feel that they are basically on their own as they work to meet expectations. As a result, they may try to keep classroom instruction as simple as possible, using multiple choice, true/false, and fill-in-the blank activities rather than giving students many opportunities for creative or analytic writing that connect what they read in class with creative expression. For instance, in their case study, Grisham and Wolsey (2011) noted that teacher candidates saw little writing instruction during literacy instruction in their student—teacher placements.

Teachers may feel that they need to take care of everything in their classrooms all by themselves while they actually have the resources of a group available at any time. If they scaffold instruction effectively and provide opportunities for group interaction among their own students, they can maximize learning in new ways.

Careful scaffolding and opportunities for group interaction empower students to help each other learn. When students verbalize what they have learned, they learn in new ways and become more engaged in what they are learning (Vygotsky, 1978, 1986). This group interaction activates schema (Bartlett, 1932; Nassaji, 2002; Rosenblatt, 1978, 2005) and can prevent the fourth-grade slump (Suhr, Hernandez, Grimes, & Warschauer, 2010). Authentic opportunities for interactive learning promote motivation and engagement (Jaramillo, 1996; Laal & Ghodsi, 2012; Yager, Johnson, & Johnson, 1986).

This chapter presents the findings of a study in which Collaborative Discovery Groups (CDG) featured both receptive and expressive language (i.e., listening, reading, speaking, and writing) for comprehending complex texts in the form of expository poetry. After students enjoyed and analyzed expository poetry, they produced well-written academic writing, which communicated their understanding and opinions with students who had read the same poems.

This study featured CDGs, which were designed to provide opportunities for interactive reading and writing. We examined the impact of the CDG and interactive pen pal letters to see if they would augment third-graders' written communication. We wanted to see whether activities of this nature had the potential to increase the level of students' communication through writing, giving teachers tools to potentially enhance their literacy instruction and ameliorate the fourth-grade slump. During this project, we provided guidelines for teachers as they used high-interest poetry, highlighting science content, to augment the quality of their students' written communication through pen pal letters. Then we used qualitative and quantitative data to determine the impact of these instructional activities. This chapter describes the design and the results of this study.

THEORETICAL FRAMEWORK

Our theoretical framework for this study aligned with cognitive constructivism as posited by Piaget (1923) and sociocultural constructivism, which is attributed to Vygotsky (1978, 1986). Thus, we used a developmental perspective, emphasizing a sociocultural foundation for the activities in the project. Following the constructivist paradigm of epistemology, the students read, comprehended, and shared their understandings of poems, generating new and more in-depth knowledge of scientific concepts. As opposed to simply accepting ready-made ideas about what was read, that is, tenets of the behaviorist paradigm (Doolittle, 2014), they were involved in actively interpreting and reshaping the text in response to their personal past experiences (Rosenblatt, 1978, 2005). Students constructed knowledge in collaboration with peers while teachers placed equal emphasis on the sociocultural contexts of the literacy events and the words, which were used to construct knowledge (Gee, 2005, 2008).

REVIEW OF LITERATURE

Throughout this project students learned about guidelines for Six Trait Writing during mini-lessons, shared their insights in CDG, and used these experiences to accomplish the objectives of the writing projects. Since the students were socially constructing knowledge in CDG, we will begin by explicating the general nature of those groups.

Collaborative Discovery Groups

There is an essential difference between CDG and traditional Literature Circles. Daniels (2002) described traditional Literature Circles as "a cooperative learning, student led experience for students around a common text" (p. 100). Literature Circles focus primarily on the reading process and include guided discussions with collaborative aspects of learning.

CDG acknowledge and celebrate the pedagogical power of linguistic synergy, that is, listening, reading, speaking, and writing of which Pearson (2012) stated, "reading and writing are synergistic processes — what we learn in the one benefits the other" (p. 101). Throughout this process students used a *Socratic Seminar* designed to produce well written, mature writing, Roberts and Billings (2008) stated that "[t]here is no question that reading, writing, speaking, and listening are interconnected skills that develop synergistically" (p. 2). Much has been written about the connection between reading and writing (Nelson & Calfee, 1998; Parr & McNaughton, 2014; Spivey, 1997). When discussions, emphasizing speaking, listening, and writing were added, it could be seen as "a process of socially shared cognition ... that results in the individual internalizing this knowledge" (Parr & McNaughton, 2014, p. 142).

As Leont'ev (1979) expressed, "higher psychological processes unique to humans can be acquired only through interaction with others." In 1989 Eeds and Wells further explained that "the internal development processes that are necessary for learning are *only* able to develop when children are interacting with people in their environment and in cooperation with their peers" (p. 6).

As this study took place in two states simultaneously, the entire group comprised a wide spectrum of cultures and lifestyles. This lent itself well to observing the social and cultural aspects of *Situated Literacy*, and its very close companion, *New Literacy Studies*, of which Street (2003) said, "[l]iteracy practices ... refer to the broader cultural conception of particular ways of thinking about and doing reading and writing in cultural contexts" (p. 79). Due to the extraordinarily rich presence of children from so many different worlds, we were mindful of the *Funds of Knowledge* (Moll, Amanti, Neff, & Gonzalez, 1992), which "draw upon the knowledge and skills found in local households" (p. 2). Bringing their traditions as well as social and cultural artifacts into the discussions enriched and authenticated the process of making and sharing of knowledge in the Situated and New Literacy traditions. As Bakhtin (1984) noted about this collaborative search for knowledge, it "is not to be found inside the head of an individual person, it is born between people collectively searching for truth, in the process of dialogic interaction" (p. 110).

METHODOLOGY

Participants

This study focuses on a total of 46 third-grade students in Title I classrooms. Males and females were represented equally. These groups were predominately White or Hispanic, and they included students who were

Black, Asian, or Pacific Islanders. Home languages of these Title I students included English, Spanish, Laotian, Thai, Vietnamese, and Bosnian. We collaborated with two teachers who were enthusiastic about using a sociocultural approach in their classrooms.

The Design of the Study

We conducted this study in two phases. The first phase emphasized *close reading of complex texts*, in the genre of expository poetry. In this phase students read and re-read poems about physics, astronomy, and biology, which were written by Brod Bagert. Then they held Grand Conversations to discuss them in their CDG. Analysis of the results, qualitatively and quantitatively, showed that close reading of complex expository poetry and opportunities for constructing personal knowledge through discussions and novel responses to literature had a positive impact on students' comprehension of science concepts.

Collaborative Discovery Groups

This mixed methods study was designed to examine the impact of a project featuring the CDG and pen pal letters. We used qualitative and quantitative data analysis of student letters and interviews with teachers to determine the influence of the CDG on communication through writing. The duration of this study was four weeks, and it included mini-lessons, poetry reading, and the exchange of pen pal letters to discuss conceptual insights. The augmentation of academic writing was studied in the CDG, which reflect the principles of socioculturalism, situated literacy, and collaborative learning. Building on the tradition of Literature Circles, CDGs emphasize opportunities for participants to expand their knowledge through a process of discovery, which van Joolingen, de Jong, Lazonder, Savelsbergh, and Manlove (2005) explained as organized "around collaborative inquiry and modeling activities [and are] student-centered forms of instructional support" (p. 672).

Grand Conversations

To accomplish synergy in the reading and writing process, the teachers initially read the poems and guided students as they reflected on the principles of situated literacy. Then the students responded to the poems in *Grand Conversations*, which were preparatory to a *Think—Pair—Share* writing activity. This type of classroom discussion contrasts with the "transmissionary mode of instruction" (Wells & Mejia, 2006, p. 379), which exemplifies what Eeds and Wells (1989) referred to as "Gentle inquisitions" (p. 4). In this traditional form of classroom discussion, the *initiate–response–evaluation* format is followed, and produces literacy results akin to what Rosenblatt (1978) termed the "efferent stance" (p. 25) of reading, that is, reading to know objectively or to take away for a specific purpose such as taking a test.

The Grand Conversations employed in the CDG used an open format in which students and teachers freely discussed their personal insights and understandings of poems, which were produced by the reaction of the text with individual schema. These active readers, speakers, and listeners exchanged ideas based on teacher-generated prompts and modified their own ideas in the process (Eeds & Wells, 1989). These discussions generated new, collective understandings of the poems and prepared students to gradually increase their communication through pen pal letters.

As students explored scientific concepts from poetry in Collaborative Discussion Groups, discussions became negotiation events as they augmented their understanding of scientific concepts. By its very nature, linguistic communication is ambiguous (Wells & Mejia, 2006). Words have different meanings, and different social situations produce different meanings for the same words or phrases (Gee, 2005, 2008). As Pica (1994) explains: "As they negotiate, they work linguistically to achieve the needed comprehensibility, whether repeating a message verbatim, adjusting its syntax, changing its words, or modifying its form and meaning in a host of other ways" (p. 494). These negotiations led to increased comprehension of the conversation, and the increased mental activity related to linguistic manipulations led to greater understanding of the concepts being communicated (Newell, 1998).

Think–Pair–Share Writing Approach
After these discussions augmented the students' understanding of the scientific concepts in the poems, the students were ready to express their ideas through academic writing. To facilitate the process, another collaborative activity was employed: a Think–Pair–Share approach to writing (Lyman, 1981). In this activity, students generated ideas individually and shared those ideas with partners. When this partnership achieved a consensus of ideas, those ideas were shared in a Collaborative Discovery Group. This was a very effective form of collaboration because the groups were small and intimate, allowing for a free, more personal exchange of ideas.

For those who were a bit timid, the personal qualities of the format also minimized shyness (Butler, Phillmann, & Smart, 2001).

Communication for Specific Purposes
Before the project began, we discussed ways to establish authentic purposes for reading and writing in the classroom. Reading and listening are receptive aspects of language; writing, and speaking are expressive. These expressive processes are continually influenced by the receptive processes as writers are influenced by others. CDG gave students opportunities to share their insights with each other and augment their understanding to communicate more effectively via reading, writing, speaking, and listening.

Collaborative Discovery Groups for Writing
Our main goal for the second phase of the project was to give students opportunities to express their augmented knowledge through writing. Teachers used mini-lessons to guide students as they began to write about what they learned from reading and discussing the poetry. They were given opportunities to draw pictures of what they learned and highlight the concepts they considered most important in pen pal letters. This gave students opportunities to learn for authentic purposes and share their knowledge in a realistic context.

Students initially wrote pen pal letters about their favorite places to share their priorities and establish relationships. A poem in which Brod Bagert introduced himself and told about his home, that is, Earth formed the basis for these letters. Then students continued to exchange pen pal letters informed by the scientific knowledge gleaned from interacting with the expository poetry.

The CDG Writing Process
After students wrote initial drafts of letters, they shared them with partners and updated the letters in pairs. Then they met in the CDG to discuss their letters in a recursive writing process with some revision and updates. Sometimes this Think–Pair–Share approach was rather limited due to time constraints. This process gave students the opportunity to share their best ideas and experience collaborative writing. Thus, students translated the concepts they learned during close reading into the writing process. Opportunities to share knowledge were designed to augment the students' understanding and insight. Sharing their knowledge through writing gave students opportunities to further augment and transfer their knowledge.

DATA ANALYSIS: THE QUANTITATIVE SIDE

In this mixed methods study, a coding system was used to analyze the development of the students' writing. The initial phase was named *Substantive Coding* (Chamarz, 2008), and was used to identify the nature of the learner's writing. The first letter was written in response to the prompt, "Tell me about your favorite place." It was inspired by Brod Baggert's poem "Home."

Substantive Coding

The initial set of codes were drawn from the first set of letters and included the following:

- *Declarative* (*D*) statements. This code usually indicated either a thesis statement, or a comment that was unrelated to the thesis and simply made a statement, such as, "My favorite place to visit is Washington."
- *Supporting Detail* (*S/D*) sentences supporting the thesis. For example, "My dogs live there."
- *Exclamation* (*E*) statements expressing sudden or strong feeling. Explaining why he liked Sea World, a student wrote about the Shamu show and exclaimed, "And you get wet!"
- *Interrogative* (*I*) sentences posing a question, such as, "What's your favorite place?"
- *Dialogical* (*D/C*) conversational statements. Frequently these were paired with interrogatives as the writer was conversationally asking a question. For example, "I'm going to tell you about food chain."
- *Dialogical Persuasive* (*D/P*) compelling conversational statements. In the initial sets of letters there were several instances in which the learner was being persuasive. For example, "You should go there."
- *Complimentary Close* (*CC*). The most common of these was, "Your friend,"

As the letters became more sophisticated, additional codes were added.

- *Reasoning* (*R*). In the latter letters, students were demonstrating cause and effect reasoning. For example, "If there were a flood, sharks will be o.k. because sharks are fish, and fish live in the water, so sharks would survive a flood."

- *Evaluative Reasoning (L/C)*. They were rare, but there were instances in the latter letters which showed the student making an evaluation. For example, after listing many things needed for survival, a student wrote, "but of all these, air is the most important thing for survival because without it we can't breath (sic)."
- *Inferential Comment (I/C)*. In the last two sets of letters learners began to make inferences. In a letter describing how a favorite animal would fare in a drought, one student wrote, "It [a jaguar] would have to go somewhere else, or dig," [inferring *dig a well*.]
- *Rhetorical Comment (RhC)*. The final set required the addition of a code for rhetorical questions. For example while discussing the effects of a disruption in the food chain, a student wrote, "but what if the fish all withered away? What do you think will happen? Well, all the penguins will die."

The Substantive coding process was accomplished by first transcribing the data verbatim, as they were written. Although it was difficult to transcribe third-graders' writing, it provided an accurate view of the data (Chamarz, 2008). After the data were transcribed, they were rewritten as codes, and whenever possible, gerunds were used "invoking a language of actions" (p. 48) to catch the sense of what was happening in the data. The next step was to assign one of the above *analytic codes* to the statement to allow for categorizing and combining. Finally, thoughts and reflections were noted in the *Memos* section.

Summative Coding

When the Substantive process was completed for all of the letters in a set, the data were entered on a Summative Data sheet where the categories were assembled. These "open-ended ... emergent processes," reflective of Grounded Theory, allowed us to draw conclusions about the writing in that set of letters (Chamarz, 2008, p. 178).

In the "Home" set, we noted that most letters followed a pattern in which the thesis was clearly stated, and then one to seven supporting details completed the paper. The dialogical elements showed that these letters were part of a sociocultural process.

The same process was employed for all subsequent sets. The set to which the first set is being compared, "Food Cheer," was radically different. Although the Thesis/Supporting details pattern was still in evidence, the writing was much more sophisticated as there were rich examples of rhetorical questions, inferential thinking, and evaluative thinking. When explaining why his favorite animal, a tiger, would survive a drought, a student wrote, "If it were a vampire tiger, he would survive the drought," implying that drinking something would permit the tiger to survive. In that same set, a learner introduced the thesis with a series of rhetorical questions, one of which was, "If, lets say, a flood came, what do you think would happen?" Finally, one student evaluated that "if you don't love pandas, you're a monster." The coding process allowed us to see the amazing growth in authentic communication which occurred over a four week period.

Comparing the Sets of Letters

The following chart is a comparison of the previously described substantive coding. Two classes participated in this project, and were designated as classes "A" and "B." The first set of letters was associated with Bagert's poem "Home" in which astrological terms were used to locate his home on this Earth. The letter served as an introduction, and the students were asked to write about their favorite places. The second set of data is from the fifth in a series of six letters and is related to Bagert's poem "Food Cheer." This short, six-line poem, which explains carnivores, herbivores, and omnivores, aligns with the school district's standard for teaching the environmental effects of floods and droughts. The prompt was to identify a favorite animal as a carnivore, herbivore, or omnivore and explain how it would fare in both a flood and a drought.

The quantitative analysis was simply a comparison of means, but was telling. In virtually every category except the use of exclamations and the ratio of dialogical comments to the number of letters produced, the second set of letters had both greater volume as well as indications of higher levels of sophistication and higher level thinking skills. The first set of letters contained an average of 1.025 simple declarative statements, which were supported by an average of 3.545 supporting statements. The second set contained an average of 1.725 declarative statements which were supported by an average of 4.14 supporting statements.

The most telling statistics were in the area of using simple reasoning for evaluative statements, inferences, and rhetorical statements. By *reasoning*, we are describing a cause and effect relationship in which a student would write something like, "lions are carnivores who eat herbivores, and in a drought the plants die, so the herbivores die, so the lions would die."

The other areas are inferences, evaluative thinking, and rhetorical comments. There were no examples of any of these in the first set, but each area was well represented in the second set. The nature of the prompt could have been a contributing factor. It is improbable that the students learned these cognitive skills over a four-week period, but it can be inferred that the strength of the synergistic process simply allowed them to express what they already were thinking and saying in conversations. Further research would be needed to investigate this.

A related topic is the volume of the writing. There was an increase in the number of sentences used, as well as a 46.1% increase in the average number of words written. This increase occurred over a four-week period of instruction. Connecting writing to reading in a social setting produced dramatic results.

FINDINGS

The Collaborative Discovery Groups, featuring specific modes of cooperative learning and research-based strategies, were highly beneficial and augmented the quality of students' writing. Grand Conversations gave students opportunities to discuss their insights, and the Think−Pair−Share approach to writing helped them to collaboratively evaluate their writing. These opportunities for thinking and working together provided support for the learners, developed diverse understandings, generated learning communities, and increased the self-esteem so needed by students (Laal & Ghodsi, 2012; Yager, Johnson, & Johnson, 1986).

Generation of Expository Knowledge with Mini-Lessons

Mini-lessons set the stage for the CDG and helped students to initially develop ideas for their writing. Teachers read the poems to the students and discussed significant vocabulary words with them. Then they used key ideas from the poems to launch the writing process. A teacher stated:

> When the poetry lined up with the writing skill I was teaching, the lesson was great. We used the poems to start a conversation about whatever we needed to study that day (science and writing), and then our letters were based off of the conversation and science subject prompt.

Throughout this study teachers used mini-lessons, featuring reading and writing strategies to generate expository knowledge. The goal was to align the divergent sets of the schema of both non-Western European students and Western European students to meet the expectations of academic writing in Western European academic institutions. These poems connected the curriculum with students' situated literacies. This connection was emphasized from the beginning of the project. Brod Bagert's poem "Home" laid the foundation for pen pal letters describing students' favorite places. A teacher noted:

> The prompts made a huge difference in how much was written by most children. The first prompt was asking a personal question that should be easy to ask: "What is your favorite place to visit?" Kids enjoyed writing about this prompt and reading the letters.

These mini-lessons were designed to align these divergent sets of schema, in the multicultural collage of academic settings, to empower students from diverse backgrounds to produce writing which strikes the Western European schematic prisms in such a way as to produce the desired results.

Construction of Knowledge — The Schematic Process as a Prism

The image of the prism conveys the interaction of cognitive and social constructivism with schema to produce a spectrum of color that enhances the writing process. In physics, sunlight is composed of many colors, but in a natural state, we see only the combined, white light. However, when a ray of sunshine passes through a prism, the velocity changes as the light bends, refraction occurs, and all of the colors of the rainbow are splayed onto the wall.

According to Vygotsky (1978), the forces which create this spectrum of color and distinguish all that we encounter mentally are primarily social, cultural, and historical in nature. As writers begin the process, they establish their purpose and their audience. Then they select the elements to be communicated, organize them, and bundle them into a metaphoric ray of light, which is sent to the audience through written words. When this light is received through the reading process, it is refracted through the audience's individual, living prisms, producing unique rainbows of new knowledge. The trick in writing is to anticipate the nature of the living, schematic prism of the intended audience and fashion a bundle of light which, when refracted, will produce the intended rainbow (Spivey, 1997). No two living prisms are the same, and no two rainbows are identical (Rosenblatt, 1978). As students exchanged pen pal letters, they learned how to communicate and relate to their friends, sharing ideas that resonated in the communication process.

Communication of Knowledge – Understanding the Schematic Process

Throughout the project we aligned the construction of knowledge with the communication of knowledge in the schematic process, demonstrating how expressive processes interact with receptive processes to produce this schematic collage. We considered ways to align the divergent, socioculturally influenced sets of schema to empower students to convey messages in meaningful, effective ways. Thus, students learned to tailor the message to interact with the schema of the desired audience. A teacher stated that this peer interaction motivated students as they wrote to communicate with peers:

> I had multiple children apply peer pressure on their pen pals who weren't finishing letters for them to read and respond to. I also noticed that some students' handwriting improved somewhat when they knew that a peer was going to read their letter ....

> One of my students usually completes little to no work in my class. She just refuses. She also doesn't have many friends because she can be difficult. However, the letters were a big hit with her. I assigned her a very sweet pen pal, and she wrote more letters than she needed to (even writing one at home). The first three or four letters were all of a personal nature rather than responding to the prompt. Soon though, she started adding in some information about the prompt, and the last letter had most of the required elements.

Academic Writing – Discovering the Nature of Academic Schema

We discussed ways to give all students access to academic schema to equip them to see themselves as writers. This process prepared students from various ethnic groups, who were linear or nonlinear thinkers, to discover ways to personalize and explore the nature of academic Capital D Discourse (Gee, 2005, 2008). When teachers emphasized students' funds of knowledge and situated literacy, this personal connection enhanced writing achievement. This promoted successful achievement as teachers focused on the multicultural collage in their academic settings. Pen pal letters aligned with situated literacy and students' funds of knowledge. A teacher explained:

> In education today, students are expected to write across the curriculum. In third grade science, it is sometimes difficult to find a way to motivate children to write about their learning. Using letters to pen pals was a very effective motivator for children.

At the beginning of this study, I had many children who "couldn't" think of more than one sentence to write about the assigned topic. As they started reading what their pen pals were writing, they were either motivated to write more like their pen pal or better than their pen pal (if he/she wrote only a short letter or boring letter). The amount of writing increased as we wrote more letters. I believe that the change came from the clarity of the topics assigned, the comparison of his/her letter to his/her pen pal's letter, and the Six Writing Traits mini-lessons. I also learned after the first lesson that my students would need more time to write good letters (about 30–40 minutes per letter and more for some reluctant writers). I started out trying to fit the lesson on one day and found that too many children didn't get anything written because of limited time.

Exemplary letters

The pen pal letters shown in Fig. 1 were written by the same student and demonstrate the amazing growth which was seen in this study. The first letter is from the first set of letters and contains 13 words. The prompt was to describe your favorite place as it related to the poem "Home."

The student wrote:

My fa pale is 711 B se yo ge lot of sodas (My favorite place is 7-Eleven because you get lots of sodas.)

The second letter is from the sixth set and was written in response to a prompt related to the food chain. There are 56 words, and this letter shows a good understanding of the food chain. It also contains a dialogic response to the partner's declaration of loving pandas. It reads:

I also like pandas to. My favorite is a pegian. If peguns eat all of the fish the the pegins will die. Because threr is no more fish. The polar bear will eat the pegins. When the die the decmopcers will eat the polar bear.

[The illustration shows the food chain with labels.] These examples demonstrate four weeks of growth through a Collaborative Discovery Group.

The Grand Conversations in the Collaborative Discovery Groups

The Grand Conversations employed in the CDG used an open format in which students and teachers freely discussed their individual schematic rainbows of insight produced by the reaction of their schematic prisms with the text. Rich, authentic discussions in CDG for reading fostered engagement, authenticity, and cultural relevance, which in turn, helped students to produce purposeful writing in creative and meaningful ways. Since the nature of these groups is social, they provided excellent opportunities to

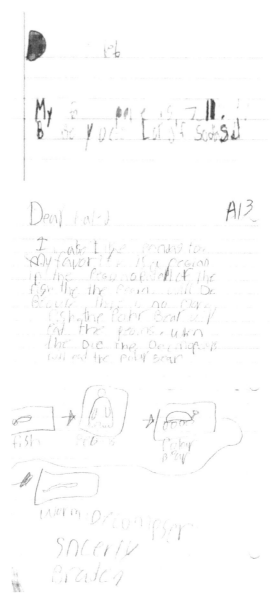

Fig. 1. Exemplary Letters.

incorporate the students' funds of knowledge, and they were reflective of situated literacy. The socioculturally dynamic process of reading and discussing expository material enriched individual schema and augmented students' ability to produce rich, informative academic writing. A teacher noted:

> Most of our discussions were focused on the language in the poetry, the "voice," and the science content. It was difficult to get the kids to talk in small groups about the poem without giving them some sort of prompt to talk about. I usually asked them to discuss something that would generate ideas of their letter writing.

Instruction and Sociocultural Interaction Tailored for Academic Writing

Partnership with teachers in K-12 classrooms, emphasizing technology and social interaction, enhanced the reading process and the resulting writing projects. The opportunity to share ideas helped them to consider their ideas from new perspectives. A teacher mentioned:

> I would read aloud the poem. Then we would take each piece and discuss what made it interesting and what science concept the author was talking about. The students really enjoyed those discussions. Many times our discussions led to trying to find additional information on the Internet – pictures, facts about animals, pictures of the Virgo Super Cluster, etc. I would eventually lead the discussion to the prompt that they would be writing about. We would brainstorm ideas to write about, and then they would write.

Mini-lessons and CDG were designed to scaffold an understanding of the poems and the scientific concepts, which Brod Bagert innovatively conveyed through his poetry. These mini-lessons and interactive sessions, using the Think–Pair–Share approach offered excellent opportunities for students to collaboratively reshape their written products into academically appropriate writing. A teacher noted students' enjoyment of the poem "Real Monsters" during her lesson:

> The writing lesson was on word choice, which I also thought fit this poem perfectly. The kids made me read through it multiple times because I used my dramatic "scary voice" and tickled some necks when reading about the different bugs. They enjoyed looking for good word choices.

Individually Produced Academic Documents

We emphasized the impact of peer discussion and peer revision as teachers explored ways to promote high-quality academic writing. The CDG were used to promoted collaborative reading and interactive writing, which in order to augmented the quality of students' academic writing. They used flow maps to study poetry, and a teacher described the ways the poems emphasized significant vocabulary from the curriculum:

> The poem was a nice way to present the vocabulary that students needed to know in order to write to their prompts. Students really enjoy writing when it is something personal like, "What is your favorite animal?" They all have favorites, and they enjoy talking about them for the most part. I put the requirements for their letters on the board for the students to reference as they wrote.

The letter in Fig. 2 is interesting for several reasons. It is in the next to the last set and shows considerable sophistication. The student starts with a series of rhetorical questions to introduce his thesis: "What do you need most in your life?" "If, let's say a flood come what do you think would happen?" and finally, "What about a drought, what do you think will happen?" Having introduced the paper, the student continues to develop a

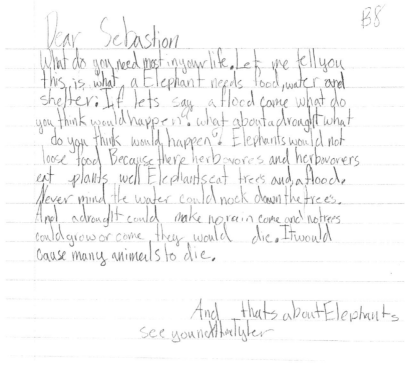

Fig. 2. Exemplary Letter.

logical series of statements that in a flood an elephant would survive because elephants are herbivores which eat trees. The flood would knock down the trees, and the student infers that this would be beneficial to elephants. However, droughts are the opposite. Without water there would be no trees, and the elephants would die [inferring that there would be no food for them].

Exploring and Interacting with the Schema for Effective Academic Writing

As students became aware of the nature of academic Discourse, they were more prepared to become writers who develop the Western European academic writing skills for success in Western European driven schools. It is well known that students learn to write by writing. We noted that mini-lessons and the weekly writing experiences in CDG helped students to become more comfortable with the writing process.

PRACTICAL IMPLICATIONS

The data revealed the importance of including the sociocultural tenants in the classroom, emphasizing that reading, writing, speaking, and listening are all a part of the same phenomenon. Together they strengthen and support each other. This has implications for classrooms teachers, tutors, and school districts because it shows the impact of collaborative writing.

CONCLUSION

This study demonstrated the impact of reading and social interaction on the quality of students' writing. As students met in CDG, they became more engaged in the writing process as they shared ideas and individually exchanged pen pal letters. It was evident that reading and collaborative discussions augmented the quality of students' writing and enhanced their enjoyment of the writing process. During these activities students shared their scientific insights with each other as they increased their ability to explain scientific phenomenon and communicate through writing. They valued their interactions and encouraged each other to write back when they wrote pen pal letters.

Throughout this writing project the teachers were guiding their students as they exchanged ideas with one another. Thus, rather than assuming the sole responsibility for the learning process as the sage on the stage, the teachers were facilitators for learning. They were interacting with their students, modeling, encouraging student interaction, and using a gradual release of responsibility model (Fisher & Frey, 2008). Opportunities increased because these teachers had the resources of a group available throughout the learning process. As they provided incremental scaffolding, their students were actively involved in learning rather than passively viewing information. Students gained new confidence as they helped each other to learn. Interactions in CDG and pen pal letters increased students' ability to explain scientific concepts and augmented their academic writing achievement.

REFERENCES

Bakhtin, M. M. (1984). *Problem of Dostoevski's poetics.* Minneapolis, MN: University of Minnesota Press.

Bartlett, F. C. (1932). *Remembering: A study in experimental and social psychology.* London: Cambridge University Press.

Butler, A., Phillmann, K.-B., & Smart, L. (2001). Active learning within a lecture: Assessing the impact of short, in-class writing exercises. *Teaching of Psychology, 28*(4), 257–259.

Chamarz, K. (2008). *Constructing grounded theory: A practical guide through qualitative analysis.* Los Angeles, CA: Sage.

Daniels, H. (2002). *Literature circles: Voice and choice in book clubs and reading groups.* Portland, ME: Stenhouse Publishers.

Eeds, M., & Wells, D. (1989). Grand conversations: An exploration of meaning construction in literature study groups. *Research in the Teaching of English, 23*(1), 4–29.

Fisher, D., & Frey, N. (2008). *Better learning through structured teaching: A framework for the gradual release of responsibility.* Alexandria, VA: Association for Supervision and Curriculum Development.

Gee, J. P. (2005). *An introduction to discourse analysis: Theory and method* (2nd ed.). New York, NY: Routledge.

Gee, J. P. (2008). *Social linguistics and literacies: Ideology in discourses* (3rd ed.). New York, NY: Routledge.

Grisham, D. L., & Wolsey, T. D. (2011). Writing instruction for teacher candidates: Strengthening a weaker curricular area. *Literacy Research and Instruction, 50*(4), 348–364. doi:10.1080/19388071.2010.532581

Jaramillo, J. A. (1996). Vygotsky's sociocultural theory and contributions to the development of constructivist curricula. *Education, 117*(1), 133–140.

Laal, M., & Ghodsi, S. M. (2012). Benefits of collaborative learning. *Procedia – Social and Behavioral Sciences, 31,* 486–490.

Lyman, F. (1981). The responsive classroom discussion: The inclusion of all students. In A. Anderson (Ed.), *Mainstreaming digest* (pp. 109–113). College Park, MD: University of Maryland Press.

Moll, L. C., Amanti, C., Neff, D., & Gonzalez, N. (1992). Funds of knowledge for teaching: Using a qualitative approach to connect homes and classrooms. *Theory into Practice, 31*(2), 132–141.

Nassaji, H. (2002). Schema theory and knowledge-based processes in second language reading comprehension: A need for alternative perspectives. *Language Learning, 52*(2), 439–481.

Nelson, N., & Calfee, R. C. (1998). *The reading-writing connection.* Chicago, IL: The University of Chicago Press.

Newell, G. E. (1998). "How much are we the wiser?": Continuity and changes in writing and learning. In N. Nelson & R. C. Calfee (Eds.), *The reading writing connection* (pp. 178–202). Chicago, IL: The University of Chicago Press.

Parr, J. M., & McNaughton, S. (2014). Making connections: The nature and occurrence of links in literacy teaching and learning. *Australian Journal of Language and Literacy, 37*, 141–150.

Pearson, P. D. (2012). Point of view: Life in the radical middle. In R. F. Flippo (Ed.), *Reading researchers in search of common ground: The expert study revisited* (2nd ed., pp. 99–106). New York, NY: Routledge.

Piaget, J. (1923). *The language and thought of the child.* London: Routledge & Kegan.

Roberts, T., & Billings, L. (2008). Thinking is literacy, literacy thinking. *Educational Leadership, 65*(5), 32–36.

Rosenblatt, L. M. (1978). *The reader, the text, the poem: The transactional theory of the literary work.* Carbondale, IL: Southern Illinois University Press.

Rosenblatt, L. M. (2005). *Making meaning with text: Selected essays.* Portsmouth, NH: Heinemann.

Spivey, N. N. (1997). *The constructivist metaphor.* San Diego, CA: Academic Press.

Street, B. (2003). What's "new" in new literacy studies? Critical approaches to literacy in theory and practice. *Current Issues in Comparative Education, 5*(2), 77–91.

Suhr, K. A., Hernandez, D. A., Grimes, D., & Warschauer, M. (2010). Laptops and fourth-grade literacy: Assisting the jump over the fourth-grade slump. *Journal of Technology, Learning, and Assessment, 9*(5), 1–46.

van Joolingen, W. R., de Jong, T., Lazonder, A. W., Savelsbergh, E. R., & Manlove, S. (2005). Co-lab: Research and development of an online learning environment for collaborative scientific discovery learning. *Computers in Human Behavior, 21*, 671–688.

Vygotsky, L. S. (1978). Mind in society*: The development of higher psychological processes*. Cambridge, MA: Harvard University Press.

Vygotsky, L. S. (1986). *Thought and language.* Cambridge, MA: The MIT Press.

Yager, S., Johnson, R. T., Johnson, D. W., & Snider, B. (1986). The impact of group processing on achievement in cooperative learning groups. *The Journal of Social Psychology, 126*(3), 389–397.

APPENDIX A

Collaborative Discovery Project: Instructions for Co-researchers

Our project to promote literacy development in the classroom will feature Collaborative Discovery Groups (CDG). This project will be approximately one month. It will include minilessons, poetry reading, and pen pal letters.

Purpose
This project is designed to promote enthusiasm for reading and writing in the classroom. Authentic writing projects and peer review will be used to encourage literacy development and enhance content knowledge in science.

Classroom Procedure
Minilessons will emphasize the Six Traits of Writing and engaging poetry to focus the CDG on ways to enhance writing. Each bi-weekly session will be approximately one hour. You may want to schedule the lessons for Tuesdays and Thursdays if those days are convenient. Feel free to do what works best for you and your class. Each minilesson will focus on the Six Traits of Writing. Although conventions will be emphasized on Day 6, writing conventions will be briefly mentioned in each minilesson to ensure students' awareness of the frameworks for writing when they write their pen pal letters.

Materials
Your team leaders will provide resources, and you may feel free to select the poems and the approach that works best for your curriculum and your class. We will use the same two poems during the first two days for consistency.

Research Participation
As a coresearcher, you will send your reflections on the progress of your students and the impact of each activity along with your notes. Feel free to plan your sessions collaboratively with a colleague or use the design that works best for your class and the expectations of your school.

Table A1. Collaborative Discovery Schedule.

Day 1 – Ideas and Content	*Day 2* – Organization
Day 3 – Voice	*Day 4* – Word Choice
Day 5 – Sentence Fluency	*Day 6* – Conventions
Day 7 – Presentation	*Day 8* – Share Presentations

Fig. A1. Collaborative Knowledge Construction.

APPENDIX B

Table of Contents

To provide an illustration of the coding process which was followed, a Substantive Coding document from the "Home" set of letters is provided in Table B1, followed by the Summative Coding document for that same set in Table B2. Table B3 is the Substantive Coding document for the "Cheers" set of letters, followed the Summative Coding document in Table B4. The two sets of summative data are compared in Table B5.

Table B1. Substantive Coding.

Analytic Codes		
Declarative –	Makes a declaration	D
Declarative/Supportive	Supports a declaration	S/D
Supportive exclamation*	An exclamation supporting the thesis	E
Interrogative*	Asks a question	I
Dialogical*	Conversational comment	D/C
Dialogical/Persuasive*	Persuasive dialog	D/P
Complimentary Close	Complimentary Close	C/C

Initial Statement	Initial Code	A/C	Memo
My favorite place to vist Six Flags because all of cool rides	Declaring that his favorite place to visit is Six Flags	D	Declarative statements
And I went on cool ride it was roaring	Explaining that it is fun because of cool rides	S/D	
	Relating that he went on a cool ride called Roaring	S/D	
I got real wet!!	Exclaiming that he got really wet	E	
but it realy fun and there was nothen ride it was Mini N train	Contradicting the previous statement by stating that it was really fun	S/D	
	There was another ride	S/D	
	Stating that the other ride was the Mini N Train	S/D	
it was fun and asole was fun visting Sixe Flags	Stating that it was fun and also was fun visiting Six Flags	S/D	
Your fren	Your friend	CC	

Table B2. Summative Coding.

Letter	D	S/D	E	I	D/C	D/P	R	L/C	#sent	Memos
A2	1	2	1		1				5	
A5	1	3			2					
A3	1	3			2				5	
A6	2	1			1				5	Beginning to be persuasive "Why, because I like the Volcano and Mt. Rainer"
A7	1	3							3	
A8	1	6	1						5	Exclamatory statement
A11	1	5	1						7	
A12	1	5							8	
A13	1	1							2	
A15	1	1							2	
A16	1								1	
A17	1	4			1				6	A declarative letter ending with a dialogical comment indicating an audience throughout
A19	1	4							5	
A20	1	4							5	
A21	1	3				2			5	Declarative statements with the supporting statements enumerated
A23	1	7	1				1		10	Good persuasive development: States a thesis, supports it with claims, concludes with persuasive comment
A4	2	4		1	2				8	This is very dialogical and assumes an Audience
										The interrogative is addressed to an audience
										The close includes a dialogical comment
Totals	19	56	4	1	11	1			82	
Mean	1.12	3.29	4/17	1/17	11/17	1/17			4.82	

Note: Letter: A; Poem: Home; Prompt: Write about favorite place; Writing Skill: Ideas. Conclusions: The basic pattern is declaring a thesis and then supporting it with one to seven supporting details. There were eight incidents of dialog in 16 letters + ½.

Table B3. Substantive Coding.

Analytic Codes		
Declarative –	Makes a declaration	D
Declarative/Supportive	Supports a declaration	S/D
Supportive Exclamation*	An exclamation supporting the thesis	E
Interrogative*	Asks a question	I
Dialogical*	Conversational comment	C
Dialogical/Persuasive*	Persuasive dialogue	D/P
Complimentary Close	Complimentary Close	C/C
Reasoning	Cause effect reasoning	R
Evaluative	Drawing logical conclusions	L/C
Inferential statement	Drawing an inference	I/SS
Rh/C	Rhetorical comment	Rh/C
*Exhibits discursive qualities		

Initial Statement	Initial Code	A/C	Memo
Dear Sebastion	Greeting		
What do you need most in your life	Asking rhetorically what is most needed in life	Rh/C Rh/C	Rhetorically stated thesis
Let me tell you this is what a Elephant needs food, water and shelter	Supplying the answer to his question: Food water and shelter	I S/D	
If lets say a flood came what do you think would happen What about a drought what do you think would happen?	Rhetorically stating the second half of the prompt – floods and drought	D/C I Rh/C D/C	
Elephants would not loose food because there herbavores and herbavorers eat plants well Elephants eat trees and a flood Never mind the water could knock down the trees	Reasoning that elephants would survive a drought because they eat plants and would not lose food Elephants eat trees Inferring that knocked down tress will benefit elephants	S/D R S/D I/S	Inference
And a drought it could make no rain come and no trees could grow or come they would die	Explaining that in a drought there would be no trees Inferring that without trees the elephants will die	S/D I/S R	Elephants will have no food No rain no trees, no trees no food (inferred) no food they die (inferred)
It would cause many animals to die	Declaring that many animals will die	S/D	
And that's about Elephants		D	
See you next time Tyler		D/C	Personalized close

Source: From Tyler.

Table B4. Summative Coding.

Letter	D	S/D	E	I	D/C	R	L/C	I/s	# Word	# SENT	Rhetorical	Memos
B1	1	3				1			59	5		Reasoning why the fish would die in a drought
												Concluding with personal address
B3	1	6			1				60	8		Personal close concerning not receiving a letter
B4	2	5			2				134	8		Domestic and wild cats
												Consideration for babies and families
B5	1	5		1	2	1		1	119	10		Implied reasoning = drink blood, survive drought
B6	1	2			1	2			39	5		
B7	2	2	1			1			44	6	1	Rhetorical
B8	2	5	3	3	3	2		2	100	10	3	Rhetorically introducing new theme
												Rhetorically introducing new theme
												Rhetorically introducing new theme
B9	1	6	1				1		96	10		Evaluating that survival in a drought depends on the length of the drought
B10	3	4			1				86	9		
B11	2	4	1	1	3				101	10		Constantly conversational
B12	1	4		1	3				103	13		
B13	2	6			1		1		115	12		Evaluating that if you don't love pandas, you're a monster
B15	1	5		1	2				75	7	1	Rhetorically initiating personal conversation
B16	2	3			1				42	6		
B17	1	3			3				74	8		
B18	1	2						1	33	3		Inferring digging for water
B19	1	5			2	1			84	5		Developing cause and effect reason for there being no food
20	2	2							27	3		Assuming the prompt (thesis)
22	1	6			2				87	9		

Note: Food Cheer B; Letter: B; Poem: Food Cheer; Prompt: Favorite animal – flood/drought.

Table B5. Comparison of First and Fifth Letters.

Analytic Coding		
Declarative –	Makes a declaration	D
Declarative/Supportive	Supports a declaration	S/D
Supportive exclamation*	An exclamation	E
Interrogative*	Asks a question	I
Dialogical*	Conversational comment	D/C

Dialogical/Persuasive*	Persuasive dialogue	D/P
Complimentary Close	Complimentary Close	C/C
Reasoning	Cause effect reasoning	R
Evaluative	Drawing logical conclusions	L/C
Inference	Making an inference	I/S
Rhetorical	Rhetorical comment	Rh/C

Letter		Number of Letters	Declarative Statement	Supporting Detail	Exclamation	Interrogative	Dialogic Comment	Dialogical Persuasive	Reasoning	Evaluation	Inference	Rhetorical Question	Total Words	Number of Sentences
Home B	Total	13	14	57	4	0	14	2					859	85
Home B	Mean		.93	3.8	3/13	0/13	7/13	2/13					66.07	5.67
Home A	Total	17	19	56	4	1	118	2					620	82
Home A	Mean		1.12	3.29	4/17	1/17	7/17	2/17					36.47	4.82
Combined Means/Ratio		30	1.025	3.545	7/30 1:4.29	1/30 1:30	4/30 1:2.24	0 1:7.5	0	0	0	0	51.32	5.25
Food Cheer A	Total	15	30	62	0	11	32	0	15	0	3	2	1139	103
Food Cheer A	Mean		2	4.13	1/15	7/15	13/15	0/15	15/15	0/15	3/15	2/15	75.93	6.86
Food Cheer B	Total	20	29	83	1	6	27	0	8	3	2	4	1511	155
Food Cheer B	Mean		1.45	4.15	1/20	6/20	15/20	0/20	8/20	3/20	2/20	4/20	75.55	7.75
Combined Means/Ratio		35	1.725	4.14	2/35 1:17.5	13/35 1:2.69	28/35 1:1.25	0/35 0:35	23/35 1:1.52	3/35 1:11.66	5/35 1:7	6/35 1:5.8	75.74	7.31